SECOND EDITION

COMMUNITY COUNSELING

EMPOWERMENT STRATEGIES FOR A DIVERSE SOCIETY

About the Cover

Interlacing designs are to be found in the art of every continent. The earliest use of interlacing symbols was by the Chinese a few thousand years B.C. Egyptians, Greeks, Romans, Byzantines, Moors, Persians, Arabs, Hebrews, Celts, and North African tribes have also used the interlacing design symbol. Commonly used as a symbol of continuity, these designs are an ancient symbol that show the twisting and turning of two forms representing the interplay between the conflicting forces of everyday life. Depending on the image, these designs symbolize many important concerns in society. For example, in Africa the Yoruba tribe has interlace designs to convey the power of their gods, the importance of leadership, fertility, and the competing powers of the world.

SECOND EDITION

COMMUNITY COUNSELING

EMPOWERMENT STRATEGIES
FOR A DIVERSE SOCIETY

Judith A. Lewis
Governors State University

Michael D. Lewis
Governors State University

Judy A. Daniels
University of Hawaii at Manoa

Michael J. D'Andrea
University of Hawaii at Manoa

Brooks/Cole Publishing Company
I(T)P® *An International Thomson Publishing Company*

PACIFIC GROVE ■ ALBANY ■ BONN ■ BOSTON ■ CINCINNATI ■ DETROIT ■ LONDON
MADRID ■ MELBOURNE ■ MEXICO CITY ■ NEW YORK ■ PARIS ■ SAN FRANCISCO
SINGAPORE ■ TOKYO ■ TORONTO ■ WASHINGTON

Sponsoring Editor: *Eileen Murphy*
Marketing Team: *Jean Thompson,*
  Christine Davis, and Deanne Brown
Editorial Assistant: *Shelley Bouhaja*
Production Coordinators: *Fiorella Ljunggren*
  and Keith Faivre
Production: *Greg Hubit Bookworks*

Manuscript Editor: *Molly D. Roth*
Permissions: *May Clark*
Interior and Cover Design: *John Edeen*
Typesetting: *Bookends Typesetting*
Cover Printing: *Phoenix Color Corp.*
Printing and Binding: *Maple-Vail Book*
  Manufacturing Group

For more information, contact:

BROOKS/COLE PUBLISHING COMPANY
511 Forest Lodge Road
Pacific Grove, CA 93950
USA

International Thomson Editores
Seneca 53
Col. Polanco
11560 México, D.F., México

International Thomson Publishing Europe
Berkshire House 168-173
High Holborn
London WC1V 7AA
England

International Thomson Publishing GmbH
Königswinterer Strasse 418
53227 Bonn
Germany

International Thomson Publishing Asia
221 Henderson Road
#05-10 Henderson Building
Singapore 0315

Thomas Nelson Australia
102 Dodds Street
South Melbourne, 3205
Victoria, Australia

International Thomson Publishing Japan
Hirakawacho Kyowa Building, 3F
2-2-1 Hirakawacho
Chiyoda-ku, Tokyo 102
Japan

Nelson Canada
1120 Birchmount Road
Scarborough, Ontario
Canada M1K 5G4

Library of Congress Cataloging-in-Publication Data
Community counseling : empowerment strategies for a diverse society /
  Judith A. Lewis . . . [et al.]. — 2nd ed.
    p. cm.
  Prev. ed. cataloged under: Lewis, Judith A.
  Includes bibliographical references and index.
  ISBN 0-534-25854-9
  1. Mental h ealth services. 2. Counseling. I. Lewis, Judith A.
RA790.5.C6 1998
362.2'2—dc   97-16993
                                                        CIP

To our families, our ohana (extended families), and the members of diverse communities everywhere who strive for collective empowerment and a more just society.

CONTENTS

CHAPTER 4

COMMUNITY COUNSELING AND THE COUNSELING PROCESS   122

CHAPTER 5

CLIENT ADVOCACY   171

CHAPTER 6

THE COMMUNITY COUNSELOR AS SOCIAL CHANGE AGENT   215

CHAPTER 7

APPLICATIONS OF THE COMMUNITY COUNSELING MODEL   250

CHAPTER 8

MANAGING THE COMMUNITY COUNSELING PROGRAM   288

FOREWORD

People live in social context. This simple but profound fact has traditionally been overlooked in individualistically oriented counseling and psychotherapy. As a result, we have three major theoretical forces (psychodynamic, cognitive-behavioral, and existential-humanistic) leading us to believe that problems reside in the individual. The social-contextual approach of the community counseling model is more sophisticated—the authors dramatically show that if counselors wish to make a permanent positive difference, they will need to expand their efforts to community and cultural concerns.

Community Counseling: Empowerment Strategies for a Diverse Society is an important book for both professionals and students. It expands their worldview, suggests many powerful strategies for counselors and therapists, and provides specifics that will enable individuals, families, groups, and communities to take charge of their own and set their own direction. As you read this book, you undertake a journey into the future.

Counseling and therapy needs a new model of "self." The old model of the contained self seems tired and obsolete. Self-actualization, once a hallowed concept, is now translated by some as "selfish actualization." The feminist theorist Jean Baker Miller (1991) talks of self-in-relation. Baker Miller reminds us that we all live in relationship—we are not alone. As we move from self to self-in-relation, we become open to the family within and around us. We become aware that multiple factors such as gender, ethnicity, and race affect our self-concept-in-relation. Counselors and therapists encounter the truth of complexity and the need to search out developmental factors that place them in context.

The vision of psychological health and well-being presented in Chapter 1 is vital to the idea of self-in-context. Note that the authors have used a wellness, competency model as contrasted with the all-too-traditional deficit paradigm. We can approach the massive social change ahead as a problem or as an opportunity. Join the authors' imaginative and insightful approach, which focuses on prevention rather than remediation, balancing individual and environment concerns rather than a simple focus on individuals, and complexity rather than oversimplification.

Preventive education and life-skills training are outlined in Chapter 2 as primary activities for the effective professional. It has become increasingly clear that cost-effective helping is a major component of community learning. Professionals can run a stress-management program, encourage intercultural skills, or engage in leadership training—all these are important dimensions of the fully functioning mental health professional.

Chapter 3 introduces you to the specifics of helping vulnerable populations such as battered women, the economically oppressed, the homeless, and the suicidal. As I read this material, I was reminded once again of how fortunate my own life is and of my responsibility to share my expertise with others. I am personally encouraged by the commitment of the authors to look at my own life and how I can increase my time in vital professional service to those in desperate need. I am sure you will find the same personal challenge. Together, we can make a difference.

You will find a powerful set of developmental models in Chapter 4. Here, the authors describe the new and substantial fourth force in counseling—multicultural counseling and therapy (MCT). MCT starts with culture at the center rather than as an "add-on" at the periphery. It also uses well-known models of development, such as those of Jane Loevinger, in a culturally sensitive way. Thus, MCT is simultaneously a culture-specific and developmentally aware framework that counselors are encouraged to use when working with persons from diverse backgrounds.

As the individual is seen in a social-cultural context, we actually are moving to a more respectful individual approach to counseling. Not too surprisingly, as we think of the true complexity of our multicultural selves, we begin to recognize the real nature of our self-in-relation.

You may find Chapter 5 a personal challenge for it speaks of client advocacy. This means a more hands-on and activist stance. For those who favor distance and counselor/therapist neutrality, this chapter may be uncomfortable. I am reminded of a story one of my graduate students told me recently. She was on internship when a woman came for her regular interview but soon broke down in tears as she had just left her husband for safety reasons and had no place to stay that evening with her family. My student did the logical thing—she immediately set up a safe place and took the client there after work. The next day, the student intern was called in and disciplined for "counter-transference" and "violation of boundaries." Advocacy involves professional transformation, so it may require personal courage.

The community counselor as a social change agent is explored in Chapter 6. Helping a client find housing is clearly an important part of advocacy, but what is the professional role in a more upstream approach? It may mean helping establish coalitions to petition community leaders and authorities to provide more adequate housing. It may mean moving out of one's office into the community to encourage contact and positive confrontation between conflicting racial and ethnic groups. One may find it important to examine the local banks' pattern of providing loans. Clearly, it means taking a risk for the betterment of all.

Chapter 7 shows how the four-component community counseling model can be used to make a difference in community mental health agencies, career development services, specialized agencies, schools, and business and industry. Direct and indirect client service as well as direct and indirect community action can be synthesized to make an important difference. I found this chapter particularly helpful in terms of conceptualizing the many interventions and activities of the previous chapters. This chapter helps readers examine their own personal expertise, goals, and strategies for networking *with others* to produce significant change in their school or community setting. I stress "with others" because it is clear that no one can do it alone.

Managing these diverse ideas and concepts will not always be easy. Chapter 8 prepares one to take this book from the classroom to the community. Though counselors and therapists do not think of themselves as managers, management skills and awareness are vital. Unless they are part of a team with a clear strategy and action plan, little will happen. It becomes easy to retreat to the individual office and wait for clients. Effective management will help balance the time in the office and in the community. Management is not something to fear; rather, it is something in which all counselors must participate, each contributing his or her own special competence and expertise.

The authors—Judy Lewis, Michael Lewis, Judy Daniels, and Michael D'Andrea—have assembled in clear form a vast literature. It is a literature and set of methods that need to become central to the practice of counselors, psychologists, and social workers. It is now time to build on the many positives of traditional counseling theories and integrate them appropriately with multicultural, developmentally oriented, and empowering approaches for the future of the profession.

My thanks and admiration to the authors for their inspiring and scholarly efforts. Let us now turn to working together to make their ideas live in ourselves and in our communities.

Allen E. Ivey, Ed.D., A.B.P.P.
Distinguished University Professor
University of Massachusetts, Amherst

PREFACE

In this revision of *Community Counseling: Empowerment Strategies for a Diverse Society*, we present our vision of what the mental health professions might do to increase their impact in terms of promoting the psychological health and personal empowerment of larger numbers of people in the 21st century. Although we have made many substantial changes in this edition, the core components of the community counseling model remain unchanged. As in the first edition, we provide practitioners with many new and comprehensive ways of thinking about themselves as mental health service providers. More specifically, the community counseling model encourages practitioners to think in creative and expansive terms regarding the multiple roles they can play and the impact they might have in their clients' lives. To foster this sort of thinking, we have presented many examples of the ways preventive education, outreach services to vulnerable populations, and advocacy services can be used to reinforce the personal well-being of many people in modern society.

Most of the changes we made from the previous edition reflect our attempts to make the model even more relevant for the types of challenges mental health professionals will face in the 21st century. These changes affect the following four areas.

First, we have tried to expand the reader's thinking regarding the broad notion of psychological health by presenting new information about personal wellness throughout the book. Much of this new information comes from the work of postmodernist thinkers and human ecology theorists in the fields of anthropology, developmental psychology, counseling, multicultural education, social psychology, and social work. We provide this new information to foster the reader's awareness of the contextual nature of human development. In doing so, we emphasize the importance of thinking about the different ways contextual (environmental) factors influence the psychological development of our clients, our students, and ourselves. Further, we hope that this emphasis will help mental health practitioners (1) be encouraged to move beyond the traditional individual-intrapsychic-remedial model of helping that has dominated the counseling profession for the past 50 years and (2) feel challenged to implement intervention strategies that we intentionally designed to create systemic changes in their clients' social environments.

Second, we have tried to define *empowerment* more precisely. However important this concept is for the work counselors, psychologists, social workers and other mental health professionals do, the term *empowerment* has lost much of its meaning and impact over the past several years. Generally speaking, we believe that too many mental health practitioners use the term without sharing a common definition of this foundational concept. For this reason, we have referred to the work of a variety of empowerment theorists in providing a clear and practical definition of the term and in describing numerous intervention strategies that have been tested and proven effective in fostering the psychological health of thousands of individuals in a variety of settings in the United States.

Third, we have infused multicultural counseling considerations throughout this revised edition. In fact, this is one of the few textbooks in which multicultural issues play a central role. Thus, rather than discussing multicultural issues in a separate section in each chapter (as many authors have done in the past), the newly revised edition of *Community Counseling: Empowerment Strategies for a Diverse Society* presents multicultural issues throughout every chapter.

Fourth, many new references have been used in this revision. This has been done to provide the reader with the most recent research findings that demonstrate the effectiveness of the community counseling model. By updating our references, we hope to underscore the point that the intervention strategies we discuss are more than just a good set of ideas for helping people realize their potential. As dozens of new research and evaluation studies show, the helping strategies described in this book have undergone extensive testing and have been found to be effective in promoting the psychological well-being of many people from diverse cultural/racial, economic, geographical, and sexual backgrounds.

The completion of this revised edition would not have been possible without the assistance of several persons to whom we are most grateful. In this regard, we thank Molly Roth, whose supportive words and skills as manuscript editor helped sharpen the way we presented many of the ideas in this book. Greg Hubit provided assistance in the overall production of this edition and helped make sure we met our deadlines. The following persons reviewed early drafts of this revised edition and offered many helpful suggestions: Ann Chapman, Eastern Kentucky University; Mary Ann Jones, Wright State University; Linda Keel, Northeastern Illinois University; Kathleen M. May, University of Virginia; Dennis L. Poole, University of Central Florida; John J. Robich, Richmond Community College; David Santoro, Cleveland State University; Nancy Sherman,

Bradley University. Eileen Murphy, our editor at Brooks/Cole, not only offered many useful suggestions that helped us reconsider some of the ways in which we presented the *Community Counseling* framework, but was a constant source of support throughout this endeavor. The completion of the second edition is in large part due to her professional expertise and personal encouragment.

We genuinely hope that the revised edition of *Community Counseling: Empowerment Strategies for a Diverse Society* will contribute to the development of a new vision of the mental health profession in the 21st century and, more specifically, that it will help expand the way counselors, psychologists, and social workers think about their professional role and purpose in modern society. In this way, we hope the book will help practitioners find new ways to increase their overall impact on large numbers of people from diverse backgrounds in schools and universities, business, mental health service agencies, and communities across the United States.

Judith A. Lewis
Michael D. Lewis
Judy A. Daniels
Michael J. D'Andrea

CHAPTER 1

THE COMMUNITY COUNSELING MODEL

THE SEARCH FOR MORE EFFECTIVE COUNSELING PARADIGMS

This book is about a vision. Specifically, it outlines the types of things counselors and other mental health practitioners might do to make a greater impact on the psychological health and well-being of large numbers of people in the United States during the 21st century.

There are three main reasons for writing a book about a new vision of counseling. First, many believe that, like most people, counselors gain a clear sense of purpose and direction when they identify with a specific vision. Senge (1994) points out that the success individuals, organizations, and professional groups achieve relates directly to the sense of purpose and direction they derive from a clearly stated vision.

Second, by developing a new vision of their professional roles, counselors can better meet the needs of clients living in a rapidly changing, culturally diverse, technological society. The willingness to reassess, renew, and transform old visions also reportedly contributes to the ongoing successes individuals and organizations achieve over time (Senge, 1994).

Third, and perhaps most important, there is an urgent need to move beyond what many consider to be an outdated vision of the counseling profession's purpose and direction (Aubrey & Lewis, 1988; D. W. Sue & Sue, 1990). Herr and McFadden (1991) echo this need by emphasizing that counseling practitioners must develop a more comprehensive vision of their role if they are to remain a relevant and viable part of this nation's mental health and educational systems in the 21st century. Further, an increasing awareness of the inherent limitations of the traditional counseling paradigm also fuels the need for a new vision.

The Traditional Counseling Paradigm

The word *paradigm* refers to a mental model or framework individuals use to make sense of their life experiences (Newton & Caple, 1985). Historically, the counseling profession has embraced a helping paradigm that emphasizes one-to-one intervention strategies that focus on clients' intrapsychic experiences. These interventions are typically time bound, office bound, and remedial in nature (Atkinson, Morten, & Sue, 1993; Aubrey, 1983).

This traditional way of thinking about counseling emphasizes facilitating change in individual clients rather than their environments. While this counseling paradigm has dominated the profession for several decades, researchers have shown ever more clearly that it is simply too narrow to address this nation's mental health needs.

In this regard, Albee (1986) notes that 43 million adults (19% of the total adult population) experience mental health problems that warrant annual professional help in the United States. This does not include patients in hospitals, mentally ill homeless people, or children. Further, youngsters constitute another 20 million in need of psychological counseling services each year in this country (Conyne, 1987).

Despite the well-documented need for mental health services, only seven million adults actually receive counseling services from trained professionals each year (Albee & Gullotta, 1986). Given the tremendous disparity between the number of people who need mental health services and the number of those who actually receive such help, numerous people suggested that the traditional one-to-one, remedial, intrapsychic counseling paradigm cannot meet this nation's psychological needs (Atkinson et al., 1993).

Beyond its quantitative ineffectiveness, this paradigm also fails to improve the overall quality of this country's mental and social health. Support for this statement comes from recent research findings that document the continued erosion of the mental and social health of U.S. citizens since 1970.

For example, Miringoff (1995) has examined changes in 17 indicators of this nation's psychological and social health from 1970 to 1993. The results of this investigation reflect positive gains in only five categories among people in the United States during this time: infant mortality rates, drug abuse statistics, the annual high-school dropout rate, the level of poverty among people over 65, and the provision of food stamps to the poor. In contrast, conditions significantly worsened in 12 other health categories during the same period. Noticeable increases took place in the total number of children living in poverty, reported cases of child abuse, teen suicides, adolescent pregnancies, and unemployment. The study also cites reduced average weekly wages; a lack of health insurance coverage among a greater number of families; more homicides, alcohol-related highway deaths, homeless individuals and families, out-of-pocket health costs for people over 65; and a greater gap between the rich and the poor in the United States (Miringoff, 1995).

Though some of these indicators may reflect problems associated with the choices individuals make (e.g., child abuse, homicide, alcohol-related deaths), others represent more complex systemic problems (e.g., unemployment, children in poverty, the gap between the rich and the poor). Regardless of the underlying causes of these problems, however, the stressors associated with all these situations negatively impact the mental health of an increasing number of people in this country each year (Miringoff, 1995).

Most important, these research findings point to the deterioration of this nation's mental and social health despite the efforts of tens of thousands of professionally trained mental health practitioners over the past three decades. This does not mean that counselors, psychologists, and social workers provide worthless or ineffective services; many studies document the benefits individuals derive from traditional counseling services. However, these results strongly suggest that relying too much on the traditional counseling paradigm has failed to promote the types of individual and systemic changes necessary to improve the overall quality of this nation's mental health and social well-being. Toward this end, counselors must develop a new vision of their responsibilities as mental health professionals in the 21st century. Developing such a vision will inevitably require a shift from the traditional counseling paradigm to one that is both more comprehensive and ultimately more effective.

Shifting Paradigms

More than 30 years ago, Kuhn (1962) popularized the notion that paradigm shifts are the inevitable results of new developments in scientific knowledge. Barclay (1983) was among the first to articulate formally the need for a paradigm shift in the counseling profession. Recognizing that the traditional counseling paradigm limits counselors' professional potential and threatens the profession's future, several others have recently discussed the importance of developing a new helping model (Ivey, Ivey, & Simek-Morgan, 1993; Pedersen, 1991; Rigazio-DiGilio, 1994; D. W. Sue & Sue, 1990).

A paradigm shift in the counseling profession requires fundamental changes in the way many counselors currently think and act. While this will likely cause a sense of confusion and resistance among some traditionally trained practitioners, such changes are necessary for the counseling profession to remain viable (Daniels & D'Andrea, 1996; Lucas, 1985).

Commenting on the dynamics associated with making a paradigm shift in the profession, Newton and Caple (1985) point out that

> The transition from an old paradigm to a new one is not simply a cumulative process or an extension of an old paradigm. It is a reordering of knowledge based on new ideas that change many of the fundamental beliefs and applications in one's world that have been held for so long. During the transition period there can be confusion and overlap about the problems that can be solved by the old paradigm and by the new paradigm. With the new paradigm, however, there will be a decisive difference in the methods used to find solutions to human problems. (p. 163)

There is considerable reason to believe that a paradigm shift is, in fact, currently taking place in counseling. Several theoretical forces that have evolved over the past 35 years are causing counselors to reconsider their roles when working with diverse client populations. These forces include the increasing awareness and acceptance of contextual (Steenbarger, 1991), ecological (Germain, 1991), and systems theories (von Bertalanffy, 1968); advancements in feminist psychology (Gilligan, 1982; J. B. Miller, 1987); the rise of multiculturalism (Locke, 1992; D. W. Sue & Sue, 1990); and the emergence of postmodern thinking (Gergen, 1992; Hayes, 1994).

The ideas and knowledge generated by these forces enrich the profession's understanding of human development in many important ways. However, these theories also promote dissonance and discomfort among some counselors as the new knowledge they have generated often conflicts with many of the premises embedded in the traditional counseling paradigm. Commenting on this situation, Rigazio-DiGilio and Ivey (1993) state that "the main task facing the counseling profession is not to continue this proliferation of diverse points of view, but rather to think about and organize these theories into some meaningful and coherent framework" (p. 208).

The community counseling model represents a transitional framework that marks a shift toward a new counseling paradigm not yet fully realized. This framework provides counselors with a practical set of guidelines for offering a broad range of mental health services among diverse client populations in a variety of settings. However, because this model incorporates a number of traditional counseling concepts and strategies, one cannot consider it a new paradigm in the truest sense of the term. Rather, it represents an integrative framework that encourages a new way of thinking about the counselor's professional purpose and purview in the 21st century.

Community Counseling Defined

We define *community counseling* as a comprehensive helping framework of intervention strategies and services that promotes the personal development and well-being of all individuals and communities. The community counseling model comprises four service components: (1) direct client, (2) indirect client, (3) direct community, and (4) indirect community services. Further, this model provides counselors with a practical intervention framework that integrates contributions from contextual, developmental, ecological, feminist, multicultural, and postmodern theorists in the the past 35 years.

These theoretical contributions have caused mental health practitioners to reconsider the validity of certain Eurocentric and individualistic principles that underlie the traditional counseling and therapy paradigm (D. W. Sue & Sue, 1990). As a result, even such time-honored values as the promotion of clients' autonomy, independence, self-esteem, and self-actualization have come into question as counselors learn more about the important role that collectivism, interdependence, and family systems serve in fostering the psychological well-being of people from diverse cultural, ethnic, and racial backgrounds (Atkinson et al., 1993; Kelly, 1989).

Many multicultural counseling theorists have raised these and other important issues in their work. As such, multiculturalism has become one of the most potent forces to challenge the traditional perspectives that have dominated counselors' thinking for most of the 20th century (Pedersen 1990; D. W. Sue, Ivey, & Pedersen, 1996; D. W. Sue & Sue, 1990). Of course, this is not a condemnation of all Eurocentric and individualistic values reflected by the traditional counseling paradigm. Rather, when used as the primary approach to counseling, the traditional framework often does not work in the context of a rapidly changing, pluralistic society.

Building Community:
The Challenge of the 21st Century

The word *community* means different things to different people. To some it may refer to people living in a specific geographical area (e.g., a rural versus an urban community). To others it may mean a group of people related by their unique cultural, ethnic, or racial background, such as the Asian-American community. Still others may use the term to refer to the interdependence each has to one another as members of a much broader "global community." In this book, we refer to *community* as "a group or gathering of people who share common interests and needs" (Paisley, 1996).

When referring to communities as *systems*, we mean that they have unity, continuity, and predictability. Individuals, groups, and organizations that compose a community are interdependent. Communities also link individuals to other communities, including the greater society. Thus, communities serve as a medium through which individuals can act on the world and through which society as a whole transmits norms. Under this working definition, families and neighborhoods can be communities, as can a school, a hospital, or a corporation. Accordingly, an individual may belong to more than one community at a time. Also, communities have such presence and power that anyone working with individuals as a helper must, at some point, examine the effects of various communities, of which they are a part, on their overall well-being.

We purposely chose a general definition because we intend it to include a wide range of human collectives—from families and schools to larger communities such as gay and lesbian groups, and further to much larger and more complex sociopolitical systems such as the North American community. Because this definition implies that community members have a direct and/or indirect impact on one another, human connections and interdependence serve as important concepts on which we base the community counseling model.

Human ecology theorists argue that people share a universal drive to belong to some sort of community. Germain (1991) indicates that this drive stems from the need to establish a sense of connection with others whereby individuals become better positioned to satisfy both their emotional and instrumental needs (Germain, 1991).

The experiences individuals have within these communities affect their psychological health and well-being in many ways. As such, while counselors will continue to play an important role in working with individuals, their greatest professional contributions rest in their willingness and ability to foster the development of healthy communities in the future.

The importance of community building and its relationship to psychological wellness has become increasingly clear as counselors gain new knowledge about human development. Feminist (Gilligan, 1982; J. B. Miller, 1987) and postmodern (Tierney, 1993) theorists have particularly helped counselors understand the importance of relatedness within significant community contexts when assessing a person's mental health. This knowledge has led counseling practitioners to better appreciate the notion of "self-in-relation" (J. B. Miller, 1987) and the inextricable role interdependence plays in determining one's overall sense of personal well-being (Gilligan, 1982; Jordan, Kaplan, Miller, Stiver, & Surrey, 1991).

Many social, economic, and political forces, however, have threatened the quality of life in U.S. communities as well as the sense of human interdependence. Lator (1993) specifically includes the rising support for cutbacks in domestic governmental spending (especially for educational and mental health programs for at-risk populations) among those factors that threaten the long-term quality of life in the United States.

These cutbacks are creating what Lator (1993) calls a "scarcity mode," which makes it increasingly more difficult to secure necessary resources. Continuing cutbacks in governmental spending for human services represent a major challenge for counselors and other mental health professionals because, as Miringoff's (1995) recent report clearly indicates, such programs desperately need more—not less—support in order to promote this country's overall mental and social health.

The need to create a new vision for the counseling profession is inexorably tied to all these factors: the dwindling governmental support for mental health services, increased knowledge about the role of interdependence and relatedness in human development, and the failure of the traditional counseling paradigm to address the mental health needs of a culturally diverse society. In light of these conditions, we believe that a new vision of counseling must reflect a dramatic shift from the current individual-remedial perspective of helping to one that emphasizes culturally sensitive, community-building initiatives that are primarily preventive. The community counseling framework provides a means for addressing these issues.

Dr. Martin Luther King (1963) insisted that developing a healthy and respectful sense of interdependence as members of a national and world community was the single most important challenge of his time. Though he presented this message more than 35 years ago, we believe that Dr. King's insight applies directly to counselors today as they search for new ways to address the mental health needs of the 21st century. We hope that counselors will find the community counseling model helpful as they strive to foster the mental health of clients as well as promoting more tolerant, responsive, and caring communities across the United States.

THE COMMUNITY COUNSELING MODEL

Overview

- At a midwestern mental health center, participants in popular workshops learn to cope with unemployment, manage chronic stress, adjust to change, or beat the holiday blues.
- Counselors in a large metropolitan area in the southeast provide comprehensive counseling services among urban, African-

American youth to address the problem of adolescent pregnancies in their communities.

- Children in a multiethnic, multiracial school participate in a program designed to increase their level of awareness and respect for cultural diversity.
- In a suburban youth project, adolescents study community issues, explore their rights and responsibilities as students, and learn to monitor and influence legislation that concerns them.
- In a large western university, students from diverse cultural and racial backgrounds take part in a variety of programs that help them acquire a host of life skills necessary to lead successful and satisfying lives.
- Latinos in Boston come together to decide on the types of services they need to help members of their community realize their human potential and develop a greater sense of cultural pride.
- Mental health practitioners in urban areas across the nation come together to plan and implement educational strategies aimed at reducing the spread of HIV/AIDS among high-risk populations in their localities.
- In an economically depressed rural part of the southwestern United States, professional counselors join with other health-care providers to address the needs of Native Americans and their families.

Although the focus, setting, and clientele of each of these programs vary widely, they share similar characteristics on which we base the community counseling model. First, they all reflect an awareness of society's effects on every member of the community in which counselors work. Second, they share a perception of clients as whole persons who possess a range of personal strengths and resources as well as limitations. Third, they reflect a desire to prevent the debilitating problems that occur daily in schools and other communities. Fourth, they strive to understand the unique needs and experiences of persons from diverse cultural, ethnic, and racial backgrounds. Above all, they reflect an understanding that individuals and communities alike become strengthened when counselors help clients learn ways to help themselves. Counselors can, in part, accomplish this when they help foster the types of knowledge and skills their clients need to lead responsible and satisfying lives.

Basic Assumptions

Although mental health practitioners who use the community counseling framework work in a variety of settings (e.g., schools, industry, community agencies), a coherent set of assumptions guides the work they do regardless of setting. These assumptions include the following beliefs:

1. People's environments may either nurture or limit them.
2. The goal of counseling is to facilitate individual and community empowerment.
3. A multifaceted approach to helping is more efficient than a single-service approach.
4. Attention to individuals' cultural, ethnic, and/or racial background is central to the planning and delivery of counseling services.
5. Prevention is more efficient than remediation.
6. One can use the community counseling model in a variety of human service, educational, and business settings.

We shall describe each of these assumptions in the following sections.

ENVIRONMENT: NEGATIVE AND POSITIVE EFFECTS   People continually interact with their surroundings in ways that help or harm them. As people develop, they rely on their environment as a source of learning and support, meeting their needs chiefly through interactions with others. Even so, the environment can also affect them negatively, stunting growth and limiting development.

Because the environment affects people so significantly, community counselors realize that attempts to promote their clients' psychological development without also dealing with their social systems are generally ineffective. As such, the community counseling model emphasizes that attempts to promote clients' well-being must include efforts to influence the contexts in which they live.

Environmental factors clearly contribute to the development of almost any kind of problem a client may face. Sometimes the connection between such factors and an individual's personal problems is clearly definable. For example, this occurs when institutionalized racism or sexism deny people career options, when abusive families victimize children, or when the ex-offender or chronically mentally ill client cannot gain free entry into the mainstream.

Though one can directly trace the vast majority of such problems to environmental interactions, many counselors continue to make the *fundamental attribution error*. This common error involves underestimating the impact of the environment on clients' development and overestimating their personal attributes. Strickland and Janoff-Bulman (1980) have described the fundamental attribution error as follows:

> Racial, economic, and social injustice force particular roles and circumstances on people which are all too often regarded and treated as psychological in nature, emanating from mental deficits within the individual. The very phrase "mental illness" connotes a disease

which must be treated by focusing one's ameliorative efforts on the individual. Psychologists, who have traditionally attributed the causes of mental disorders to the personal dispositions of their clients, have no doubt been unwitting perpetrators of the fundamental attribution error. (pp. 105–106)

When clients have developed in a psychologically noxious environment but counselors primarily focus on their clients' personal attributes (such as depression, apathy, and anger), they often inadvertently undermine their clients' own sense of personal power. Without the support to deal with and change environmental conditions that negatively impact their lives, clients usually feel increasingly powerless, lack a sense of purpose in counseling, and continue to feel trapped in highly restricted roles and unrewarding relationships.

While the environment can work against an individual's growth, however, it can just as surely aid personal development. In this regard, people vary in their ability to cope with life's stress. At least some of this variation proceeds from differences in the degree and type of social support available to them. An actively supportive social environment tends to foster healthy development by helping people cope well with stress (Dakof & Taylor, 1990; D'Andrea, 1994; Tedeschi & Calhoun, 1993). Because the environment affects people in so many ways, one must recognize its impact as the first step in planning strategies intentionally designed to foster individual and community empowerment.

EMPOWERMENT: PROMOTING SYSTEMIC AND INDIVIDUAL CHANGE *Empowerment* has become the buzzword of the 1990s among many mental health professionals. Unfortunately, ambiguity has often accompanied this popularity. When used to explain the goals of the community counseling model, however, the term has a very specific meaning. E. H. McWhirter's (1994) definition effectively captures the type of empowerment that underlies the community counseling framework:

> Empowerment is the process by which people, organizations,
> or groups who are powerless or marginalized (a) become aware
> of the power dynamics at work in their life context, (b) develop the
> skills and capacity for gaining some reasonable control over their
> lives, (c) which they exercise, (d) without infringing on the rights
> of others, and (e) which coincides with actively supporting the
> empowerment of others in the community. (p. 12)

This definition implies that counseling can be empowering when it promotes individual and systemic changes—that is, changes in those groups, organizations, and systems that impact clients' lives.

Although the community counseling framework emphasizes practical ways to promote empowerment, it rests firmly on a rich theoretical foundation that integrates work from many fields, including counseling, psychology, social work, community organizing, public health, organizational development, and multicultural counseling. In drawing on the perspectives of theorists in these areas, we have formulated a new vision of the multiple roles counselors can play in the future. The ultimate goal of the community counseling model is to promote positive changes in both clients and their environmental systems. To accomplish these goals, counselors must use a multifaceted and culturally sensitive approach in their work.

A *MULTIFACETED APPROACH TO HELPING*   The community counseling model emphasizes a multifaceted environmental approach to helping people. This approach sharply contrasts with the type of professional training many counselors have received, or the one-to-one method that primarily focuses on intrapsychic experiences.

Given the nature of our rapidly changing society and the relative ineffectiveness of the traditional one-to-one approach, counselors must be encouraged to develop a more expansive and systems-oriented method to promote their clients' well-being.

Failure of Traditional Approaches.   Aubrey and Lewis (1988) describe how traditional counseling approaches fail to meet the needs of clients affected by the rapid social change that began in the 1960s. In commenting on the pervasive use of the individual-remedial approach to counseling, these theorists state,

> The perspective was myopic, concentrating on intrapsychic
> functioning to the exclusion of environmental influences. In turn,
> applications focused on individual self-discovery and insight when, for
> many, this process failed to alleviate the presenting condition. What
> seemed called for, therefore, was both a broadening of perspective and
> a wider array of intervention techniques. (pp. 286–287)

The traditional approach to counseling seems particularly limiting when one considers the implications of the rapid demographic transformation in the United States. In light of this change, many multicultural counseling experts have argued that a single-focused, one-to-one, remedial approach is inappropriate—and unethical—in work with those with psychological problems that are directly tied to oppression in their environments (Atkinson et al., 1993; Locke, 1992; White & Parham, 1990). Further, the greatest challenge facing counseling practitioners in the 21st century involves finding new and more effective ways to help people from diverse cultural/ethnic/racial populations realize a greater sense of individual health and collective well-being (Ivey, Ivey, & Simek-Morgan, 1993; Lee & Richardson, 1991; Locke, 1992; Parham & McDavis, 1987).

New Approaches.   In attempting to respond to this important challenge, mental health practitioners have begun to use various types of group counseling and psychoeducational interventions to meet the needs of culturally diverse client populations. Research indicates that these alternative strategies offer much promise in terms of promoting the psychological well-being of people from diverse cultural, ethnic, and racial backgrounds (Daniels, 1995; Vargas & Koss-Chioino, 1992). Despite the usefulness of these interventions, though, many practitioners continue to adhere to a traditional approach in their work. Commenting on this situation, Aubrey and Lewis (1988) state,

> Many counselors have learned to feel comfortable dealing with groups, as well as individuals. They have come to regard training as a natural ally of counseling. They have ventured into new settings and dealt with new audiences. Despite the increase in the number and focus of group interventions, however, the basic perspective of counselors has not changed to the extent one might expect. Counselors still tend to overlook the impact of environmental factors on individual functioning, to distrust the efficacy of prevention interventions, and narrow the scope of their attention to the individual psyche. (p. 296)

To move beyond the narrow scope of the traditional paradigm, the community counseling framework emphasizes using a variety of approaches and services to promote psychological development. The model stresses the need to make changes in the environment that foster clients' physical, mental, cultural, and spiritual health and well-being. This model encourages practitioners to use what D'Andrea (1988) calls

> a multi-method framework wherein the counselor becomes a sort of architect. As an architect in this sense, the counselor consciously designs and structures various experiences in ways that are aimed at maximizing the client's opportunity to develop psychologically, emotionally, cognitively, morally, and physically. (p. 30)

From an ethical perspective, counselors must pay particular attention to their clients' cultural traditions, values, and worldviews to design interventions that complement their unique backgrounds (American Counseling Association, 1995; American Psychological Association, 1991).

MULTICULTURAL COUNSELING CONSIDERATIONS   Over the past 20 years, the counseling profession has been severely criticized for failing to address adequately the unique cultural differences that characterize the psychological development of people from diverse backgrounds (D'Andrea, 1992; Lee & Richardson, 1991; Locke, 1992; Pedersen, 1990; D. W. Sue & Sue, 1990). This failure has been compounded by the tendency of many counselors to impose their own values, preferences, and worldviews when working with clients from culturally diverse populations. Wrenn (1985) notes that this sort of professional imposition stems largely from the counselor's own unwillingness to consider respectfully and sensitively the implications of a client's cultural background in the context of counseling. He further states that this resistance typifies the counselor's own "cultural encapsulation."

Despite the growing awareness of the changing ethnic and racial demography of the United States, many mental health practitioners still resist addressing their clients' cultural uniqueness within the context of counseling. Recognizing the detrimental effects of such resistance, multicultural counseling advocates have worked hard to catalyze a host of theoretical and practical changes in the counseling profession (Atkinson et al., 1993; Lee & Richardson, 1991; Locke, 1992; D. W. Sue et al., 1996).

Three main factors have led to the rise of the multicultural counseling movement over the past two and a half decades. First, the number of Asian Americans, African Americans, Latinos, and Native Americans residing in the United States has dramatically increased because of changing immigration patterns and differential birthrates (Atkinson et al., 1993). Some predict that by 2050, the majority of citizens will come from various "minority" groups (D. W. Sue & Sue, 1990). Many counselors have already experienced this demographic transformation through an increase in work with people whose cultural background, values, and worldviews differ greatly from their own.

Second, researchers have noted that counselors have generally been ineffective when working with people from culturally diverse client populations (Atkinson et al., 1993; D. W. Sue & Sue, 1990). They have traced this ineffectiveness to the overall lack of cultural awareness, knowledge, and skills many counselors exhibit (D. W. Sue, Arredondo, & McDavis, 1992).

Third, many have argued that the conventional individual-intrapsychic-remedial approach to helping often conflicts with the traditions, values, and worldviews of many clients from diverse cultural backgrounds (Ivey et al., 1993; Locke, 1992). To overcome this ineffectiveness and the questionable ethics of using traditional models with certain clients, counselors have tried to incorporate a multifaceted, preventive approach that requires awareness, sensitivity, and flexibility when working with culturally different people (Atkinson et al., 1993; Lee & Richardson, 1991).

The multicultural counseling movement has made many mental health practitioners more aware of the importance of changing the traditional counseling paradigm. Because of multicultural counseling's powerful influence and potential to shift mental health practice, Pedersen (1990) has recently referred to it as the "fourth force" in the counseling profession. In light of the changing demography of the United States and the rising interest in multiculturalism, several theorists have argued that the profession needs a comprehensive and practical model that bridges the knowledge and techniques of traditional Western approaches and new strategies that complement the unique needs and values of people from diverse backgrounds (D. W. Sue, Ivey, & Pedersen, 1996).

The community counseling framework represents one response to this explicitly stated need. This model synthesizes many conventional and preventive counseling theories with knowledge generated from the multicultural movement into a practical and expansive framework.

EMPHASIS ON PREVENTION   As we have noted, counselors usually spend a disproportionate amount of time providing individual counseling services to clients. Though counselors do help individuals in this way, one to-one counseling alone does not offer a way to reach people before the onset of problems. Such a narrow focus wastes human resources and makes it impossible to reach today's increasing number of people who need help.

With the escalating need for mental health services among culturally diverse client populations, now more than ever counselors must consider new ways to reach larger numbers of people *before* psychological distress has debilitated them. The community counseling model attempts to address this challenge by making preventive counseling strategies an integral part of its framework.

Preventive counseling strives to lower the incidence of specific types of problems among a given population. Mental health professionals have borrowed terminology from the field of public health to differentiate *primary, secondary,* and *tertiary prevention:*

> Primary prevention . . . focuses on lowering the incidence of
> emotional problems and on promoting positive mental health
> among people not identified as having any special difficulty. It
> can be distinguished from secondary prevention, which aims
> toward early identification and treatment of problems, and from
> tertiary prevention, which attempts to decrease the long-term
> effects of disabilities. In essence, primary prevention involves
> activities designed to reduce environmental stressors or to build
> people's competencies and life skills. (Lewis & Lewis, 1981, p. 173)

Primary prevention is a multidimensional construct central to the community counseling model. In defining primary prevention, Conyne (1994) outlines ten qualities particularly relevant to this model:

1. Primary prevention counseling efforts occur "before the fact." That is, preventive counseling represents proactive efforts which are instituted before psychological dysfunction, illness, or problems occur.

2. Primary prevention focuses on healthy people or people at-risk. Some examples of individuals likely to be at-risk for future psychological problems include persons who are victims of racial or cultural discrimination, children of divorce or alcoholics, people growing up in poverty, family members of a newly unemployed worker, HIV patients, and survivors of a recently deceased loved one.

3. Preventive counseling is implemented to stop or reduce the incidence of new dysfunctions from occurring among specific groups of people.

4. Preventive counseling is group-oriented and population based. While preventive services can be used with one person, they are intended to be utilized with many people such as a group, neighborhood, school, or an at-risk population.

5. Primary prevention efforts are designed to reduce specific risk factors while simultaneously increasing protective factors. Risk factors may include destructive family dynamics, emotional difficulties, low self-esteem, school-related problems, unemployment, poverty, interpersonal problems, and delays in skill development. [Conyne here cites Coie et al., 1993.]

6. Preventive counseling is ecological and systemic as it occurs within a complex context of interacting levels of influence including but not limited to family, school, business, and community interventions.

7. Primary prevention is culturally sensitive and valid. Thus, when working with large groups of people in their natural settings, counselors must strive to be respectful of the cultural norms, beliefs, and practices of the population and setting.

8. Preventive counseling is concerned with social justice and intended to include persons from traditionally underrepresented populations. It is an inclusive process in which people from diverse cultural, ethnic, and racial groups and communities are routinely invited to develop strategies that are designed to help individuals avoid major debilitating problems and enhance their overall psychological functioning.

9. Primary prevention is collaborative and educative. The primary tools of this form of intervention are those of education, not therapy or rehabilitation, although some insights for its models and programs grow out of the wisdom derived from clinical experience.

10. Preventive counseling is empowering. Education and collaboration promotes empowerment because it affords individuals real opportunities for involvement in activities that build on their personal strengths and psychological assets in culturally sensitive and respectful ways (pp. 2–4)

Preventive counseling may involve *direct services*, offering individuals opportunities to participate in competency-building experiences. Counseling approaches that are prevention-oriented are also characterized by the provision of *indirect services*. Indirect counseling services focus on changing the social surroundings that affect people's lives.

No matter the approach, if a program aims at serving a group of people who have not developed specific problems or dysfunctions, one calls it preventive rather than remedial. The community counseling model emphasizes the importance of combining direct and indirect services to meet the needs of the population being served, regardless of the setting in which counselors work.

From a human service planning perspective, one clearly sees that preventing problems allows helpers to reallocate resources according to logical priorities. Thus, instead of directing objectives toward current crises, the community counseling framework encourages practitioners and community members to work together to determine goals and then identify the resources needed to accomplish them.

APPLICABILITY IN A VARIETY OF SETTINGS   Anyone offering psychological, social, educational, or vocational services to individuals or groups has a responsibility to some community. This is obvious to a counselor in a community mental health center, whose clients reside in geographically defined or catchment areas, where the agency has a clear mandate to identify and address the specific needs of those communities. This responsibility is less obvious, however, where the community is not well defined. For example, school counselors who intentionally strive to influence the interplay between students and their environments—their families, peers, neighborhoods, classrooms—in effect act as "community counselors." Any counselor or helping professional, though, may find the community counseling model useful if they

1. Understand the dynamic interplay between individual clients and their environments.
2. Accept that clients are continuously affected by their environments
3. Strive to empower clients and their respective communities by intentionally designing and implementing strategies that foster individual and environmental changes
4. Use culturally appropriate interventions

THE ROLE OF THE COMMUNITY COUNSELOR

The community counseling model requires practitioners to develop new ways of organizing and delivering services to clients. Counselors must take on roles that extend beyond what professional helpers have traditionally been trained to do and have grown comfortable using in the past.

This new model, however, represents an expansion of ways to think about the helping process. For this reason, you should consider the framework discussed in the following chapters as an extension and not a replacement of the traditional approach. Because this model is comprehensive, community counselors direct attention to both the individual and the environment when providing services that foster clients' well-being.

The Individual and the Environment

That the social environment affects every individual by either enhancing or stunting one's personal development is a relatively simple proposition with which most counselors would readily agree. However, despite such agreement, counselors and other helping professionals still typically promote changes with individual clients and spend little time and energy to impact their environments.

The community counseling model encourages practitioners to expand their view of themselves as professional helpers by altering the types of strategies and services they use with their clients. In traditional counseling, practitioners help clients examine their behavior, take responsibility for their actions, and change that which can most easily be changed: themselves. Community counselors take these activities further, seeing the environment not as a static reality to which clients must adjust but as a dynamic structure that—like the client—can change.

In this relationship, counselor and client together explore the following questions:

1. To what extent can the client resolve the issue through personal change?
2. What environmental resources can help the client grow?
3. To what extent does the solution depend on changing the environment rather than the individual?
4. How can the counselor, the client, or both bring about necessary changes in the environment?

The counselor also considers these questions in terms of all the members of a given community, such as what problems African Americans face in general. With practice, the counselor can discern factors that might also affect other current or potential clients. Becoming aware of these forces is easy when many clients present problems exacerbated by a common set of environmental conditions. More difficult, but just as important, is sensing the potential for such problems before they arise, or being so attuned to what is going on within a school or other community that one can take action before casualties appear.

Working to bring about positive environmental changes that prevent mental health problems is a key part of the community counselor's role. To do so, practitioners must become familiar with and make themselves available to those communities, such as families, schools, neighborhoods, community centers, and workplaces, that impact their clients' psychological development and personal well-being.

Taking the time to become involved with their clients' communities is especially important when working with people from diverse cultural, ethnic, and racial backgrounds. By doing so, counselors become better positioned to

1. Understand their clients' cultural/ethnic/racial experiences
2. Observe the types of environmental factors and conditions that directly contribute to their problems
3. Gain a greater appreciation of their clients' unique sources of strength and support.

Recognizing the importance of the environment, the community counselor must plan strategies that bring about positive community changes. To realize this role, practitioners must develop and implement a multifaceted approach to working with clients.

A Multifaceted Approach Within a Multicultural Society

Using a multifaceted approach in counseling practice challenges practitioners to develop new skills for confronting negative environmental forces and fostering those conditions that promote health. More specifically, this approach to counseling compels practitioners to deal with large groups as well as individuals, to become an educator as well as a counselor, and to deal with the environment as well as the affected person. However, letting go of the familiar and conventional ways of working is not always easy. As Lewis, Lewis, and Souflee (1991) point out,

> [There is] a tendency for human service deliverers to concentrate more on the nature of the services being delivered than on the ultimate purposes of these services. Familiar methods are often used long after changes in the community needs or agency mission should have dictated changes in services. (p. 21)

Community counselors recognize that they need a variety of resources, techniques, and roles. To meet the diverse needs of their clients, practitioners must develop expertise in areas that often go beyond their formal training. Those who adopt the community counseling model in practice must be committed to becoming perpetual learners—developing new skills in consultation, advocacy, advising, and community organizing, as well as facilitating indigenous support systems and healing methods.

Atkinson et al. (1993) note that "for the most part, these skills are not really new, since they have been proposed and to some degree implemented in the past" (p. 300). Rather than viewing these skills as radical departures from the roles many counselors have played in the past, one might most aptly think of them as "old wine in new bottles" (Pine, 1972, p. 35).

They are new, however, in the sense that they have not yet gained widespread acceptance within human service professions. By accepting the role of client advocate, consultant, adviser, community organizer, and/or facilitator of indigenous support systems and healing methods, community counselors become more actively involved in their clients' life experiences than do most practitioners who adhere to the traditional counseling paradigm. Those who use the community counseling model also differ from other helping professionals in that they generally direct more time and energy toward preventive rather than remedial issues and concerns.

Promoting Prevention

Community counseling's emphasis on healthy development and preventing problems calls for a continually fresh perspective on problems and potential solutions. Community counselors must look beyond the problems themselves to how clients' environments have caused them.

Although a more traditional approach to counseling might treat dysfunction as belonging to individuals, and though community counselors certainly work with individuals in trouble, the preventive dimension of the community counseling model involves evaluating dysfunctions in the context of larger systems. Prevention implies bringing about changes in the community rather than concentrating primarily on individual diagnoses.

The emphasis on prevention makes community counseling highly active. One cannot wait passively for the next task, the next problem, the next crisis to appear. Instead, practitioners continually look for situations in which they can help, planning and initiating new programs to meet the needs of clients and their communities. This emphasis on prevention also makes the community counseling model a more viable and relevant framework than the traditional model for working with minority groups. *Minority group* is defined here as the following:

A group of people who, because of physical or cultural characteristics, are singled out from others in the society in which they live for differential and unequal treatment, and who therefore regard themselves as objects of collective discrimination. . . . Minority group status carries with it the exclusion from full participation in the life of the society." (Wirth, 1945, cited in Ponterotto & Pedersen, 1993, p. 7)

While ethnic minority groups experience as many mental health problems as European Americans do, several researchers have reported that minority-group members frequently avoid using conventional counseling services (Atkinson et al., 1993; Cheung & Snowden, 1990; S. Sue, 1988). Specific cultural values, such as saving face for oneself or one's family, often contribute to the minority-group person's reluctance to talk about personal and sensitive issues with a stranger (i.e., a professional counselor) (Esquivel & Keitel, 1990).

Also, the problems many clients from minority groups experience often begin with the external environment. Smith (1985) has identified several environmental stressors including prejudice, discrimination, poverty, racism, and sexism that he believes contribute to the mental health problems people from minority groups commonly face. Given the persistence of these systemic stressors and the reluctance of such groups to use conventional counseling services, the preventive dimension of the community counseling model represents a culturally responsive and respectful way of serving diverse client populations in the 1990s and beyond.

FROM MODEL CONCEPT TO MODEL PROGRAM

Having examined the assumptions underlying the community counseling framework and their implications for the counselor's role we can begin to define the model in more concrete terms. We define *community counseling* as a multifaceted approach combining direct and indirect services to help community members live more effectively and to prevent those problems most frequently faced by people who use the services.

Although community counselors clearly need to be creative and flexible in their approach, they do not lack guidelines for action. The activities that make up a comprehensive community counseling approach to helping fall into distinct categories.

First, as noted earlier in the chapter, we can distinguish between direct and indirect services. *Direct services* provide community members opportunities to learn new skills or develop fresh understandings that can help them live more effectively and independently. *Indirect services* address the settings that affect people's well-being. When using indirect services, the community counselor intervenes, or enters into a situation in order to bring about change that will make the environment more suitable for individual growth. Thus, direct services and programs focus on specific target populations; indirect interventions, on the environment.

Second, we can distinguish between community and client services. Available to each member of the general community or target population, *community services* provide help to large numbers of people who have not been identified as having specific dysfunctions. In contrast, *client services* are more concentrated, aimed at people identified as needing more active assistance.

Combining these categories, we find that the community counseling approach has, in practice, four distinct facets:

1. **Direct community services** (preventive education): Community-wide educational programs that provide direct experiences and are made available to the population as a whole
2. **Direct client services** (outreach and counseling): Programs that provide direct assistance to clients or potential clients who might be at risk for developing mental health problems
3. **Indirect community services** (promoting systemic changes and influencing public policy): Efforts to make the social environment more responsive to the needs of the population as a whole
4. **Indirect client services** (advocacy and consultation): Programs that intervene in the environments of specific individuals or groups, allowing their special needs to be met

Each facet of the comprehensive community counseling program is associated with specific modes of service, as shown in Table 1.1. To provide a truly comprehensive program, the community counselor must offer services pertaining to all four quadrants of the table.

TABLE 1.1

THE FOUR FACETS OF COMMUNITY COUNSELING AND THEIR SERVICE MODES

	COMMUNITY SERVICES	CLIENT SERVICES
Direct	Preventive education	Counseling Outreach to vulnerable clients
Indirect	Influencing public policy	Client advocacy Consultation

Direct Community Services: Preventive Education

Counselors providing direct community services work to educate or train the population at large. In these interventions, they aim at sharing psychological knowledge and skills that help lessen the need for professional helpers. Ideally, through participating in these experiences, community members gain skills to help themselves.

Voluntary education programs provide individuals and groups with opportunities to increase their awareness and develop skills that can help them live more effectively and deal with their problems more competently. Such programs may run the gamut from values-clarification seminars to assertiveness training, from courses in decision making and life planning to workshops in cross-cultural understanding, from relaxation training for adults to prejudice-reduction activities for children and adolescents.

The possibilities are endless. For each of these and many other programs, counselors have developed techniques, concepts, and even course outlines. The simple challenge for practitioners is to implement these programs, techniques, and concepts among a broad range of people. Through preventive educational programs such as these, community counselors can help people experience their own competence and can come to recognize that effective life skills serve to prevent a variety of problems.

Direct Client Services: Outreach and Counseling for Vulnerable Populations

Though the principles and values of community counseling bring a new perspective to the healing process (see Chapter 4), counseling itself remains an important tool in the community counselor's repertoire of skills. It remains necessary for a simple reason: Not all problems can be prevented. However, by identifying those situations that make particular individuals susceptible to developing dysfunctions, counselors can reach those people especially vulnerable at particular times—and intervene before problems occur.

Instead of searching for a specific underlying precondition associated with a particular pattern of maladaptive behavior, researchers have begun to focus their interests directly on the stressful life events that can trigger patterns of maladaptive behavior in a portion of the population that experiences those events. Thus, over the past 20 years, researchers have begun to shift their attention from high-risk populations to high-risk situations and events (Price, Badger, & Keterer, 1980, p. 80).

Stressful situations can trigger a variety of physical, psychological, and social dysfunctions, however transient the stressful reaction itself may be. "What follows after the immediate, transient stress reaction depends on the mediation of situational and psychological factors that define the context in which this reaction occurs" (Dohrenwend, 1978, p. 4).

Whether individuals can withstand a high degree of stress depends, at least in part, on factors that serve as buffers to protect the individual's sense of well-being. Such buffers include social support systems (Gottlieb, 1981; Holahan & Moos, 1982; Wehlage, Rutter, Smith, Lesko, & Fernandez, 1989), a sense of control over life events (Bandura, 1989; Johnson & Sarason, 1979), and cognitive problem-solving skills (Shure & Spivack, 1982). Furthermore, people can develop what Kobasa (1979) calls *hardiness*, which refers to one's strength to withstand stressful situations.

People facing difficult situations need to develop new and practical problem-solving strategies and approaches to everyday living. Also, such people need close contact with others, links to human beings who can provide support and encouragement.

Community counselors can address these needs directly by providing outreach services to people identified as needing personal counseling but who cannot or will not access the existing mental health system. By directly reaching out to those schools and communities that would welcome their help, practitioners can provide a variety of career, family, academic, and personal counseling services to individuals in at-risk and vulnerable groups.

Indirect Community Services: Systemic Changes and Public Policy

In addition to helping individuals, the community counselor often tries to intervene consistently and intentionally in the environment. This is particularly important when environmental conditions limit instead of facilitate the psychological growth, well-being, and confidence of community members.

Though anyone may suffer as a result of toxic environmental conditions, members of some groups are more vulnerable to negative external forces than others. Researchers have noted that women (Worell & Remer, 1992), children and adolescents (E. H. McWhirter, 1994), people of color (D. W. Sue & Sue, 1990), poor people (Kozol, 1991), the elderly (Waters & Goodman, 1990), gays and lesbians (Dworkin & Gutierrez, 1992), and physically challenged people (J. F. Miller, 1992) more likely experience deleterious effects on their physical and psychological well-being than other groups.

As counselors attempt to respond to the needs of all community members, particularly the most vulnerable people, the need to negotiate environmental changes becomes apparent. Their work brings community counselors face to face with the victims of poverty, racism, sexism, and stigmatization; of political, economic, and social systems that leave individuals feeling powerless; of governing bodies that deny their responsibility to respond; of social norms that encourage isolation. In the face of these realities, counselors have no choice but to promote positive changes in those systems that directly impact the psychological well-being of their clients or that blame the victims.

One important reason for counselors to get involved in community action is to promote systemic changes by influencing public policy. This activism is critical because there is often no other way to prevent the increasing number of serious mental or physical health problems that people in vulnerable populations experience.

Many counseling practitioners have not been trained, are not encouraged, and consequently do not direct much energy toward intentionally influencing the systems that profoundly affect their clients. This is perplexing, because most of the stressors that promote mental health problems come from people's environments.

> Most mental conditions are not identifiable by objective tests, and most have not been shown to be real organic diseases. Rather, epidemiological studies find clear correlations between most forms of psychopathology and one or more of the following: (a) emotionally damaging infant and childhood experiences; (b) poverty and degrading life experiences; (c) powerless and low self-esteem; and (d) loneliness, social isolation, and social marginality. (Albee, 1986, p. 891)

Given the impact of the environment on the well-being of clients, counselors need to influence educational, corporate-industrial, social, and political systems. They can do this by raising the general awareness of the problems common to their clients, gaining support from policy makers, and encouraging positive community action.

By working directly with educational administrators, business leaders, and policy makers, community counselors can more effectively solicit support for the development and implementation of programs regarding human development and psychological wellness. Unlike traditional counseling approaches, which focus on changing clients' perceptions about situations, the community counseling model emphasizes the importance of promoting positive systemic changes and influencing public policy to prevent or reduce the occurrence of mental and physical health problems.

Indirect Client Services: Advocacy and Consultation

The impact of the environment becomes especially clear when counselors work with individuals and groups who have special needs. To help such clients get their needs met, counselors must become advocates, speaking up on their clients' behalf and actively intervening in their clients' surroundings.

Such advocacy begins with identifying groups of people who might benefit from increasing their own strength. For example, society devalues some people because they are different in some way, such as racially, ethnically, physically, or sexually. Referred to as "socially devalued populations" (Locke, 1992), they find their worth as people not fully appreciated by others, and they typically become separated from and stigmatized by the mainstream community.

The community counseling model strives to create conditions that lead to what McWhirter (1994) refers to as the "empowerment of vulnerable persons" (p. 4). The counselor encourages such clients to help themselves, tries to boost their sense of independence and effectiveness, and helps them use available community resources.

To access community resources effectively, counselors must inform individuals about the helping networks that can help them meet their specific needs. These networks include the following: human service agencies, adult continuing-education programs, career training and placement centers, and governmental agencies that serve the needs of special populations, such as elderly assistance programs, Aid to Families with Dependent Children (AFDC), Women and Infant Care, and Foodstamps services.

Besides referring clients to such services, counselors must often engage in more active support and client advocacy. Frequently, people in vulnerable populations must face rigid bureaucratic systems and individuals with negative attitudes. Both impinge on a person's right to healthy physical and psychological growth. When these basic human rights are violated in these ways or others, helping professionals may need to act as personal advocates for their clients.

Suppose, for example, that a pregnant teenager has been barred from public school. A traditional counselor might help her find private tutoring or plan a career in a field requiring few academic qualifications. In contrast, the community counseling model encourages mental health practitioners to confront the policy of exclusion. By taking this sort of action, the community counselor acts as an advocate for the individual as well as others who might experience similar barriers in the future. There are countless situations in which client advocacy can make a difference to large segments of the population. In later chapters, we shall discuss other examples of indirect services that reflect client advocacy.

The four components of the community counseling model—*direct client, direct community, indirect client,* and *indirect community services*—represent complementary and interdependent elements of a comprehensive counseling framework. Helping professionals interested in using this model must effectively integrate these components in ways that promote their clients' healthy development.

A Unified Approach

By combining the four components of community counseling into a unified framework, counselors can begin to conceptualize the types of intervention strategies likely to have the greatest impact on the largest number of clients. When using the community counseling model, counselors do not need to choose between helping individuals or acting as agents of social change. Instead, they are encouraged to implement an *ecological perspective* into the work they do:

> An ecological perspective lies somewhere at the nexus of system and person change. The ecological perspective views people and environments as being in reciprocal transaction, each mutually influencing the other in subtle and obvious ways. Thus, understanding, growth, and change would emanate from and within the relevant ecological transaction (Conyne, 1985, p. 1).

The skills involved in facilitating individual development and influencing environments complement each other. Although an individual counselor cannot implement a multifaceted program alone, he or she must be aware of the continuous and complex interplay between clients and their environments and work with others to develop a combination of programs that offer an appropriate array of services.

The idea of providing multifaceted, preventive services strikes some traditional caregivers as idealistic. In fact, more and more schools, human service agencies, and businesses are implementing programs that exemplify the community counseling model. Aunt Martha's Youth Service Center in Forest Park, Illinois, and the "I Have a Future" program in Nashville, Tennessee, demonstrate how.

THE COMMUNITY COUNSELING MODEL IN ACTION

Aunt Martha's Youth Service Center

In 1986, the board of trustees of Aunt Martha's Youth Service Center in Park Forest, Illinois, considered making drastic cuts in the funding allocated for the center's programs. Within days, an outpouring of public support for the agency compelled the board to reconsider. Typical of the community's response was a petition signed by 15 local clergymen:

We the undersigned clergymen of Park Forest are painfully aware of the growing needs Aunt Martha's has been fulfilling in our community. We are, therefore, most alarmed that recent draft budgets could even contemplate the idea of decreased funding for our youth services agency. We strongly urge that there be no decrease in allocation, and that instead the village trustees search for ways to restore Aunt Martha's allocation to what it was three years ago. ("Clergy Asks," 1986, p. A3)

A broad range of individuals, groups, and organizations throughout the area served by Aunt Martha's expressed similar sentiments. As a result, though many agencies have floundered in an era of continued financial cutbacks, the center has flourished and maintained an impressive level of community support over the past ten years. This success proceeds largely from the agency's close ties to the community, its efforts to provide a welcoming environment for young people, its responsiveness to the real needs of its clients, and the comprehensiveness of its services. In short, because it embodies the community counseling concept in many practical ways, Aunt Martha's is healthy as well as effective. The founders' own words express the agency's philosophy most clearly:[1]

"You've Got a Friend" is the theme of Aunt Martha's Youth Service Center, Inc., a community-based youth-serving organization which offers comprehensive programs to meet the needs of young people and families residing in a fifteen-township region of metropolitan Chicago. Established in 1972, Aunt Martha's offers a range of services for young people and their families and has created innovative programs which enable young people to participate as positive contributing members of their communities. The initial community commission which led to the creation of Aunt Martha's was composed of both young people and adults.

The name *Aunt Martha's* was chosen to reflect the quality of warmth and concern one would find in the home of a close relative and which the community hoped young people would find at Aunt Martha's Youth Center. Since its beginning, Aunt Martha's has grown from a simple counseling center to a complex, highly structured agency serving a wide geographic area through a dozen programs, a staff of 89 and over 250 community volunteers. Aunt Martha's serves a richly varied population, including both suburban and rural residents, as well as persons from a broad range of ethnic, racial, and economic groups. The service area also encompasses industrial areas with many of the characteristics of an urban setting.

Aunt Martha's founding principles strongly advocated for

---

[1]From *You've Got A Friend* by E. Mazer and C. G. Leofanti, 1980, Park Forest, IL: Aunt Martha's Youth Service Center. Copyright 1980 by Aunt Martha's Youth Service Center. Reprinted by permission.

community participation, particularly with regard to the involvement of young people in the planning and operations of programs. Additionally, every effort was made to ensure that services were accessible to all young people in the community and that the bulk of service delivery was to be accomplished by community volunteers. These principles have been followed in the development of Aunt Martha's programs. Youth and adult volunteers are the heart of Aunt Martha's service delivery system. . . . Thus, Aunt Martha's offers the community, especially youth, the opportunity to give as well as to receive help and to advocate on their own behalf.

Community and youth participation assure the development of programs which are responsive to young people and to the community. Volunteers are involved at all levels of the agency's operations— service delivery, program planning and policy making. Most of the staff are long-time residents of the communities they serve; many were previously volunteers. Volunteer training and supervision are crucial aspects of Aunt Martha's programs.

Aunt Martha's Youth Service's commitment to youth participation both within the organization and throughout the community is based on the belief that the majority of youth problems which communities experience are caused by alienation and the perceived lack of access to meaningful social roles on the part of young people. Thus, Aunt Martha's comprehensive approach not only offers assistance to those who are experiencing problems but also seeks to provide vehicles through which young people may experience a sense of competence, usefulness, belonging, and potency that is needed to develop healthy, productive adults who are integrated members of the community. (Mazer & Leofanti, 1980, pp. 1–4)

Aunt Martha's demonstrates how one can effectively put the community counseling model into practice. The agency provides programs using each of the service modes that compose a comprehensive community counseling program: (1) offering preventive education, (2) bringing counseling and outreach services to vulnerable populations, (3) influencing public policy, and (4) providing client advocacy and consultation.

PREVENTIVE EDUCATION   Aunt Martha's has traditionally offered programs aimed at preventing problems that young people will likely encounter. These programs all focus on building competency and emphasize youth participation in problem identification, planning, and implementation.

In Project Listen, for instance, young people use dramatic presentations to encourage other teenagers to talk about issues important to them. *Changes*, for example, a play written by teenagers, deals with decisions in regard to sexuality; it addresses such issues as birth control, teen pregnancy, homosexuality, and taking responsibility for one's actions. *Different People*,

Different Times focuses on youth participation and was written to increase the community's awareness of young people's talents and potential. *Who Needs It* is a series of skits and improvisations designed to elicit audience participation in a discussion of alcohol and other drugs. Project Listen performances are designed not just to provide information but also to encourage frank discussions among young people and between parents and children.

These and other activities foster the participation of young people who come to Aunt Martha's not because they have problems but because they enjoy feeling involved. Because the agency attracts a broad range of people, individuals need not feel stigmatized when they seek help through the center's more intensive mental health programs.

COUNSELING AND OUTREACH   By training community volunteers as counselors, Aunt Martha's offers highly accessible counseling services. These services include general counseling, drop-in counseling, substance-abuse treatment, and 24-hour crisis intervention.

Among other programs sponsored by Aunt Martha's and designed to meet the needs of specific client groups, EDGE (Employment-Direction-Growth-Experience) is an employment training program for economically disadvantaged youths. Project Truck Stop is an outreach program for interstate runaways, and Transition to Independence provides shelter for homeless youths.

INFLUENCING PUBLIC POLICY   In addition to offering innovative direct services, Aunt Martha's works with other youth-serving systems, increasing the access young people have to those systems and demonstrating their right to be involved in community affairs. The Center for Student Citizenship, Rights, and Responsibilities (CSCRR) is a youth leadership, involvement, and advocacy program sponsored by Aunt Martha's that promotes the development of leadership skills among young people. The activities of the CSCRR include the following:

- Publication of a book designed to raise consciousness about issues affecting young people
- Publication of a newsletter to increase awareness of the program's advocacy efforts
- Seminars on educational issues, including alternatives to suspension from school
- Educational forums on issues selected by the youths themselves
- School-based study groups that deal with such issues as student rights and responsibilities, school attendance policies, student representation on school boards, and gang activities

- Training programs in skills such as negotiation, conflict resolution, and public speaking
- Formation of a legislative committee to identify issues of concern to young people and to help teens learn how to monitor related legislation. (Committee members sometimes help organize young people to write legislators, testify at hearings, visit legislators, or draft legislation.)

The center also conducted a survey of high-school dropouts that resulted in a report and recommendations to help school districts prevent dropouts and better meet the needs of young people experiencing personal problems. Other efforts related to school policies and practices include training parent-student teams to monitor legislation related to educational reform.

CLIENT ADVOCACY AND CONSULTATION   School policies affect most of the young people who make up Aunt Martha's clientele. However, a smaller number of the agency's clients need more specific and active types of advocacy services. Sometimes, this advocacy is provided on an individual basis. For example, volunteer attorneys offer their initial legal consultations free of charge.

Frequently, however, Aunt Martha's and other youth-serving agencies must join together to ensure that young people with special needs are treated equitably and to protect the quality and availability of youth services. Thus, the administration, staff, and volunteers of Aunt Martha's play an active role in the work of such organizations as the American Youth Work Center, the Youth Network Council, the Illinois Collaboration of Youth, and the Children's Defense Fund Youth Lobby. Aunt Martha's director has also chaired the Illinois Governor's Task Force on Youth Employment, as well as a number of other advocacy-related committees and commissions.

When Aunt Martha's staff recognize that a problem exists, they join with people in the appropriate systems to take action. They actively consult with other agencies and with the many systems that affect young people. In Aunt Martha's service area, for example, troubled young people who could not be reunited with their families were once served only through the court system. That they can now be referred to a community-based alternative mental health program attests to this agency's effectiveness, not just as a service provider but also as an advocate for disenfranchised youth and as a consulting resource for the community.

AUNT MARTHA'S UNIFIED APPROACH   Regardless of their work setting, community counselors make a conscious effort to use a unified approach. That is, they develop interventions in which they use direct and indirect as

TABLE 1.2
THE FOUR FACETS OF COMMUNITY COUNSELING:
AUNT MARTHA'S YOUTH SERVICE CENTER

	COMMUNITY SERVICES	CLIENT SERVICES
Direct	Project Listen Students Involved in Pregnancy Prevention	Counseling Substance-abuse treatment Crisis intervention Project New Chance Head Start EDGE Project Truck Stop Transition to Independence
Indirect	Center for Student Citizenship, Rights, & Responsibilities Participation in the Illinois Fair Schools Coalition	Legal advocacy Affiliations with the American Youth Work Center, Youth Network Council, Illinois Collaboration on Youth, and Children's Defense Fund Youth Lobby Juvenile justice alternatives

well as community-wide and client-focused services in complementary ways. Counseling practitioners who work in agencies like Aunt Martha's recognize the importance of combining direct services to individuals with indirect methods that focus on public policy.

Table 1.2 shows how comprehensive and complementary Aunt Martha's services are. Aunt Martha's exemplifies the multifaceted nature of the community counseling framework in action. While directly helping young people at risk or in trouble, the staff and volunteers of the agency also work to prevent serious problems from developing. They do this by providing services that foster problem-solving skills and by actively advocating their cause among influential people in the greater community.

The Community Counseling Model in Action: The "I Have a Future" Program

While Aunt Martha's exemplifies a program designed to address multiple developmental concerns and issues, one can also apply the community counseling model to specific issues. The "I Have a Future" program (IHAF) in Nashville, Tennessee, serves as a clear example of how this framework can address a specific adolescent problem.

Although the IHAF program focuses on one problem—high rates of pregnancy among poor, African-American adolescents—its approach is comprehensive. That is, it aims services at various segments of the broader community, including the clients' family members, school officials, church leaders, and representatives from other local human services agencies.

The IHAF program provides services that stimulate changes in those environments where high rates of repeated adolescent pregnancies occur, such as poor urban areas. These services include providing outreach counseling and preventive education services as well as seeking to influence public policy, promoting client advocacy, and offering consultation services in targeted poor, urban, African-American communities. This comprehensive and unified approach to adolescent pregnancy prevention offers another example of how one might use the community counseling framework in a culturally sensitive way.

OUTREACH AND COUNSELING   The IHAF program was developed by personnel affiliated with the Department of Obstetrics and Gynecology at Meharry Medical College in Nashville, Tennessee (Foster, Arthur, & D'Andrea, 1987). One of the few African-American medical centers in the United States, Meharry historically has tried to serve the physical and mental health-care needs of communities comprising primarily poor, African-American families in Nashville.

Recognizing the chronic problem of teen pregnancy in the city's low-income areas, the IHAF founders received funding to develop a comprehensive community-based program designed to serve youth in low-income areas. The first step in developing this program involved conducting outreach services to the targeted communities. In these outreach efforts, staff members conducted a needs assessment that directly involved the parents and adolescents in the chosen communities.

In conducting this assessment among 500 parents, the IHAF counselors learned which specific services they would need in a comprehensive youth program to prevent teen pregnancies (D'Andrea, Foster, & Arthur, 1987). The IHAF program's planners also surveyed over 1100 adolescents to evaluate their general health and educational status as well as to assess the types of problems young people experienced in the targeted communities. This sort of outreach not only resulted in their gaining much information about residents in targeted neighborhoods, but it also allowed members of the assessment team to interact with residents who already needed various medical, mental health, and social services.

The reluctance of many poor, urban African Americans to use traditional mental health services is well documented (Atkinson et al., 1993; White & Parham, 1990). However, the IHAF staff found that by intentionally extending themselves through these initial outreach efforts, they could collect useful data about the adolescents and their families and offer practical counseling and referral services to people who expressed specific personal needs.

Because they conducted the surveys in the residents' homes, the counselors could provide support and referral information in a personal and confidential environment. These spontaneous consultation services did much to help the program planners gain parental support for IHAF at the early stage of its development.

PREVENTION   Using the data generated from the community needs assessment, the IHAF program planners designed a set of services for reducing teen pregnancies among African-American youth. To achieve this goal, the IHAF staff emphasized preventive education and training interventions. While past efforts had focused on African-American teenagers who were already pregnant (D'Andrea, 1994), the IHAF program geared its resources primarily toward prevention through impacting the adolescents' communities.

Many prevention experts have pointed out that adolescent pregnancy rates go down when youth can identify realistic and positive alternatives to becoming a teenage parent. In this regard, providing teenagers with the education, training, and support they need to complete their education and secure satisfying careers has consistently been mentioned as an essential component of an effective adolescent pregnancy prevention program (J. J. McWhirter, McWhirter, McWhirter, & McWhirter, 1993). Further, the results of the community needs survey indicated that parents also identified career counseling as one of the most desirable services they would like to see initiated in their communities to help reduce the high rate of teen pregnancies (D'Andrea, 1995). Consequently, the initial program development efforts were directed toward creating a career education project for this group of at-risk youth.

The IHAF Career Development Project was designed to serve four specific purposes:

1. Promoting adolescents' career awareness
2. Facilitating the acquisition of a number of preemployment skills
3. Increasing participants' level of personal discipline
4. Cultivating effective problem-solving skills

To accomplish these goals, the IHAF counselors designed a culturally appropriate curriculum and initiated career development classes in the low-income housing areas where the adolescents resided (D'Andrea, 1995).

The IHAF staff used a variety of educational and counseling services in these career development classes, including the following:

- Consulting with and recruiting several successful African Americans viewed as experts in local businesses and economic endeavors. Considered as positive role models, these people volunteered to share their knowledge about career opportunities and future employment trends in the community.
- Using a number of structured group activities to stimulate adolescents' critical-thinking skills by posing a variety of "career problems" that were discussed in small-group settings.
- Role-playing job interviews to help the adolescents develop more effective communication skills in this sort of situation.
- Reviewing specific strategies for conducting a job search and helping the teenagers develop effective resume-writing skills.

SYSTEMIC CHANGE AND PUBLIC POLICY   Although direct educational and counseling services played an important role in the IHAF program, their effectiveness largely depended on the environment within which the problem of teen pregnancy occurs. Thus, the IHAF staff also tried to foster environmental changes toward increasing positive life options within the teenagers' communities. This included using a variety of indirect counseling services to influence public policies that affected the young persons' lives.

The specific efforts initiated by the IHAF counselors in this regard included these:

- Meeting with local and state elected officials to lobby for pending legislation that would affect the welfare of urban, African-American youth in Tennessee
- Networking with human service agencies in the targeted areas to enhance interagency communication and develop cooperative working relationships with other community agencies in order to avoid duplicating services
- Working with African-American church leaders to explore ways that the religious community might help the youth to become successful and responsible adults
- Recruiting a number of African-American adults in the business community who were viewed as positive career role models to speak with adolescents in the IHAF Career Development Project
- Soliciting support from leaders in private industry to secure job opportunities for those youth who had successfully completed the IHAF Career Development Project

CLIENT ADVOCACY AND CONSULTATION   By working with these individuals and organizations, the IHAF counselors actively advocated for the rights and well-being of the targeted adolescents. Client-advocacy strategies in this project generally involved three fundamental steps.

First, one had to identify key persons in the environment who directly and/or indirectly affected the lives of adolescents in the targeted areas. Government officials were chosen because their decisions often made a direct impact on this vulnerable population. Also, respecting the important historical role the Black church plays in African-American communities, the IHAF counselors extended their outreach services by consulting with numerous ministers about the problem of adolescent pregnancies in the targeted communities.

Second, these strategies were designed to stimulate greater awareness and knowledge of the teenagers' needs and interests among key persons in the community. To accomplish this goal, the IHAF staff set up meetings with elected officials, ministers, parents, and other leaders to discuss the results of the community needs assessment survey and to explain the goals of the IHAF program.

Third, the program staff understood that effective advocacy should ultimately lead to new helping networks that involve collaborative inter-actions with people who can positively affect clients' lives. Recognizing the importance of this step, the IHAF staff set up meetings with government officials, African-American ministers, and parents in the targeted areas to advocate for the adolescents' rights and well-being. These efforts resulted in the formation of several formal and informal support networks. Those involved in these networks spent much time discussing strategies for increasing the number of positive life options available to the African-American youth participating in IHAF programs.

MULTICULTURAL COUNSELING CONSIDERATIONS Like IHAF, programs designed to serve the mental health needs of urban, African-American youth work best when they reflect sensitivity to the unique ethnic racial backgrounds of the target group (Lee & Richardson, 1991). Advances in the fields of developmental and multicultural counseling over the past two decades have resulted in many theoretical models that are useful to implement when working with people from different cultural, ethnic, and racial backgrounds. What follows is a brief description of ways the IHAF program implemented these models.

In their preventive education services, the IHAF staff integrated a variety of traditional career development services (such as providing job-search and interview training) within a context that reflected an Afro-centric worldview (Asante, 1988). This multicultural venue was built around seven life principles called *Nguzo Saba* (Kunjufu, 1986). In providing the career development classes, the IHAF counselors made a consistent effort to integrate discussions of these life principles among the program participants.

For example, one of the *Nguzo Saba* life principles is referred to as *Nia*, meaning one's "purpose in life." From an Afrocentric perspective, an individual's purpose directly involves helping to build and strengthen one's family and community. Thus, in the IHAF career development classes, the counselors initiated group discussions that related the adolescents' sense of responsibility and their personal and career achievements to their *Nia*.

Another one of these life principles, *Kujichagulia*, reflects the importance of self-determination. It shows when African Americans define themselves, create for themselves, and speak for themselves rather than being defined, created, and spoken for by others (Kunjufu, 1986). To accommodate *Kujichagulia* into the career education project, the IHAF counselors helped clients clarify values and develop assertiveness skills.

Other *Nguzo Saba* principles incorporated into the program include *Umoja* (a sense of unity), *Ujima* (the importance of collective work and responsibility), *Ujamaa* (*cooperative economics*), Kuumba (the need for creativity), and *Imani* (the importance of faith in others). Collectively, these principles represent cultural values that reinforce the healthy development of African-American youth. With these principles integrated into the preventive education component of the program, the adolescents could develop career skills in a context that reinforced pride and respect for their cultural background.

Another important multicultural consideration relates to the milieu in which the IHAF services were provided. Multicultural theorists have suggested that expecting poor youth from diverse cultural backgrounds to participate in programs set up in predominantly white, middle-class areas creates a host of problems that typically reduce the effectiveness of the services offered (D. W. Sue, 1981). By using the community counseling model and providing neighborhood-based interventions that emphasize outreach and counseling, preventive education, client advocacy, and consultation services, the IHAF program had a positive impact on both clients and their environments.

IHAF'S UNIFIED APPROACH   The outreach, educational, and consultative services provided by the IHAF program are truly comprehensive, encompassing prevention as well as intervention and advocacy. The scope of the program's services is made clear in Table 1.3.

Like Aunt Martha's Youth Service Center, the IHAF program demonstrates the applicability of the multifaceted approach of the community counseling model to real-life settings and situations.

TABLE 1.3
IMPLEMENTING THE FOUR FACETS OF COMMUNITY
COUNSELING: THE I HAVE A FUTURE PROGRAM

	COMMUNITY SERVICES	CLIENT SERVICES
Direct	Consultation with African-American role models and soliciting their input about the needs of the community	Client assessment Client referrals
	Networking with other mental health agencies to foster the development of other community-wide youth programs	Career development education and counseling
	Networking with black religious leaders to develop constructive community initiatives	
Indirect	Lobbying for youth programs with state legislators	Consultation with parents Consulting with school officials

SUMMARY

The community counseling model represents a multifaceted approach to combining direct and indirect services to help people live more effective and satisfying lives. This model emphasizes directing efforts toward the prevention of problems rather than focusing primarily on clients experiencing serious mental health problems as a result of debilitating factors in their environments.

Though one can use the community counseling model in a wide variety of settings, three philosophical tenets underlie each situation. These tenets are (1) the demonstration of a strong commitment to prevention, (2) an awareness of the potential effects of the social environment, and (3) the explicit understanding that one can most effectively serve people by helping them develop the skills and resources to help themselves.

Further, these tenets are fueled by five assumptions that guide community counseling:

1. People's environments may either nurture or limit their developmental potential

2. A multifaceted service approach is more efficient than a single-service approach.
3. In the long run, prevention is more efficient than remediation.
4. Effective intervention efforts must explicitly demonstrate sensitivity and respect for clients' cultural, ethnic, and racial backgrounds.
5. The community counseling model can be adapted and applied in any human service setting.

When put into practice, the community counseling framework involves four distinct components that represent different service modalities:

1. **Direct community services** provide educational experiences to the community as a whole. Counselors typically accomplish this through preventive education.

2. **Direct client services** address the immediate needs of clients as well as people identified as at risk for developing future mental health problems. The specific types of services used in this component of the model include outreach and counseling to vulnerable populations.

3. **Indirect community services** comprise efforts deliberately designed to make the social environment more responsive to the needs of the population as a whole. In attempting to promote these sorts of constructive environmental changes, counselors collaborate with key people in targeted areas to cultivate positive systemic changes by influencing public policy.

4. **Indirect client services** represent those environmental interventions aimed at meeting the special needs of people in vulnerable populations. These services primarily work to create new helping networks by providing consultation and client-advocacy services to people and agencies within the areas where clients live.

The stresses of modern society clearly stretch many people beyond their ability to cope. This situation has resulted in a rise in the number and severity of mental health problems manifested by people in the United States (Miringoff, 1995).

Frequently, these problems show up disproportionately among people who make up what counseling professionals refer to as vulnerable or at-risk populations. To complicate matters further, mental health practitioners increasingly acknowledge that many traditional counseling models are woefully inadequate in addressing the types of problems people in these vulnerable populations commonly experience.

The community counseling model provides a pragmatic alternative to these traditional helping paradigms. The discussion of Aunt Martha's Youth Service Center and the I Have a Future (IHAF) program have been presented to describe specific ways in which this comprehensive counseling framework can be used in real-life situations.

SUPPLEMENTAL ACTIVITIES

1. Visit a local community agency or school. Using the community counseling model as a tool, think about the agency or school in these terms:
   a. What kinds of direct, community-wide services are offered?
   b. To what degree is the agency or school involved in efforts to create systemic changes in the community?
   c. What direct client services does it offer? To what degree do these services take environmental factors into consideration?
   d. Is the agency or school involved in providing indirect counseling services? If so, what types of indirect services does the staff commonly use and how does the program manifest them?
   e. In what ways does the agency or school address the unique cultural, ethnic, and/or racial backgrounds of the clients? In many instances, you may find some types of services missing from a program. If that is the case, can you think of specific services that might enhance the agency's or school's overall effectiveness in meeting its goals?
2. Think about a particular group or population, such as adults with physical disabilities, survivors of child abuse, unemployed professionals, gays and lesbians, women, people with HIV, or high-school students. What social, economic, political, or psychological pressures affect the well-being of this population? Taking these factors into account, develop some ideas for appropriate services for the population you have selected.

   You will probably notice that direct counseling services alone are unlikely to meet the group's needs. Beginning with a clear statement of your goals, develop a hypothetical community counseling program incorporating services that fall in each of the four quadrants described in Chapter 1. At this point, concentrate on the thrust of each quadrant rather than the details of each service. As you become more familiar with the community counseling model in the following chapters, you will be better able to conceptualize specific services in each quadrant.

REFERENCES

Albee, G. W. (1986). Toward a just society: Lessons from observations on the primary prevention of psychopathology. *American Psychologist, 41*, 891–898.
Albee, G., & Gullotta, T. (1986). Facts and fallacies about primary prevention. *Journal of Primary Prevention, 6*, 207–218.

American Counseling Association. (1995). *Code of ethics and standards of practice.* Alexandria, VA: Author.

American Psychological Association. (1991). *Guidelines for providers of psychological services to ethnic, linguistic, and culturally diverse populations.* Washington, DC: Author.

Asante, M. K. (1988). *Afrocentricity.* Trenton, NJ: Africa World Press.

Atkinson, D. R., Morten, G., & Sue, D. W. (1993). *Counseling American minorities: A crosscultural perspective* (4th ed.). Dubuque, IA: Brown.

Aubrey, R. (1983). The odyssey of counseling and images of the future. *Personnel and Guidance Journal, 61,* 78–82.

Aubrey, R., & Lewis, J. (1988). Social issues and the counseling profession in the 1980s and 1990s. In R. Hayes & R. Aubrey (Eds.), *New directions for counseling and human development* (pp. 286–303). Denver, CO: Love Publishing.

Bandura, A. (1989). Human agency in social cognitive theory. *American Psychologist, 44,* 1175–1184.

Barclay, J. R. (1983). Searching for a new paradigm in counseling. *Personnel and Guidance Journal, 62,* 2.

Cheung, F. K., & Snowden, L. R. (1990). Community mental health and ethnic minority populations. *Community Mental Health Journal, 26,* 277–291.

Clergy asks Aunt Martha's funding. (1986, June 15). *Park Forest Star,* p. A-3.

Coie, J., Watt, N., West, S., Hawkins, J., Asarnow, J., Markman, H., Ramey, S., Shure, M., & Long, B. (1993). The science of prevention: A conceptual framework and some directions for a national research program. *American Psychologist, 48,* 1013–1022.

Conyne, R. K. (1985). The counseling ecologist: Helping people and environments. *Counseling and Human Development, 18*(2), 1–12.

Conyne, R. K. (1987). *Primary preventive counseling: Empowering people and systems.* Muncie, IN: Accelerated Development.

Conyne, R. K. (1994). Preventive counseling. *Counseling and Human Development, 27*(1), 1–10.

Dakof, G. A., & Taylor, S. E. (1990). Victims' perceptions of social support: What is helpful from whom? *Journal of Personality and Social Psychology, 58,* 80–89.

D'Andrea, M. (1988). The counselor as pacer: A model for revitalization of the counseling profession. In R. Hayes & R. Aubrey (Eds.), *New directions for counseling and human development* (pp. 22–44). Denver, CO: Love Publishing.

D'Andrea, M. (1992). The violence of our silence: Some thoughts about racism, counseling and development. *Guidepost, 35*(4), 31.

D'Andrea, M. (1994). The Family Development Project: A comprehensive mental health counseling program for pregnant adolescents. *Journal of Mental Health Counseling, 16*(2), 184–195.

D'Andrea, M. (1995). Addressing the developmental needs of urban, African-American youth: A preventive intervention. *Journal of Multicultural Counseling and Development, 23,* 57–64.

D'Andrea, M., Foster, H., & Arthur, C. (1987). *The quality of life needs assessment survey.* Nashville, TN: Meharry Medical College.

Daniels, J. (1995). Building respectful connections among culturally-diverse students in Hawai'i. *Educational Perspectives, 29*(2), 23–28.

Daniels, J., & D'Andrea, M. (1996). MCT theory and ethnocentrism in counseling. In D. W. Sue, A. E. Ivey, & P. D. Pedersen, *A theory of multicultural counseling and therapy* (pp. 155–174). Pacific Grove, CA: Brooks/Cole.

Dohrenwend, B. S. (1978). Social stress and community psychology. *American Journal of Community Psychology, 11*(2), 1–14.

Dworkin, S. H., & Gutierrez, F. J. (1992). *Counseling gay men and lesbians: Journey to the end of the rainbow.* Alexandria, VA: American Association of Counseling and Development.

Esquivel, G. B., & Keitel, M. A. (1990). Counseling immigrant children in the schools. *Elementary School Guidance and Counseling Journal, 24,* 213–221.

Foster, H., Arthur, C., & D'Andrea, M. (1987). *The "I Have a Future" (IHAF) program.* Nashville, TN: Meharry Medical College.

Gergen, K. J. (1992). The postmodern adventure. *Family Therapy Networker, 16*(6), 52, 56–57.

Germain, C. B. (1991). *Human behavior in the social environment: An ecological view.* New York: Columbia University Press.

Gilligan, C. (1982). *In a different voice: Psychological theory and women's development.* Cambridge, MA: Harvard University Press.

Gottlieb, B. H. (1981). *Social networks and social support.* Beverly Hills, CA: Sage.

Hayes, R. L. (1994). Counseling in a postmodern world: Origins and implications of a constructivist developmental approach. *Counseling and Human Development, 26*(6), 1–12.

Herr, E., & McFadden, J. (1991). *Challenges of cultural and racial diversity to counseling.* Alexandria, VA: American Association for Counseling and Development.

Holahan, C. J., & Moos, R. H. (1982). Social support and adjustment. *American Journal of Community Psychology, 10,* 403–413.

Ivey, A., Ivey, M., & Simek-Morgan, L. (1993). *Counseling and psychotherapy: A multicultural perspective* (3rd. ed.). Needham Heights, MA: Allyn and Bacon.

Johnson, J. H., & Sarason, I. G. (1979). Moderator variables in life stress research. In I. G. Sarason & C. D. Spielberg (Eds.), *Stress and anxiety* (pp. 151–167). Washington, DC: Hemisphere.

Jordan, J. V., Kaplan, A. G., Miller, J. B., Stiver, I. P., & Surrey, J. L. (1991). *Women's growth in connection: Writings from the Stone Center.* New York: Guilford Press.

Kobasa, S. C. (1979). Stressful life events, personality and health: An inquiry into hardiness. *Journal of Personality and Social Psychology, 37,* 1–11.

Kelly, E. W. (1989). Social commitment and individualism in counseling. *Journal of Counseling and Development, 67*(2), 341–344.

King, M. L. (1963). *Strength to love.* New York: Walker.

Kozol, J. (1991). *Savage inequities: Children in America's schools.* New York: Crown.

Kuhn, T. (1962). *The structure of scientific revolutions.* Chicago: University of Chicago Press.

Kunjufu, J. (1986). *Motivating and preparing black youth to work.* Chicago: African American Images.

Lator, B. (1993). *We have never been modern.* Cambridge, MA: Harvard University Press.

Lee, C. C., & Richardson, B. L. (Eds.) (1991). *Multicultural issues in counseling: New approaches to diversity.* Alexandria, VA: American Association for Counseling and Development.

Lewis, J. A., & Lewis, M. D. (1981). Educating counselors for primary prevention. *Counselor Education and Supervision, 20,* 172–181.

Lewis, J. A., Lewis, M. D., & Souflee, F. (1991). *Management of human service programs* (2nd ed.). Pacific Grove, CA: Brooks/Cole.

Locke, D. C. (1992). *Increasing multicultural understanding: A comprehensive model.* Newbury Park, CA: Sage.

Lucas, C. (1985). Out at the edge: Notes on a paradigm shift. *Journal of Counseling and Development, 64*(2), 165–171.

Mazer, E., & Leofanti, C. G. (1980). *You've got a friend.* Park Forest, IL: Aunt Martha's Youth Service Center.

McWhirter, E. H. (1994). *Counseling for empowerment.* Alexandria, VA: American Counseling Association.

McWhirter, J. J., McWhirter, B. T., McWhirter, A. M., & McWhirter, E. H. (1993). *At-risk youth: A comprehensive response.* Pacific Grove, CA: Brooks/Cole.

Miller, J. B. (1987). *Toward a new psychology of women* (2nd ed.). Boston: Beacon Press.

Miller, J. F. (Ed.). (1992). *Coping with chronic illness: Overcoming powerlessness* (2nd ed.). Philadelphia: F. A. Davis.

Miringoff, M. L. (1995). Toward a national standard of social health: The need for progress in social indicators. *American Journal of Orthopsychiatry, 65*(4), 462–467.

Newton, F. B., & Caple, R. B. (1985). Once the world was flat: Introduction and overview. *Journal of Counseling and Development, 64,* 163–184.

Paisley, P. O. (1996, January). *Creating community: Group work and the arts.* Presentation made at the annual meeting of the Association for Specialists in Group Work, Athens, GA.

Parham, T. A., & McDavis, R. J. (1987). Black men, an endangered species: Who's really pulling the trigger? *Journal of Counseling and Development, 66,* 24–27.

Pedersen, P. B. (1990). The multicultural perspective as a fourth force in counseling. *Journal of Counseling and Development, 64*(5), 430–434.

Pedersen, P. B. (1991). Multiculturalism as a generic approach to counseling. *Journal of Counseling and Development, 70*(1), 6–12.

Pine, G. J. (1972). Counseling minority groups: A review of the literature. *Counseling and Values, 17,* 35–44.

Ponterotto, J. G., & Pedersen, P. B. (1993). *Preventing prejudice: A guide for counselors and educators.* Newbury Park, CA: Sage.

Price, R. H., Badger, B. C., & Keterer, R. F. (1980). *Prevention in mental health: Research, policy, and practice.* Beverly Hills, CA: Sage.

Rigazio-DiGilio, S. A. (1994). A co-constructive-developmental approach to ecosystemic treatment. *Journal of Mental Health Counseling, 16*(1), 43–74.

Rigazio-DiGilio, S. A., & Ivey, A. E. (1993). Systemic cognitive-developmental therapy: An integrative framework. *Family Journal: Counseling and Therapy for Couples and Families, 1*, 208–219.

Scarr, S., & Ricciuti, A. (1991). What effects do parents have on their children? In L. Okagaki & J. Sternberg (Eds.), *Directors of development: Influences on the development of children's thinking* (pp. 3–22). Hillsdale, NJ: Erlbaum.

Senge, P. M. (1994). *The fifth discipline: The art and practice of the learning organization*. New York: Doubleday.

Shure, M. B., & Spivack, G. (1982). Interpersonal problem solving in young children: A cognitive approach to prevention. *American Journal of Community Psychology, 10*, 341–356.

Smith, E. M. J. (1985). Ethnic minorities: Life stress, social support, and mental health issues. *The Counseling Psychologist, 13*, 537–579.

Steenbarger, B. N. (1991). Emerging contextualist themes in counseling and development. *Journal of Counseling and Development, 70*, 288–296.

Strickland, B. R., & Janoff-Bulman, R. (1980). Expectancies and attributions: Implications for community mental health. In G. S. Gibbs, J. R. Lachenmeyer, & J. Sigal (Eds.), *Community psychology: Theoretical and empirical approaches* (pp. 97–119). New York: Gardner Press.

Sue, D. W. (1981). *Counseling the culturally different: Theory and practice*. New York: Wiley.

Sue, D. W., Arredondo, P., & McDavis, R. J. (1992). Multicultural counseling competencies and standards: A call to the profession. *Journal of Counseling and Development, 70*(5), 477–486.

Sue, D. W., Ivey, A. E., & Pedersen, P. B. (Eds.). (1996). *A theory of multicultural counseling and therapy*. Pacific Grove, CA: Brooks/Cole.

Sue, D. W., & Sue, D. (1990). *Counseling the culturally different*. New York: Wiley.

Sue, S. (1988). Psychotherapeutic services for ethnic minorities: Two decades of research findings. *American Psychologist, 43*(2), 301–308.

Tedeschi, R. G., & Calhoun, L. G. (1993). Using the support group to respond to the isolation of bereavement. *Journal of Mental Health Counseling, 15*(1), 47–54.

Tierney, W. G. (1993). *Building communities of difference: Higher education in the twenty-first century*. Westport, CT: Bergin & Garvey.

Vargas, L. A., & Koss-Chioino, J. D. (Eds.). (1992). *Working with culture: Psychotherapeutic interventions with ethnic minority children and adolescents*. San Francisco: Jossey-Bass.

von Bertalanffy, L. (1968). *General system theory: Foundations, development, applications*. New York: Braziller.

Waters, E. B., & Goodman, J. (1990). *Empowering older adults: Practical strategies for counselors*. San Fancisco: Jossey-Bass.

Wehlage, G. G., Rutter, R. A., Smith, G. A., Lesko, N., & Fernandez, R. R. (1989). *Reducing the risk: Schools as communities of support*. New York: Falmer Press.

White, J. L., & Parham, T. A. (1990). *The psychology of blacks: An African-American perspective*. Englewood Cliffs, NJ: Prentice-Hall.

Wirth, L. (1945). The problem of minority groups. In R. Linton (Ed.), *The science of man in world crisis* (pp. 347–372). New York: Columbia University Press.

Worell, J., & Remer, P. (1992). *Feminist perspectives in therapy: An empowerment model for women*. Chincester, England: Wiley.

Wrenn, G. (1985). The culturally encapsulated counselor revisited. In P. Pedersen (Ed.), *Handbook of cross-cultural counseling and therapy* (pp. 323–329). Westport, CT: Greenwood Press.

CHAPTER 2

PREVENTIVE EDUCATION

A RATIONALE FOR PREVENTION

People in the United States are rapidly becoming more conscious of prevention. It makes sense that individuals want to learn about and implement preventive strategies that affect their daily lives positively. Simply stated, more and more people see it as smarter, more economical, and more fun to avoid developing an addiction to cigarettes than it is to have lung cancer, to brush their teeth with fluoride than to lose teeth, and to exercise regularly than to develop a stress-related illness.

Counselors are well positioned in the educational and health-care systems to initiate preventive programs and services that positively impact their clients' development. Whether employed in schools, universities, agencies, or other institutional settings, counselors often work with clients who as a group manifest similar difficulties and challenges. This includes people whose psychological problems stem from their inability to effectively manage stress, individuals who lack information about their physical and psychological wellness, and people who have not developed an adequate array of life skills to meet the demands of a highly complex, rapidly changing, 21st-century society.

The Limitations of Individual Counseling

Working with individuals who demonstrate similar difficulties can be somewhat comforting to helping professionals, because it increases their familiarity with a set of common problems. Indeed, using the same counseling interventions with these people may boost the counselor's confidence even more. However, though repetition of the same method of counseling may promote counselors' competence in that particular problem area, it often breeds redundancy and long-term ineffectiveness.

Professionals who counsel clients on a one-to-one basis often spend hours upon hours helping them solve problems the clients might have avoided if they had developed certain life skills earlier on. Commenting on the overuse of the traditional counseling paradigm, Conyne (1987) discusses several reasons why the repeated use of individual counseling services does not work:

> It is a no-win proposition because these remedial services are after-the-fact approaches that can do nothing to stem the tide of new cases. It is no-win because the access to traditional clinical services is becoming increasingly more difficult and expensive as cost containment and efforts to monopolize the health care industry become commonplace. It has always been a no-win situation for the typically underserved–or nonserved–in our society. Thus, the poor, the unemployed, the culturally different, the homeless, and the untold others who are most in need are least able to get this sort of help. And it is a no-win situation because professional counseling, counseling psychology, and other helping professions are restricting the list of available practitioners in their efforts to protect consumer (and the provider) through licensing, registries, and the like. (p. 12)

Recognition of these limitations has caused many counselors to reassess the overall effectiveness of individual counseling. This reassessment has also led them to consider using alternative professional roles to foster clients' development. In this regard, many have noted that professional counselors are particularly well-suited to take on the roles of *psychological educator* and *life-skills trainer* to foster the mental health and well-being of people in at-risk populations (Donaghy, 1995; Goldstein, 1992; Robinson & Howard-Hamilton, 1994). The community counseling model strongly supports these alternative roles because they reflect the proactive and preventive values on which the framework is based.

Resistance to Prevention

Not surprisingly, many administrators and even some counselors resist implementing preventive services at their schools, agencies, or businesses. Three main factors contribute to this hesitancy. First, their professional identity has historically been associated with providing remedial, one-to-one counseling services to people experiencing personal crises (Steenbarger & LeClair, 1995). Second, much of the current funding for mental health services goes to remedial, individual, and small-group counseling services that emphasize an intrapsychic approach to problem solving and personal development. Third, professional training programs have generally failed to address the importance of using preventive counseling strategies in the field. As a result, many practitioners lack the knowledge base and skills necessary to incorporate a preventive approach in their work.

Incorporating Preventive Strategies in Counseling Practice

Two changes must occur in the counseling profession for preventive intervention strategies to become more integral to counselors' work. First, professional preparation programs must demonstrate a new commitment to this area of study. Second, practitioners must be willing to use their understanding of the benefits of preventive counseling to expand the types of services they provide clients.

This latter change requires a shift from the individual-remedial method to more comprehensive and effective ways of operating. For many practitioners, this shift will inevitably require a redefinition or expansion of their professional identity to include new roles and responsibilities as *community health educators* and *mental health consultants*.

Used interchangeably in this book, *preventive counseling* and *preventive education* refer to services intentionally designed both to promote clients' development and to prevent problems. In Chapter 1, we distinguished three types of preventive counseling services—primary, secondary, and tertiary. Unless otherwise stated, preventive counseling and preventive education specifically refer to primary prevention interventions.

In terms of the four service components that make up the community counseling framework, preventive education falls under *direct community counseling services*. As such, it represents those proactive interventions specifically designed to facilitate the empowerment of at-risk groups. Examples include family members of a newly unemployed worker, children of divorce, children of alcoholic parents, people growing up in poverty, and individuals victimized by racial or cultural discrimination.

Multicultural Considerations

Preventive counseling involves helping people develop effective ways of dealing with daily stress. All human beings experience similar needs that, when left unsatisfied, stimulate heightened stress levels. Maslow's (1968) description of the hierarchy of human needs provides a useful framework to conceptualize those needs common to all people.

According to Maslow (1970), individuals experience stress when their basic needs (e.g., the need for food) go unsatisfied for an extended time. This is also true when their sense of personal safety and/or self-esteem is threatened over prolonged periods. Clearly, universal stressors exist. Even so, many people of color, for example, experience unique stressors because of the various types of interactions, discrimination, and oppression they experience (Locke, Daniels, & D'Andrea, 1995).

People of color have a long history of oppression, discrimination, and marginalization in the United States. Although much of the current rhetoric in the counseling profession embraces cultural diversity, most practitioners would readily agree that racism and prejudice continue as institutionalized sources of stress for many people (Huang, 1989; Locke et al., 1995).

The recent rise in racially based violence in the United States is a particularly destructive source of stress (Boland, 1992; D'Andrea & Daniels, 1995; Harvey, 1991). Beyond the threat of physical violence, people of color must also routinely face unique environmental barriers that limit their ability to realize their own occupational (Arbona, 1990; McWhirter, 1992), educational (Carter & Wilson, 1993; National Research Council, 1991), and economic (Kozol, 1991) potential. Given the unique stressors people of color experience in a racist society and the ineffectiveness of many traditional remedial counseling services to meet their needs, preventive counseling interventions present a much more useful and ethical way to promote the psychological well-being of persons in at-risk, culturally diverse populations (Locke et al., 1995; D. Sue & Sue, 1991).

Whether providing preventive or remedial counseling services to people from diverse backgrounds, counselors must become culturally competent service providers in the 21st century. Recognizing the importance of this issue, the community counseling model emphasizes that ethical counseling practice in a pluralistic society requires practitioners to develop the specific competencies outlined by the Association for Multicultural Counseling and Development (Arredondo et al., 1996; D. W. Sue, Arredondo, & McDavis, 1992).

By developing these competencies, counselors can best help people from diverse backgrounds learn ways to prevent problems in their lives. Typically, this involves assisting individuals to expand their repertoire of coping and life skills. Some of the many promising preventive strategies found effective across a broad range of client populations include stress-management programs, health-promotion projects, life-skills training, parenting classes, prejudice-reduction programs, and various school-based interventions specifically designed for at-risk children and youth. Table 2.1 illustrates the place of such strategies in the community counseling model.

TABLE 2.1
PREVENTIVE EDUCATIONAL STRATEGIES
AND THE COMMUNITY COUNSELING MODEL

	COMMUNITY SERVICES	CLIENT SERVICES
Direct	Stress management	
	Health promotion	
	Life skills training	
	Life planning	
	Parenting education	
	Prejudice reduction programs	
	Primary prevention work with	
	children	
Indirect		

STRESS: AN OVERVIEW[1]

Stress is an inevitable part of life. While people have directed much attention to the debilitating effects of stress, some level of stress is necessary for growth and development to occur. Thus, the community counseling model is not designed to help people live a "stress-free life," but rather to help create opportunities in which individuals learn to develop a broad range of stress-management skills they can use in different situations throughout their lives.

Two fundamental premises underlie this approach to counseling. First, individuals can best realize their own optimal level of personal health and well-being when they learn how to manage their unique life stressors. Second, physical illness and psychological disorders can often be avoided by strengthening an individual's or group's capacity to handle environmental stressors and life crises effectively (Conyne, 1991).

Romano (1992) states that stress-management programs are exceptionally well suited for preventive counseling and educational interventions. Mental health practitioners should, however, have a well-defined understanding of what stress is before attempting to train others to manage their reactions to stressful life events and situations.

Ivancevich and Matteson (1980) define *stress* as "an adaptive response, mediated by individual characteristics and/or psychological processes, that is a consequence of any external action, situation or event

---

[1]The following sections are based on material from *Counseling Programs for Employees in the Workplace* by J. A. Lewis and M. D. Lewis, 1986, Pacific Grove, CA: Brooks/Cole.

that places special physical and/or psychological demands upon a person" (pp. 8–9). Using this definition as a guide, the following section provides a brief overview of three different theories of stress that are useful for one to keep in mind when planning preventive interventions among a broad range of clients.

Theories of Stress

Knowledge of stress has dramatically increased over the past 35 years. During this time, three theoretical models have been commonly used in the professional counseling literature to describe stress: the physiological response model (Selye, 1976), the life events model (Holmes & Rahe, 1967; Romano, 1992), and the environmental-interactional model (Lazarus & Folkman, 1984; Lewis, Sperry, & Carlson, 1993) .

The *physiological response model* defines stress in terms of the body's physical response to an environmental demand. Selye (1976) states that, while it is advisable to distinguish between adaptive and nonadaptive stress, such as eustress and distress, respectively, the body inevitably responds to different stressors in ways readily identifiable by most people. Collo-quialisms describe some of these common physiological reactions, such as "My heart is racing," "He's a pain in the neck," and "I have butterflies in my stomach."

Where the physiological model directs attention to a person's physical responses to stress, other researchers focus on specific life events as stressors. The *life events model* suggests that stress results predictably from certain events that occur at different points during a person's development. Several instruments have been developed to assess the degree to which stress may be occurring in one's life. The Holmes and Rahe Readjustment Scale is one of the best-known instruments used to measure adults' stress levels (Holmes & Rahe, 1967). Similar instruments have also been developed to assess the stress levels of college-age students (Marx, Garrity, & Bowers, 1975) as well as children and adolescents (Coddington, 1972).

The third major stress theory is the *environmental-interactional model* (Lazarus & Folkman, 1984). According to this theory, one's appraisal of a stressful event in terms of its potential risk and one's ability to cope with it mediate its impact (Romano, 1992). Further, Lazarus and Folkman (1984) define *coping* as "the process of managing demands (external or internal) that are appraised as taxing or exceeding the resources of the person" (p. 283). This definition suggests that stress-related problems occur when individuals interpret events or situations as personally threatening. The degree to which individuals perceive situations as stressful depends on a number of factors such as their sense of competence to handle the stressor, previous success in dealing with similar situations, the degree to which they feel in control of events, their perceptions of being overloaded or having conflicting needs, and expectations that are either self-imposed or imposed by others (Lewis, et al., 1993).

The Cultural Specificity of Stress Reactions

Many events and interactions can cause stress-related problems and challenge a person's sense of well-being. However, few experiences are universally stressful. Only those situations an individual *views* as personally threatening seem stressful to him or her.

Stressors often relate to such contextual factors as gender (Jordan, Kaplan, Miller, Stiver, & Surrey, 1991), age (Craig, 1992), socioeconomic class (Bassuk, 1993; Knitzer & Aber, 1995), and cultural/ethnic/racial background (Slavin, Rainier, McCreary, & Gowda, 1991). Despite the importance of considering these variables when planning stress-management interventions, counselors frequently fail to address one or more of these factors when working with clients (D'Andrea, 1995).

Slavin et al. (1991) point out that traditional models of psychological stress minimize or completely fail to address the role that one's cultural, ethnic, and/or racial background plays in determining stressful situations. Given the rapid cultural diversification of the United States, counselors must expand their understanding of stress from an ethnic/racial perspective.

In attempting to extend the monocultural frameworks that have dominated the thinking of most mental health professionals in the past, Slavin et al. (1991) have developed a more expansive, culturally sensitive theoretical framework of stress. By identifying several culturally relevant issues that many people of color routinely experience in their lives, these researchers provide a more accurate and comprehensive understanding of some of the underlying cultural and racial determinants of stress.

These investigators identify four specific variables that contribute to an increased level of stress but frequently go unnoticed by white counselors. First, many people in underrepresented groups in the United States experience stress simply because they are identified as members of a "minority group." For example,

> African American adolescents may often find themselves to be
> the only one of their race in a restaurant, store, or classroom; they
> may have difficulty finding a hairdresser who is skilled in handling
> their hair; or they may find themselves called upon regularly in
> classroom discussions to represent their race. (Slavin et al., 1991,
> p. 158)

Second, these researchers refer to the stress that occurs from discrimination and prejudice that plague people of color. Discriminatory acts may be overt and intentional, such as being taunted with racial slurs or stopped by the police for no apparent reason, or they may be covert, such as being addressed in a patronizing manner by white people (D'Andrea, 1996; Locke, 1992; Ridley, 1995).

Third, a disproportionate number of people from nonwhite cultural groups are often overrepresented in the lowest socioeconomic class. Without political or financial clout, these economically disadvantaged persons are more vulnerable to such stressful life events as criminal victimization, eviction, interference by state agencies in family life, not having enough money to eat, and not being able to secure adequate health care. Because these factors are often interrelated, Slavin et al. (1991) report that the occurrence of one of these events tends to catalyze other stressful situations.

Fourth, members of some cultural groups experience unique stressors directly related to the customs of their group. For instance, a Cambodian-American woman may experience heightened stress because of her parents' expectations of an arranged marriage (Slavin et al., 1991).

The community counseling model not only emphasizes the environmental-interactional dimensions of stress but also recognizes that a person's interpretation of stressful situations is often culturally determined. Thus, a particular cultural, ethnic, or racial group may find certain events as stressful, but others may not interpret them as such.

When using the community counseling framework to help clients learn more effective ways of coping with life's challenges, counselors must conceptualize stress from an *environmental-interactional-cultural* or a *contextual perspective*. In doing so, mental health practitioners will gain a better understanding of how clients' cultural, ethnic, and racial backgrounds relate to the unique stressors they experience in their lives.

The Universality of Stress Reactions

While one's cultural background, gender, socioeconomic status, and age usually affect the types of situations one finds stressful, one's physiological responses to threatening events are universal. That is, given an event perceived as personally threatening, all people show similar physical reactions.

To cope with stressful situations, the human body automatically prepares for vigorous physical activity. This involuntary reaction, or "fight-or-flight" response, occurs regardless of the nature of the stressor. Here is a description of the complex, universal physiological reactions to stress:

> It starts in the hypothalamus, a tiny bundle of nerve cells at the
> center of the brain. Messages race from that command post and
> spread the alarm throughout the nervous system. Muscles tense. Blood
> vessels constrict. The tiny capillaries under the skin shut down
> altogether. The pituitary gland sends out two hormones that move

through the bloodstream to stimulate the thyroid and adrenal glands. The adrenals send some thirty additional hormones to nearly every organ in the body. This automatic stress response causes the pulse rate to shoot up; blood pressure soars. The stomach and intestines stop all the busy activity of digestion. Hearing and smell become more acute. Hundreds of other physical changes occur without us even knowing it. (Veninga & Spradley, 1981, p. 11)

These physical reactions stimulate one to take adaptive action when confronted with a stressful situation. However, when these stress responses build up tension that is not released, they use energy that is not restored. Over time, this can ultimately lead to physical and psychological exhaustion. When this occurs, the stress response is not adaptive and tends to cause problems instead of helping one solve them.

The ongoing effects of stress are many. Individuals consistently under stress may find themselves troubled with such physical symptoms as respiratory problems, backaches, chronic high blood pressure, generally low energy levels, and even cardiovascular diseases. Stress also affects psychological health, frequently resulting in depression and anxiety.

STRESS-MANAGEMENT INTERVENTIONS

Because stress-related difficulties result from a combination of external demands, individual perceptions, cultural factors, and physiological responses, one can reduce them by providing interventions at any of these points. Counselors can help individuals examine the stressors in their lives, study their own responses, and make purposeful choices to manage and reduce the stress they will likely experience.

Table 2.2 lists several ways to break the stress cycle. These counseling strategies help clients do the following:

1. Develop insights and skills that help them learn new ways of altering their environment
2. Change the mental processes they use to interpret external events
3. Make healthy changes in the way they live
4. Learn new ways to modify their own physiological responses to stress

Controlling the Environment

People can lower stress by learning to control their environments effectively. As a first step toward this end, counselors can help clients examine

TABLE 2.2
BREAKING THE STRESS CYCLE:
METHODS OF INTERVENTION

| | INTERNAL PROCESSES: | |
EXTERNAL PROCESS	PSYCHOLOGICAL	PHYSIOLOGICAL
Altering the environment	Altering the mental processes	Altering the physiological processes
Counseling focused on decision making and problem solving	Cognitive modification	Relaxation training
		Training in self-hypnosis
	Clarification of values	
Time management counseling	Training in goal setting	Training in meditation
		Training in biofeedback
Training in interpersonal skills (assertiveness, leadership, helping)	Lifestyle assessment and counseling	Sensory awareness training
Training in self-management procedures	Training in problem-solving skills	
Support groups		

Note: Adapted from "A Model of Stress and Counseling Interventions: by J. C. Barrow and S. S. Prosen, 1981, *Personnel and Guidance Journal, 60,* p. 7. Copyright 1981 ACA (formerly the American Personnel and Guidance Asociation). Adapted with permission. No further reproduction authorized without written permission of the American Counseling Association.

those stressors amenable to change. Although they will always experience some stress, individuals can learn to control environmental stressors by developing and implementing problem-solving, time management, and interpersonal skills in their daily lives.

Another important mechanism people use to cope with stress involves their reliance on what psychologists have called *social support systems* (Koeske & Koeske, 1990). A person's social support system typically includes family members, relatives, friends, church members, and co-workers. These people not only provide a buffer from life stressors, but also can encourage and reinforce change (Cohen & Adler, 1986; Koeske & Koeske, 1990).

Helping clients develop strategies aimed at expanding their social support networks is especially important in work with people who value collectivism over individualism. While European Americans extol the latter, those from non-European backgrounds tend to favor a collectivistic orientation (Carter, 1991; D. Sue & Sue, 1990). Thus, strengthening existing support networks and encouraging people to participate in support groups can help culturally diverse clients alter some of the stressful conditions associated with their environments (White & Parham, 1990).

African Americans, Asian Americans, Latinos/Latinas, Native Americans, and people from Pacific Island groups often experience stressors directly related to their membership in a minority group in the United States. As we have mentioned earlier, ethnic discrimination and racism continue to represent insidious sources of stress for many.

The community counseling model emphasizes the importance of addressing these culturally based stressors from a preventive perspective. This may involve helping expand oppressed clients' social support by referring them to culturally specific self-help, political, or social action groups that strive to create changes at the community, state, or national levels. Clients' involvement in such groups offers a powerful way to help them become a part of broad-based environmental modification efforts (Martin, 1991; McWhirter, 1994).

Altering Mental Processes

Besides learning to influence external conditions, people can also learn stress-management skills and techniques that give them greater control over the way they react to environmental situations. For example, counselors can teach clients how to reframe the way they think about stressful situations in their lives.

Ellis (1993) has written extensively about the types of dysfunctional thinking that lead people to experience self-induced stress. According to Ellis's Rational Emotive Behavior theory, stress reactions can be self-induced when individuals use faulty thinking to interpret their situations and experiences.

Beck and Weishaar (1995) discuss several types of dysfunctional thinking that create stress reactions:

1. **All or nothing thinking** leads people to think in dualistic terms; that is, they view situations and/or people as being either good or bad, right or wrong; they do not consider a middle position.
2. **Perfectionistic thinking** causes people to believe that anything less than perfect is unacceptable.
3. **Overgeneralizations** occur when individuals make broad generalizations about other people and/or experiences, with little evidence to back them up.
4. **Catastrophizing** refers to interpreting events and bodily sensations as much worse than the available information suggests.

5. *Self-punishing thinking* involves excessive blaming of oneself when events do not happen as one wishes.

Each type of faulty thinking produces heightened levels of self-induced stress. Thus, counseling aims at helping clients restructure the way they have learned to think about themselves, others, and events in their lives. In doing so, individuals begin to gain a greater sense of internal control over the types of stress they experience. This process is referred to as *cognitive* or *rational restructuring* (Goldfried & Goldfried, 1980; Neimeyer, 1993).

The use of cognitive restructuring techniques to help clients alter their mental processes involves five steps:

1. Counselors help clients recognize that cognitions mediate emotional arousal.
2. Clients examine the irrationality of their dysfunctional thinking style.
3. Counselors help their clients understand the ways unrealistic cognitions affect clients' maladaptive emotions and promote stress reactions.
4. Clients explore ways to change their faulty thinking.
5. Counselors support clients as they strive to restructure their thinking; they also help clients evaluate the outcomes of these efforts.

Changing Lifestyles

Another major component of stress management relates to a person's ability to maintain a healthy lifestyle. While providing clients information about the dangers of smoking, using drugs and alcohol, eating poorly, and refraining from exercising may not be new for many counselors, identifying the relationship between living a healthy lifestyle and managing stress may be (Romano, 1992).

Psychoeducational and life-skills training interventions are excellent strategies for reaching more people in at-risk populations, who will benefit from learning how to manage stress effectively. When providing these services, counselors must help clients understand that unhealthy lifestyle behaviors represent faulty attempts to manage stress, such as using alcohol to reduce social anxiety (Romano, 1992). Psychoeducational interventions that encourage people to develop a broad range of health-promoting, stress-management behaviors work particularly well in school, business, and community-agency settings.

Some examples of the types of psychoeducational interventions that help clients learn to alter their lifestyles constructively include cigarette cessation programs; classes that focus on weight reduction and healthy nutrition; parental training; assertiveness training; conflict-resolution classes; comprehensive health courses in the elementary, middle, and secondary schools; and classes designed to promote problem-solving and decision-making skills.

Altering Physiological Responses to Stress

One cannot always control environmental factors or one's cognitive responses. Counselors, however, can help individuals learn to intervene at the physiological level of the stress response. Through such techniques as biofeedback training, relaxation training, mental imagery, self-hypnosis, and meditation, people can constructively deal with stressors and, thus, avoid the long-term negative effects stress could have on their physical health and psychological well-being.

Biofeedback training teaches individuals ways to control their physiological functioning when they experience stress. By using instruments that provide immediate feedback about certain physiological functions less involuntary than scientists once thought, clients can learn to bring stress-related physical symptoms under control and achieve an increased state of calm at will (Wolpe, 1990).

Similarly, *relaxation training* can help people gain control over the physical tension that occurs from acute or chronic stress. Counselors can use a variety of relaxation training techniques in aiding clients of all ages to alter their physiological reactions to stress (Foreman, 1993).

Mental imagery involves teaching people to relax by picturing scenes they associate with comfort and ease or through related techniques, such as muscle relaxation. In this method, clients alternately tense and relax each of their major muscle groups as they picture this movement in their minds. After clients learn to distinguish between tensed and relaxed states, they can consciously trigger physical relaxation during stressful situations by focusing on muscle groups (Forman, 1993).

Intentionally striving to achieve a relaxed state is the first step in *self-hypnosis*. However, this technique differs from relaxation training in that in self-hypnosis, individuals imagine that what is being suggested is actually happening.

> Doing hypnosis successfully requires the subject to shift into a literally extraordinary frame of mind. While ordinarily we direct our mental processes toward coping with the outer world as we reconstruct or define it within our self-interactions, in hypnosis you shift your attention away from the objective universe, to focus instead upon the imaginary universe you construct internally. In doing so, you literally forget about the "real world" and concentrate upon the ever-shifting

> inner reality you are creating for yourself as you think, feel, and
> imagine along with the suggestions. (Straus, 1982, p. 51)

The suggestions used in self-hypnosis training can relate to changing behavior, modifying attitudes and perceptions, or learning to manage specific environmental stressors.

> A very important set of self-suggestions are those for absolute
> calmness and total relaxation. These kinds of deep-relaxation
> suggestions, which are typically given subvocally to oneself while
> alone, with eyes closed, are especially helpful for relieving stress
> and tension and for alleviating psychosomatic ailments. (Barber,
> 1982, p. v)

Another effective tool for relieving stress and tension involves the use of *meditation.* The meditative experience produces a level of consciousness best described as a state of inner calmness and clarity, which is both self-empowering and pleasurable. One can meditate in many ways, including the popularized breath meditation, transcendental meditation techniques, and other more sophisticated approaches (Jaffe & Scott, 1984).

Breath meditation is an easy way for clients to gain control over stress-related physiological reactions. This technique requires approximately 10 to 20 minutes per day and involves four basic steps. First, clients must locate a quiet, safe place where they will be free from interruptions.

Second, after finding a comfortable sitting position, they must close their eyes and consciously shift their attention from the outside world to their own breathing. Their concentration should specifically focus on the air going into their lungs and out again. While directing their attention this way, they continue to concentrate on their breathing patterns for the first few minutes. If their mind begins to wander, they should gently refocus attention on their breathing.

Third, after taking a few minutes to focus on their breathing, individuals then begin silently to count, "One," as they inhale through their nose and mouth. As they begin to exhale, they say, "And." At the next inhalation they continue their count—"Two—and as they exhale silently count, "And." When they have counted to four, they begin the count over again, following this procedure in a focused and relaxed manner for about 10 to 15 minutes or as long as they feel comfortable doing so.

Finally, they slowly open their eyes and sit still for about a minute to reflect on their own inner feelings. It is important to remind clients (particularly those new to meditation) that distracting thoughts usually occur when one initially begins practicing these sorts of exercises. So they don't get frustrated with these normal distractions, individuals need the counselor's encouragement to accept them when they do occur and to let them go as they turn their attention back to their breathing (Jaffe & Scott, 1984).

These and other meditation techniques are largely derived from Eastern religious groups and traditions. As a result, they may prove particularly helpful for people with Asian backgrounds. The increased popularity that various forms of meditation have received in the United States over the past several decades provides counselors with additional resources for helping others learn new ways of altering their physiological reactions to stress.

The Stress-Management Workshop

Providing stress-management workshops in school, business, and community settings is a practical way of fostering this important life skill among people of different ages and backgrounds. Stress-management workshops generally use a preventive education format designed to provide a safe and mutually supportive environment in which clients can develop new insights and skills to cope with stress. While one clearly needs to tailor these workshops to meet the participants' unique developmental and cultural needs, most share the following characteristics:

1. *Identifying stressors:* Stress management begins with accurately recognizing the stressors that occur in one's life. To promote self-awareness and build mutual support within stress-management groups, the workshop leader can divide participants into small groups and ask them to generate lists of typical work, school, or social stressors. After sharing their lists of stressors in the small groups, the workshop participants discuss commonalties and potential solutions to the problems presented by the group members.

2. *Cognitive restructuring:* The workshop leader can deepen participants' self-awareness by inviting them to look for patterns in how they deal with stressful situations. To accomplish this, the leader asks participants to list recent events that made them anxious. By analyzing these situations and their reactions to them, clients can discover what kinds of events they tend to perceive as threatening and stressful. A short lecture and discussion can then help them consider alternative ways to deal with stress in their lives.

3. *Stress reduction:* The workshop leader usually provides an overview of the universal physiological reactions people have to stress. Once participants know more about the body's physical fight-or-flight response to stress, they are better positioned to learn new ways of coping with their particular life stressors. By focusing on ways to relieve anxiety, such as enhancing their own ability to relax, workshop participants receive the opportunity to explore the methods that work best for them.

4. *Identifying successful strategies:* This exercise requires participants to talk about ways they have successfully dealt with specific stressors

in their own lives. As they discuss these strategies, participants often notice that the commonly used stress reduction tactics run the gamut from environmental problem solving through changes in one's thoughts to physical relaxation methods. Because this exercise invites participants to talk about their successes rather than their problems, it provides an encouraging counterpoint to the workshop's early focus on their stressors and problems.

5. *Making stress-management plans:* Creating personalized stress-management plans can enhance the long-term benefits of the stress management workshop. Counselors encourage each participant to select several stress-related situations and generate immediate strategies for dealing with them. A follow-up session helps monitor and reinforce clients' successes in managing stress.

HEALTH-PROMOTION PROGRAMS

Overview: A Holistic Approach

Many contemporary health problems are preventable. To prevent health problems, however, clients often need assistance in developing new attitudes and behaviors that enhance wellness. The importance of using preventive educational interventions seems clear if only because vast expenditures on traditional remedial health-care services have not reduced the occurrence of preventable health problems that millions of people experience in the United States each year.

A century ago, infectious diseases were the leading cause of death in this country. During the 20th century, however, health patterns have changed. Because of scientific advancements, diseases such as tuberculosis, measles, poliomyelitis, influenza, and pneumonia are no longer the killers they once were.

While these diseases have mostly subsided, other threats to people's health and well-being have greatly increased. This includes a rise in the number of people whose health is seriously compromised by conditions linked to their lifestyle. Such conditions include lung cancer, major cardiovascular disease, drug and alcohol abuse, and motorcycle and drug-related automobile accidents (Lewis et al., 1993). Even those infectious diseases currently on the rise in the general population, such as Acquired Immune Deficiency Syndrome (AIDS), highly correlate with lifestyle variables.

Today, most deaths can often be avoided or at least mitigated by changes in the way one lives (Witmer & Sweeney, 1992). Cardiovascular disease alone accounts for half the annual mortalities among Americans. Cancer and accidents are also major causes of death in the United States.

Often preventable, these problems do not respond well to traditional medical interventions (Lewis et al., 1993).

Experts have noted how individuals can both improve the state of their health and reduce the costs of medical care during their life span (Zimpfer, 1992). These health-promoting behaviors include eliminating cigarettes and misuse of alcohol, minimizing excess calories and fats, exercising moderately each day, undergoing periodic screening for the early detection of major disorders such as high blood pressure and certain cancers, adhering to traffic laws, and using seat belts (Lewis et al., 1993).

In the community counseling model, counselors foster these types of behaviors by developing programs designed to promote the well-being of targeted populations. When developed in schools, community agencies, hospitals, or business settings, health-promotion programs affect large numbers of people.

More important than a program's setting, a holistic approach to the enhancement of wellness requires two fundamental considerations. First, one must consider the physiological, environmental, psychological, and cultural factors that affect a client's health and well-being. Second, at its core, the holistic approach involves encouraging clients to take personal responsibility for their own health. Thus, a key element in this preventive approach is the individual's willingness and ability to take greater control of his or her wellness.

Wellness refers to a holistic way of thinking about one's overall well-being. Witmer and Sweeney (1992) claim,

> The concept of wellness is inextricably connected with several major themes related to wholeness in mind, body, spirit, and community. As individuals and families strive to meet their daily responsibilities in work, friendships, and love relationships, there is a need to maintain a perspective not only on what is adequate health and what is normal but also what is necessary and desirable for optimum health and functioning. (p. 140)

Health-promotion programs designed to promote "optimal functioning" direct counselors to foster a greater understanding of wellness, to help clients discover their power to prevent illness through personal initiative, and to encourage clients to take responsibility for meeting their own health needs. In these ways, counselors can help clients acquire a sense of personal power that enhances what Kobasa (1979) has referred to as "psychological hardiness."

Many have cited psychological hardiness as one of the most important factors in helping people avoid chronic illness (Lichtenberg, Johnson, & Arachtingi, 1992). Kobasa (1979) has also pointed out that, among people facing comparable degrees of stress, the factors distinguishing those who remained healthy from those who became ill included a vigorous attitude toward the world, a strong self-commitment, a sense of meaning in life, and an internal locus of control.

Over the past 15 years, other researchers have added to Kobasa's list by pointing out that people who had faith in themselves, believed that they could control events through their own behavior, and experienced a sense of mutual support within the context of a meaningful community, manifested a psychological hardiness that protected them against psychological stress and illness (Lewis et al., 1993).

These observations suggest that health-promotion programs should be designed to accomplish two central purposes:

1. Helping clients develop attitudes that foster an increased sense of psychological hardiness
2. Helping them acquire the life skills needed to maintain their optimal level of health and well-being

Health-promotion programs typically consist of services that focus on specific issues, such as smoking-cessation groups, weight loss programs, and exercise classes. Just as important, however, is the emphasis health programs place on the idea of wellness. The following discussion describes two health-promotion programs developed in quite different geographic locations among groups identified as at risk for certain physical and psychological problems.

Health Promotion in an Urban Setting: A Health Center for At-Risk Youth

Poor children often have limited access to quality medical care. Because of economic and personal hardships and a lack of low-cost prevention services, parents may too often delay seeking primary and preventive health care for their children. This delay frequently leads them to rely on costly hospital emergency room visits when health problems escalate.

Recognizing the importance of providing services that enhance youngsters' physical health and psychological well-being, Aunt Martha's School-Linked Health Center (SLHC) was developed to foster the wellness of an at-risk group of children and youths in Chicago, Illinois. This innovative, community-based project targeted students in School District 170, part of an economically depressed area known as Chicago Heights.

In an extensive assessment of these students' health needs, the SLHC program planners found that many of them were at-risk for many health problems. Planners determined that the students could avoid most of these problems if they could more easily access certain types of primary and preventive health care services. Then, school nurses, social workers, counselors, parents, and others affiliated with the superintendent's office participated in a needs assessment study designed to generate information about the students' health-care needs.

The results provided a grim picture of the physical and psychological health of many of the youngsters in Chicago Heights. The following sections provide brief descriptions of the top health priorities identified by the assessment; then, we discuss the ways the counselors, social workers, and school nurses who worked with the SLHC project came together to enhance the physical and psychological wellness of the students in School District 170.

ACCESS TO MEDICAL CARE   Many of the children in District 170 lacked access to routine medical care. Despite the availability of health-care services in Chicago Heights, the school nurses estimated that 20% of all students in the district who were recommended for outside medical follow-up services never received them. A major factor contributing to this lack of follow-up care was the limited number of health-care providers who accepted medicaid reimbursement payments. To address this problem, the SLHC program began providing community-based health services to students in the fall of 1995.

The program planners successfully negotiated rental space in a building across the street from Washington Elementary School, Washington Junior High School, and the school district's administrative offices. Shortly thereafter, the Community Health Center opened, offering a variety of primary and preventive health-care services at low cost or free of charge to students in the district. In addition to these services, the staff at the Community Health Center made referrals for those who needed specialized services.

The results of the needs assessment also indicated that many students relied heavily on the school nurses to meet their health-care needs. In this regard, the head nurse at the school reported that most of the nursing staff saw an average of 30 students per day. She further estimated that the demand to provide a variety of health-care services to the students left her staff with less than 7 minutes to spend on each child, including the time it took to make referrals, provide follow-up services, and complete paperwork. Recognizing the important role the nurses played, the SLHC counselors and social workers began working closely with them, supporting and supplementing their duties and periodically relieving them of some of the overwhelming responsibilities they encountered on a daily basis.

IMMUNIZATIONS   Another important finding generated from the needs assessment was the number of students who needed but did not receive immunizations. The results of the needs assessment indicated that 8% of all students entering the first and fifth grades could not begin school on time because of noncompliance with immunization regulations. Further, these children faced a particular risk in that Chicago Heights had one of the highest rates of measles in the state.

To address this problem, the SLHC counselors designed an action plan that included (1) working with the students' parents to show them the importance of having children immunized and (2) developing a program that provided free or low-cost immunizations.

ADOLESCENT PREGNANCIES   Though the needs assessment was conducted only two months into the school year, three girls in the eighth grade were already pregnant. Five pregnancies were also reported among students in the ninth-grade classes. The preceding year, 12 ninth-graders had become pregnant. Although the adolescent pregnancy problem was not new, school personnel indicated an urgent need for more pregnancy prevention services. Many of the teachers and parents strongly recommended services that emphasized the importance of abstinence and promoted the development of more effective decision-making skills.

In reviewing these recommendations, the SLHC counselors and social workers drew on their extensive experience as prevention educators and family planning consultants to develop an educational intervention that addressed these concerns. The SLHC nurse also agreed to provide one-on-one health and sex education services for those students at particularly high risk for pregnancy. Referral and transportation services were provided to those pregnant teenagers who needed but did not have access to comprehensive, prenatal, postnatal, and well-baby care services.

PERSONAL HYGIENE AND NUTRITION   Another need consistently identified by the teachers, school counselors, nurses, and social workers involved the chronic lack of knowledge students had about basic personal hygiene and good nutrition. They thought problems with students' hygiene and nutrition often related to frequent health complaints such as headaches, stomachaches, ear infections, rashes, and head lice.

To address these concerns, the SLHC counselors initiated a cooperative venture with other school personnel to address prevention issues specifically related to personal hygiene and nutrition. They planned to meet with students individually and in groups to increase their awareness of hygiene and nutrition. Other local resources were identified and referrals made for those students found to be diabetic, obese, malnourished, allergic, or otherwise needing special dietary education services.

STRESS   Many of the children and adolescents in the school district suffered from emotional and physical stressors precipitated by poverty and other environmental factors such as crime, domestic violence, drug abuse among family members, and inferior housing conditions. One indicator showed that nearly 10% of junior-high students voluntarily sought personal counseling from the school counselors. Further, practitioners claimed that many more students than those who were self-referred needed such services; they reported consistently having as many as 20 students on waiting lists for stress-related counseling services at a given time.

The SLHC staff developed several strategies to help meet the students' need for such counseling. These included working with school counselors to provide direct services to students in immediate need; assistance in making referral arrangements for neurological, psychiatric, and psychological services; and preventive mental health education services to students and families.

Regarding this last point, the SLHC staff began working closely with the school personnel to develop a monthly prevention calendar that targeted groups of students from kindergarten through the eighth grade. Topics covered in these age-appropriate group sessions included sexually transmitted diseases and HIV/AIDS prevention; alcohol/drug/tobacco and nutritional education; personal safety; conflict resolution and anger management; violence prevention; and decision-making, peer pressure, and refusal strategies.

MULTICULTURAL ISSUES   Recognizing that 80% of the students attending the schools served by SLHC came from multiethnic backgrounds, the staff acknowledged the importance of providing culturally sensitive services. They specifically noted that more than one-third of the students in the district were Latino. This suggested that communication differences might be a potential barrier to the effective delivery of human services in this community. To help address this concern, pamphlets and parental permission forms were translated into Spanish to enhance more effective communication between the SLHC staff and Latino parents.

Another potential barrier related to the staff's level of multicultural counseling awareness, knowledge, and skills (D. W. Sue et al., 1992). The SLHC staff themselves readily acknowledged that the project's overall effectiveness related directly to the workers' ability to provide services in a culturally sensitive manner. As such, they implemented two strategies. First, the program planners made the recruitment and hiring of a bilingual/bicultural staff member a top priority. Second, all SLHC staff were expected to attend Aunt Martha's regularly scheduled cultural awareness training sessions as part of their ongoing professional and personal development activities.

The SLHC provides an excellent example of a comprehensive health-promotion program for at-risk youth residing in economically depressed urban areas. The needs assessment proved vital in providing the community counselors with useful information about the types of services that would be most helpful to students and their families.

Although these sorts of urban-based interventions are vital, many counselors work in suburban and rural settings. The psychological and physical health needs of people who live there often differ from those of their urban counterparts. Because people in different target groups usually have different needs, mental health practitioners should assess the needs of their target population before developing and implementing a health-promotion program (Braucht & Weime, 1990).

In discussing the urgency of providing more effective health-promotion services in rural areas of the United States, Human and Wasem (1991) note that many counselors simply lack an accurate understanding of the unique needs of rural clients. The following discussion examines how strategies used in secluded parts of South Africa helped planners develop a health-promotion program in rural North Carolina.

Health Promotion in a Rural Setting: The Madison County Health Project

A good example of a health-promotion program for an at-risk population in a rural setting is the Madison County Health Project (MCHP). This community-based health initiative began in 1989. Located in the mountainous western region of North Carolina, Madison County consists of a 456-square-mile rural area where 16,953 people live in some 6514 households (Landis, Trevor, Futch, & Plaut, 1995). Madison County has historically comprised primarily family farmers who raised tobacco as their main cash crop.

During the 1980s, the economy hurt many rural counties, including Madison. At that time, the demand for tobacco decreased in general, and major U. S. tobacco companies increasingly turned to cheaper overseas suppliers. The subsequent lack of economic opportunity in Madison County led to a tremendous flight of younger workers to other parts of the country in search of better career options.

As a result, a disproportionate number of poor families with school-aged children and elderly people remained in Madison. Concern about the possible health problems these individuals might face and the lack of resources available to address their needs led to the formation of the MCHP.

A FIVE-STAGE PROCESS   The development of the MCHP involved a five-stage process:

1. Exploring what "community" meant to the residents of the
   targeted area and directing particular attention to identifying

the specific human resources and key "helpers" within their community

2. Identifying specific health problems common among residents of Madison County
3. Prioritizing their health needs
4. Designing and implementing health-promotion interventions
5. Evaluating the effectiveness of the health-promotion programs to enable their ongoing improvement (Landis et al., 1995; Nutting, 1990)

These intervention guidelines followed similar strategies used by two physicians, Sidney and Emily Kark, committed to promoting preventive health-care services in rural parts of South Africa (Plaut, Landis, & Trevor, 1991).

Like the Chicago-based program previously described, the MCHP coordinators recognized that assessing the needs of the community was a logical starting point. In attempting to gather meaningful information regarding the physical and mental health of the county residents, the coordinators decided to use focus groups to survey them.

They chose this method for a number of reasons. First, several members of the MCHP planning committee pointed out that many of the residents in the target group expressed no desire to participate in a traditional community needs assessment project, because they had already "been surveyed to death" by other researchers in the past (Landis et al., 1995).

Second, though time consuming, focus groups provide a useful method of overcoming many barriers associated with conducting assessments among the rural poor. These barriers include suspicion and mistrust of traditional research procedures and researchers they do not know, fear of self-disclosure, an internalized sense of marginality, high illiteracy rates, and a general fear of the assessment process.

The sense of safety that typically characterizes focus groups makes it easier for such people, who would feel vulnerable and intimidated in a one-to-one encounter with a researcher, to express their thoughts and feelings more freely (Crabtree, Yanoshik, Miller, & O'Conner, 1993). Although the MCHP staff did encounter suspicion (and even hostility), especially among some of the men who participated, the focus groups did generate valuable information about the health-care needs and types of interventions preferred by the community residents.

NEEDS ASSESSMENT The specific health concerns receiving the highest ratings included the diseases that afflicted many elderly persons in the county, alcohol-related problems among adolescents and adults, stress-related health problems (e.g., headaches and stomachaches) among many of the farmers in the county, concern for young parents in the community, and stress-related problems (especially clinical depression) among high-school students who indicated they would have few opportunities after they graduated (Landis et al., 1995). Using the results of the needs assessment as a guide, the MCHP's Community Advisory Board (CAB) initiated the following grassroots interventions in Madison County.

The Elderly.   In light of the concerns expressed about the physical well-being of the elderly, representatives from various human services organizations in the county began meeting to discuss ways they might work together to address this need. This collaboration resulted in a series of health fairs for seniors, which have been held annually since 1991.

The health fairs provide a variety of services to people over 65, who can there receive flu and pneumonia vaccinations, blood pressure screening, and eye and hearing examinations. They can also attend stress-management workshops. A community resource guide identifying safety tips for seniors has also been developed and is distributed free of charge at the fairs.

The health fairs also strengthen the community members' sense of social support by providing the opportunity to socialize and see old friends. More than 500 people attend the health fairs each year.

Adolescents.   To address the identified health-care needs of adolescents in the targeted area, counselors and educators in the community helped organize a series of forums for high-school seniors. These forums examined a broad range of teenage health issues including alcohol/drug/tobacco misuse and abuse, AIDS and other sexually transmitted diseases, and stress-related health problems.

New Parents.   In addition to these projects and services, parents of newborn children also received preventive education and supportive services. Women were recruited as "community volunteers" from the greater county area. These volunteers were trained to provide parents with information about agencies in the area that offered various types of family services. In addition to this community education service, the volunteers were trained to talk with the new parents specifically about making sure their infants receive proper preventive health-care services. In encouraging parents to address this need, the community volunteers informed them of the immunization schedules at hospitals and health-care clinics in the county. The volunteers also provided new parents with home-safety kits, which included practical items such as forehead-tape thermometers, electrical outlet caps, and smoke detectors to help them take care of themselves.

Children.   Recently, the MCHP initiated another prevention project that addressed a particular need of the children living in the county. In this area, most drinking water comes from wells or springs; the lack of fluoride in the water had an adverse affect on children's dental health. To help prevent serious dental problems, a school-based oral health prevention program was initiated. It included putting sealants on the teeth of elementary-school students in the area (Landis et al., 1995).

The services offered by the MCHP complement the community counseling model's emphasis on prevention education as a basic health-promotion strategy. Counselors may find the five-step plan, which the MCHP program planners followed in developing their projects and services, useful as they consider ways to initiate health-promotion projects in their own communities.

As we mentioned earlier, the success of any health-promotion program is fundamentally linked to helping clients develop and maintain a positive attitude regarding their physical and psychological wellness. However, in addition to a positive attitude, people need to acquire a broad range of life skills for maintaining a healthy lifestyle. Recognizing the importance of fostering such competencies, the community counseling model places a special emphasis on life-skills training projects.

LIFE-SKILLS TRAINING: PROMOTING PERSONAL COMPETENCE

Everyone faces myriad challenges, conflicts, confusion, and difficult choices in life. How people react to these challenges frequently impacts their physical health and psychological well-being. In attempting to navigate through the various environmental demands and stressors they encounter at different points in their development, people rely on many life skills.

Definition and Importance of Life Skills

Life skills refer to those competencies that enhance one's ability to realize a personally satisfying and productive life in the face of challenging and stressful times. Though acquiring a broad range of such skills does not guarantee personal success and satisfaction, an absence of these skills clearly makes it more likely that individuals will experience unhealthy levels of psychological stress over which they have little control.

The idea that helping professionals should help people develop life skills that enhance their sense of personal empowerment and well-being is not new. In fact, the importance of teaching desirable behaviors that promote psychological health was supported by many in the American educational establishment during the early part of the 20th century. The Character Education Movement in the 1920s represents one of the first organized efforts to help youngsters systematically acquire such important life competencies as effective decision-making and problem-solving skills within the public school system (Goldstein, 1992).

The Character Education Movement foreshadowed other life-skills projects including the moral education and values clarification programs implemented in public schools during the 1970s and 1980s (Kirschenbaum, 1975; Kohlberg & Turiel, 1971). These programs were specifically designed to help students develop the cognitive reasoning abilities necessary to make responsible decisions (Lickona, 1991).

Several other innovative life-skills training projects also found a tremendous degree of popularity during the 1970s. Often referred to as "psychological skills training" (Goldstein, 1992) or "deliberate psychological education" (Mosher & Sprinthall, 1971), these programs gained a strong foothold in counseling and psychology at a time when the public had begun to doubt seriously the effectiveness of many traditional counseling and psychotherapeutic interventions.

Various types of life-skills training programs currently operate in public schools, community colleges, universities, mental health agencies, hospitals, and businesses across the United States. Some of these skill-building programs center on family planning (Pransky, 1991), leadership training (Astin, 1989), public speaking and assertiveness training (Powell & Collier, 1990), career planning (Herr & Niles, 1994), computer training (Gerler, 1995), and diversity training (Lee, 1995).

Further, hundreds of thousands of people purchase self-help books to learn how to realize their human potential, develop healthy lifestyles, acquire effective interpersonal skills, and become proficient decision makers and life planners. Given the increasing demands of a rapidly changing, complex, technological society and the broad-based interest in life-skills training among the general public, counselors must develop a clear understanding of this popular and important area of work.

Effectiveness of Life-Skills Training Programs

Empirical evidence supporting the effectiveness of life-skills training programs, especially those designed to promote clients' social and problem-solving abilities, has steadily increased. Researchers have noted that the emphasis on prevention and the development of personal competencies—the core of most life-skills training programs—has substantially enhanced the successful adjustment and personal satisfaction of people of diverse backgrounds and ages (Albee, Bond, & Monsey, 1992; Albee & Rynn-Finn, 1993; Bond & Compas, 1989; Commission on Prevention of Mental/ Emotional Disorders, 1987).

Bloom (1984) asserts that an individual's level of personal competence, particularly in social situations, can moderate many of the negative effects of stressful life events. From his own research, Bloom concludes,

> Much human misery appears to be the result of a lack of competence–that is, a lack of control over one's life, a lack of effective coping strategies, and the lowered self-esteem that accompanies these deficiencies. This opinion is emerging out of an analysis of a substantial body of research from a variety of domains that appears to converge on competence building as one of the most persuasive preventive strategies for dealing with individual and social issues in many communities. (p. 270)

Thus, even without knowing the unique biological, social, or psychological source of a particular problem, one may be able to prevent that problem, along with others, by strengthening the coping skills and general competency of people who have not yet developed dysfunctions. Preventive intervention strategies found to be effective include stress management (Romano, 1992), health promotion (Gebhardt & Crump, 1990; Winett, 1995), parenting (D'Andrea, 1994), prejudice reduction (Ponterotto & Pedersen, 1993), and school-based (Baker, 1996) and community-based life-skills training (Gazda, 1984; Goldstein, 1992).

Promoting Intrapersonal and Interpersonal Competencies

The life-skills training perspective is primarily preventive in theory and practice. Interventions designed to promote life skills view individuals less as clients than students who would benefit from opportunities to foster various intrapersonal and interpersonal competencies.

Intrapersonal competencies refer to those attitudes and skills that allow individuals to negotiate their social environments in constructive, responsible, and assertive ways (Kieffer, 1984; McWhirter, 1994). This includes but is not limited to developing a positive sense of self-esteem (Bowman, 1992), self-efficacy (Bandura, 1982), and self-management skills (Jaffe & Scott, 1984). The intrapersonal dimension of life-skills training also involves acquiring a broad range of decision-making skills and coping strategies that one can use in stressful situations.

Interpersonal competencies, on the other hand, include skills that increase one's ability to communicate effectively with others. To do so, individuals must learn to converse with others in ways that reflect an understanding of one's own perspective as well as respect for that of any other person with whom one interacts (Selman, 1980). McWhirter (1994) points to interventions designed to help individuals from diverse cultural backgrounds develop the types of interpersonal skills that "facilitate an individual's efforts toward greater self-direction, an increased sense of personal competency and mastery, and greater effectiveness in communicating, relating to, and working with others" (p. 51).

These interventions include school-based leadership training for culturally diverse student populations (Fertman & Long, 1990); school-based conflict resolution, mediation training, and violence prevention among youngsters from multiracial backgrounds (D'Andrea & Daniels, 1996; Larson, 1994); public-speaking classes for culturally diverse adult clients (Powell & Collier, 1990); and assertiveness training for Asian Americans (D. Sue & Sue, 1991). Although many psychological and life-skills training models have appeared over the past several decades, the developmental approach (Gazda, 1984; Ivey, 1993) is particularly consistent with the community counseling framework.

Gazda's Life-Skills Training Model

A training model designed by Gazda and others (Gazda, 1984; Gazda, Childers, & Brooks, 1987), which they call "Life Skills Training," successfully applies developmental theory to the task of building personal competence. This model emphasizes four basic skills: (1) interpersonal communication and human relations, (2) problem solving and decision making, (3) physical fitness and health maintenance, and (4) identity development.

ASSUMPTIONS   Gazda and his colleagues have identified over 300 life skills, categorizing them according to their age appropriateness and the area of human development to which they relate. Here is a summary of the basic assumptions that underlie the Life Skills Training model:

1. Across the seven dimensions of human development—psychosocial, physical-sexual, vocational/career, cognitive, ego, moral, and affective—there are stages through which all people must progress to lead effective lives. Some of these are age related; some are not.

2. Satisfactory progression through each stage depends on the successful accomplishment of developmental tasks specific to each.

3. Accomplishment of these developmental tasks depends on the mastery of life skills appropriate to a given stage and task.

4. Each person encounters many agents (parents, siblings, teachers, peers, social institutions, and so on) through which she or he may learn life skills.

5. There are certain age ranges during which particular life skills can be most easily learned.

6. Though individuals inherit their capacity for learning, the degree to which they can achieve their maximum potential depends on their environment and life experiences.

7. Individuals achieve optimal functioning when they fully acquire fundamental life skills.

8. Neuroses and functional psychoses result from a failure to develop life skills. Persons experiencing such dysfunctions usually suffer from multiple life-skills deficits.

9. Life skills can be taught most effectively through small groups, provided members are developmentally ready. Therefore, the most satisfactory means of ensuring positive mental health and of remediating psychological dysfunction is through direct teaching/training in life skills, especially if two or more life-skills deficits are addressed concurrently. (Gazda, 1984, p. 93)

FOUR STEPS In accordance with these general principles, Gazda's Life Skills Training program fosters various competencies by analyzing the coping behaviors appropriate to the tasks of a given age or stage across the seven dimensions of human development mentioned in the first assumption. Gazda and his colleagues use small-group settings to teach life skills appropriate to the needs and strengths of the individual participants. The same approach applies to both prevention and remediation work. Regardless of the degree of dysfunction among the trainees, the goal of the training is the same: to escort the participants through a series of group sessions that help them move from being trainees through gaining competencies to becoming trainers themselves. Here are four steps that make up this training format:

STEP 1: Training in generic life skills.
1. *Tell.* The trainers explain the purpose of teaching the generic life skill to be taught.
2. *Show.* The trainers model the behavior(s) or response(s) to be mastered.
3. *Do.* The trainees practice the skills in the group setting mastered.
4. *Transfer.* The trainees receive homework assignments and try to apply the new skill(s) in their daily life.
5. *Feedback.* The trainers and trainees assess the progress the students have made toward achieving the skills.

STEP 2: The trainees are encouraged to help other students develop those life skills they themselves have successfully learned during the group training sessions—*peer bonding*. This involves cotraining with a "master" trainer (usually a staff member or trainee who has "graduated" from Step 4).

STEP 3: Training other trainees under the supervision of a "master" trainer.

STEP 4: Conduct group training sessions alone. (Gazda, 1984, p. 95)

The Prepare Curriculum: Goldstein's Problem-Solving Program

Another example of a systematic approach to life-skills training is the Prepare Curriculum (PC) (Goldstein, 1992). The PC is based on more than 20 years of research on the effectiveness of interventions designed to promote the psychological competencies and prosocial behaviors of children and adolescents (Spivack & Levine, 1973; Spivack & Shure, 1974; Strain, 1981). Although originally designed to teach an array of prosocial skills to youngsters who manifested interpersonal deficits, the PC provides a useful preventive framework as well.

The PC comprises 10 courses in which youngsters participate in structured learning activities designed to foster their cognitive, interpersonal, and moral development. These courses include training in the following areas: problem solving, interpersonal relations, situational perception, anger control, moral reasoning, stress management, empathy, cooperative learning and behaving, and understanding and participating in groups (Goldstein, 1992). These courses aim at building skills that will do the following:

1. Help youngsters develop realistic ways to achieve personal and interpersonal goals and acquire a better understanding of their self-concepts, emotions, and conflicts, as well as their wishes and goals

2. Help them learn more effective ways to elicit the help and cooperation that will enable them to meet their personal and career goals

3. Help youngsters learn ways to become more personally appealing to others who are important to them

4. Help them to understand others' self-concepts, emotions, conflicts, problems, desires, and goals

5. Help youth to more effectively help others by learning to offer suggestions for constructive change appropriately

6. Help youngsters to understand and resolve problems between themselves and others in a constructive and enduring way—a way that takes all realities, including emotional ones, into account and that comes closest to satisfying all parties

7. Increase participants' ability to enrich their relationships with people important to them in love, work, and play—that is, enable them to discover more ways to increase the enjoyment and productivity they experience in such relationships
8. Help participants increase their ability to generalize and transfer these skills to their daily life and to maintain them over time
9. Help participants increase their ability to teach significant others the skills necessary to accomplish these nine goals (Goldstein, 1992, pp. 8–9)

The PC framework assumes that effective living depends on an individual's ability to give understanding, to empathize with others, and to generate their empathy in return. In short, this training model teaches youngsters how to respond more effectively to others. To accomplish this, cognitive and behavioral instruction are systematically combined to help foster the following:

1. *Expressive skills* to promote self-understanding and the ability to communicate this understanding effectively to others
2. *Empathic skills* to help youngsters see the world as others see it, emotionally identify the feelings of others, and show respect and compassion to others
3. *Mode switching* to help them learn to use expressive and empathic skills appropriately
4. *Interpersonal conflict and problem-resolution skills* to foster tolerance, understanding, and respect for human diversity
5. *Facilitation abilities* to help youngsters learn to elicit reactions from others that enrich their relationship with them as well as contribute to their own personal growth
6. *Generalization and maintenance* to encourage the youngsters to make the newly learned behaviors integral parts of their lives

Although traditional counseling and therapy can nurture many of these attitudes and behaviors, Goldstein (1992) emphasizes the importance of basing this sort of training on educational models rather than clinical or medical ones. Consequently, the counselor acts as a trainer by (1) motivating, (2) explaining, (3) demonstrating, (4) modeling/prompting, (5) supervising skill practice within the training sessions, (6) preparing the learner to be successful with homework, (7) assessing homework assignments, (8) preparing the learner to use the skills spontaneously in everyday living, (9) supervising the transfer of skills into everyday living, and (10) supervising the acquisition of maintenance skills.

School-Based Preventive Life-Skills Programs

People concerned with primary prevention have come to recognize that programs can and should focus on the developmental and cultural needs of children and adolescents. As such, the school setting is an ideal environment to implement the community counseling framework.

In this setting, youngsters have multiple opportunities to discuss rationales for using a wide variety of life skills, to practice using them, and to receive feedback on their efforts to acquire these skills. Furthermore, classroom-based efforts to enhance life-skills development are desirable because most students find these group settings more attractive than the relatively infrequent interactions they have with school counselors (Baker, 1996).

Further, regarding the many positive aspects of developing preventive interventions within educational settings, Weissberg and Allen (1986) note,

> School-based prevention approaches reduce the possibility that students will be stigmatized, because youngsters receiving training need not be labeled as emotionally disturbed or mentally ill. Without direct intervention to promote adaptive interpersonal behavior, the adjustment of too many children who have social relationship problems gets worse, or at best, remains unchanged, and these untreated children continue to be vulnerable to later problems. (p. 157)

School-based programs allow counselors to reach children efficiently at the ages most appropriate for learning particular life skills. More important, because they target a broad range of young people who have not necessarily exhibited problems, such programs promote competency building.

To help students acquire the types of life skills they will need in a rapidly changing, pluralistic society, many counselors have implemented developmental guidance and counseling programs in their schools. These programs emphasize preventive education strategies (Baker, 1996; Muro & Kottman, 1995; Myrick, 1987). Although the focus differs from school to school, most school-based developmental guidance programs address the following: self-esteem, motivation to achieve, decision making and goal setting, interpersonal problem solving and conflict resolution, and social-multicultural awareness.

MULTICULTURALISM IN SCHOOL-BASED PROGRAMS As mentioned in Chapter 1, one of the main challenges facing mental health professionals in the 21st century involves facilitating community-building initiatives among people from diverse cultural, ethnic, and racial backgrounds. Because the future prosperity and tranquility of society largely depends on the successful accomplishment of this task, schools will be increasingly called on to help students embrace cultural diversification and avoid falling prey to prejudice and stereotyping.

To promote these positive developmental outcomes, counselors in Hawai'i implemented an innovative school-based program to foster elementary-school students' awareness and respect for cultural diversification. Over 140 African-American, European-American, Hawaiian, Japanese-American, Chinese-American, Filipino, Korean, and Samoan students from four different third-grade classes participated in the Multicultural Guidance Program (MGP) (Daniels, 1995). This developmental guidance program comprised ten class sessions in which the youngsters actively engaged in a variety of learning activities that focused on positive aspects of their own and their classmates' cultural backgrounds. Researchers reported significant gains in the children's empathy and social-skills development as a result of participating in the MGP (D'Andrea & Daniels, 1995).

In another school-based primary prevention program, Locke and Faubert (1993) conducted a series of psychoeducational classes among students traditionally identified as at-risk for a host of physical and psychological problems. The Getting on the Right Track Project targeted African-American high-school students from rural North Carolina.

Meeting in small groups, these counselors used an African-centered perspective in designing the curriculum for the project. As a result of participating in this project, the participants demonstrated an increased sense of pride and awareness in their cultural background, improved grades, and developed new leadership and social skills (Locke & Faubert, 1993).

Violence Prevention and Conflict Resolution

Acts of violence in the United States have reached epidemic proportions. This is shown by the number of reported homicides and assaults (Federal Bureau of Investigation, 1994); the rising incidence of domestic violence (Browne, 1993; Kilpatrick, Edmunds, & Seymore, 1992); the escalation of hate crimes directed toward people from diverse ethnic/racial backgrounds (D'Andrea & Daniels, 1994); and the increasing number of violent acts perpetuated by secondary-, middle-, and even elementary-school students (Ferrara, 1992; Johnson & Johnson, 1995).

While public support has increased for harsher punishments for perpetrators of violence, such reactive policies have done little to reduce destructive conflicts in schools and communities. Other solutions therefore need to be explored and implemented. The prevention of violence and the effective resolution of interpersonal conflicts involve using a complex array of life skills. These skills need to be nurtured throughout one's life—from the elementary school years through adulthood.

To help stem the tide of violence, many counselors have initiated conflict resolution and peer mediation programs in the public schools. These programs reflect the community counseling model in many ways. First, they help students of all ages develop the types of life skills they will need to resolve interpersonal conflicts peacefully and respectfully in the future. Second, they use educational approaches to foster youngsters' social and moral development. Third, these programs are fundamentally preventive because they help children and youth learn nonviolent ways to deal with interpersonal conflicts that may occur later in their lives.

Johnson and Johnson (1995) describe a framework for implementing a school-based program designed to reduce violence through conflict-resolution training. Their model consists of three main components:

1. Helping teachers and students learn ways to create a cooperative context within their classrooms and schools
2. Teaching students negotiation and mediation skills
3. Implementing peer mediation programs in the schools

D'Andrea and Daniels (1996) emphasize the importance of being responsive to students' unique developmental and cultural needs when one plans violence-prevention programs in the schools. They also note that because conflict-resolution competencies relate closely to several other important life skills, one should address them simultaneously. In this regard, they encourage counselors to help students develop stress- and anger-management skills, acquire effective problem-solving and decision-making skills, learn cooperative work strategies, and develop the skills necessary to communicate in an assertive rather than an aggressive manner (D'Andrea & Daniels, 1996).

SUMMARY

Central components of community counseling include identifying the needs of the community or school in which one works and implementing prevention programs capable of reaching large numbers of people who have not yet manifested dysfunctional behaviors. Preventive education programs can particularly help people of all ages to acquire the types of life skills and competencies that will buffer the negative effects of stress and help maintain their physical and mental health.

Such programs work best when they are tailored to the unique personal and cultural needs of people in the community or school where counselors work. One can, however, identify several general preventive approaches that hold a great deal of promise for people in at-risk groups. Some of the most useful intervention strategies for a broad range of client populations include stress-management training, health and wellness promotion, life-skills training, and school-based mental health programs.

SUPPLEMENTAL ACTIVITIES

1. Community counselors must frequently develop and implement workshops to foster physical health and psychological wellness. They can do this most effectively if they plan them step by step. Think of a particular topic and audience you would like to address and develop a workshop plan by following these steps:
    a. Consider the specific audience you will be addressing. Direct particular attention to the developmental and cultural characteristics and needs of your audience.
    b. State the specific objectives of the workshop. For instance, you should ask yourself how the participants will be affected by participating in the workshop. What new skills, attitudes, or knowledge are you trying to instill?
    c. Select the kinds of activities you think are most likely to meet your objectives. Consider lectures, discussion groups, case conferences, creative use of computers and other types of media, role playing, simulations, or other preventive education approaches that might meet the developmental and cultural needs of your participants. Which activities would increase the participants' active involvement and ensure their interest in the workshop?
    d. In planning the workshop, be sure to consider the resources likely to be available to you, including your own skills.
    e. Based on your analysis so far, develop a detailed design for the workshop.
    f. Design an evaluation component that will help you determine whether or not the workshop's objectives have been met.

2. At the end of Chapter 1, you were encouraged to develop an outline of a community counseling program to meet the needs of a particular population. Now, consider in detail the kinds of community education or school-based programs that might be appropriate for this target group. What preventive education activities might help your clients/students acquire the types of competencies necessary for them to realize a greater sense of psychological wellness?

REFERENCES

Albee, G. W., Bond, L. A., & Monsey, T. V. C. (Eds.). (1992). *Improving children's lives: Global perspectives on prevention*. Newbury Park, CA: Sage.

Albee, G. W., & Ryan-Finn, K. D. (1993). An overview of primary prevention. *Journal of Counseling and Development, 72*, 115–123.

Arbona, C. (1990). Career counseling research and Hispanics: A review of the literature. *The Counseling Psychologist, 18*(2), 300–323.

Arredondo, P., Toporek, R., Brown, S. P., Jones, J., Locke, D. C., Sanchez, J., & Stadler, H. (1996). Operationalization of the multicultural counseling competencies. *Journal of Multicultural Counseling and Development, 24*(1), 42–78.

Astin, H. S. (1989, November). *Women and power: Collective and empowering leadership*. Paper presented at the annual meeting of the American Education Research Association, San Diego, CA.

Atkinson, D. R., Morten, G., & Sue, D. W. (Eds.). (1993). *Counseling American minorities* (4th ed.). Dubuque, IA: Brown.

Baker, S. (1996). *School counseling for the twenty-first century* (2nd ed.). New York: Merrill-Macmillan.

Bandura, A. (1982). Self-efficacy mechanism in human agency. *American Psychologist, 37*(2), 122–147.

Barber, T. X. (1982). Foreword. In R. G. Straus, *Strategic self-hypnosis* (p. v). Englewood Cliffs, NJ: Prentice-Hall.

Bassuk, E. (1993). Social and economic hardships of homeless and other poor women. *American Journal of Orthopsychiatry, 63*(3), 340–357.

Beck, A. T., & Weishaar, M. E. (1995). Cognitive therapy. In R. J. Corsini & D. Wedding (Eds.), *Current psychotherapies* (5th ed., pp. 229–261). Itasca, IL: Peacock.

Berger, K. S. (1994). *The developing person through the lifespan*. New York: Worth.

Bloom, B. L. (1984). *Community mental health* (2nd ed.). Pacific Grove, CA: Brooks/Cole.

Boland, M. L. (1992). "Mainstream" hatred. *The Police Chief, 59*, 30–32.

Bond, L. A., & Compas, B. E. (Eds.). (1989). *Primary prevention and promotion in the schools*. Newbury Park, CA: Sage.

Bowman, J. (1992, March). *Empowering black males through positive self-esteem*. Paper presented at the annual convention of the American Association for Counseling and Development, Baltimore.

Braucht, S., & Weime, B. (1990). Establishing a rural school counseling agenda: A multiagency needs assessment model. *The School Counselor, 37*, 179–183.

Browne, A. (1993). Family violence and homelessness: The relevance of trauma histories in the lives of homeless women. *American Journal of Orthopsychiatry, 63*(3), 370–384.

Carter, R. T. (1991). Cultural values: A review of empirical research and implications for counseling. *Journal of Counseling and Development, 70*(1), 164–173.

Carter, D. J., & Wilson, R. (1993). *Minorities in higher education*. Washington, DC: American Council of Education, Office of Minorities in Higher Education.

Coddington, R. R. (1972). The significance of life events as etiologic factors in the disease of children—II: A study of a normal population. *Journal of Psychosomatic Research, 16,* 205–213.

Cohen, C. I., & Adler, A. (1986). Assessing the role of social network interventions with inner-city populations. *American Journal of Orthopsychiatry, 56*(2 , 278–288.

Commission of Prevention of Mental/Emotional Disorders. (1987). National Health Association report. *Journal of Primary Prevention, 7*(4), 175–241.

Conyne, R. (1987). *Primary preventive counseling: Empowering people and systems.* Muncie, IN: Accelereated Press.

Conyne, R. (1991). Gains in primary prevention: Implications for the counseling profession. *Journal of Counseling and Development, 69,* 277–279.

Crabtree, B. F., Yanoshik, M. K., Miller, W. M., & O'Conner, P. J. (1993). *Successful focus groups: Advancing the state of the art.* Newbury Park, CA: Sage.

Craig, G. J. (1992). *Human development* (6th ed.). Englewood Cliffs, NJ: Prentice-Hall.

D'Andrea, M. (1994). The family development project: A comprehensive mental health counseling program for pregnant adolescents. *Journal of Mental Counseling, 16*(2), 184–195.

D'Andrea, M. (1995, April). *Respectful counseling: An integrative framework for diversity counseling.* Paper presented at the annual meeting of the American Counseling Association, Denver, CO.

D'Andrea, M. (1996). White racism. In P. B. Pedersen & D. C. Locke (Eds.), *Cultural and diversity issues in counseling* (pp. 55–58). Greensboro, NC: ERIC/ CASS Publications.

D'Andrea, M., & Daniels, J. (1994). The different faces of racism in higher education. *Thought and Action, 10*(1), 73–89.

D'Andrea, M., & Daniels, J. (1995). Helping students learn to get along: Assessing the effectiveness of a multicultural developmental guidance project. *Elementary School Guidance and Counseling Journal, 30*(2), 143–154.

D'Andrea, M., & Daniels, J. (1996). Promoting peace in our schools: Developmental, preventive, and multicultural considerations. *School Counselor, 44*(1) 55–64.

Daniels, J. (1995). Building respectful connections among culturally-diverse students in Hawai'i. *Educational Perspectives, 29*(2), 23–28.

Donaghy, K. B. (1995). Beyond survival: Applying wellness interventions in battered women's shelters. *Journal of Mental Health Counseling, 17*(1), 3–17.

Ellis, A. (1993). *Fundamentals of rational-emotive therapy.* Newbury Park, CA: Sage.

Federal Bureau of Investigation. (1994). *Uniform crime reports.* Washington, DC: Department of Justice.

Ferrara, M. L. (1992). *Group counseling with juvenile delinquents.* Newbury Park, CA: Sage.

Fertman, C. I., & Long, J. A. (1990). All students are leaders. *School Counselor, 37,* 391–396.

Forman, S. G. (1993). *Coping skills interventions for children and adolescents.* San Francisco: Jossey-Bass.

Gazda, G. M. (1984). Multiple impact training: A life skills approach. In D. Larson (Ed.), *Teaching psychological skills: Models for giving psychology away* (pp. 87–103). Pacific Grove, CA: Brooks/Cole.

Gazda, G. M., Childers, W. C., & Brooks, D. K. (1987). *Foundations of counseling and human services*. New York: McGraw-Hill.

Gebhardt, D. L., & Crump, C. E. (1990). Employee fitness and wellness programs in the workplace. *American Psychologist, 45*(2), 262–272.

Gerler, E. R. (Ed.). (1995). Applications of computer technology [Special issue]. *Elementary School Guidance and Counseling Journal, 30*(1).

Goldfried, M. R., & Goldfried, A. P. (1980). Cognitive change methods. In F. H. Kanfer & A. P. Goldstein (Eds.), *Helping people change* (2nd ed., pp. 97–130). New York: Pergamon Press.

Goldstein, A. P. (1992). *The prepare curriculum: Teaching prosocial competencies* (5th ed.). Champaign, IL: Research Press.

Harvey, W. B. (1991). Faculty responsibility and racial tolerance. *Thought and Action, 7*(2), 115–136.

Herr, E. L., & Niles, S. G. (1994). Multicultural career guidance in schools. In P. Pedersen & J. C. Carey (Eds.), *Multicultural counseling in schools* (pp. 177–194). Boston: Allyn and Bacon.

Holmes, T., & Rahe, R. (1967). The social readjustment rating scale. *Journal of Psychosomatic Research, 11*, 213–218.

Huang, L. N. (1989). Southeast Asian refugee children and adolescents. In J. T. Gibbs & L. N. Huang (Eds.), *Children of color: Psychological interventions with minority children* (pp. 278–321). San Francisco: Jossey-Bass.

Human, J., & Wasem, C. (1991). Rural mental health in American. *American Psychologist, 46*(3). 232–239.

Ivancevich, J. M., & Matteson, M. T. (1980). *Stress and work: A managerial perspective*. Glenview, IL: Scott, Foresman.

Ivey, A. E. (1993). *Developmental strategies for helpers: Individual, family, and network interventions*. North Amherst, MA: Microtraining Associates.

Jaffe, D. T., & Scott, C. D. (1984). *Self-renewal: A workbook for achieving high performance and health in a high-stress environment*. New York: Simon & Schuster.

Johnson, D. W., & Johnson, R. T. (1995). *Reducing school violence through conflict resolution*. Alexandria, VA: Association for Supervisors and Curriculum Development.

Jordan, J. V., Kaplan, A. G., Miller, J. B., Stiver, I. P., & Surrey, J. L. (Eds.). (1991). *Women's growth in connection: Writings from the Stone Center*. New York: Guilford Press.

Kieffer, C. H. (1984). Citizen empowerment: A developmental perspective. *Prevention in Human Services, 3*(2/3), 9–30.

Kilpatrick, D. G., Edmunds, C. S., & Seymore, A. K. (1992). *Rape in America: A report to the nation*. Arlington, VA: National Victims Center and Medical University of South Carolina.

Kirschenbaum, H. (1975). Recent research in values education. In J. R. Meyer, B. Burnham, & J. Chotvat (Eds.), *Values education: Theory, practice, problems prospects* (pp. 207–241). Waterloo, Ontario: Wilfrid Laurier University Press.

Knitzer, J., & Aber, J. L. (1995). Young children in poverty: Facing the facts. *American Journal of Orthopsychiatry, 65*(2), 174–176.

Kobasa, S. C. (1979). Stressful life events, personality, and health: An inquiry into hardiness. *Journal of Personality and Social Psychology, 36*, 1–11.

Koeska, G. F., & Koeske, R. D. (1990). The buffering effect of social support on parental stress. *American Journal of Orthopsychiatry, 60*(3), 440–451.

Kohlberg, L., & Turiel, E. (1971). Moral development and moral education. In G. S. Lesser (Ed.), *Psychology and educational practice* (pp. 18–45). Chicago: Scott, Foresman.

Kozol, J. (1991). *Savage inequalities: Children in America's schools.* New York: Crown.

Landis, S., Trevor, J., Futch, J., & Plaut, T. (1995). *Building a healthier tomorrow: A manual for coalition building.* Asheville, NC: Mountain Area Health Education Center.

Larson, J. (1994). Violence prevention in the schools: A review of selected programs and procedures. *School Psychology Review, 23*, 151–164.

Lazarus, R. S., & Folkman, S. (1984). *Stress, appraisal, and coping.* New York: Springer.

Lee, C. C. (Ed.). (1995). *Counseling for diversity: A guide for counselors and related professionals.* Boston: Allyn and Bacon.

Lewis, J. A., Sperry, L., & Carlson, J. (1993). *Health counseling.* Pacific Grove, CA: Brooks/Cole.

Lichtenberg, J. W., Johnson, D. D., & Arachtingi, B. M. (1992). Physical illness and subscription to Ellis' irrational beliefs. *Journal of Counseling and Development, 71*(2), 157–163.

Lickona, T. (1991). *Educating for character: How our schools can teach respect and responsibility.* New York: Bantam.

Locke, D. C. (1992). *Increasing multicultural understanding: A comprehensive model.* Newbury Park, CA: Sage.

Locke, D. C., Daniels, J., & D'Andrea, M. (1995, April). *Dealing with racism: Implications for counseling.* Paper presented at the annual meeting of the American Counseling Association, Denver, CO.

Locke, D. C., & Faubert, M. (1993). Getting on the right track: A program for African American high school students. *School Counselor, 41*, 129–133.

Martin, J. (1991). The mental health professional and social action. *American Journal of Orthopsychiatry, 61*(4), 484–488.

Marx, M. B., Garrity, T. F., & Bowers, F. R. (1975). The influence of recent life experiences on the health of college freshmen. *Journal of Psychosomatic Research, 19*, 87–98.

Maslow, A. (1968). *Toward a psychology of being* (2nd ed.). New York: Van Nostrand.

Maslow, A. (1970). *Motivation and personality* (2nd ed.). New York: Harper & Row.

McWhirter, E. H. (1992). *A test of a model of the career commitment and aspirations of Mexican American high school girls.* Unpublished doctoral dissertation, Arizona State University, Tempe.

McWhirter, E. H. (1994). *Counseling for empowerment.* Alexandria, VA: American Counseling Association.

Mosher, R. L., & Sprinthall, N. A. (1971). Deliberate psychological education. *Counseling Psychologist*, 2(4), 3–82.

Muro, J. J., & Kottman, T. (1995). *Guidance and counseling in the elementary schools: A practical approach.* Dubuque, IA: Brown & Benchmark.

Myrick, R. (1987). *Developmental school guidance and counseling: A practical approach.* Minneapolis, MN: Educational Media.

National Research Council. (1991, June). *Doctorate records file.*

Neimeyer, R. A. (1993). Constructivism and the cognitive psychotherapies: Some conceptual and strategic contrasts. *Journal of Cognitive Psychotherapy*, 7(3), 159–171.

Nutting, P. A. (1990). *Community-oriented primary care in the United States: A status report.* Albuquerque, NM: University of New Mexico Press.

Plaut, T., Landis, S., & Trevor, J. (1991). Combining sociology with epidemiology: Community-oriented primary care in a rural mountain county. *Clinical Sociology Review*, 7, 87–105.

Ponterotto, J. G., & Pedersen, P. B. (1993). *Preventing prejudice: A guide for counselors and educators.* Newbury Park, CA: Sage.

Powell, R., & Collier, M. J. (1990). Public speaking instruction and cultural bias. *American Behavioral Scientist*, 34(2), 240–250.

Pransky, J. (1991). *Prevention: The critical need.* Springfield, MO: Burrell Foundation and Paradigm Press.

Ridley, C. R. (1995). *Overcoming unintentional racism in counseling and therapy.* Newbury Park, CA: Sage.

Robinson, T. L., & Howard-Hamilton, M. (1994). An Afrocentric paradigm: Foundation for a healthy self-image and healthy interpersonal relationships. *Journal of Mental Health Counseling*, 16(3), 327–339.

Romano, J. L. (1992). Psychoeducational interventions for stress management and well-being. *Journal of Counseling and Development*, 71(2), 199–202.

Selman, R. L. (1980). *The growth of interpersonal understanding.* Orlando, FL: Academic Press.

Selye, H. (1976). *The stress of life.* New York: McGraw-Hill.

Slavin, L. A., Rainer, K. L., McCreary, M. L., & Gowda, K. K. (1991). Toward a multicultural model of stress process. *Journal of Counseling and Development*, 70(1), 156–163.

Spivack, G., & Levine, M. (1973). *Self-regulation in acting out and normal adolescents* (Report No. M-4531). Washington, DC: National Institute of Mental Health.

Spivack, G., & Shure, M. B. (1974). *Social adjustment of young children.* San Francisco: Jossey-Bass.

Steenbarger, B. N., & LeClair, S. (1995). Beyond remediation and development: Mental health counseling in context. *Journal of Mental Health Counseling*, 17(2), 173–187.

Strain, P. (Ed.). (1981). *The utilization of classroom peers as behavior change agents.* New York: Plenum.

Straus, R. G. (1982). *Strategic self-hypnosis.* Englewood Cliffs, NJ: Prentice-Hall.

Sue, D. W., Arredondo, P., & McDavis, R. J. (1992). Multicultural counseling competencies: A call to the profession. *Journal of Counseling and Development, 70*, 477–486.

Sue, D., & Sue, D. W. (1990). *Counseling the culturally different.* New York: Wiley.

Sue, D., & Sue, D. W. (1991). Counseling strategies for Chinese Americans. In C. C. Lee & B. L. Richardson (Eds.), *Multicultural issues in counseling: New approaches to diversity* (pp. 79–90). Alexandria, VA: American Association for Counseling and Development Press.

Veninga, R. L., & Spradley, J. P. (1981). *The work/stress connection: How to cope with job burnout.* Boston: Little, Brown.

Weissberg, R. P., & Allen, J. P. (1986). Promoting children's social skills and adaptive interpersonal behavior. In B. A. Edelstein & L. Michelson (Eds.), *Handbook of prevention* (pp. 153–175). New York: Plenum.

White, J. L., & Parham, T. A. (1990). *The psychology of blacks: An African-American perspective.* Englewood Cliffs, NJ: Prentice-Hall.

Winett, R. A. (1995). A framework for health promotion and disease prevention programs. *American Psychologist, 50*(5), 341–350.

Witmer, J. M., & Sweeney, T. J. (1992). A holistic model for wellness and prevention over the lifespan. *Journal of counseling and Development, 71*(2), 140–148.

Wolpe, J. (1990). *The practice of behavior therapy* (4th ed.). Elmsford, NY: Pergamon Press.

Zimpfer, D. G. (1992). Psychosocial treatment of life-threatening disease: A wellness model. *Journal of Counseling and Development. 71*(2), 203–209.

CHAPTER 3

OUTREACH TO VULNERABLE POPULATIONS

At the same time community counselors strive to prevent problems by strengthening the life competencies of the population they serve, they recognize that some people may need additional services. People under severe stress—whether from chronic stressors such as poverty or from an immediate crisis such as the breakup of a family—tend to develop physical or mental health problems more than the general population.

DEFINING VULNERABLE POPULATIONS

When individuals experience a similar kind of stressor for extended periods, they are collectively referred to as a *vulnerable population*. Counselors commonly work with such vulnerable populations as poor, homeless, and unemployed people; adults and children in families undergoing divorce; pregnant teenagers; survivors of violence; individuals with HIV or AIDS; and people victimized by ageism, racism, and sexism. Although these vulnerable populations differ greatly from each of the others, they all routinely experience high levels of environmental stress that outweigh their personal resources and coping abilities.

Many studies confirm the widely held belief that people subjected to severe stress over extended periods experience a higher risk of physical and mental health problems (Stokols, 1992; U.S. Department of Health and Human Services, 1990). This is true whether the origin of the stress is linked to an immediate crisis—such as an unexpected pregnancy during adolescence—or rooted in more subtle but no less destructive forms of chronic stress—such as regular subjection to racism or sexism.

An Equation for Psychological Health

One can use the following equation to conceptualize the delicate balance between people's resources and their life circumstances in the development of mental health problems:

$$\text{Psychological Health} = \frac{\text{Organic Factors} + \text{Stress} + \text{Powerlessness}}{\text{Coping Skills} + \text{Self-esteem} + \text{Social Support} + \text{Personal Power}}$$

This equation represents a modified version of one devised by George Albee and cited by the National Mental Health Association (NMHA) Commission on the Prevention of Mental-Emotional Disabilities (1986, p. 13). We have added two factors, powerlessness and personal power, to Albee's original equation.

THE PARTS DEFINED In the previous chapters, we have discussed many parts of this equation: stress, coping skills, social support, and self-esteem. However, we have not yet defined what is meant by organic factors, feelings of powerlessness, and personal power, nor have we examined how these variables usually impact one's mental health and psychological well-being.

Organic factors refer to those biological conditions that compromise a person's mental or physical functioning. Examples include individuals born with congenital defects or natural brain damage. A combination of these conditions and ineffective and inappropriate environmental responses to them produces stress that tends to affect adversely a person's overall psychological well-being and frequently nurtures a sense of personal hopelessness and powerlessness.

McWhirter (1994) describes *powerlessness* as a condition in which individuals cannot direct the course of their own lives because of societal conditions and/or power dynamics that place them in devalued positions in society. These power dynamics often hinder many individuals from acquiring the life skills needed to lead satisfying and productive lives. These dynamics also frequently undermine a person's belief in his or her own ability to develop the personal competencies needed to prevent negative situations.

Finally, as used in the equation, *personal power* refers to two important processes. First, it reflects the belief that one can control one's life in ways that lead to positive and health-promoting outcomes. Bandura (1989) refers to this aspect of personal power as "self-efficacy."

Second, personal power largely depends on the acquisition of a variety of life skills one can use to negotiate effectively developmental and environmental challenges.

Many environmental factors influence a person's ability to develop a broad range of life skills and use these skills productively in society. For example, it has been well established that the complex set of variables associated with living in poverty negatively impacts an individual's ability to realize her or his career/economic, educational, social, and psychological potential (Langston, 1995; Persell, 1993).

HELPING AT-RISK GROUPS   The community counseling model recognizes that the cultural, economic, political, psychological, and social arrangements that characterize life in the United States affect all its citizens. However, as numerous multicultural counseling experts have pointed out, the ones who have historically benefited most by the structure of Western society are white men (Banks & Banks, 1993; Sue & Sue, 1990).

Further, two particular groups—people of color and women—have been consistently devalued and marginalized as a result of the way U.S. economic, educational, political, and social institutions have been structured (Banks & Banks, 1993; Ivey, 1995). Such treatment often leads to an erosion in these groups' sense of personal power, an increased sense of powerlessness, and a heightening of their vulnerability to a host of physical and mental health problems (McWhirter, 1994).

Community counselors can help clients develop a greater sense of personal power in two fundamental ways. First, they can provide various types of direct counseling services intentionally designed to enhance their clients' self-efficacy and foster the development of a broad range of life competencies. This may include, but is not limited to, helping clients learn effective coping strategies, providing assertiveness training, promoting decision-making and problem-solving skills, helping individuals with college and/or career searches, developing programs that teach individuals conflict resolution skills, and providing other supportive outreach services for people experiencing major life stressors and transitions. Such stressors and transitions include marital disruptions, becoming a single parent, unemployment, and various forms of discrimination, prejudice, and unfair social policies and practices.

Second, counselors can also try to influence those systems (such as families, schools, workplaces, universities, churches, neighborhood agencies, and recreation centers) that directly impact their clients' lives. While Chapter 6 examines issues and strategies related to the counselor's role in creating systemic changes, this chapter focuses on the types of direct client services that mental health professionals can use to promote the personal power of individuals in vulnerable populations.

TABLE 3.1
OUTREACH STRATEGIES
AND THE COMMUNITY COUNSELING MODEL

	COMMUNITY SERVICES	CLIENT SERVICES
Direct		Outreach to vulnerable clients: High-risk situations Crises
Indirect		

Helping Clients Learn New Coping Strategies

Community counselors can help prevent or mitigate many problems by rec-ognizing potentially stressful situations and reaching out to people when they are most vulnerable. By *reaching out*, we mean that counselors will leave the office and work directly with clients in their homes, schools, churches, neighborhoods, and workplaces to help them learn new ways of coping with their life stressors. Table 3.1 shows how outreach programs and services to vulnerable populations fit into the community counseling framework.

As indicated in Table 3.1, outreach programs fall under the heading of direct client services. Such programs target individuals and groups that, at particular times, might be more vulnerable to stress than the general popu-lation and therefore need intensive programming.

Preventive outreach occurs when community counselors identify cer-tain situations as particularly stressful and intervene to help healthy indi-viduals develop the resources to cope with them. When prevention is not possible and chronic problems or crises occur, community counselors use outreach services to provide support and assistance.

Counselors can help clients significantly improve their own well-being by helping them learn better ways to cope with new or difficult situ-ations. Any situation that makes demands on an individual can cause stress or damage. However, whether or not a situation will cause stress depends on such factors as one's view of one's own ability to handle new demands, pre-vious success in dealing with similar situations, the degree to which one feels in control of events, one's perception of being overloaded or having conflicting needs, and the standards one sets for one's own performance (Lewis, Sperry, & Carlson, 1993).

Lazarus (1980) describes three types of situations people find stressful: (1) those that represent harm and loss, (2) those viewed as threats to one's own well-being, and (3) those perceived as potentially positive challenges in one's life, such as moving to another community, having a baby, or starting a new career.

> The distinction between harm, loss, threat, and challenge may be very important not only in affecting the coping process itself and the effectiveness with which coping skills are utilized in social transactions, but also in their divergent consequences for morale and somatic health. . . . A working hypothesis about the causal antecedents of threat and challenge is that the former is more likely to occur when a person assumes that his or her environment is hostile and dangerous and that he or she lacks the resources for mastering it, while a sense of challenge arises when the environmental demands are seen as difficult but not impossible to manage, and that drawing upon existing or acquirable skills offers a genuine prospect for mastery. (Lazarus, 1980, pp. 47–48)

Stensrud and Stensrud (1983) emphasize that one must keep these distinctions in mind when helping people in vulnerable populations learn better ways of "taking personal control of their lives, accepting stress as a challenge rather than a harm-loss-threat factor, and finding personal meaning within stressful situations" (p. 216). Fostering this sort of attitude helps clients gain a sense of hopefulness, even when facing difficult problems or transitions in their lives (Snyder, 1995).

In choosing methods to enhance their clients' positive coping abilities and decrease stress-related dysfunctions, counselors need to consider those factors that mediate the effects of potential crises. Once mental health practitioners become aware of the personal characteristics and situations that favor successful coping, they can intentionally design counseling strategies that foster similar conditions with their clients.

Lewis and Lewis (1986) have identified several factors that characterize people who successfully adapt to trying conditions:

I. *Successful persons tend to have strong social support systems.* The availability of supportive associates serves as a buffer against the effects of stressful situations. These relationships provide both personal validation and practical assistance. For instance, when faced with troublesome situations, successful copers reportedly turned to family members, friends, or associates for information, advice, and concrete resources as well as emotional sustenance.

II. *Successful copers tend to have a sense of control over the environment.* Whether we term this factor "self efficacy" or "internal locus of control," we know that people who cope effectively do so because they believe their actions can have an effect on the world. Individuals differ in their general belief systems concerning their ability to exert power and control when needed. In addition, the sense of control in a specific situation can be affected by the appraisal of the stressor and the presence or absence of adequate personal and environmental resources.

III. *Successful copers have the information and tools needed for effective problem-solving.* Individuals' coping success depends, at least in part, on their ability to solve immediate problems and develop appropriate new behaviors. This factor involves both general life competencies and situation-specific knowledge.

IV. *Successful copers tend to be confident that they can adapt to new situations.* Realistic feelings of confidence come from the fact that adequate personal and financial resources are available and that the individual has coped successfully with similar transitions in the past. One aspect of confidence-building, then, is recognizing commonalities between the current situation and prior experiences. For example, while the victim of a job loss may never have been fired in the past, he or she has been successful in obtaining a position. Thus, the planning skills that were used to secure past employment positions may still be valid and useful in the current situation. (pp. 177–178 [italics added])

These factors are interrelated. People's support systems help them solve problems, increasing both their sense of control and their confidence. Confident people are more likely to have strong social support systems and to apply their problem-solving skills effectively.

Recognizing that social support systems help buffer the debilitating effects of environmental stressors, community counselors can strive to become "buffer builders" (Aubrey & Lewis, 1988, p. 298). They can do this by creating new opportunities for clients to develop the social resources they need to survive and grow during periods of heightened stress. For example, when counselors help clients form peer support groups, they simultaneously help build new social support systems, provide the context for skill development, and help people experience a greater sense of control over their lives. In this way, counselors can help their clients create and maintain buffers against present and future stressors (Aubrey & Lewis, 1988, p. 298).

Buffer-building efforts can assist people dealing with expected transitions, unexpected crises, or ongoing stressors. However, the key to providing this sort of outreach service is the ability to recognize those stressors and situations likely to lead to major personal crises. For instance, research has shown that certain life events place heavy demands on individuals. In their now classic study, Holmes and Rahe (1967) identify and rank many particularly stressful life events:[1]

---

[1] Reprinted with permission from "The Social Readjustment Rating Scale," by T. Holmes and R. Rahe, 1967, *Journal of Psychosomatic Research, 11.* Copyright 1967 Pergamon Press. Reprinted with permission of Elsevier Science Inc.

Death of spouse
Divorce
Marital separation
Jail term
Death of close family member
Personal injury or illness
Marriage
Fired at work
Marital reconciliation
Retirement
Change in health of family member
Pregnancy
Sex difficulties
Gain of new family member
Change in financial state
Death of close friend
Change to different line of work
Change in the number of arguments with spouse
Foreclosure of mortgage or loan
Change in responsibilities at work
Son or daughter leaving home
Trouble with in-laws
Outstanding personal achievement
[Spouse] beginning or stopping work
Beginning or ending school
Revision of personal habits
Trouble with boss
Change in hours or work conditions
Change in residence
Change in schools
Change in recreation
Change in social activities
Change in sleeping habits
Change in number of family get-togethers
Change in eating habits
Planning for a vacation
Minor violations of the law

Many of the highest-ranked life events can cause other stressors to emerge. For instance, the death of or separation from a spouse, a jail term, personal injury, retirement, or the addition of a new family member may also bring about new financial demands that can themselves trigger an unexpected personal crisis.

MODEL OUTREACH PROGRAMS

Successful community counseling programs build on what is known about high-risk situations and the resources that enable people to cope with them. Ideally, outreach programs for vulnerable clients should adhere to the following guidelines:

1. Use all available sources of client support, including family members, extended family members, peers, co-workers, church affiliates, counselors, and others who can serve as role models for successful coping.
2. Provide opportunities for clients to help themselves and one another.
3. Inform clients about the nature of the new roles or situations they face.
4. Help clients develop the coping skills they will need to manage their specific situations effectively.
5. Use methods that enhance clients' sense of control over their situations and their lives.
6. Implement services that reflect an accurate understanding of and demonstrate a genuine respect for the cultural integrity and needs of clients. Such actions help clients gain confidence and a greater sense of control as they learn to cope with life's challenges more effectively.

Many programs that serve diverse populations have successfully helped clients face high-risk situations. These programs commonly use various types of outreach services to help empower people in vulnerable populations.

The following sections discuss several programs designed to empower people in specific at-risk groups. The diverse populations served by these programs include adults and children dealing with marital disruptions, teenagers making the transition to parenthood, at-risk high-school students, and battered women.

However, before moving to a discussion of these programs, please consider again the equation presented earlier in this chapter. By keeping this equation in mind, you will note that all those involved in the following programs needed to strengthen their "denominator values" (coping skills, self-esteem, social support, and personal power) to withstand the negative forces in the numerator. Thus, what the following programs have in common, and part of the reason for their success, is that they combine timely intervention with a clear focus on the denominator values.

Here, then, are several models of outreach interventions used to address the needs of vulnerable populations. Keep in mind, however, that community counselors must adapt such programs to meet the special needs and characteristics of their own clients.

Helping People Cope with Marital Disruption

Marital separation and divorce are consistently identified as among the most stressful events of an adult's life (Sprenkle, 1990). It is no wonder that marital disruptions put people at risk for mental and physical health problems. When a marriage breaks up, family members must cope with radical life changes while their social support systems are severely disrupted. On reviewing several epidemiological and clinical studies, Bloom (1984) summarizes the types of problems commonly associated with marital separation and divorce:

> The findings of these studies converge on identifying a small
> but important number of problems faced by persons undergoing
> marital disruption. Such a list would include a generally weakened
> support system; the need to work through the variety of psychological
> reactions to the disruption; problems with child rearing,
> resocialization, finances, education and employment planning,
> housing, and homemaking; and protection of legal rights.
> (p. 272)

Newly separated people commonly report anger, depression, loneliness, financial problems, disequilibrium, and difficulty in resolving their emotional attachment to their spouses (Sprenkle, 1990). Such problems heighten the likelihood of various physical and mental health problems. As Cherlin's (1992) research indicates, separated and divorced people manifest more frequent incidences of psychopathology, physical illnesses, accident proneness, alcoholism, suicide, and homicide when compared with people still married.

PROGRAMS FOR ADULTS   Given the general agreement that marital disruption is a high-risk situation, counselors can intervene preventively by developing programs for people going through this transition. Ideally, such programs should focus on (1) "fostering on-going support mechanisms" and (2) "building practical, situationally relevant problem-solving skills" (Cowen, 1985, p. 36). Bloom, Hodges, and Caldwell (1982) have developed one such program. With this six-month preventive program, they focused on recently separated people living in Boulder, Colorado. Using mass media and mailings, targeted for appropriate referral sources, the program developers recruited 153 people, 101 of whom were assigned to the intervention program and 52 of whom composed the untreated control group. Participants in the separation and divorce program were offered two types of services: individual assistance from paraprofessional helpers and study groups that addressed issues of special concern to newly separated people.

Each participant was assigned to a paraprofessional counselor who was to provide emotional support, intervene in possible crises, and link the individual with other components of the program. Referred to as "program representatives," these paraprofessionals played an active outreach role—contacting the participants on a regular basis, developing opportunities for social interaction on both a group and an individual basis, making referrals to other parts of the program and to appropriate community agencies, and following up with their clients throughout their participation in the intervention program (Bloom et al., 1982).

As mentioned, the program participants were encouraged to take part in regularly scheduled study groups that focused on practical issues commonly faced by recently separated or divorced persons. These groups included the following:

- *Career planning and employment:* This study group helped participants find or change jobs, make long-range career plans, and develop marketable skills.
- *Legal and financial issues:* Led by an attorney, this group explored ways to establish credit, loan eligibility, child custody and visitation, child support, and the divorce litigation process, among other issues.
- *Child-rearing and single-parenting:* In this group, participants could discuss their children's reactions, visitation issues, behavior problems, and ways to help their children adjust to the separation or divorce.
- *Housing and homemaking:* This group led by a home economist stressed such issues as finding a new place to live, making home repairs, managing money, purchasing and preparing food, and managing time.
- *Socialization and personal self-esteem:* This group helped participants deal with their loneliness, damaged self-concepts, and feelings of social and personal inadequacy.

A formal evaluation of this program indicated that those who participated in the intervention group reported significantly fewer physical and mental health problems than the control group six months after their separation or divorce. Members of the intervention group also demonstrated a significant decrease in general psychological problems across time, along with a reduction in psychological distress, maladjustment, and anxiety (Bloom et al., 1982).

A separate study was also conducted to determine the long-term impact of the program two and a half years after the participants completed their involvement in the project. The results of this investigation indicated that "the early gains were either maintained or increased over time. These findings suggested that the program achieved its primary prevention objective, i.e., to forestall the psychological fallout that often follows marital dissolution" (Cowen, 1985, p. 36).

PROGRAMS FOR CHILDREN   Researchers have identified a number of cognitive, affective, behavioral, and psychological problems commonly manifested among children whose parents have divorced (Amato, 1993; Behrman & Quinn, 1994; Carbone, 1994). Recognizing the special needs that children may have during the transition from an intact to a separated family has led counselors to develop several preventive outreach projects.

One such intervention is the Divorce Adjustment Project, a "structured two-part primary prevention program intended to enhance prosocial skills and to prevent acting out, the development of a poor self-concept, and academic failure among children of divorced families" (Stolberg & Garrison, 1985, p. 113). Designed for psychologically healthy children who had never before used mental health services, the program offered both school-based Children's Support Groups (CSG) and community-based Single Parents' Support Groups (SPSG).

The CSGs taught cognitive-behavioral skills to and provided emotional support for 7- to 13-year-olds, to help them adjust to their parents' divorces. In this highly structured, 12-session program, the children discussed issues directly related to divorce and received training in skills such as problem-solving, controlling anger, communication, and relaxation.

The assumption underlying the complementary SPSGs was that the children's ability to adjust could be enhanced indirectly by improving the parenting skills and postdivorce adjustment of their primary caregivers. This support and skill-building program—also 12 weeks long—assisted divorced mothers who had custody of their children to develop new skills and attitudes that would help them meet the challenges of being single persons and parents. Personal development topics incorporated into these study groups included "The Social Me," "The Working Me," "The Sexual Me," and "Controlling My Feelings." Parenting topics included "Communicating with My Child," "Disciplining My Child," and "Communicating with My Former Spouse About Child-Rearing Matters" (Stolberg & Garrison, 1985).

This well-researched project evaluated outcomes among four different groups of children: (1) children who participated in the CSG alone, (2) children who participated in the CSG and whose parents took part in the SPSG, (3) children whose only treatment was their parents' participation in the SPSG, and (4) a control group of children receiving no treatment. The researchers found that the self-concepts and social skills of the children who participated in the CSG alone (group 1) improved substantially.

Further, the children in group 3 appeared more psychologically adjusted in follow-up studies than the children in the other groups. Thus, the combination of the two interventions did not necessarily bring about the strong improvements expected.

A modified version of the Children's Support Group was implemented in Pedro-Carroll and Cowen's (1985) Children of Divorce Intervention Program. While helping youngsters develop new skills that would increase their ability to cope with their parents' divorces, this intervention also included activities designed to enhance the children's emotional adjustment and development. These activities included group discussions and role playing, which encouraged the children to explore their emotional responses to their parents' divorces.

In the first three sessions, the children concentrated on getting to know one another, sharing common experiences, and discussing divorce-related anxieties and other feelings. Sessions 4 through 6 focused on problem solving and cognitive-skill building. These group sessions specifically involved teaching the youngsters various methods for resolving interpersonal problems and dealing with negative feelings related to their parents' divorce.

During these sessions, counselors directed particular attention toward helping the children understand that they were not responsible for their parents' divorce. The counselors also focused on increasing the youngsters' understanding of the types of problems that were beyond their control and thus not solvable (e.g., parental reconciliation) versus those that lay within their control (e.g., appropriately communicating their feelings to others). Once the children understood the importance of disengaging from their parents' conflicts, they began to work more diligently on expressing and controlling their anger. In the last session, the children had a chance to evaluate their group experience and discuss their feelings about its ending.

The program evaluation indicated that the participants made significantly greater gains in adjustment than did youngsters in a comparable control group. Pedro-Carroll and Cowen (1985) have attributed these gains, in part, to the supportive group context that allowed the children to break through their sense of isolation and talk about their feelings about their parents' divorce. The researchers also consider the skill-building aspects of the program to be equally important in promoting these positive outcomes. As they point out,

> However important a supportive environment is in helping children
> to identify, express, and deal with salient feelings about their parents'
> divorce, it may not by itself be enough. . . . Acquiring specific

competencies for dealing with the concrete challenges that parental divorce poses is a co-equal need. Interpersonal problem-solving strategies, including the communication and anger control skills that the program offered, stressed a differentiation between problems that could and could not be solved and, for the latter, stressed ways of disengaging from their parents' disagreements. Thus, the intervention's positive effects appear to reflect a combination of its support and skill building components. (p. 609)

PROGRAMS FOR STEPFAMILIES   Effective coping skills are also needed to deal with the new stressors brought about when one or both partners remarry. Stepfamilies—that is, families formed through remarriage—represent a promising, though sparsely researched, area of intervention.

Because remarriage families start with children and yet have had no time to build a history, the family must deal with the tasks required of more mature families while possessing the skills of a family just starting out. Because they lack a common set of experiences, remarriage families typically hold limited or unrealistic expectations that paralyze them into inaction or galvanize them into a reaction against people or events they little understand. (Hayes & Hayes, 1988, pp. 473–474)

Such blended families need to clarify and stabilize members' roles and relationships, replace myths with realistic expectations, develop appropriate limits for children, and acknowledge the impact of children's allegiances to noncustodial parents. Hayes and Hayes (1988) suggest that counselors can help blended families accomplish these tasks in the following ways:

- Encouraging family members to identify and relinquish myths they may hold about the remarriage family
- Helping blended family members understand their new family system, its differences from their past family, and involvement of nonfamily members in the new system
- Teaching members more effective communication skills
- Helping blended family members, especially children, to mourn the loss of previous relationships and encouraging the development of new relationships
- Providing a forum in which blended family members can work out their relationship differences with new family members and explore their feelings about the absent parent
- Offering structured programs of parent training and lists of readings that family members can use as self-instructional devices

- Informing members of the latest research findings and clinical evidence that may be helpful in understanding the blended family reorganization process
- Identifying the tasks of parenting and the relationships that are necessary to enact those roles
- Running groups for remarriage parents in the community or for stepchildren in the schools (pp. 474–475)

The comprehensiveness of such an approach to working with blended families makes it an appropriate model for preventive outreach.

The Family Development Project: Helping Pregnant Adolescents

Each year, one million adolescent girls get pregnant in the United States (U.S. Bureau of the Census, 1994). Researchers have identified a variety of negative outcomes that can follow pregnancy during the high-school years. These include forgoing one's education by dropping out of school prematurely, becoming dependent on government support at a young age, and attempting to deal with one's own personal and social development while simultaneously trying to meet an infant's 24-hour needs (Hanson, 1992).

The community counseling model's emphasis on outreach and preventive services particularly suits this vulnerable population because it stresses positive prevention, for example, assisting young parents in developing new coping skills. Providing such services implies going beyond a crisis-oriented and restorative intervention orientation and, essentially, focuses on strengthening and adding to the client's set of skills and competencies.

Thus, rather than viewing a teenage pregnancy as a personal deficit or a psychological problem, community counselors interpret this phenomenon as a unique developmental crisis that can result in either negative or positive outcomes. The following discussion of the Family Development Project (FDP) demonstrates how the community counseling framework was used to promote the well-being of a group of pregnant African-American adolescents residing in an economically impoverished urban area.

Sponsored by the Meharry Community Mental Health Center in Nashville, Tennessee, the FDP was entirely funded by private donations. Using the community counseling model as their guide, program developers built on several theoretical premises:

1. Adolescents' interactions with their environment can have either negative or positive effects on their mental health and personal development.
2. A multifaceted approach is more efficient than a single service approach.

3. Outreach, prevention, and educational services are more appropriate to use in promoting the personal development of teenage mothers than remedial services.

4. When providing counseling services to vulnerable populations, counselors need to be sensitive and responsive to the unique cultural, ethnic, and racial characteristics of the persons in the targeted group. (D'Andrea, 1994, p. 186)

FDP'S DIRECT COMMUNITY SERVICES   The first step in planning the FDP program involved soliciting input and support from several key persons in the schools and community within the targeted service area. With this in mind, the program's counseling coordinator set up several "community meetings" with key persons in the targeted areas to see if they perceived a need for a primary prevention program for pregnant youth in their schools and community. The persons who attended these meetings included an obstetrical-gynecological physician, a clinical psychologist, a licensed nurse-midwife, several social workers, three school counselors, four high-school teachers, and the FDP counseling coordinator (D'Andrea, 1994).

During these community meetings, participants not only indicated the vital need for such a program but also expressed a willingness to plan the FDP. After several meetings, which primarily focused on community assessment and program-planning issues, all agreed that a preventive counseling program would best meet the needs of the pregnant adolescents in the community.

As a prevention program, the FDP emphasized the need to support teenagers who, while in the midst of a major life crisis, had not yet manifested any outstanding psychological problems. The program developers also hoped that by providing this at-risk group of youth with opportunities to develop basic parenting skills, the new parents could learn to care for their infants in ways that would enhance their children's overall health and avert potential problems.

While those who attended the program-planning meetings unanimously agreed that the FDP should focus primarily on prevention, they also indicated that many pregnant teenagers experience personal crises during their pregnancy and shortly after the birth of their babies. Thus, the need to incorporate remedial counseling services within the FDP program was clearly acknowledged and supported.

Based on these and other suggestions, a comprehensive program plan developed. This plan included the following components: preventive education, outreach-consultation, individual counseling, and program research and evaluation.

Given their limited financial resources, the program planners agreed that they must immediately recruit and train paraprofessionals in the community. To address this need, the FDP coordinator set up meetings with several officials at a local university. This outreach effort aimed at identifying undergraduate students willing to help adolescents in the program. With the university's permission, the FDP counselors visited undergraduate classes at Tennessee State University to solicit support. As a result, 15 African-American women from the departments of education, psychology, and social work volunteered.

These students agreed to take part in 32 hours of training (8 hours per week for 4 weeks) during which they covered issues related to early childhood and adolescent development. These training sessions also introduced the volunteers to the community counseling framework and helped them develop basic individual counseling and interviewing skills.

Having successfully completed this training, the university students began direct work with the adolescents who were referred to the FDP. The program coordinator provided clinical supervision to these volunteers throughout their involvement in the project (D'Andrea, 1994).

FDP'S DIRECT CLIENT SERVICES   The adolescents who participated in the FDP were referred from the Department of Obstetrics and Gynecology at Meharry Medical College and the Nashville Metropolitan School System's Office of Guidance and Counseling. To qualify as a participant in the project, one had to be at or below the federal guidelines for poverty, between 12 and 18 years old, pregnant for the first time, a resident of one of the city's public subsidized housing communities, and currently enrolled in high school.

On entering the program, the teenagers were assigned to one of the paraprofessionals, who were directly responsible for their case management. The paraprofessionals' duties included setting up individual interviews with the adolescents to assess their personal concerns and needs (e.g., medical, food, housing, financial), evaluate their educational needs and develop a plan to help them avoid dropping out of school, and identify community resources.

By consulting with the other FDP counselors and the program coordinator about the information gathered from those interviews, the paraprofessionals developed an individualized action plan for each participant. These plans included making referrals to local human service agencies such as medicaid and the Metropolitan Public Housing Office, consulting with the schools' counselors and teachers about their clients' academic progress, and setting up individual counseling sessions to give the adolescents additional opportunities to explore other personal concerns, interests, and goals in a supportive and confidential environment (D'Andrea, 1994).

All the adolescents in the FDP project were also encouraged to participate in a series of parenting classes. The classes met every other Thursday evening and lasted 2 hours. Transportation was provided. Because the classes overlapped with most of the participants' dinner times, a nutritious meal was also provided.

These classes helped the adolescents understand healthy prenatal care and the birth process, as well as examine ways they could promote their infants' overall health and well-being. Particular attention was given to the types of things the teenagers themselves could do to help cope with the stress of raising a child. Further, these parenting classes offered opportunities for the teenagers to learn about helpful community resources. Finally, the classes provided a source of mutual support; the participants became increasingly comfortable discussing common interests, concerns, frustrations, personal fears, goals, and values with others experiencing similar challenges. As a result, the class meetings evolved into what was later referred to as an "empowerment group," where new friendships were established and maintained months after the adolescents gave birth.

FDP'S INDIRECT CLIENT SERVICES   The FDP used a systems approach to promote the participants' development. For instance, by participating in the FDP parenting classes, the adolescents became an integral part of a new human system (the class) that provided opportunities to increase their sense of self-esteem and personal power. The direct client services just mentioned were designed to promote these positive developmental outcomes.

In addition to these services, the FDP staff sought to strengthen the natural social support networks to which the pregnant teenagers already belonged. To accomplish this objective, the counselors and paraprofessionals used several outreach-consultation services, including visiting the adolescents' homes and consulting with school personnel. These efforts aimed at fostering environments in which the teenagers would find greater support and respect.

The FDP staff made home visits throughout the duration of the project, with the paraprofessionals making at least one home visit per month. However, they often made two and even three visits a month as the adolescents' parents found how resourceful the paraprofessionals were in supporting their daughters' needs as well as serving as a sounding board for many of the parents' own frustrations and concerns. For instance, most parents wanted their daughters to graduate from high school. To address this concern, the FDP staff regularly consulted with the adolescents' teachers and school counselors regarding their academic performance. They often found that the teenagers needed tutorial help to keep up with their teachers' expectations and academic assignments.

This need became particularly apparent when the adolescents' schooling was temporarily interrupted by their infants' birth. As such, the FDP counselors and paraprofessionals worked especially hard to maintain the link between the new mothers and their schools by continuing to make regular home visits and having ongoing contact with teachers. These efforts aimed at preventing the adolescents from dropping out of school for an extended period.

FDP'S INDIRECT COMMUNITY SERVICES   Program evaluation formed another important component of the FDP. The results of these evaluative efforts indicate that the FDP participants manifested higher positive self-concept scores and a significant increase in the level of social support they experienced during their pregnancies, compared with a control group of teenage parents who did not take part in the program (D'Andrea, 1994).

Beyond these formal evaluation efforts, the counselors and paraprofessionals obtained additional data from numerous other sources, including comments made by the participants and their parents, teachers, and school counselors. Reactions to the program consistently reflected strong support for it. The adolescents themselves stated that they had learned a great deal about their infants' needs and reported acquiring many useful parenting skills. They had also learned many new ways to cope with the multiple stressors associated with the transition to parenthood. The adolescents' parents consistently expressed appreciation for the types of outreach services that the program offered and the genuine sense of concern extended by the staff.

The teachers and school counselors noted that the project provided a host of mental health services that, although clearly important for pregnant adolescents, simply lay beyond the purview of the schools' resources. These school officials also said that the project's success was largely due to the high level of commitment manifested by the FDP counselors and paraprofessionals, who had initiated and maintained numerous types of outreach services on behalf of the teenagers.

These program evaluation efforts were important for three reasons. First, they provided the program planners with data that allowed an assessment of the FDP's overall effectiveness. Second, these efforts generated valuable information about the program's strengths as well as weaknesses. Third, the evaluation results provided documentation of the FDP's success, which was used to lobby for additional funding from persons in the public and private sectors.

The results of these formal and informal evaluations demonstrate that the strategies employed by the FDP staff helped strengthen several variables listed in the denominator of the equation presented earlier in this chapter. As a result of participating in a program that offered a variety of individual, preventive, outreach, and consultative services, members of this vulnerable population reported developing new coping skills, increased self-esteem, greater social support, and a heightened sense of personal power.

Addressing the Mental Health Needs of Latinos/Latinas: The Inquilinos Boricuas en Acción (IBA)

The United States has a long legacy of racial divide, which continues in the various forms of individual, institutionalized, and cultural racism that are manifested in many communities and campuses across this country (D'Andrea & Daniels, 1994). Such racism sometimes results in physical violence. More often, however, people of color experience increased psychological stress from regular exposure to subtler types of discrimination and prejudice (Atkinson, Morten, & Sue, 1993; Locke, 1992; Sue & Sue, 1990).

In spite of this psychological vulnerability, the U.S. mental health-care system has generally failed to address effectively the unique mental health needs of people from diverse cultural, ethnic, and racial backgrounds (Atkinson et al., 1993). As a result, individuals with non-European backgrounds have had to choose between two relatively negative options when they need psychological services:

1. Choosing treatment that is not provided in a culturally sensitive or appropriate manner.
2. Refusing to work with mental health practitioners at all, even when in obvious need of such services (Sue & Sue, 1990).

Fortunately, over the past three decades, the number of organizations that serve the unique needs of diverse cultural, ethnic, and/or racial groups has increased. One such model program, Inquilinos Boricuas en Acción (IBA), was designed to support the needs of Latinos and Latinas residing in a major urban setting in the eastern part of the United States.

IBA is a private, nonprofit organization established in 1968 to empower a predominately Latino community called Villa Victoria, located in Boston's South End. IBA emerged when the Latino community came together in the mid-1960s to fight the city's proposal to displace most of the people residing in the Villa Victoria area.

The community rallied to lobby support for an alternative plan—to create subsidized housing units for low- to moderate-income Latino families who resided in the area. These efforts ultimately led to the building of 857 apartments, which currently house more than 3000 residents (Merced, 1994).

IBA has evolved and changed since its inception in 1986. Today, this community organization is dedicated to three goals:

1. Promoting the psychological, social, and economic well-being of the Villa Victoria residents
2. Advocating for Latinos and Latinas citywide
3. Perpetuating the rich Latino cultural and artistic heritage in the greater Boston area (IBA Factsheet, 1994)

This community organization uses a proactive, holistic approach that includes a wide range of outreach, educational, and counseling services to promote the psychological and cultural well-being of the residents in Villa Victoria. These services primarily aim at fostering the leadership skills of adolescents and adults living in the community, providing support for resident-driven community-change projects, and organizing other socio-cultural-awareness programs designed to enhance the empowerment of the families in the area. The following discussion briefly examines some of the services offered by the IBA staff and explains how these services fit into the community counseling model.

IBA'S DIRECT COMMUNITY SERVICES   IBA's mission is shaped by the belief that community members are the ideal agents for solving the critical psychological, social, and economic problems occurring in their neighborhoods. This organization's philosophy stems from three general premises about the health of their community. That is, the overall health of the entire community improves when residents (1) strive to lead healthy lifestyles, (2) participate in projects that elevate the community from a devalued to a valued status, and (3) avoid behaviors that put them at risk for physical and/or mental health problems (IBA Factsheet, 1994).

To help the Villa Victoria residents achieve these goals, IBA provides leadership training services and peer counseling projects for children, adolescents, and adults living in the community. The emphasis that is placed on these training opportunities reflects IBA's strong commitment to preventive education as well as to the strong value the organization places on working with local residents to enhance their sense of pride and responsibility for the entire community.

In the IBA youth programs, youngsters learn to help their peers see the dangers of leading an unhealthy lifestyle and see ways to cope with various developmental and cultural stressors. Topics covered in these peer counseling programs include the physical and psychological effects of abusing alcohol, tobacco, and other drugs; unsafe sex; school desertion; alternatives to violence; and issues related to racism and discrimination. These adolescents frequently work with adults learning how to organize various community projects, including workshops, dances, neighborhood video projects, and other events that send a positive message and encourage healthy choices among their peers (Merced, 1994).

IBA'S DIRECT CLIENT SERVICES   In addition to providing leadership train-ing and preventive-education services, IBA also offers one-to-one and small-group counseling services, support groups, academic tutoring, crisis-intervention services for adolescents and adults, translating for adults, recreational programming, and art classes. These direct client services com-plement IBA's community-wide prevention programs by extending assis-tance and support to those individuals who manifest various personal, educational, and social needs or problems (Merced, 1994).

IBA'S INDIRECT COMMUNITY SERVICES   Those who try to empower com-munity residents must face many environmental factors counterproductive to their clients' physical health and psychological well-being. These factors include the following: racism and discrimination; poverty; language and cultural barriers; high unemployment rates; and a lack of sensitivity in and responsiveness by many elected city officials regarding these problems.

The IBA counselors use several indirect community services to address these negative environmental conditions. In commenting on these services, Merced (1994) notes:

> IBA politicizes residents, builds coalitions with persons and organizations in other communities, collaborates with human service providers, registers and educates voters, trains residents to be community leaders, supports members of the community in their efforts to become elected representatives on the City Board of Directors, and conducts public demonstrations against or in support of policies which affect the Villa Victoria community. (p. 2)

IBA'S INDIRECT CLIENT SERVICES   Many of the IBA clients have gone through experiences that have left them feeling personally devalued. This is especially true for clients living with the negative social stigma imposed on people with chronic mental health difficulties and/or clients who have been involved in antisocial behaviors such as illegal, violent acts. The devaluation that these people experience in society tends to both under-mine their sense of personal power and heighten their sense of power-lessness.

Recognizing the negative long-term consequences that these environ-mental dynamics tend to have on clients' psychological well-being, the IBA counselors work to help guarantee that they receive the treatment and ser-vices to which they are entitled. In attempting to support clients' rights, the IBA counselors spend a great deal of time and energy advocating with other community officials for housing services, entitlement benefits, family ser-vices, health-care services, appropriate school services, and legal aid for these clients.

IBA presents an excellent example of the community counseling model in action. It offers a broad range of mental health services to a culturally distinct group historically subjected to psychological distress as a result of numerous social/political/environmental stressors in their environments. We have presented the direct and indirect client and community services offered by the IBA counselors with the hope that other practitioners can gain a better idea of the types of interventions considered important in developing comprehensive, culturally appropriate services among diverse client populations.

Promoting the Wellness of Battered Women

Although domestic violence has existed for centuries, communities across the United States have only recently begun to address this problem in any substantial way. In response to the rising number of women who report domestic violence each year, many human service agencies and shelters have been established to address the needs of battered women and their children.

Hotaling and Sugarman (1990) report that since the 1970s, the battered women's movement has resulted in the formation of over 1000 shelters for victims of domestic violence in the United States. Shelters for battered women and their children fall generally into one of two categories: first-stage or second-stage shelters.

In describing the difference between these two categories, Donaghy (1995) explains that "first-stage shelters primarily focus on short-term, immediate care, and second-stage shelters focus on integrating women into society after they have left their batterers" (p. 4). An increasing number of domestic violence shelters incorporate "transitional second-stage" intervention strategies into their programs by providing women with opportunities to move toward independent living at their own rate (Russell, 1990; Sullivan, 1991).

Along with the trend to help battered women move toward independent living, interest in the total wellness of this population has recently risen. Adopting a wellness perspective in battered women's shelters means making a commitment to using multidimensional interventions intentionally designed to increase clients' coping abilities, social support, self-esteem, and sense of personal power. This approach requires counselors to provide a broad range of direct and indirect client and community services.

Donaghy (1995) discusses a model program for victims of domestic violence. This program originated at the University of Wisconsin-Stevens Point. Like the other projects described in this book, it reflects the goals and objectives of the community counseling framework, exemplifying ways that counselors can use preventive and wellness strategies while also providing remedial and supportive counseling to battered women.

In discussing the types of programs available to battered women in the United States, Davis (1988) notes that, with the exception of occasional support groups, few wellness-oriented programs exist for survivors of domestic battery. Thus, the preventive and wellness counseling strategies that Donaghy (1995) describes represent new ways of thinking about and working to empower the victims of domestic violence. In discussing reasons to use a wellness approach with this population, she notes,

> An advantage of a wellness program is that many of its components reflect a preventive orientation. Not only can a person's enhanced well-being work to reduce the chance for future incidents, but the empowerment arising from a sense of enhanced personal well-being can serve to reduce the chance that women will be placed in a position of economic or emotional vulnerability in the first place. (p. 7)

A wellness approach to counseling battered women starts with an initial assessment of each client's needs. By taking the time to assess these needs, counselors can design counseling strategies tailored to their clients' unique situations.

ASSESSING THE NEEDS OF BATTERED WOMEN   Counselors interested in using a wellness model in battered women's shelters should conduct a holistic appraisal of their clients' disposition, which includes the following:

1. Assessing each woman's history of being battered
2. Identifying each client's short- and long-term needs and goals
3. Evaluating each battered woman's overall state of wellness

Unstructured intake interviews provide excellent opportunities to gather this sort of evaluative information. Donaghy (1995) recommends two structured assessment tools to complement this evaluation process: the Lifestyle Assessment Questionnaire (LAQ) (Elsenrath, Hettler, & Leafgren, 1988) and the Conflict Tactics Scale (CTS) (Herzberger, 1991; Straus, 1989). The results of these instruments provide much useful information, which a counselor should share with the client as they work together to develop a plan of action. Program administrators may also find these instruments useful for evaluating the impact of wellness programming on this population.

These instruments generate information related to five dimensions of a person's wellness: physical, emotional, intellectual, occupational/career, and spiritual. The following discussion examines these dimensions in more detail and outlines the types of community counseling services that help victims of domestic violence realize a greater degree of physical health and psychological wellness in their lives.

The Physical Dimension of Wellness.   The physical dimension of wellness encompasses many behaviors and factors that directly and indirectly affect a person's physical health. Nutrition, alcohol and drug misuse, stressors, frequency of physical exercise, sexual activity, body esteem, and average amount of sleep all influence physical wellness.

Further, a battered woman's overall physical wellness is clearly compromised by the threat of being subjected to domestic violence in the future. Both the actual battering and the psychological stress that accompany domestic violence adversely affect the client's general physical health and body esteem.

Interventions to enhance battered women's physical wellness may include helping them obtain a temporary restraining order to increase their sense of personal safety, offering stress-management workshops, securing free passes to the YWCA and other organizations that have exercise facilities, and providing direct counseling services that help clients address issues and plan strategies for improving their body esteem.

The Emotional Dimension of Wellness.   Emotional wellness involves "the person's ability to own and express one's emotions in a healthy manner" (Donaghy, 1995, p. 10). To help nurture this wellness, survivors learn to express a full range of feelings and reactions regarding the violence their spouses have inflicted on them. This important work counselors do with battered women usually occurs during individual and group counseling sessions.

When provided with opportunities to examine the emotional dimension of their own wellness, battered women not only gain important insights into themselves and their interpersonal needs, but also begin to change the way they relate to people in their environment. Because family members and friends are often surprised and perhaps even confused by these sorts of changes, offering indirect client services (e.g., consultations) to them is important. By sharing with family members and close friends the emotional needs and changes battered women normally experience, counselors can help expand the family's understanding and encourage their continued support.

The Intellectual Dimension of Wellness.   One can easily overlook the importance of battered women's intellectual development while addressing other, more basic needs. However, the cognitive-intellectual dimension is an important component of wellness. This sort of wellness involves using "formal and informal means that enhance an individual's level of knowledge and enlightenment" (Donaghy, 1995, p. 10). Strategies counselors might use to stimulate growth in this dimension include

1. Working with educational professionals in the community to set up a General Education Degree (GED) program at battered women's shelters
2. Offering psychoeducational workshops that specifically focus on relationship issues
3. Providing small peer counseling groups where battered women can discuss their concerns and learn from others' experiences
4. Using bibliotherapy as a way to help survivors understand the dynamics of abusive relationships

The Occupational/Career Dimension of Wellness.   Occupational wellness refers to a person's vocational/career experiences and skills, past and present employment satisfaction, and past and current income levels. As Donaghy (1995) emphasizes,

> Many unskilled, unemployed battered women remain in abusive situations due to economic dependency on their abusers. Another deterrent for many women is that the salary of an unskilled laborer is insufficient to live on with the added expense of child care; therefore, many of them enter the welfare system and remain dependent. (p. 9)

Counselors can do much to support occupational wellness by offering vocational/career counseling services, encouraging and assisting survivors to enroll in occupational training programs, and recruiting volunteers from the greater community to provide instruction in writing resumes and help clients develop employment interview skills.

The Spiritual Dimension of Wellness.   This psychological domain is the most elusive and least discussed dimension of wellness. In attempting to define the spiritual dimension of wellness, Donaghy (1995) states,

> Because spirituality carries with it many different connotations, it can be perceived in as many ways as there are individuals. Spirituality can be expressed within the tradition and structure of a church setting, or experienced simply through an engagement with nature, in a moment of quiet contemplation, or while engaging in a simple day-to-day activity such as changing a baby's diaper. (p. 9)

McFadden (1992) adds that spiritual wellness can be experienced within the self, in meaningful and healthy relationships with others, in connections with one's environment, or with a higher being.

During the recovery process, battered women may experience the need to reconnect with their own spirituality. Counselors can help address this need simply by acknowledging the importance of the spiritual dimension for a person's overall well-being.

The ethics of community counseling, however, do not allow mental health professionals to impose any religious beliefs on clients. Instead, they can encourage battered women to take time for themselves (perhaps even away from their children and the shelter) to reflect on their own spiritual development.

CRISIS INTERVENTION AND SUICIDE PREVENTION

The recommendations and strategies outlined in the models we have presented target specific populations. Individuals in the general population, though, also experience various types of crises. When individuals whose personal assets (i.e., coping skills, self-esteem, social support, and sense of personal power) are low experience crises, they frequently lose sight of or underestimate their potential options, become depressed, and perhaps even contemplate suicide. The community counseling framework includes practical strategies for working with clients in crisis. This includes planning and implementing suicide prevention programs.

Definition of Crisis

A *crisis* is a critical phase in a person's life when his or her normal ways of dealing with the world are suddenly interrupted. Personal crises may stem from a sudden, life-affecting change or from a combination of problems. Counseling theorists have differentiated various types of crises. These distinctions are often based on the unpredictability of a given crisis as well as its level of severity.

Poland (1990) conceptualizes crises along a continuum, ranging from normal developmental transitions (such as entering school, beginning adolescence, getting married, or retiring from one's career), to unexpected events (such as suddenly losing a job, experiencing a disabling injury, or the death of a close family member). Life crises can also be thought of as *intratemporal* (specific to particular life stages), *intertemporal* (occurring as an individual moves from one developmental stage to the next), and *extratemporal* (occurring independently of developmental stages) (American Association of Suicidology, 1989).

Regardless of the cause, people in crisis find they have lost an even keel. They typically need help from others in exploring the immediate problem, finding appropriate resources, and developing a practical plan to deal effectively with the crisis. People in crisis also need personal support and encouragement to cope with their feelings of helplessness and frustration.

Though crises represent highly stressful situations, they do not imply pathology. Rather, personal crises can occur at any time to any person who is in a situation that requires problem-solving abilities and other resources he or she has not yet developed or used.

Personal crises are usually temporary. They can, however, have long-lasting effects on individuals' physical health and psychological wellness. The likelihood that long-term negative outcomes will occur largely depends on the way individuals respond to their particular crisis. It is useful, therefore, for counselors to help clients think of a crisis as a process that follows a set of predictable phases.

The Phases of Crisis

In the first phase in crisis, a person is confronted with a new or unexpected event that causes anxiety, depression, and/or other types of stress. Second, individuals often find that their usual problem-solving methods do not work. Third, this leads most people to try new ways of dealing with the immediate problem. Finally, individuals either emerge stronger if the new approaches were effective, or they experience continued and perhaps even greater levels of stress than before, if the new approaches were not effective.

Elaborating on the potential positive and negative outcomes of a personal crisis, Aguilera and Messick (1981) further note,

> The Chinese characters that represent the word "crisis" mean both danger and opportunity. Crisis is a danger because it threatens to overwhelm the individual and may result in suicide or a psychotic break. It is also an opportunity because during times of crises, individuals are more receptive to therapeutic influence. Therefore, prompt and skillful intervention may not only prevent the development of a serious long-term disability but may allow new coping patterns to emerge that can help the individual function at a higher level of equilibrium than before the crisis. (p. 1)

In a crisis, then, the timeliness of the intervention is very important. Accordingly, crisis counseling serves mainly to affect the outcome of the crisis positively. This sort of counseling is, of course, temporary; it aims at helping clients (1) regain a sense of control over their lives and (2) develop the resources they need to experience an increased level of wellness after the crisis has passed. Crisis interventions may take place in an agency specifically designed for that purpose, such as domestic violence centers, in an organization with a wider service mandate, such as community mental health centers, or in school counseling programs.

Regardless of the setting, crisis counseling adheres to the same principles:

1. It focuses on specific, time-limited treatment goals. Attention is particularly directed to helping clients reduce the level of tension that currently exists in their lives. The time limits associated with crisis counseling can enhance and maintain clients' motivation to examine new ways of dealing with the crisis and attain specified goals.

2. Crisis interventions involve helping clients clarify and accurately assess their perceptions of the source and the meaning of the stressors. This method of counseling entails an active and directive approach that facilitates clients' cognitive restructuring of the perceived stressors.

3. Crisis counseling is designed to help clients develop more effective and adaptive problem-solving mechanisms so that they can return to their precrisis level of functioning.

4. Because crisis intervention is reality oriented, it is specifically designed to help clarify clients' cognitive perceptions, to confront denial and distortions, and to offer emotional support without providing false reassurances.

5. Whenever possible, and especially when working with people from diverse cultural, ethnic, and racial backgrounds, crisis intervention strategies usually include members of the client's existing relationship networks to help determine and implement effective coping strategies.

6. Crisis interventions may serve as a prelude for further counseling and development services in the future. (Okun, 1982, p. 216)

These principles all point to the importance of making crisis counseling practical and realistic. As such, counselors need to focus on the client's current situation, encouraging the client to identify the salient points of the problem as he or she experiences it.

Because the client may have difficulty focusing on the problem and identifying alternative solutions, the counselor should be prepared to use a directive approach, following organized problem-solving procedures to help the client identify relatively permanent sources of support in his or her environment. This process typically includes the following steps:

1. **Assess the nature of the crisis.** The counselor's first step in crisis counseling is to learn as much as possible about what precipitated the crisis, what coping mechanisms have been attempted, and what patterns of coping the individual usually follows. Of course, counselors must also assess the seriousness of the situation by asking the question, "Is the individual or

family in any immediate danger?" If the answer to this question is yes, mental health practitioners are ethically responsible to take whatever action is necessary to help protect the safety of the client and his or her family.

    2. *Help the client clarify the immediate problem.* As mentioned earlier, clients in crisis usually find it hard to make a realistic assessment of the major issues associated with their crisis. Counselors can help clients frame problems in concrete and realistic terms.

    3. *Make the problem manageable.* Individuals in crisis typically feel overwhelmed by the demands they must face. However, clients can begin to increase their sense of control and personal power over the problem once they have broken it down into manageable parts. As action is taken to resolve aspects of the problem, individuals can begin to regain equilibrium and a sense of personal power.

    4. *Identify additional sources of support.* As clients prepare to address the crisis, counselors should encourage them to identify sources of social support from family members, friends, and others. In reaching out, clients can gain emotional support and assistance.

    5. *Identify personal strengths.* In a crisis, individuals can lose sight of their own positive attributes. Helping them identify personal resources can increase their sense of their personal assets and self-responsibility.

    6. *Explore feelings.* Normally, a crisis stirs up deep emotions. Clients can deal with these feelings most effectively if they can identify and express them.

    7. *Develop a strategy for coping with the situation.* The counselor should work to increase the client's problem-solving abilities. The strategies employed during this phase of crisis counseling resemble those used with clients not in crisis. However, the client in crisis needs concrete direction and more emotional support when examining and trying out new problem-solving strategies.

    8. *Plan for the prevention of future crises.* As clients return to a less stressful level of functioning, counselors can encourage them to take stock of the crisis situation and identify possible ways to prevent problems. If new problem-solving skills are accompanied by attempts to maintain an increased level of personal resources, the crisis can cause the client to grow. (Lewis & Lewis, 1986, pp. 100–101)

Suicide Prevention

The early development of crisis-counseling models in the late 1950s and early 1960s paralleled an increased interest in suicide prevention. Contemporary approaches to suicide prevention are largely based on the groundbreaking work of Farberow and Shneidman at the Los Angeles Suicide Prevention Center (Farberow, 1974; Farberow & Shneidman,

1961). This center developed the concept of the 24-hour telephone crisis line and was the first to train volunteers to provide crisis counseling services by telephone.

After workers at the center studied and developed effective methods of telephone counseling, they shared this information widely so that crisis-intervention programs could be initiated throughout the nation. The escalating number of suicides and suicide attempts reportedly occurring among people of all ages and backgrounds in the United States at that time was viewed as an urgent national problem, one needing study as well as active preventive measures.

The Los Angeles Suicide Prevention Center served as a model not only because it broke ground in developing scientific methods of intervention but also because it consistently generated significant research on the nature of suicidal thinking and behavior. This research began with Farberow and Shneidman's (1961) discovery and analysis of hundreds of suicide notes. McGee (1974) provided the following comments about the pioneering efforts of these two researchers:

> However one chooses to tell the story, certain elements must be included, such as the fortuitous discovery by two behavioral scientists of several hundred actual suicide notes filed in the office of the Los Angeles County Medical Examiner-Coroner. This discovery, together with the realization of its scientific worth, led Norman Farberow and Edwin Shneidman to make the first of many explorations into the psychological processes of a person [who takes] his own life. They analyzed the thinking processes and identified the "logic of suicide"; they looked into affective states and uncovered the ambivalence; they dissected the communications and discovered the clues which foretell an act of self-destruction. Thus, they became convinced that suicide could be prevented. (p. 5)

These initial research efforts continued, with Shneidman (1987) developing a detailed postmortem mental history that provided much insight into the thoughts of people who chose suicide as their only option. Shneidman (1987) coined the term *psychological autopsy* when referring to these findings. The highly personalized nature of the information Shneidman gathered in conducting his studies led him to draw the following conclusions:

> Suicide, I have learned, is not a bizarre or incomprehensible act of self-destruction. Rather, suicidal people use a particular logic, a style of thinking that brings them to the conclusion that death is the only solution to their problems. This style can be readily seen, and there are steps we can take to stop suicide, if we know where to look. (Shneidman, 1987, p. 56)

Shneidman used his research findings to develop a number of guidelines for preventing suicide. For example, he pointed out that because suicidal people usually experience a great deal of unendurable pain in their lives, counselors should work to reduce that feeling of distress as quickly as possible. Sometimes this requires them to include significant others in the suicide prevention strategy.

Furthermore, since Shneidman's (1987) research findings clearly indicate that suicidal people act out of different needs, mental health practitioners must remember to tailor their crisis-counseling interventions to each individual. Because suicidal people cannot themselves find alternative solutions, counselors need to point out repeatedly that other options are indeed available. Finally, because many suicidal people hint at their intention, counselors can learn to read some of the warning signs of suicide accurately and intervene in time.

Though people of all ages commit suicide, its occurrence among adolescents has dramatically escalated over the past few decades (Recklitis, Noam, & Borst, 1992). In fact, the actual number of adolescent suicides in the United States has risen 300% during the past 30 years (Frymier, 1988; Kush, 1991).

Drawing a single portrait of the typical teenage suicide victim is nearly impossible. However,

> some of the conditions most often linked with adolescent suicide include families plagued by divorce; communication barriers between parents and teenagers; dual-career families; drug and alcohol addiction; parental, academic, and peer pressures; rootlessness and family mobility; fear of future jobs and opportunities; and personal relationship problems. (Peach & Reddick, 1991, p. 108)

Researchers have noted that some teenagers tend toward suicide more than others. The characteristics associated with such at-risk adolescents include the following:

- A previous suicide attempt
- Suicidal gestures (e.g., cutting off one's hair, self-inflicted cigarette burns, other abuse of self)
- A tendency to be socially isolated (having no friends or only one friend)
- A record of school failure or truancy
- A broken home or a broken relationship with a significant other (family member, boy/girlfriend)
- Talk of suicide, either one's own or that of others
- A close friend or relative who was a suicide victim
- Not living at home

- Preoccupation with death or dying
- A recent significant loss or the anniversary of one
- Sudden disruptive or violent behaviors
- Being more withdrawn or uncommunicative and isolated from others than usual (Friedrich, Matus, & Rinn, 1985)

Schools are excellent settings for implementing suicide prevention programs. The professional counseling literature suggests that to be effective, school-based suicide prevention programs must be comprehensive and systematic. Using the community counseling framework as a guide, school counselors can implement the following direct and indirect client and community services when developing a suicide prevention program in their schools:

- *Direct client services:* Provide individual and small-group counseling, as well as educational and referral services, to students identified as at risk for suicide
- *Indirect client services:* Offer in-service training that helps teachers identify suicide warning signs; develop a written statement that describes specific criteria that administrators, counselors, and teachers can use to assess the lethality of suicidal students; make suicide prevention materials available to parents
- *Direct community services:* Develop and distribute suicide prevention materials to students; implement classroom-based prevention projects; conduct schoolwide psychological screening activities to identify at-risk students
- *Indirect community services:* Work with school administrators and teachers to develop a written formal suicide policy for the school; develop a set of written procedures to address the needs of students identified as at-risk for suicide; consult with people in the greater community who have expertise in suicide prevention counseling

SUMMARY

In addition to developing and implementing educational projects to prevent dysfunctions, community counselors offer more intensive counseling services to groups of individuals identified as especially vulnerable to mental health problems. One can conceptualize vulnerability by using an equation that balances the deficits of organic factors, stress, and powerlessness against the resources of coping skills, self-esteem, social support, and the individual's sense of personal power. A change in any of these factors affects a person's degree of vulnerability at any given time. Clients may thus need extra help when their life circumstances could overwhelm their coping resources.

Severe stress can cause many physical, psychological, and social problems. One can intervene in these stressful, high-risk situations even without connecting a specific stressor to a specific disorder. Whether or not individuals can cope with chronic or acute stress may depend on buffers such as their social support systems, sense of self-efficacy, and problem-solving skills. The community counseling framework helps mental health practitioners identify groups of at-risk individuals and plan strategies designed to enhance these clients' life skills and sense of personal power.

A number of community- and school-based programs have begun to demonstrate the tremendous potential of outreach to vulnerable clients. The examples presented in this chapter include the following:

1. Programs designed to help families going through separation and divorce
2. A program that assisted pregnant adolescents making the transition to parenthood
3. An agency devoted to meeting the psychological and cultural needs of Latinos and Latinas
4. An innovative wellness program for working with victims of domestic violence
5. Crisis-intervention and suicide prevention strategies

These examples illustrate general approaches counselors can adapt to the situations they face in their own community or school setting.

SUPPLEMENTAL ACTIVITIES

1. Think about a specific vulnerable population. What particular transitions or situations might make members of this population likely to develop problems? Can these high-risk situations be prevented? If not, how can individuals' ability to cope with them be strengthened?
2. Consider again your own hypothetical community counseling program (see Chapter 1). For the client population you have identified, what would you do to help reduce the occurrence of crisis situations? Develop in more detail the facet of your program involving outreach to vulnerable populations.

REFERENCES

Aguilera, D. C., & Messick, J. M. (1981). *Crisis intervention: Theory and methodology*. St. Louis, MO: Mosby.

Albee, G. W. (1986). Advocates and adversaries of prevention. In M. Kessler & S. E. Goldston (Eds.), *A decade of progress in primary prevention* (pp. 309–332). Hanover, NH: University Press of New England.

Amato, P. R. (1993). Children's adjustment to divorce: Theories, hypotheses, empirical support. *Journal of Marriage and the Family, 55,* 23–38.

American Association of Suicidology. (1989). *Postvention guidelines, school suicide prevention program committee.* Boulder, CO: Author.

Atkinson, D. R., Morten, G., & Sue, D. W. (1993). *Counseling American minorities: A crosscultural perspective. (4th ed.).* Dubuque, IA: Brown.

Aubrey, R., & Lewis, J. A. (1988). Social issues and the counseling profession. In R. Hayes & R. Aubrey (Eds.), *New Directions for counseling and human development* (pp. 286–303). Denver, CO: Love Publishing.

Bandura, A. (1989). Human agency in social cognitive theory. *American Psychologist, 44*(9), 1175–1184.

Banks, J. A., & Banks, C. A. (1993). *Multicultural education: Issues and perspectives* (2nd ed.). Boston: Allyn and Bacon.

Behrman, R. E., & Quinn, L. S. (1994). Children and divorce: Overview and analysis. *The Future of Children, 4*(1), 4–14.

Bloom, B. L. (1984). *Community mental health: A general introduction.* Pacific Grove, CA: Brooks/Cole.

Bloom, B. L., Hodges, W. F., & Caldwell, R. A. (1982). A preventive program for the newly separated. *American Journal of Community Psychology, 10,* 251–264.

Capuzzi, D. (1988). *Counseling and intervention strategies for adolescent suicide prevention.* Educational Resources Information Center, Counseling and Personnel Services Clearinghouse (ERIC/CAPS). Ann Arbor: School of Education, University of Michigan.

Carbone, J. R. (1994). A feminist perspective on divorce. *The Future of Children, 4*(1), 183–209.

Cherlin, A. (1992). *Marriage, divorce, and remarriage.* Cambridge, MA: Harvard University Press.

Cowen, E. L. (1985). Person-centered approaches to primary prevention in mental health: Situation-focused and competence-enhancement. *American Journal of Community Psychology, 33,* 31–48.

D'Andrea, M. (1994). The Family Development Project (FDP): A comprehensive mental health counseling program for pregnant adolescents. *Journal of Mental Health Counseling, 16*(2), 184–195.

D'Andrea, M., & Daniels, J. (1994). The different faces of racism in higher education. *Thought and Action, 10*(1), 73–90.

Davis, N. J. (1988). Shelters for battered women: Social policy response to interpersonal violence. *Social Science Journal, 25,* 401–419.

Donaghy, K. (1995). Beyond survival: Applying wellness interventions in battered women's shelters. *Journal of Mental Health Counseling, 17*(1), 3–17.

Elsenrath, D., Hettler, B., & Leafgren, F. (1988). *Lifestyle assessment questionnaire* (5th ed.). Stevens Point, WI: National Wellness Institute.

Farberow, N. L. (1974). *Suicide.* Morristown, NJ: General Learning Press.

Farberow, N. L., & Shneidman, E. S. (1961). *The cry for help.* New York: McGraw-Hill.

Friedrich, M. C., Matus, A. L., & Rinn, R. (1985). *An interdisciplinary supervised student program focused on depression and suicide awareness.* New York: New York Department of Education.

Frymier, J. (1988). Understanding and preventing teen suicide. *Phi Delta Kappan, 4,* 290.

Hanson. S. L. (1992). Involving families in programs for pregnant teens: Consequences for teens and their families. *Family Relations, 41,* 303–311.

Hayes, R. L., & Hayes, B. A. (1988). Remarriage families: Counseling parents, stepparents, and their children. In R. Hayes & R. Aubrey (Eds.), *New directions for counseling and human development* (pp. 465–477). Denver, CO: Love Publishing.

Herzberger, S. D. (1991). Conflict tactics scale. In D. J. Keyser & R. C. Sweetland (Eds.), *Test critiques* (Vol. 8, pp. 98–103). Austin, TX: Pro-Ed.

Holmes, T., & Rahe, R. (1967). The social readjustment rating scale. *Journal of Psychosomatic Research, 11,* 121–128.

Hotaling, G. T., & Sugarman, D. B. (1990). Prevention of wife assault. In R. T. Ammerman & M. Hersen (Eds.), *Treatment of family violence* (pp. 425–437). New York: Wiley Interscience.

IBA factsheet. (1994). *IBA VIVA!* (Brochure). Boston Author.

Ivey, A. (1995). Psychotherapy as liberation: Toward specific skills and strategies in multicultural counseling and therapy. In J. G. Ponterotto, J. M. Casas, L. A. Suzuki, & C. M. Alexander (Eds.) *Handbook of multicultural counseling* (pp. 53–72). Newbury Park, CA: Sage.

Kush, F. R. (1991). A descriptive study of school-based adolescent suicide prevention/intervention programs: Program components and the role of the school counselor. *Dissertation Abstracts International, 52,* 1692A.

Langston, D. (1995). Class and inequality: Tired of playing monopoly? In M. L. Andersen & P. H. Collins (Eds.), *Race, class, and gender: An anthology* (pp. 17–100). Dubuque, IA: Brown.

Lazarus, R. (1980). The stress and coping paradigm. In L. A. Bond & J. C. Rosen (Eds.), *Competence and coping in adulthood* (pp. 28–74). Hanover, NH: University Press of New England.

Lewis, J. A., & Lewis, M. D. (1986). *Counseling programs for employees in the workplace.* Pacific Grove, CA: Brooks/Cole.

Lewis, J. A., Sperry, L., & Carlson, J. (1993). *Health counseling.* Pacific Grove, CA: Brooks/Cole.

Locke, D. (1992). *Increasing multicultural understanding: A comprehensive model.* Newbury Park, CA: Sage.

McFadden, S. (1992, April). *The spiritual dimensions of a "good old age."* Paper presented at the 38th Annual Kirkpatrick Memorial Conference on Mental Health and Aging, Ball State University, Muncie, IN.

McGee, T. F. (1974). *Crisis intervention in the community.* Baltimore: University Park Press.

McWhirter, E. H. (1994). *Counseling for empowerment.* Alexandria, VA: American Counseling Association.

Merced, N. (1994). *Description of IBA's community counseling strategy.* Boston: Inquilinos Boricuas en Acción.

National Mental Health Association Commission on the Prevention of Mental-Emotional Disabilities. (1986). *The prevention of mental-emotional disabilities: Report of the National Mental Health Association Commission of the Prevention of Mental-Emotional Disabilities.* Alexandria, VA: National Mental Health Association.

Okun, B. F. (1982). *Effective helping: Interviewing and counseling techniques* (2nd ed.). Pacific Grove, CA: Brooks/Cole.

Peach, L., & Reddick, T. L. (1991). Counselors can make a difference in preventing adolescent suicide. *School Counselor, 39,* 107–110.

Pedro-Carroll, J. L., & Cowen, E. L. (1985). The children of divorce intervention program: An investigation of the efficacy of a school-based prevention program. *Journal of Consulting and Clinical Psychology, 53,* 603–611.

Persell, C. H. (1993). Social class and educational equality. In J. A. Banks & C. A. Banks (Eds.), *Multicultural education: Issues and perspectives* (2nd ed., pp. 71–89). Boston: Allyn and Bacon.

Poland, S. (1990). *Suicide intervention in the schools.* New York: Guilford Press.

Recklitis, C. J., Noam, G. G., & Borst, S. R. (1992). Adolescent suicide and defensive style. *Suicide and Life-threatening Behavior, 22*(3).

Russell, M. (1990). Second-stage shelters: A consumer's report. *Canada's Mental Health, 38*(2/3), 24–26.

Shneidman, E. S. (1987, March). At the point of no return. *Psychology Today,* 54–58.

Snyder, C. R. (1995). Conceptualizing, measuring, and nurturing hope. *Journal of Counseling and Development, 73*(3), 355–360.

Sprenkle, D. H. (1990). The clinical practice of divorce therapy. In M. R. Textor (Ed.), *The divorce and divorce therapy book* (pp. 37–91). Northvale, NY: Aronson.

Stensrud, R., & Stensrud, K. (1983). Coping skills training: A systematic approach to stress management counseling. *Personnel and Guidance Journal, 62,* 214–218.

Stokols, D. (1992). Establishing and maintaining healthy environments: Toward a social ecology of health promotion. *American Psychologist, 47*(1), 6–22.

Stolberg, A. L., & Garrison, K. M. (1985). Evaluating a primary prevention program for children of divorce. *American Journal of Community Psychology, 13,* 111–124.

Straus, M. A. (1989). *Manual for the conflict tactics scale (CTS).* Durham: Family Research Laboratory, University of New Hampshire.

Sue, D. W., & Sue, D. (1990). *Counseling the culturally different: Theory and Practice* (2nd. ed.). New York: Wiley.

Sullivan, C. M. (1991). The provision of advocacy services to women leaving abusive partners: An exploratory study. *Journal of Interpersonal Violence, 6,* 45–54.

U. S. Bureau of the Census. (1994). *Household and family characteristics, 1993.* Washington, DC: U. S. Government Printing Office.

U. S. Department of Health and Human Services. (1990). *Healthy people 2000: National health promotion and disease prevention objectives* (PHS Publication No. 91-50212). Washington, DC: Author.

CHAPTER 4

COMMUNITY COUNSELING AND THE COUNSELING PROCESS

The community counseling model follows a set of values that unify a variety of services, even in highly diverse settings. Community counselors emphasize their clients' strengths instead of focusing on their deficits. They recognize that the social environment significantly affects each individual's development. Further, they seek to help prevent problems, not just react to them. Within the community counseling framework, practitioners acknowledge that they act most effectively when they provide individuals with opportunities to acquire skills and resources to help themselves.

Consistent with these values, community counselors create multifaceted programs that go far beyond individual counseling to include preventive education, outreach to people coping with high-risk situations, advocacy for stigmatized populations, and efforts to influence public policy. The preceding chapters have emphasized the importance of expanding the counselor's role and responsibilities to more effectively promote the psychological health and wellness of larger numbers of people than many practitioners have traditionally done.

This chapter examines the role of direct counseling services—that is, individual and small-group counseling—in the community counseling framework. In particular, this chapter emphasizes the need to address empowerment as well as developmental, coping, and multicultural issues when counseling people from diverse client populations.

THE ROLE OF DIRECT COUNSELING

Despite the importance of prevention and outreach, made clear in Chapters 2 and 3, direct counseling intervention strategies remain an essential part of the community counseling model. Counselors by definition *counsel*, or help clients directly, one-to-one. Thus, while mental health practitioners would be ill advised to view the individual counseling interview as the primary means of promoting their clients' psychological wellness, it remains a basic building block in the community counseling framework.

The values promoted by the community counseling model—the promotion of human development, empowerment, and wellness—strongly impact the nature of the counseling process. In following this model, counselors recognize clients' responsibility for their own lives and the influence of environmental factors on human behavior. Accordingly, community counselors work to strengthen their clients' sense of hope and personal mastery by encouraging them to take responsibility for solving each problem but not necessarily to shoulder the blame for it.

Four Models of Responsibility

As Brickman et al. (1982) have made clear, how counselors attribute responsibility for clients' problems largely determines their approach to the helping process:

> Whether or not people are held responsible for causing their problems and whether or not they are held responsible for solving these problems are the factors determining four fundamentally different orientations to the world, each internally coherent, each in some measure incompatible with the other three. (p. 369)

Brickman and his colleagues define these four orientations as follows:

1. **The moral model:** People are responsible for both creating and solving their problems.
2. **The medical model:** People are responsible for neither creating their problems nor solving them.
3. **The enlightenment model:** People are responsible for creating their problems but not for solving them.
4. **The compensatory model:** People are not responsible for creating their problems but are responsible for solving them.

Using substance abuse as an example, one can see how differently supporters of these four models would conceptualize the same problem (Lewis, Dana, & Blevins, 1988). For example, adherents of the moral model attribute full responsibility of substance abuse to the individual. Therefore, if drinking or drug use is the problem, willpower is the solution. In contrast, supporters of the medical model hold that the client controls neither the problem nor the solution; thus though such clients are not to blame for their disease, they cannot recover without treatment.

According to the enlightenment model, though people bear the responsibility for their past actions, and for any resulting problems, they can find help in surrendering to an outside force stronger than themselves. Consequently, Alcoholics Anonymous encourages its members to "make amends" for past actions and turn their lives over to a "higher power."

Finally, adherents of the compensatory model expect individuals to assume responsibility for solving their own problems despite the fact that these problems may not have been of their own making. Describing this perspective in more detail, Lewis (1994) suggests that the etiology of an addiction may involve entirely different factors than the process of recovery does and that a sense of detachment between the problem behavior and the individual's personal identity and self-concept can help substance-abusing clients change their behavior.

One can apply the models described by Brickman and his colleagues (1982) to any human problem. Regardless of the problem, "models in which people are held responsible for solutions . . . are more likely to increase people's competence than models in which they are not held responsible for solutions" (p. 375). At the same time, models in which problems are attributed to external causes tend not to provoke guilt or self-blame, which can be debilitating.

The compensatory model thus offers a double advantage. As Brickman and his colleagues (1982) explain, "The strength of the compensatory model for coping is that it allows people to direct their energies outward, working on trying to solve problems or transform their environment without berating themselves for their role in creating these problems" (p. 372). In this way, the compensatory model balances one's recognition of the impact of environmental influences with a sense of individual responsibility and personal hope that is clearly consistent with the community counseling model.

Understanding and Nurturing Hope

Clients who seek counseling services have typically experienced problems that they were ill-prepared to address effectively. These problems often result in depression, frustration, and/or anger. When allowed to continue over time, such problems frequently lead to an erosion of clients' hope for a better future. Because the absence of such hopefulness compromises one's psychological health and well-being in many ways, the community counseling model emphasizes that counselors serve a crucial function in promoting hopefulness among their clients. Despite the importance of facilitating a hopeful disposition among clients, however, this issue has received little attention in the professional counseling literature.

Hopefulness refers to an inner anticipation of new potentials and a greater sense of satisfaction and connection with life. It fuels the belief that though we are who we are at the present time, we are also capable of actualizing new potentials, new insights, and new skills that will promote a greater sense of personal well-being and interdependence with others.

HOPE AND MENTAL HEALTH   The correlation between hopefulness and mental health is readily observed. Researchers have reported that those who experience high levels of hopelessness consistently manifest heightened levels of depression, frustration, substance abuse, and suicidal ideation. On the other hand, hopeful people have reported greater happiness and less distress in their lives, demonstrated superior coping skills, recovered better from physical injury, and manifested less burnout at work than their "low hope" counterparts (Elliott, Witty, Herrick & Hoffman, 1991; Sherwin, Elliott, Frank, & Hoffman, 1992).

Again, although hopefulness has been found to correlate highly with a person's mental health, this topic has received little attention from counseling theorists, researchers, and practitioners in the field. Attempting to explain this lack of attention, Snyder (1995) points out that mental health professionals have been "skeptical and ambivalent about hope, suggesting that it is too vague to measure, and useless to measure if we could" (p. 355). Recently, a number of professionals have begun looking at ways in which counselors might begin to conceptualize, measure, and nurture hope among their clients (Elliott et al., 1991; Sherwin et al., 1992; Snyder, 1995). We present the results of these efforts here to help mental health practitioners gain a better understanding of the importance of promoting hope in their clients.

RESEARCH ON HOPE   Hope comprises two components, a sense of agency and a person's ability to conceptualize and act on what Snyder (1995) calls "pathways." *Human agency* refers to an individual's willpower or level of psychological energy to move toward her or his goals. Human agency is usually affected by self-efficacy (Bandura, 1989) and optimism about the future (Scheier & Carver, 1987). The second aspect of hope involves using one's *pathways*, or one's knowledge and ability to lead a healthy and satisfying life (Gazda, 1984; Goldstein, 1992).

Counselors can do much to nurture their clients' hope by fostering an increased sense of agency and creating opportunities for clients to develop new pathways that enhance their level of optimal functioning and personal satisfaction. Helping clients develop new goals, increase their self-confidence, and develop new life skills can raise their hope.

Progress in each of these areas, though, does not need to occur all at once to foster hope. Often, enhancing one of these areas catalyzes change in other components. For example, a person's agency and pathways may increase merely by clarifying a goal in counseling. Likewise, counselors will commonly find that when a person identifies a realistic personal goal, his or her motivation to develop pathways related to a specific goal often increases as well (Snyder, 1995).

It is important to note, however, that hope, in and of itself, is not always positive. As Synder (1995) states,

> Hope is ultimately counterproductive to the extent that individuals
> pursue goals to maximize their outcomes to the comparative
> detriment of other people. Hope in this context, may fuel the pursuit
> of egocentric goals. What is needed are environments in which
> people living and working together can interact in a supportive
> atmosphere so that both individual and collective goals can be met.
> This would mean that people, in whatever settings they reside, could
> increasingly perceive that they have the agency and pathways to
> succeed. Our role as counselors is to help people to think in more
> hopeful ways and to help them build more hopeful environments for
> themselves and those around them. (p. 359)

From this perspective then, counselors nurture hope ultimately to increase clients' sense of both individual and social responsibility.

The traditional counseling paradigm has led many practitioners to pay disproportionate attention to issues related to clients' individual responsibilities (Kelly, 1989). The community counseling model clearly values the importance of fostering an increased sense of personal responsibility among clients. However, it also emphasizes the need to move beyond the traditional emphasis by nurturing the internalization of a greater sense of social responsibility among clients.

PROMOTING PERSONAL RESPONSIBILITY

Young-Eisendrath (1988) has indicated that one's sense of personal responsibility increases when one can "conceive of [oneself] as an agent or actor in making life happen" (p. 82). To foster such responsibility, counselors must create opportunities for clients to experience success and thus recognize their own power. This may include learning social skills, developing interviewing skills, and learning to make more effective decisions. After clients have experienced these or other types of success through counseling, practitioners should help them learn to exercise this new sense of personal power in other settings.

Encouraging clients to apply their newly developed power to their social environments helps clients recognize and accept responsibility for their lives. This, in turn, fosters an increased sense of self-efficacy and the acquisition of a host of self-management skills.

Self-Efficacy

Bandura's (1989) definition of *self-efficacy* refers to a person's ability to mobilize the cognitive and behavioral skills he or she needs in order to deal with the environment. *Perceived self-efficacy* refers to a person's beliefs about his or her ability to deal with life's challenges. How people judge their self-efficacy greatly affects their behavior. For instance, people who think they lack efficacy tend to avoid challenges or give up quickly when encountering obstacles, while those with a strong sense of self-efficacy tend to persevere through difficulties (McWhirter, 1994). As Bandura (1982) points out,

> In any given activity, skills and self-beliefs that ensure optimal use of capabilities are required for successful functioning. If self-efficacy is lacking, people tend to behave ineffectually even though they know what to do. . . . The higher the level of perceived self-efficacy, the greater the performance accomplishments. Strength of efficacy also predicts behavior change. The stronger the perceived efficacy, the more likely are people to persist in their efforts until they succeed. (pp. 127–128)

Clients are most likely to resolve their problems if they believe they have self-efficacy. Consequently, self-efficacy is important both as an end in itself and as a means to continued success. Counselors can help strengthen their clients' sense of self-efficacy within individual and small-group counseling sessions by encouraging them to see their problematic behavior as controllable and themselves as capable.

Self-Managed Behavior Change

Many people seek counseling because they want to change their behavior but cannot do so on their own. If clients can learn the principles of behavior change, however, they can gain greater control over their own lives. Ideally, counselors can use behavioral counseling strategies to teach clients skills for managing their own behavior.

> Training in self-management requires strong and early support from the helper, with the client gradually relying more and more on his [or her] newly developed skills. These include skills in

(1) self-monitoring; (2) establishment of specific rules of conduct by contracts with oneself or others; (3) seeking support from the environment for fulfillment; (4) self-evaluation; and (5) generating strong reinforcing consequences for engaging in behaviors which achieve the goals of self-control. The concept of self-control implies that an individual can be taught to rearrange powerful contingencies that influence behavior in such a way that he [or she] experiences long-range benefits. (Kanfer, 1980, p. 344)

Behavioral management is based on established learning principles. In simple terms, people learn to repeat or to avoid particular behaviors according to the consequences of those behaviors. If a behavior is positively reinforced, a person will likely attempt it again. The more regular the reinforcement, the more likely the response. On the other hand, if a behavior is either punished or never reinforced, it will occur fewer times in the future and may eventually be extinguished. People can also learn to associate a behavior with a specific stimulus from the environment. In these situations, the stimulus serves as a cue that a given action will most likely be positively reinforced, making that action more likely to be repeated.

Individuals can learn to change their behavior by purposefully manipulating cues and reinforcements in their environment. They can increase their performance of positive behaviors by choosing special rewards given only for successful performance of desired behaviors. They can decrease the repetition of negative behaviors by changing the environmental cues, eliminating or nullifying consequences they have identified as reinforcing, or substituting positive behaviors that are incompatible with the undesired ones.

From a self-management perspective, the first step in changing behavior is to establish measurable objectives. This involves helping clients identify and describe specific behaviors they want to learn, translating what may at first be vague goals into concrete, measurable terms. The client can then select a positive reinforcement to follow the successful performance of a given behavior. If the desired behavior is difficult or complex, counselors should help clients establish subgoals designed to promote incremental behavioral change that culminates in the successful achievement of a broader personal goal within a chosen time-span.

Before people can set realistic personal goals, they must obtain base rates for their activities, observing and recording how frequently they currently perform the behavior they want to change. Once counselors have collected baseline data and established specific behavioral objectives, they can better help clients plan their own interventions.

As clients implement their plans they should keep a record of their progress so that changes from the baseline will be readily apparent. At first, target behaviors should be reinforced each time they occur. Later, reinforcement should be intermittent. Eventually, intrinsic reinforcers should replace the extrinsic reinforcement, at which point keeping records is no longer necessary or desirable. By this time, clients will have learned the behavioral-management skills that enable them to feel that life can, indeed, be better controlled. Throughout this process, the counselor plays an educational and supportive role, providing the initial encouragement, training, and ongoing support that clients need to make self-determined behavioral changes (Watson & Tharp, 1993).

Effective use of the self-managed behavioral change approach also depends on the counselor's ability to model desirable self-regulatory behaviors. Thus, as Lewis, Sperry, and Carlson (1993) state, "If we are to help our clients become self-regulators, we must ourselves be self-regulators. If wellness is to become part of our clients' lives, it must also be part of our own" (p. 290).

Social Responsibility

The combination of the limited resources and the escalating demands that accompany the rising number of people who live on this planet are forging a heightened awareness of our interconnectedness and interdependence as a global community (Lator, 1993). The way we lead our lives directly and indirectly impacts our environment and other people in many more ways than most imagined in the past.

In some situations, individuals can easily notice the social impact they have on others, as in parenting, teaching, or counseling. On a much broader scale, though, the strength of a modern democratic society and, ultimately, the viability of a global ecosystem largely depends on people's ability and willingness to extend their sense of social responsiveness.

MOVING AWAY FROM TRADITIONAL MODELS   The emphasis that the community counseling model places on promoting social responsibility in clinical practice clearly distinguishes it from the traditional individual-intrapsychic counseling paradigm. As mentioned earlier, community counseling involves fostering positive community-building attitudes and skills among clients. This necessitates providing opportunities for counselors and clients to engage in collaborative discussions about their own social responsibilities—for example, as parents, students, members of the workforce, or U.S. citizens. These discussions should foster both parties' learning, sensitivity, caring, and responsiveness to others.

However, because the idea of using the counseling process to help clients develop a heightened sense of social responsibility sharply contrasts with many traditional counseling approaches, especially those emphasizing the importance of nurturing individual responsibility as a vehicle to self-actualization, counselors must have a clear understanding of social responsibility and how they might promote it through counseling.

Social responsibility literally refers to one's ability and willingness to respond to others by paying attention to them and actively responding to their needs. It emphasizes respect and care for other people and the environment in which one lives. The term *respect* means showing regard for the worth of someone or something. In the context of the community counseling model, the term takes three major forms: "respect for oneself, respect for other people, and respect for all forms of life and the environment that sustains them" (Lickona, 1992, p. 43).

One can view the development of social responsibility as an ongoing process that requires a shift from an egocentric to an allocentric (other-centered) orientation. Thus, helping clients develop a greater sense of social responsibility involves facilitating this shift. Helping clients achieve an allocentric perspective does not, however, mean that practitioners should abandon their efforts to stimulate individual responsibility. Rather than viewing the importance of promoting individual responsibility and social responsibility as opposing or unrelated goals, the community counseling model embraces both as complementary and interrelated dimensions of the helping process.

METHODS FOR DEVELOPING SOCIAL RESPONSIBILITY   McWhirter (1994) describes a variety of ways practitioners can help nurture a sense of individual and social responsibility in counseling. Her model of "empowerment counseling" outlines a host of practical strategies counselors can use to promote the individual and social responsibility of clients victimized by racism or physical violence and those discriminated against because of their sexual identity, age, or physical disability.

Other counseling interventions that stimulate individual and social responsibility include peer mediation and counseling programs in the schools (Lupton-Smith, Carruthers, Flythe, Modest, & Goettee, 1995). Counselors strive to foster an increased level of individual responsibility in these programs by following two steps:

1. Meeting with students (individually or in small groups) to discuss the importance of developing a broad range of life competencies and leadership skills that will enable them to communicate more effectively with people experiencing conflicts and/or other difficulties in their lives
2. Providing training that facilitates the development of a broad range of interpersonal problem-solving skills within the schools

Besides helping students develop the interpersonal skills they need for a greater sense of personal competence and responsibility, these programs also try to increase the peer mediators' or counselors' sense of social responsibility. This is accomplished by creating opportunities for students to see how their new skills and competencies help create a more positive and responsive school environment. By encouraging students to use their newly acquired human-relations skills to help their peers learn more effective ways of resolving conflicts and coping with stress, they directly experience the connection between their own personal development and the benefits that people in their community or school can derive from it.

D'Andrea (1994) outlines counseling strategies used to foster an increased sense of individual and social responsibility among adults who had been diagnosed with chronic mental health problems. Working within a partial hospitalization setting, counselors set up regular psychotherapy groups to facilitate an exploration of specific client concerns as well as to initiate discussions about their adult responsibilities.

The latter discussions included an in-depth examination of clients' responsibilities to themselves, their families, their therapeutic community, and their broader socio-political community. Much time was spent talking about the relationship between people's psychological well-being and their level of individual and social responsibility (D'Andrea, 1994).

In attempting to identify specific ways to become more responsive and engaged in their social environments, the group members discussed the various volunteer programs, social action projects, and self-help organizations in the community. The clients were then encouraged to select one of them and to participate in at least two of their meetings.

The information, support, and encouragement generated in these psychotherapy groups resulted in several members joining various local volunteer organizations (such as church groups and school tutorial programs), volunteering to work in local voter registration campaigns, and testifying at public hearings to protest proposed cutbacks in governmental spending for statewide mental health programs. The clients who participated in these activities reported an increased sense of personal worth and psychological well-being as a result of their involvement (D'Andrea, 1994).

Developmental Stages

Many factors influence a person's readiness to become more personally and socially responsible. These include self-confidence, life skills, coping abilities, and environmental support. One of the most important is psychological maturity. Being able to assess accurately the developmental stages clients grow through as they change is a vital prerequisite for planning and implementing individual and group counseling interventions (D'Andrea & Daniels, 1994).

Becoming more personally and socially responsible requires *developmental* changes, or persistent and complex transitions that lead to qualitative differentiation. Thus, developmental changes represent transformational shifts in a person's previous manner of thinking, perceiving, feeling, and acting.

In the past, developmental theorists have deemphasized the value of higher-stage functioning, arguing that one should not construe it as "better than" lower-stage functioning (Loevinger, 1976). Recently, however, some have suggested that acquiring the psychological skills and characteristics associated with more mature stages of psychological development is particularly important, given the complex demands and challenges of the current sociopolitical environment. In this regard, D'Andrea (1988) states that "from a developmental point of view, higher stage functioning is discerningly 'better' in the long run in terms of effectively coping with the demands of a sophisticated post-industrial society" (p. 24).

If this is true, counselors would do well to promote their clients' psychological development by intentionally fostering the acquisition of greater reasoning abilities and behavioral competencies. Accordingly, while the community counseling framework emphasizes the need to strengthen each client's sense of personal power and self-efficacy, it also acknowledges the importance of creating conditions within the counseling process that intentionally stimulate movement to higher stages of psychological development.

However, to implement this sort of developmental approach effectively, counselors must first have a clear theoretical understanding of both the process and the content of human development. Several structural developmental theories have emerged over the past 30 years; these useful theories can help counselors better understand both the "how" and the "what" of human development (Kegan, 1982; Kohlberg, 1984; Loevinger, 1976).

STRUCTURAL DEVELOPMENT   Structural developmental models are based on several fundamental theoretical propositions:

1. The impetus for development is based on an inherent drive to construct meaning from one's life experiences (Kegan, 1982).
2. Psychological development is manifested by a series of stages that are identifiable, invariant, and hierarchical (Kohlberg, 1984).
3. Movement from stage to stage is characterized by more complex ways of thinking, acting, and feeling (Loevinger, 1976).

These developmental stages represent qualitatively different ways of looking at oneself and the world at large. Each stage provides a unique frame of reference for *meaning-making,* or the innate human propensity to construct meaning out of one's life experiences actively rather than passively receiving meaning from the environment.

Movement from one developmental stage to the next is marked by a sense of greater personal competence and maturity. As individuals develop psychologically, they demonstrate an increased capacity to interpret life experiences in differentiated, comprehensive, and integrated ways (D'Andrea & Daniels, 1994). Their perspective also moves from centering on themselves to taking into mind the views and needs of others. Consequently, higher-stage functioning results in more accurate interpretations of situations and events than lower-stage functioning (Hayes, 1986).

Structural theories of psychological development also state that developmental stages emerge in a predictable and sequential pattern in which each stage integrates and reorganizes the elements and characteristics of the preceding stages. This pattern presents itself as a succession of qualitatively different developmental turning points referred to as *milestone sequences* (Loevinger, 1976, p. 55).

From a structuralist perspective, though stages of development do not entirely depend on chronological maturation, they do rely somewhat on chronology. As Young-Eisendrath (1988) points out,

> Early stages typically evolve with chronology when supportive
> environments are present. . . . [However], when further development
> is not supported by environmental factors, a person may stop
> developing. Hence, some adults function at stages that are more
> typical of childhood or adolescence than adulthood. (p 71)

Support for these developmental premises has emerged from a variety of empirical studies conducted among people from diverse settings and cultural backgrounds (Kohlberg, 1984; Loevinger, 1976).

Although all structuralists use hierarchical models to describe the process of psychological growth, they apply their models to different aspects of human development. For instance, Loevinger (1976) describes the stages of ego development, while Kohlberg (1984) explains the process and levels of moral reasoning. Underutilized by many counseling practitioners, these developmental theories offer much potential in terms of understanding the content and process of healthy psychological development and maturation within the context of counseling.

Ego Development.   Loevinger's (1976) research has resulted in the identification of the stages of ego development. One can understand *ego develop-*

ment as a process in which individuals evolve psychologically from less to more complexity, differentiation, and self-reflection. This process involves a shift from an impulsive and egocentric orientation to a more self-controlled and allocentric one (Young-Eisendrath, 1988).

As defined by Loevinger, the ego provides a way for individuals to make sense of their life experiences. As a person moves to higher levels of ego development, she or he becomes better able to deal with complex concepts. Loevinger's framework consists of seven developmental stages and two levels, briefly described as follows:

1. **The Presocial Stage:** People cannot psychologically differentiate themselves from others at this point in their development. Although this is a normal stage for infants, children who fail to move beyond it are referred to as *autistic*.

2. **The Impulsive Stage:** Here, people are preoccupied with their own impulses, bodily feelings, and aggressiveness. In light of the limited cognitive abilities and the lack of impulse control that characterizes this developmental stage, people cannot comprehend the rudiments of individual or social responsibility.

3. **The Self-Protective Stage:** At this point in their development, individuals can control their impulses better, usually out of fear of being caught or punished by others. They are manipulative and demonstrate a heightened sense of self-protection. At this stage, individuals begin to form basic ideas of individual responsibility. However, the dominance of self-centeredness (egocentrism), which characterizes this stage, greatly limits their understanding of and interest in social responsibility.

4. **The Conformist Stage:** At this stage, a person's cognitive capacities are based on simple and concrete operations. This cognitive style is accompanied by a preoccupation with conforming to external rules and being accepted by others. This strong need to conform to group standards represents the emergence of an elementary sense of social responsibility.

5. **The Self-Aware Level:** People begin to manifest the capacity to differentiate their own norms, values, and goals from those of the group. A more mature understanding of a person's individual and social responsibilities is intentionally reflected in his or her thoughts and behaviors at this stage.

6. **The Conscientious Stage:** Here, developing more complex cognitive capacities increases people's ability to act consistently according to their own self-determined standards. At this stage, people exhibit heightened feelings of guilt and shame when they fail to fulfill their personal or social responsibilities.

7. **The Individualistic Level:** Heightened interest and concern about independence-dependence, personal obligations, and loyalty mark

this stage. Internal conflicts regarding personal, social, and familial responsibilities often emerge at this level.

8. The Autonomous Stage: Here, people have learned to cope with conflicting inner needs and tolerate ambiguity, to demonstrate respect for others' autonomy, to show greater concern about their social impact and self-fulfillment, to be more objective, to understand complex concepts, and to approach issues broadly with an increasing awareness of the social contexts that shape human dynamics.

9. The Integrated Stage: Individuals operating at this stage resolve inner conflicts well and renounce the unattainable, cherish individuality, and demonstrate greater concern and respect for the integrity and identity of others.

Although these stages always occur in the same order, people do not necessarily move through them all. In fact only about 1% of the adult population is thought to demonstrate the psychological competencies and characteristics associated with the Integrated Stage of ego development (Loevinger, 1976).

Moral Development.   *Moral development* refers to the process by which individuals acquire a sense of "right and wrong" in society. Furthermore, it explains the ways people develop the cognitive abilities necessary to facilitate a more complex understanding of ethical principles and behavior (Gilligan, 1982; Gilligan, Ward, & Taylor, 1988; Kohlberg, 1984).

Over the past 40 years, two figures have made particularly significant theoretical and empirical contributions in the area of moral development. Kohlberg (1969, 1971) has pioneered much of the modern psychological thinking about the stages people pass through as they develop a more sophisticated understanding of moral issues. More recently, Gilligan (1982) has added to Kohlberg's theory by describing differences in the way men and women make sense of and try to resolve moral dilemmas.

For Kohlberg, *moral development* refers to "the reasoning process by which individuals determine what is right or fair in resolving moral conflicts, which are really conflicts of perspective or interest" (Hayes, 1986, p. 74). The reasoning an individual uses in dealing with moral dilemmas determines his or her stage of development. Kohlberg (1984) has identified three levels of moral development, with each level comprising two distinct stages:

LEVEL 1: Preconventional
          Stage 1 *Heteronomous Morality:* At this stage in their
                   development, people try to avoid punishment, and
                   they accept the power of authorities in making moral

choices. Furthermore, they consider the rights of others only in relation to actual physical damage and punishment.

Stage 2 *Individualism, Instrumental Purpose, and Exchange:* People judge behavior to be right or wrong based on self-interest while recognizing that others also have interests. Human rights are basically associated with the equal exchange of products, services, resources, possessions, etc.

LEVEL 2: Conventional

Stage 3 *Mutual Interpersonal Expectations, Relationships, and Conformity:* People are concerned with living up to the expectations of others. Caring for others and following the "Golden Rule" mark this stage.

Stage 4 *Social System and Conscience:* People are concerned with upholding laws, performing their social duties, and preventing the breakdown of the system.

LEVEL 3: Postconventional, or Principled

Stage 5 *Social Contract and Individual Rights:* The individual understands that most values and opinions are relative but tries to uphold them in the interest of the social contract. At this stage, people try to identify the greatest good for the greatest number.

Stage 6 *Universal Ethical Principles:* People choose their own ethical principles and maintain a personal commitment to them. Principles such as justice and the dignity of human beings override the law in cases of conflict.

APPLYING DEVELOPMENTAL THEORY IN COUNSELING PRACTICE Kohlberg's (1984) and Gilligan's (1982) theories of moral development as well as Loevinger's (1976) theory of ego development have tremendous implications for counseling. Several practitioners have outlined ways one can use these developmental theories to promote clients' psychological maturity in counseling practice, including the following:

1. Intentionally matching specific counseling approaches to the current developmental stages of their clients (D'Andrea & Daniels, 1992, 1994)
2. Presenting clients with cognitive conflicts in the form of moral dilemmas and exposing them to higher levels of thinking during individual and group counseling sessions (Kuhmerker, 1991)

The most comprehensive integration of structural developmental theories for counseling practice to date is Ivey's (1986, 1991, 1994) Developmental Counseling and Therapy (DCT) framework. Ivey (1994) highlights two aspects of the counseling process thought to particularly foster clients' psychological development:

1. **Conducting a developmental evaluation:** This involves assessing the way clients "organize the world—how they think and feel about themselves, other people, and situations" (Ivey, 1994, p. 265).

2. **Using developmental questioning skills:** After becoming familiar with the client's meaning-making system (Kegan, 1982), practitioners can proceed by intentionally matching their language and communication style to the individual's developmental perspective.

The DCT model provides counselors with an excellent and detailed overview of specific counseling methods they might use in attempting to stimulate a client's psychological development.

Multicultural Counseling and Therapy (MCT)

Ivey (1994) has recently extended his thinking about DCT by directing particular attention to the cultural dimension of counseling. As a result, he and others have developed a new model called Multicultural Counseling and Therapy (MCT) (Sue, Ivey, & Pedersen, 1996). The many theoretical and practical considerations addressed in this model apply particularly well to the counseling profession, especially in light of the rapid cultural diversification of the United States and the increasing need for counselors to implement culturally specific approaches.

The product of many minds, MCT has emerged over the past several years as a synthesis of ideas shared by various developmental (Piaget, 1970), cultural identity (Cross, 1971, 1991; Helms, 1990; Sue & Sue, 1990), and educational (Freire, 1972) theorists. Although MCT is a relatively new approach to counseling, it is gaining recognition among theorists, researchers, and practitioners in the field (Ivey, Ivey, & Simek-Morgan, 1993; Rigazio-DiGilio, 1989).

When working with clients from diverse populations, counselors must understand how a person's cultural, ethnic, and racial background affects his or her psychological development (Sue & Sue, 1990). Over the past ten years, multicultural counseling theorists and researchers have outlined several new developmental models that help explain this effect (Ponterotto & Pedersen, 1993).

Although these models do not fall under the same classification as structural developmental theories, they comprise a set of stages that relate to one's identity development as part of a cultural group in the United States. The descriptions of these stages provide counselors with useful ways of thinking about clients' ethnic (Phinney, 1990), racial (Carter, 1995; Helms, 1990), and minority identity development (Atkinson, Morten, & Sue, 1993). The following section provides a brief overview of one of these models and discusses its implications for counseling practice.

STAGES OF MINORITY IDENTITY DEVELOPMENT   The Minority Identity Development (MID) model (Atkinson et al., 1993) provides an interesting explanation of the ways in which people from nonwhite minority groups develop a sense of personal identity within the context of a social environment that frequently devalues their cultural, ethnic, and racial background. In this model, *minority* refers to people who continue to be oppressed by the dominant societal group "primarily because of their group membership" (Atkinson et al., 1993, p. 13). Although they focus on people from diverse backgrounds, the authors note that this definition allows women to be considered "minority group members" even though they constitute a numerical majority in the United States, because they continue to endure various forms of oppression.

This model is "anchored in the belief that all minority groups experience the common force of oppression, and as a result, will all generate a strong sense of self- and group-identity in spite of their oppressive conditions" (Ponterotto & Pedersen, 1993, p. 45). Although the MID framework presents stages, the authors point out that one can best conceptualize it as a continuous process in which the characteristics of the various stages blend into one another without clear or abrupt demarcations (Atkinson et al., 1993).

The MID model comprises five stages. Each of these stages is defined with respect to one's (1) attitudes toward oneself, (2) attitudes toward others from the same racial-ethnic background, (3) attitudes toward people in other minority groups, and (4) attitudes toward the white majority in the United States.

Though not intended to serve as a comprehensive personality theory, the MID model serves as a framework to help counselors understand minority clients' attitudes and behaviors. The model can help counselors become more sensitized to the following:

1. The role oppression plays in a minority person's psychological development
2. The differences that can exist between members of the same minority group with respect to their cultural identity
3. The potential developmental changes that persons from various cultural, ethnic, and racial groups may manifest during their lifespan

These developmental changes have been described in the following stages.

1. The Conformist Stage.   Minority individuals operating at the Conformist Stage show an unequivocal preference for the dominant cultural values over those of their own cultural-racial group. Their choice of role models, life-styles, and values all follow the lead of the dominant societal group. Those physical and cultural characteristics that single them out as minorities cause them pain and embarrassment; they often view these characteristics with disdain or repress them from consciousness.

Implications for Counseling.   Unlikely to seek counseling services for issues related to their cultural identity, clients at the Conformist Stage instead tend to seek out counselors from the dominant cultural group rather than those with the same minority background as themselves. Such clients usually present issues amenable to decision-making, problem-solving, and goal-oriented counseling approaches and techniques.

2. The Dissonance Stage.   In the Dissonance Stage, people from minority groups encounter information and experiences inconsistent with the values and beliefs associated with the Conformist Stage. These experiences and information stimulate an increased level of cognitive dissonance that leads these people to question and perhaps even challenge attitudes acquired in the Conformist Stage.

Implications for Counseling.   At the Dissonance Stage, individuals are preoccupied with questions concerning their personal identity, self-concept, and self-esteem. They typically perceive personal problems as related to their cultural identity and background. Emotional problems may develop when they cannot resolve conflicts that arise when dominant cultural views and values conflict with those of their minority group.

Clients at this stage prefer to work with counselors who possess a good working knowledge of their cultural, ethnic, and/or racial group. Recommended counseling approaches for clients operating at this stage include those that facilitate self-exploration and the acquisition of stress-management skills.

3. The Resistance and Immersion Stage.   In this stage of development, clients experience strong discontent and discomfort with the views and values of the dominant cultural group. These feelings are accompanied with a heightened desire to eliminate the oppression and injustice minority groups experience. At this stage, clients typically express negative reactions and anger toward members of the dominant societal group.

Implications for Counseling.   The likelihood that people functioning at this stage will seek formal counseling is slim. However, those instances when counseling is sought tend to occur as responses to immediate personal crises and with a counselor from the same minority group as the client.

Clients at this stage usually view all psychological problems as a product of their oppression. Useful counseling strategies include group process interventions and referrals to community- or social-action groups and organizations.

4. The Introspection Stage.   Clients operating at this stage manifest discontent and discomfort with many of the rigidly held views associated with the Resistance and Immersion Stage. As such, they often focus on their personal and psychological autonomy.

Implications for Counseling.   Clients at the Introspection Stage are torn between identification with their minority group and the need to exercise greater personal freedom and decision making. Much more likely to seek counseling than those at the Resistance and Immersion Stage, people at the Introspection Stage generally prefer counselors from their own cultural group. These clients, however, may view counselors from other cultural backgrounds as credible sources of help if their worldviews resemble those of the clients. Counseling approaches recommended at this stage include problem-solving and decision-making methods as well as techniques that promote stress-management skills and encourage self-exploration of culturally relevant issues and concerns.

5. The Synergistic Articulation and Awareness Stage.   At this stage, clients feel self-fulfillment regarding their personal and cultural identity. The conflicts and discomforts manifested at the Introspection Stage have generally been resolved, allowing individuals to experience a greater sense of personal control and flexibility in their lives. Clients objectively examine the cultural values of other minority groups as well as the dominant group and accept or rejected them on the basis of experience gained in earlier developmental stages.

Implications for Counseling.   Clients at the Synergistic Articulation and Awareness Stage manifest a heightened desire for psychological freedom. Their sense of minority identity is well balanced by a genuine appreciation of other cultures. Attitudinal similarity between the counselor and the client, rather than issues related to the client and counselor's group membership similarity, becomes an important determinant of successful counseling outcomes (Atkinson et al., 1993).

The MID model complements the community counseling framework because it focuses on how the broader sociopolitical environment influences the psychological development of people from devalued groups. As mentioned in the preceding chapters, the community counseling model centers on the belief that counselors need to do the following:

1. Be keenly aware of the ways in which the environment impacts clients' development, and
2. Be able to provide counseling services that foster their ability to constructively negotiate oppressive environmental circumstances

Using the MID model can greatly help counselors understand how participation in various environmental institutions, organizations, and systems can affect the culturally diverse clients' psychological development.

SYSTEMS THEORY AND ENVIRONMENTAL INFLUENCES

With its attention to environmental factors, community counseling is influenced by systems theory. General systems theory (von Bertalanffy, 1968) presents an alternative to the linear reductionistic thinking underlying Newtonian science. Newtonian thought is reductionistic in that it attempts to study complex phenomena by breaking them down into their smallest components. It is linear because it attempts to understand these smaller parts as a series of cause-and-effect relationships that are less complex than the phenomenon itself.

In contrast, von Bertalanffy's general systems theory views all living things as open systems, or systems that interact with their environment. When using general systems theory in counseling practice, counselors focus on discovering consistent patterns of interaction, interrelationships, probabilities, and organizing principles rather than identifying linear, causal relationships. In commenting on general systems theory, Steinglass (1978) states,

> If a system is defined as a set of units or elements standing in some consistent relationship or interactional stance with each other, then the first concept is the notion that any system is composed of elements that are organized by the consistent nature of the relationship between these elements. Consistency is the key; consistent elements are related to each other in a consistently predictable fashion. (p. 305)

One can define organisms as open systems because their boundaries allow them to take and give information during environmental interactions.

Within these living systems, subsystems interact in a moderately predictable manner within the context of the larger system. Umbarger (1983) describes additional characteristics of living systems as follows:

1. **Part and whole:** The system as a whole is greater than the sum of its parts.
2. **Information, error, and feedback:** Feedback loops within living systems indicate error when the system encounters dissimilarities to the system's overall design.
3. **Feedback and homeostasis:** The feedback loops enable the system to maintain a steady state.
4. **Feedback and growth:** Feedback can also trigger changes that may be necessary to the system's continued life.
5. **Life and tension:** Periods of growth alternate with periods of stability.
6. **Circularity:** Cause-and-effect relationships, which are linear, are secondary to ongoing processes, which are circular.
7. **Change:** Change in one part of the system affects changes in other parts and in the system as a whole.

A systems perspective shapes the way counselors interpret their clients' issues and problems. To date, family therapy and counseling models represent the most widespread application of systems theory in the profession. During the past 20 years, however, two additional theoretical forces—postmodernism and contextualism—have gained noticeable popularity as offshoots of systems thinking. Collectively, these three forces will continue to exert a significant impact on the practice of professional counseling well into the 21st century.

Family Counseling

Because family systems have such an obvious impact on their clients' development, many counselors view the family system itself as the most appropriate target for intervention. Counselors who concentrate on working with families feel that the individual cannot really be separated from the family, or the sick from the well, or the cause of a dysfunction from its effect.

In family counseling, practitioners recast clients' problems in terms of the behavior's context (family environment), without which one cannot understand the problem. Rather than seeing the source of problems or symptoms as the "sick" individual, the family counseling approach views the person simply as a symptom-bearer who expresses his or her family's disequilibrium (Goldenberg & Goldenberg, 1985).

Lewis et al. (1988) note that one can characterize families as open systems according to the principles listed by Umbarger (1983). According to

Lewis and her colleagues, every family has its own homeostasis, or preferred steady state, that may or may not be "healthy" but that is monitored through feedback and control mechanisms and protected by the system as a whole.

Each family has a set of rules that governs its interactions and makes them predictable. Each family system includes subsystems (such as spouses, parents, siblings) that carry out specialized functions and attempt to preserve the integrity of the overall system. Each is part of an organized whole, making it impossible to consider intervening in one part without taking the others into account (Lewis et al., 1988). Thus, attention directed to the client's personal context is a key consideration in family counseling, as it is in the community counseling model.

There exist as many approaches to family counseling as to individual counseling. Satir (1967, 1972) focuses on improving the family's communication patterns to enhance the self-esteem and growth of each member. Bowen (1982) emphasizes increasing the differentiation of each member. Minuchin's structural approach (1979, 1984) helps family counselors understand the structure of specific family systems and ways to make such systems more functional. The strategic therapy of Haley (1976) and Madanes (1981) exemplifies the communications approach to family therapy, which is derived from Gregory Bateson's work in Palo Alto in the 1950s. In the communications approach, counselors work with family members to "discover the social situation that makes the problem necessary" (Haley, 1976, p. 9). Finally, in behavioral family counseling (Liberman, 1981), problem behaviors are considered as socially reinforced, learned behaviors malleable to environmental change.

Postmodernism and Family Counseling

Traditional family counseling theories are all based on "modernistic thinking" (Lewis, 1993). Cheal (1993) defines *modernism* as a worldview that depends on rationality for solving problems and assumes that progress will bring about improvements in the human condition. The dominance of modernistic thinking in the 20th century has led family counselors to view the process of change as moving from temporary disintegration and disequilibrium to adaptive reorganization and the reestablishment of a sense of psychological equilibrium and normality among family members (Lewis, 1993).

As Gergen (1992) further explains,

> We now seem to be witnessing an erosion of modernism and
> confronting a slide into a new kind of intellectual and moral chaos
> that challenges all existing ideas of who we are and what we want,
> which undermines all previous assumptions about truth and order,

> that perhaps even pronounces the coup de grace on the traditional
> family as we have known it. (p. 52)

The rise of postmodernistic thinking during the past decade sharply contrasts with the modernistic perspective and is beginning to influence
the way counselors conceptualize the purpose and process of family counseling.

Counseling practitioners who operate from a postmodernistic perspective recognize the legitimacy of diverse worldviews that people from different cultural backgrounds exhibit. As a result, these professionals accept the
relativity of the meaning of such concepts as human development, psychological well-being, and family life.

In discussing postmodernistic thinking and family counseling,
Bernardes (1993) points out that, although a minority of families actually
fit the definition of the "normal nuclear family," this traditional concept
remains an integral part of U.S. society's discourse and notion of normality.
In fact, the traditional concept of the normal family is so deeply ingrained
into the public's consciousness that many counselors have difficulty relating
and supporting alternative family structures such as single-mother or gay-
parent families in their professional endeavors.

Lewis (1993) stresses that the continued attachment to the traditional
family model leads counselors to collaborate in oppression by reinforcing
the idea that people can (and perhaps even should) make their own families fit a particular norm. In discussing the effects of this thinking on the
victims of domestic abuse, Bernardes (1993) explains that these clients frequently view themselves at fault for the abuse they have suffered:

> The guilt and shame of these victims is the direct consequence of our
> own refusal, thus far, to recognize our responsibility in portraying the
> image of the normal nuclear family that has become such a popular
> yardstick against which ordinary people measure personal success and
> failure. (p. 48)

The increasing recognition and acceptance of the relativity of such
terms as *family, human development,* and *psychological well-being* among
people in diverse client populations will likely create confusion, anxiety,
and resistance among many modernistic-thinking counselors. Lewis (1993)
notes that despite this reaction to postmodern thinking, the 21st-century
counselor must understand that the contemporary experience of theoretical
pluralism and fragmentation is not a temporary stop on the road to reorganization but, rather, a permanent state that mental health practitioners
must accept.

By adopting a postmodernistic perspective in their work, counselors
can recognize, confront, and move beyond the culturally embedded meanings and images of the "normal family," "mental health," and "human devel-

opment" that are often disguised as universal truths. Given the increasing diversification of the United States, the future viability of the counseling profession largely depends on counselors' ability and willingness to develop intervention strategies that reflect a postmodernistic and relativistic perspective in their work (Daniels & D'Andrea, 1996). In doing so, counselors would avoid inadvertently contributing to their clients' psychological oppression.

The community counseling model embraces psychological empowerment and personal liberation as the ultimate goals of individual, small-group, and family counseling. Systems theories can help counselors gain a more accurate and comprehensive understanding of various client problems. In that vein, another off shoot of systems theory, contextualism, has emerged over the past ten years.

Contextualism

The contextual perspective views human development as a process in which individuals undergo continuous changes stimulated by their unique biological, environmental, social, and cultural contexts (Steenbarger & LeClair, 1995; Thomas, 1996). With this definition in mind, the similarity between contextualism, human ecological theories (Blocher, 1966; Germain, 1991), and the community counseling model is apparent.

These theoretical perspectives share the belief that counselors cannot effectively help clients by viewing them as individuals detached from the multiple contexts that continuously influence their development. In this sense, the notion of the "self-in-relation," which emerges from the work of female psychologists (Miller, 1991), replaces the traditional counseling conception of the individual and the autonomous self.

Several important differences exist between the structural-developmental theories mentioned earlier in this chapter and the contextual view of counseling. First, contextual theorists have criticized the structural developmental models for failing to explain the open-endedness and plasticity of human development, as noted in several longitudinal studies (Lerner & Kauffman, 1985; Steenbarger, 1993). In this regard, Steenbarger and LeClair (1995) point out that relatively little empirical evidence exists to confirm the fundamental structural developmental claim that

> individuals march in linear fashion down a series of stages toward increasing cognitive and psychosocial complexity. Personality research (Magnusson & Allen, 1983), as well as developmental studies of intelligence (Gelman & Baillargeon, 1983), suggest that our traditional theories of human development artificially constrain the range of possible developmental outcomes, limiting their explanatory utility. (pp. 177–178)

Thus, from a contextual perspective, one sees psychological growth as much more plastic, varied, and open than from a structural point of view.

Second, the contextually oriented counselor views change, not growth, as the fundamental developmental event counseling needs to facilitate. The emphasis contextualists place on psychological variation and change complements the postmodern notion that individuals construct various meanings out of their life experiences, resulting in the creation of multiple realities. For this reason, again, an increasing acceptance of contextualist principles will undoubtedly result in a heightened sense of chaos within the counseling profession as linear explanations of human development, perpetuated by the traditional counseling paradigm, come into question.

Third, one should refer to contextualism as a "metatheory," because it operates at a higher level of abstraction than traditional counseling theories do. In attempting to clarify the relationship between contextualism and counseling practice, Steenbarger and LeClair (1995) note the following:

> Although there are many current theories that try to put a contextualist worldview into practice, only a certain class of theories—those of a systems nature—truly qualify as contextualist. This is because any theory that seeks to address the fit between person and context must embrace both of these elements, elaborating the linkages among them. Many well-known contextualist theories in counseling limit their consideration of context to a single domain, including interactional-interpersonal (Claiborn & Lichtenberg, 1989); cultural (Sue & Sue, 1990); and ecological (Blocher, 1966) contexts. As developmental theorists have observed, however, development is inherently multicontextual, affected by overlapping biological, psychological, social, cultural, and historical contexts. (p. 181)

Contextualism represents the type of comprehensive thinking counselors will need to impact the psychological well-being of larger numbers of people in the 21st century. This metatheory offers an exciting alternative to the simplistic, linear, and remedial counseling theories that have dominated the profession for the past 50 years. By incorporating a contextual perspective in their work, counselors will enable themselves to move beyond the limitations of the traditional counseling paradigm as they strive to find more effective ways of fostering their clients' personal empowerment and liberation.

Counseling for Personal Liberation

Counseling for liberation is part of the broader framework of Multicultural Counseling and Therapy (MCT) discussed earlier (Ivey, 1995). Counselors who use this liberation approach to counseling help clients understand how their relationship with their social/political/cultural contexts influence their psychological development. The attention that Ivey's liberation counseling model directs to clients' contextual relationships sharply contrasts with most traditional counseling approaches, which emphasize individualism, autonomy, and self-actualization. Commenting on this departure, Ivey (1995) states, "Not helping clients see how their difficulties are the logical result of developmental, social, and contextual history constitutes a major failing of today's psychotherapy and counseling" (p. 54).

Using a personal liberation approach in counseling requires a shift from an individualistic framework to a *self-in-relation* perspective (Miller, 1991). Over the past 20 years, several feminist psychologists have explored issues counselors need to address when counseling from such a perspective (Amaro, 1995; Gilligan, 1982; Marecek, 1995; Miller, 1986).

To promote clients' personal liberation, Ivey (1995) claims that counselors must develop a collaborative relationship with their clients. Thus, rather than establishing and maintaining a doctor-patient or therapist-client relationship, counselors must build "egalitarian relationships in which the client becomes a partner, exploring with the other . . . new meaning and new ways of being. In doing so, the person who 'helps' may learn as much as the person being 'helped' " (Ivey, 1995, p. 57).

Given (1) its emphasis on the context of a person's life and (2) its reluctance to acknowledge that any problem lies totally in the client, Ivey's personal liberation model clearly fits into the community counseling framework. Further, both are designed to foster clients' empowerment by helping them learn about the ways their unique personal contexts affect their cognitions, emotions, and actions.

Another major task in liberation counseling is to increase what Ivey calls the *critical consciousness* of both the counselor and the client. To develop this consciousness, both must use counseling to increase their own understanding of themselves as contextual beings.

Increasing one's critical consciousness through counseling involves two overlapping tasks. First, one must take the time to examine how one's psychological development, self-esteem, sense of personal power, and behavior stem from environmental-interpersonal experiences. Second, one must examine how such important contextual characteristics as gender, socioeconomic class, and cultural, ethnic, and racial background necessarily influence one's experiences.

In the final step of liberation counseling, practitioners help individuals implement new actions that address the unhealthy environmental conditions that underlie their difficulties. This is followed by a period of reflection and assessment of these actions. The combination of action and reflection is vital to liberation counseling because they present opportunities for clients to develop a greater understanding of the interconnection between their daily contextual experiences, level of psychological well-being, and sense of internal locus of control (Ivey, 1995).

CONTRAST WITH TRADITIONAL APPROACHES   The rise of multicultural and feminist theories over the past 30 years has increased criticism aimed at traditional counseling approaches. In providing a critical analysis of psychoanalytic counseling approaches, Ivey (1995) refers to the work of Brown (1959), who has pointed out that "human consciousness can be liberated from the parental (Oedipal) complex only by being liberated from its cultural [contextual] derivatives, the paternalistic state, and patriarchal God" (Brown, 1959, p. 155).

Humanistic and cognitive-behavioral theories have met with similar criticism from advocates of the liberation counseling perspective. For example, Lerman (1992) points out that humanistic theories have generally "failed to recognize that no person constructs their own reality without external influences" (p. 13). She further notes that such hallowed humanistic concepts as self-actualization and autonomy are middle-class, Euro-centric products simply not relevant to the many groups who value collectivism and interdependence.

Cognitive-behavioral approaches do take into consideration many of the client's contextual characteristics. However, as Kantrowitz and Ballou (1992) explain, when counselors use this approach in practice, "individuals are fundamentally expected to improve their adaptive capacities to meet the environmental conditions, which serve to reinforce the dominant social standards" (p. 79). Rather than accepting the primacy of external conditions, liberation counseling encourages clients to use their newly developed critical consciousness to influence their environments and, ultimately, to help transform the status quo.

Ivey (1995) provides the following case vignettes to help explain the difference between traditional counseling interventions and liberation counseling:

> Consider the African American client who comes for therapy to
> seek stress management techniques to control his hypertension. We
> know cognitive-behavioral techniques can be both emotionally
> and physically beneficial. Liberation counselors and psychotherapists
> would support and utilize a cognitive-behavioral approach but would
> consider these techniques insufficient. They would also consider it
> necessary to help this client examine his cultural context and
> consider how the constant barrage of racist acts in society contributes
> to his concerns. Similarly, women who are diagnosed as depressed
> or "borderline" need to be helped to see family and cultural issues
> of sexism as underlying much of their difficulty. (Ivey, 1995,
> p. 54)

STRATEGIES: LIBERATION COUNSELING IN ACTION The following brief description of two clients provides examples of some of the strategies and benefits of implementing the liberation counseling model in practice.

> Two male clients were referred to counseling. While both of the clients were employed in similar management positions by the same company and were the same age, one was White and the other was an African American.
>
> Both clients indicated feeling exhausted and depressed as a result of the intense demands of their job. However, in addition to the stresses that were directly associated with the demands of the job, the African American client talked about the pressure he experienced as a result of being the only non-White employee in the company. In this regard, he reported constantly feeling pressured to do better than the other managers in his division to overcome the negative stereotypes he believed some of his co-workers and supervisor had about African Americans.
>
> The counselor utilized a variety of stress management techniques with both of these clients to help them develop new skills to deal with the demands of their careers. However, additional time and energy was directed towards exploring a number of concerns expressed by the African American client regarding his perceptions of racial discrimination on the job. In doing so, the counseling sessions included an examination of the client's and the counselor's beliefs about racism, discussion of their past experiences and knowledge of racism, their feelings about these experiences, and an examination of the power dynamics that were linked to the racial discrimination and prejudice the client experienced at work.
>
> Recognizing that it was very likely that he would encounter other types of racism in the future, the client and counselor worked together to develop new insights and skills for dealing with the sort of stress that will predictably accompany future negative racial experiences. This included exploring issues related to the client's level of minority identity development, using a variety of relaxation techniques, utilizing assertiveness training to enhance his ability to confront racism and discrimination in an assertive rather than an aggressive manner in the workplace, and encouraging him to join an African-American men's group comprised of individuals who were experiencing similar stresses in various aspects of their lives.
>
> During his last meeting with the counselor, this client reflected on the positive benefits he derived from this approach to counseling. He specifically indicated that he was able to more effectively reduce the stress-induced reactions he was having at work by using the relaxation techniques and the assertiveness training to discuss some of his frustrations with his co-workers and supervisor. "I have learned a lot about myself and how to better deal with some of the things that

stress me out. I really feel like I understand myself better and appreciate knowing how I can change some of the things going on around me in positive ways instead of just letting situations and people stress me out. I just wish I had learned these things earlier in my life." (D'Andrea, 1995, pp. 2–4).

The issues covered in the preceding sections of this chapter reflect important considerations underlying the various approaches and strategies counselors might use with their clients. However, the specific direction counselors take with their clients—family counseling, contextual approaches, or Ivey's liberation counseling framework—depends on their assessment of clients' needs and strengths.

PRACTICAL APPLICATIONS OF COMMUNITY COUNSELING

The community counseling framework stresses the importance of conducting a comprehensive and holistic assessment of a client's developmental, cultural, and environmental strengths and challenges before one plans an intervention. By using the results of such an assessment to select and implement direct counseling services, counselors demonstrate particular sophistication and intentionality in their work (D'Andrea & Daniels, 1994; Ivey et al., 1993).

Assessment

CLIENTS' INVOLVEMENT   Because the community counseling framework operates from an empowerment perspective, assessment is guided by the premise that clients are responsible for running their own lives. Counselors can help identify problem areas and suggest possible solutions; however, to be most effective, the assessment process must elicit the client's active participation. By participating in assessment, clients can both learn about themselves and begin to increase their sense of control over their actions. These benefits can occur only through a practical, multifaceted, culturally sensitive assessment process easily understood by clients.

In community counseling, assessment does not necessarily aim at placing clients in appropriate treatment; rather, it helps them devise a plan by which they can transcend problematic situations and improve the quality of their lives. From this perspective, the question to be answered through assessment is not "What is wrong with this person?" but "What is keeping this person from effectively managing his or her life right now?" The best way to answer this question is through an assessment process with the following characteristics:

1. Procedures that focus on individuals' strengths and resources as well as their deficits and challenges
2. The active involvement and understanding of clients
3. A natural flow into the planning process, so that each identified difficulty comes to be addressed in an individualized action plan
4. A procedure that takes into account both the stressors and the support available to clients
5. Attention to clients' cultural/ethnic/racial identity development and the potential strengths and stressors associated with their ethnic/racial background

Whatever issues might bring them to a counselor's office, most clients have in common the need to increase their sense of control over events going on in their lives. To paraphrase Bandura (1989), they need to strengthen their perceived self-efficacy—that is, their expectation that they can act in ways that will lead to positive outcomes.

If the assessment process is taken out of their hands and performed by an "expert," the client's presenting problem(s) might be identified, but their sense of control and personal responsibility will ultimately be damaged. Assessment in the community counseling context, then, is a mutual effort in which both counselors and clients strive to identify components of clients' lives that can be changed as clients work to gain mastery over their lives, to increase their sense of self-efficacy, and to learn better ways to withstand stress.

THE WELL-BEING EQUATION   As noted in Chapter 3, the following equation can be applied equally well to individuals, high risk populations, schools, organizations, and whole communities.

$$\text{Psychological Well-being} = \frac{\text{Organic Factors} + \text{Stress} + \text{Powerlessness}}{\text{Coping Skills} + \text{Self-esteem} + \text{Social Support} + \text{Personal Power}}$$

This equation is particularly well suited for both the assessment and prevention of mental health problems. As a tool for assessing clients' psychological well-being, it provides (1) a way to organize data and (2) a method of teaching people how stress and coping factors interrelate.

When using this equation in assessment, counselors must first teach the client how to use it as a guide for thinking about her or his own circumstances. Clients generally have no trouble understanding that anyone might, because of genetic or other physiological factors, be vulnerable to specific stress-related problems or disorders.

This susceptibility might never be triggered if the individual is never subjected to severe and prolonged levels of stress. But even under such stress, people protect themselves from dysfunction by mobilizing social support, using effective coping skills, and maintaining their self-esteem, all of which stimulate increased feelings of personal power.

Seeing this equation can help clients understand that they can take steps to reduce stress, thereby decreasing the values in the numerator, and to strengthen their own sense of personal power by increasing their resources, thereby increasing the values in the denominator. Moreover, analyzing their own situations according to the variables in the equation shows clients what strengths they can build on and what areas they need to change. They can then more responsibly plan action strategies that address the issues that have come to light during assessment.

STRUCTURED FORMS   Counselors can use structured forms to help them in conducting a holistic client assessment. An example from a particularly helpful form, the Lewis-Fussell Case Conceptualization Form, is provided in Figure 4.1.

This version of the Lewis-Fussell Case Conceptualization Form provides counseling practitioners with a handy means of keeping track of the information generated in the community counseling assessment process. This form (1) helps counselors focus on specific variables to be assessed and (2) reminds them to evaluate all aspects of the individual's well-being.

This form also helps counselors to clearly conceptualize their recommendations. The form represents a practical, though unorthodox, record-keeping tool. Its open-ended questionnaire format helps counselors systematically track the information generated in assessment. In doing so, the form enables counselors to proceed naturally from assessment to problem solving.

Individual and Environmental Change

When community counselors work with individual clients, they are expected to work with the whole person as well as with the client's environment, attending both to detrimental factors and to possible sources of help and support. If an individual's natural support systems cannot meet her or his needs, additional sources of support must be sought. If aspects of the individual's environment are destructive, then those aspects must, if possible, be changed.

Troubled individuals must, of course, examine and perhaps change those aspects of their own behavior that add to their problems. Obviously, people have more control over their own actions than over those of others. And if individuals can resolve their problems through personal change, they may not need to change the environment.

Usually, however, the individual, the family, and the community are so closely interrelated that the client's entire social system must be taken into account to ensure his or her long-term psychological wellness. Purely personal change may be impossible, impractical, or damaging to the individual's integrity. Community counselors, therefore, should help the client (1) identify sources of help in the environment, (2) create additional sources of support if necessary, and (3) learn to reduce or eliminate stressful elements in the environment by either avoiding them or directly confronting and changing them.

The counselor and the client must jointly identify possible sources of support. No one can tell another person what his or her support system should be. Relationships prove supportive and helpful only if people experience them that way. Thus, no objective standard can help one distinguish between a "good" environment and a "bad" one. Rather, the interaction between individuals and their surroundings determines this distinction; therefore, only the people involved can know when their own needs are being met in ways that promote positive and constructive psychological outcomes.

RELATIONSHIP OF PERSONAL AND ENVIRONMENTAL FACTORS   The attention given to the environment distinguishes the community counseling model from other traditional counseling approaches. Most counselors have, in the past, assumed that the attitudes, feelings, or behavior of the client should be the objects of change. Counselors are becoming more aware, however, that the obstacles to clients' meeting their goals may lie in the environment rather than in the clients themselves. Intervention in the environment is therefore often imperative if an individual's problems are to be truly resolved.

At the same time, even when environmental factors have clearly contributed to the development of a problem, as when economic changes cause an individual's unemployment, one must separate responsibility for the *etiology* of the problem from responsibility for the *resolution* of the problem. Otherwise, as Monahan and Vaux (1980) note, clients may suffer feelings of passivity, helplessness, and immobilization if they are portrayed as victims of economic and social circumstances beyond their control. When used in individual-counseling settings, this perspective accords with the compensatory model of Brickman et al. (1982), defined earlier, which communicates that while clients should not be blamed for their predicaments, they must be encouraged to take effective action to resolve them.

JUNCTURES   As is clear from the well-being equation presented earlier, personal and environmental factors are closely interrelated. To choose sides, that is, to insist that most client problems arise either within the individual

Client: _____	Dates Seen:
Address: _____	_____

| Telephone: Work   Home | |

Employer Providing Coverage:	Employment:
_____	Present Job Title _____
_____	How Long in Present Position?_____
_____ Employee	How Long with Company?_____
_____ Family Member of Employee	Referred by: _____

Marital Status:	Dependents:	Age:	Cultural/Racial Background:	_____ Male
				_____ Female

Reason for Referral (Presenting Problem):

Physical Vulnerabilities

Physician:

Medical Problems/Medications:

Pattern of Alcohol Use (Self and/or Family):

Pattern of Drug Use (Self and/or Family):

Previous Treatment (for Substance Abuse):

Level of Health/Fitness:

General Impressions (Physical Strengths/Vulnerabilities):

Assessor's Recommendations for Decreasing Physical Vulnerabilities:

FIGURE 4.1   The Lewis-Fussell Case Conceptualization Form

Stress
Significant Life Changes (Last 12 Months):
Marital/Family Stressors:
Cultural/Racial Stressors:
Work-Related Stressors:
Client's Perception of Stress Factors:
General Level of Stress:
Recommendations for Decreasing Stress:
Life Skills
Professional/Educational Level:
Problem-Solving/Decision-Making Skills:
Interpersonal Skills:
Life Planning Skills
Apritudes/Interests/Hobbies:
Ability to Handle Life Situations:

FIGURE 4.1   (continued)

General Impressions of Life Skills:

Recommendations for Increasing Life Skills:

Self-Concept

Levels of Cultural/Racial Identity:

Level of Life Satisfaction:

Client's Perception of Strengths:

Client's Perception of Weaknesses/Problems:

Level of Self-Esteem:

Level of Work Satisfaction/Perceived Competence:

General Impressions:

Recommendations for Increasing Self-Esteem:

Social Supports

Stability of Present Home Situation:

Relationship to Family:

Family-Related Problems:

FIGURE 4.1   (continued)

Degree of Family Support for Problem Resolution:

Significant Other Relationships/Support:

Work Relationships/Support:

General Level of Available Support:

Recommendations for Increasing/Using Social Support:

General Level of Adjustment

Psychosocial Problem Areas:

Developmental History of Problems:

Previous Treatment/Response to Treatment:

General Assessment

Nature of Problem	Recommendation/Referral
____ Everyday Living Issue (No Long-Term Treatment Needed	
____ Psychological	
____ Substance Abuse _____	
____ Family	
____ Medical _____	
____ Legal/Financial	
____ Other _____	
Date of Referral:	Date of Follow-up:

FIGURE 4.1   (continued)

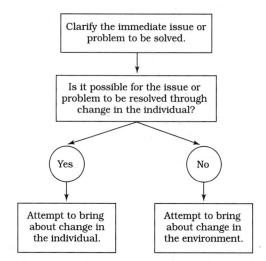

FIGURE 4.2   The first juncture in the counseling process

or from a destructive environment is unrealistic and counterproductive. In fact, sometimes individuals can solve their own problems, sometimes not. It is helpful, therefore, to look at the counseling process as a series of junctures, or points at which the counselor and the client together decide who has the power to address the issue at hand. The first juncture in the counseling process is shown in Figure 4.2.

Working together, the counselor and the client examine the types of changes the client can make to deal with specific problems and challenges identified during assessment. In considering alternatives to the current situation, the counselor and the client must initially consider whether or not the client actually has the power to implement the best possible solution.

If the issue can be resolved and other challenges met by making personal changes, the client and the counselor work to bring about those changes. But if at this point in the counseling process the individual seems unable to change—if some destructive force in the environment is blocking change—then the two of them try to develop strategies aimed at influencing and changing the environment.

Suppose, for example, that a counselor and client have decided that the client can change in a way that will solve the immediate problem. Figure 4.3 indicates various considerations in following this juncture in the counseling process. In this situation, the next step is to choose interventions that will best facilitate the client's change. For some clients, continuing one-to-one counseling may suffice; others may need more help. Counselors may try to foster closer ties between such clients and the people in their natural support systems or work directly with them in a group setting. Direct counseling and consultation with a specialized helper might both be used. Additional opportunities for clients to develop other life skills

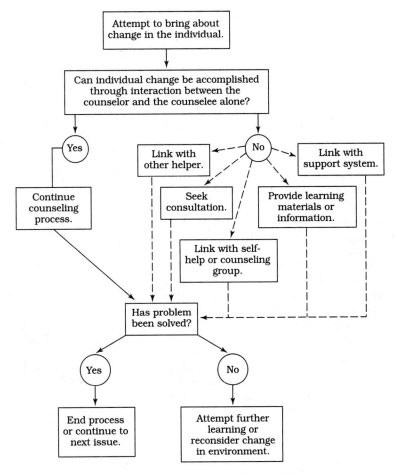

FIGURE 4.3   Juncture in individual change

should also be discussed. In this regard, counselors could inform their clients of programmed materials in decision making and encourage their participation in seminars dealing with ways to increase self-motivation or interpersonal effectiveness.

Whatever methods are used, the counselor and the client must ultimately evaluate the success of their action plan. If the client has been able to solve the problem, he or she can either end the counseling relationship or go on to deal with another issue or challenge. If the initial problem remains unresolved, both parties must decide whether the client needs additional help or whether, in fact, they need to change the environment.

If both decide to change an external factor, they must ask new questions. Figure 4.4 illustrates this juncture.

If the client does not have the power to solve the immediate problem, who does? If a change in the attitudes or behavior of another person or group would solve the problem, an appropriate step might be to consult

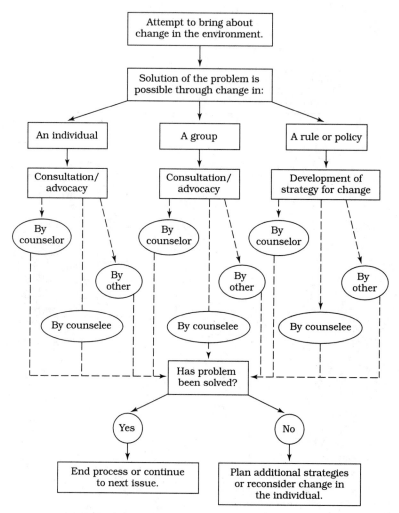

FIGURE 4.4   Juncture in environmental change

with that person or group. The person who speaks on behalf of the client might be the counselor, the client, or someone else, such as a citizen advocate or a school official.

If solving the problem requires a change in the rules or policies of some agency or institution, then a strategy for bringing about that sort of change must be devised. The appropriate person to lead this process might, again, be the counselor, the client, or another person or group. The counselor will most likely take an active role in promoting such a change if the rule or policy in question affects several clients.

If the environment changes and the problem is solved, then counseling can end or else it can continue with other issues and challenges. If the problem is not solved, the counselor and the client can collaborate further about new ways to deal with the environment or consider once more the possibility that the individual must change.

At each juncture, both decide what elements and action strategies they will emphasize at that time. When a counselor helps individuals make changes, she or he remains sensitive to the ways in which the clients' changes might impact their environmental systems.

This latter point is particularly important to consider when counselors help clients make changes that others in their environment may notice but not understand. For example, when counseling people whose cultural background encourages humility and discourages direct interpersonal conflict (such as many Asian and Native-American groups), counselors need to discuss with the client how family members might react when they exercise their newly developed assertive skills.

When counselors direct attention to environmental changes, they remain aware of the individual's complex responses. By working with clients to examine ways to change specific aspects of the environment that lead toward positive outcomes, counselors help increase clients' sense of hope and personal power.

One should not, of course, oversimplify the interactive counseling process. At each juncture, the counselor and client must determine not only what kind of change—individual, environmental, or both— will most effectively solve the problem at hand, but also how ready the individual or significant others in the environment are for such changes. Thus, they must ask not only what change is possible, but also what change is preferable.

Community counselors need not choose between strengthening individuals' personal resources or confronting environmental conditions; they need not choose between being counselors or agents of environmental change. Rather, the roles constantly interact. Dealing with the environment can and should be an important part of counseling individuals. As clients recognize that more than their own behavior must change, they learn to confront actively the systems that affect their lives. As a result, their attitudes and behavior also change.

CHOOSING STRATEGIES: THREE EXAMPLES   The following examples illustrate the need to examine both personal and environmental factors in choosing strategies for change in counseling.

Example 1: A Runaway Youth.   An adolescent boy runs away from home and finds himself alone in an unfamiliar neighborhood. He turns to the local runaway center, where a counselor asks questions similar to the following:

1. Does your family give you emotional support? Can they?
2. What changes in your family might make your home supportive enough for you to consider returning?
3. What changes in your behavior might make the family more supportive of you? Can you make those changes yourself?
4. If the conflicts at home cannot be resolved, what alternative living situations are available? Do you know of a family or a group home where you could be comfortable?
5. What kinds of relationships do you have with relatives outside of your immediate family? Are any of them potential sources of support?
6. Have you gotten into trouble with the police or been arrested in the past?
7. Can you support yourself? What work skills do you have? What job opportunities are or might be open to you?
8. Do you or your family need financial aid? What sources of aid might be appropriate?
9. Do you have a group of friends you identify strongly with? How can they help you now?
10. What is your situation at school? Is that where the real conflict or support lies? Are there any people or programs at school that can provide additional support? Can any negative factors be changed?
11. Has anyone else tried to help you in the past? Have you two established any kind of relationship?
12. Is child abuse or substance abuse a factor in this situation? If so, what steps have been taken to deal with either issue in the past?

These questions seem obvious, but it is surprising how many of them remain unasked in the immediacy of a crisis. The questions reflect a clear recognition that children do not run away in isolation from the context of their lives. They are usually running to or from something. It is more than coincidence that many youth runaway centers that initially concentrated on individual counseling have now developed group-counseling programs for parents as well as youths. These group interventions are usually designed to affect the adolescent's environment by working to build more effective support systems within his or her life.

Example 2: A Physically Disabled Adult.   A recent accident has left a young, single woman physically disabled. As she prepares to leave the hospital, a counselor on the staff tries to help her answer the following questions:

1. What living situation would best suit you? Can you live alone? Are members of your family available to provide attendant care? Do you need to hire an attendant?
2. What financial assistance is available, not only to help you meet your basic needs but also to cover attendants' salaries or technical necessities? Do you need an advocate to obtain assistance in this regard?
3. What are your career goals? What work can you do? Do you need additional skills? What educational resources are available to you?
4. How are your relationships with family members and friends? Have they been able to offer psychological support throughout the crisis? How have they adjusted to your disability? Are they allowing you to be as independent as possible?
5. How can you maintain social relationships and continue to enjoy recreation?
6. Do you need help and information to deal with a potential crisis in your sexuality?
7. Do you have ready access to whatever legal and medical assistance you need?
8. How can you maintain the greatest possible degree of physical mobility and independence?
9. To what degree does the community provide the resources and accessibility you are entitled to?

Following traditional approaches, one counselor might help this woman with her vocational goals, another with her physical needs, and still another with her psychological adjustment. Most likely, though, none would address her needs for socializing and recreation.

In contrast, the community counselor sees this woman as a whole person whose interactions with the total environment constitute her potential support system. The basic questions thus become: "Is her former support system holding up under the pressures of change, or does she need supplemental help to meet all her needs effectively?" "Where can she find additional support, and how can she be helped to make the most of the opportunities that now exist for her?" "To what degree does she need an advocate to maximize these opportunities?"

Example 3: A Mature Woman Continuing Her Education.   A woman who has worked full time at raising a family and maintaining a household decides to return to school to complete schooling interrupted by the birth of her first child. Her success, of course, depends on her own motivation, talent, and good fortune, but the environment does make an important dif-ference. The community counselor asks the following questions:

1. Does your family support and show enthusiasm about your new endeavor? If not, how can they be helped to understand your situation more fully?
2. Do your friends and associates understand your goals? Are any of them in similar situations, or do their values differ? Are they likely to encourage or to discourage you?
3. Do you know of any other women taking similar steps who might offer support?
4. How does your move affect the family's immediate finances? Is financial aid available?
5. Does the educational institution meet your special needs by providing such services as day care, flexible scheduling, and career counseling?
6. Are extracurricular activities on campus aimed solely at young, resident students or do some apply to older students? Can new activities be developed?
7. What steps have been taken to integrate older students into campus life? What kinds of interaction exist between students of different age groups?
8. Who is handling the household tasks that you used to do? Do other family members understand their responsibilities?
9. When you have completed your education, what job opportunities will you find? Do local businesses discriminate against women or middle-aged people in hiring? Is a part-time or flexible job possible? Could it be?

In this instance, what appears to be an individual step really involves the family, the educational institution, and the community. A change in this one individual's behavior creates stress on all her interactions. Her sup-port system, which might have been strong, must adapt. If her former sup-port system proves inadequate, new sources of help must be created or found, or some changes must be made.

Each of these examples makes clear that counseling cannot focus merely on individual, intrapsychic change. Instead, one must consider mul-tiple levels of the whole system, from the family to the culture as a whole. As Keeney (1983) points out, "The limits of individual growth, evolution, or health are constrained by the health of their immediate contexts—their families. Families in turn must help to maintain the health of the contexts which embody them; and so on until we can conceive of a healthy planet" (p. 37).

Summary

Community counseling values the strengths and competencies of clients, recognizes the impact of the social environment, emphasizes prevention, and promotes the belief that one can help people most effectively if they receive the resources to help themselves. These values lead community counselors to develop multifaceted programs that include preventive education, outreach efforts, attention to public policy issues, and client advocacy.

By definition, of course, counselors also provide direct, one-to-one counseling services. In the community counseling model, however, the nature of the counseling process changes to emphasize both individual responsibility and environmental influences.

Brickman and his colleagues have defined four models of helping and coping based on how responsibility is attributed: (1) the moral model, where people are responsible both for creating and for solving their own problems; (2) the medical model, where people are responsible neither for creating nor for solving their problems; (3) the enlightenment model, where people are responsible for creating their problems but are not responsible for solving them; and (4) the compensatory model, which allows a dual focus on individual responsibility and environmental influences. This last model is the most compatible with community counseling.

At its most effective level, community counseling enhances the client's sense of personal power and responsibility. By training them in the principles of behavioral change, community counselors can help clients gain mastery over their lives. By following various structural developmental models, counselors can also promote clients' progress toward higher levels of development. Such models trace the development of psychological competencies through specific invariant stages.

Loevinger identifies the stages of ego development; Kohlberg outlines three levels of moral reasoning. In general, the later stages of these models are thought to promote greater adaptive responses to the world than earlier, less complex stages.

The community counseling framework is further characterized by an attention to systems theory. Such theory focuses on consistent patterns of interaction, on interrelationships, and on general organizing principles. Although many systems or levels of systems may affect clients, the system counselors have addressed most successfully in the past is the family.

Counselors who work with families see the family system itself as the target of their interventions. They identify the source of difficulties within a dysfunctional system rather than see the client as a "sick" individual. Each of the many approaches to family counseling recognizes the importance of the family as a social system that affects and is affected by the behavior of its members.

Currently, systems thinking is greatly expanding the purview of the counseling profession. The increasing influence of such forces as contextualism, postmodern thinking, and the counseling for personal liberation model represent exciting new complements to the community counseling framework.

SUPPLEMENTAL ACTIVITIES

1. Find a friend, colleague, or student willing to work with you. Ask the individual to act as a client, either role playing an imaginary problem or sharing a real concern. Analyze the presenting problem from a community counseling perspective (i.e., from an environmental-contextual perspective).

2. Consider once more your own hypothetical community counseling program. Given what you have read in this chapter, what are the salient issues to consider when counseling people in this group? How might the community counseling model affect your approach to these individuals?

REFERENCES

Amaro, H. (1995). Love, sex, and power: Considering women's realities in HIV prevention. *American Psychologist, 50*(6), 437–447.

Atkinson, D. R., Morten, G., & Sue, D. W. (1993). *Counseling American minorities: A crosscultural perspective* (4th ed.). Dubuque, IA: Brown & Benchmark.

Bandura, A. (1982). Self-efficacy mechanism in human agency. *American Psychologist, 37*, 122–147.

Bandura, A. (1989). Human agency in social cognitive theory. *American Psychologist, 44*, 1175–1184.

Bernardes, J. (1993). Responsibilities in studying postmodern families. *Journal of Family Issues, 14*(1), 35–49.

Blocher, D. (1966). *Developmental counseling*. New York: Ronald Press.

Bowen, M. (1982). *Family therapy in clinical practice*. New York: Aronson.

Brickman, P., Rabinowitz, V. C., Karuza, J., Coates, D., Cohn, E., & Kidder, L. (1982). Four models of helping and coping. *American Psychologist, 37*(2), 368–384.

Brown, N. (1959). *Life against death: The psychoanalytic meaning of history*. Middletown, CT: Wesleyan University Press.

Carter, R. T. (1995). *The influence of race and racial identity in psychotherapy: Toward a racially inclusive model*. New York: Wiley.

Cheal, D. (1993). Unity and difference in postmodern families. *Journal of Family Issues, 14*(1), 5–19.

Claiborn, C. D., & Lichtenberg, J. W. (1989). Interactional counseling. *Counseling Psychologist, 17*(2), 355–453.

Cross, W. (1971). The negro to black conversion experience. *Black World, 20,* 13–25.

Cross, W. (1991). *Shades of black.* Philadelphia: Temple University Press.

D'Andrea, M. (1988). The counselor as pacer: A model for the revitalization of the counseling profession. In R. Hayes & R. Aubrey (Eds.), *New directions for counseling and human development* (pp. 22–44). Denver, CO: Love Publishers.

D'Andrea, M. (1994, April). *Creating a vision for our future: The challenges and promise of the counseling profession.* Paper presented at the meeting of the American Counseling Association, Minneapolis, MN.

DAndrea, M. (1995). *Notes on counseling practice at Meharry Medical College.* Unpublished manuscript, University of Hawai'i at Manoa.

D'Andrea, M., & Daniels, J. (1992) Measuring ego development for counseling practice: Implementing developmental eclecticism. *Journal of Humanistic Education and Development, 31,* 12–21.

D'Andrea, M., & Daniels, J. (1994). Group pacing: A developmental eclectic approach to group work. *Journal of Counseling and Development, 72*(6), 585–590.

Daniels, J., & D'Andrea, M. (1996). MCT theory and ethnocentrism in counseling. In D. W. Sue, A. E. Ivey, & P. D. Pedersen (Eds.), *A theory of multicultural counseling and therapy* (pp. 155–173). Pacific Grove, CA: Brooks/Cole.

Elliott, T. R., Witty, T. E., Herrick, S., & Hoffman, J. T. (1991). Negotiating reality after physical loss: Hope, depression, and disability. *Journal of Personality and Social Psychology, 61,* 608–613.

Freire, P. (1972). *Pedagogy of the oppressed.* New York: Herder & Herder.

Gazda, G. M. (1984). Multiple impact training: A life skills approach. In D. Larson (Ed.), *Teaching psychological skills: Models for giving psychology away* (pp. 87–103). Pacific Grove, CA: Brooks/Cole.

Gelman, R., & Baillargeon, R. (1983). A review of some Piagetian concepts. In P. H. Mussen (Series Ed.) & J. H. Flavell & E. M. Markman (Vol. Eds.), *Handbook of child psychology: Vol. 3. Cognitive development* (pp. 167–230). Philadelphia: Dorrance.

Gergen, K. J. (1992). The postmodern adventure. *Family Therapy Networker, 16*(6), 52, 56–57.

Germain, C. B. (1991). *Human behavior in the social environment: An ecological view.* New York: Columbia University Press.

Gilligan, C. (1982). *In a different voice.* Cambridge, MA: Harvard University Press.

Gilligan, C., Ward, J. V., & Taylor, J. M. (1988). *Mapping the moral domain: A contribution of women's thinking to psychological theory and education.* Cambridge, MA: Harvard University Press.

Goldenberg, I., & Goldenberg, H. (1985). *Family therapy: An overview.* Pacific Grove, CA: Brooks/Cole.

Goldstein, A. P. (1992). *The prepare curriculum: Teaching prosocial competencies* (5th ed.). Champaign, IL: Research Press.

Haley, J. (Ed.). (1976). *People-solving therapy*. San Francisco: Jossey-Bass.

Hayes, R. L. (1986). Human growth and development. In M. D. Lewis & J. A. Lewis (Eds.), *An introduction to the counseling profession* (pp. 36–95). Itasca, IL: Peacock.

Helms, J. (1990). *Black and white racial identity*. Westport, CT: Greenwood Press.

Ivey, A. E. (1986). *Developmental therapy: Theory into practice*. San Francisco: Jossey-Bass.

Ivey, A. E. (1991). *Developmental strategies for helpers: Individual, family, and network interviewing*. Pacific Grove, CA: Brooks/Cole.

Ivey, A. E. (1994). *Intentional interviewing and counseling: Facilitating client development in a multicultural society* (3rd ed.). Pacific Grove, CA: Brooks/Cole.

Ivey, A. E. (1995). Psychotherapy as liberation: Towards specific skills and strategies in multicultural counseling and therapy. In J. G. Ponterotto, J. M. Casas, L. A. Suzuki, & C. M. Alexander (Eds.), *Handbook of multicultural counseling* (pp. 53–72). Newbury Park, CA: Sage.

Ivey, A. E. Ivey, M., & Simek-Morgan, L. (Eds.). (1993). *Counseling and psychotherapy: A multicultural perspective*. Boston: Allyn and Bacon.

Kanfer, F. H. (1980). Self-management methods. In F. H. Kanfer & A. P. Goldstein (Eds.), *Helping people change* (pp. 334–389). New York: Pergamon Press.

Kantrowitz, R., & Ballou, M. (1992). A feminist critique of cognitive-behavioral theory. In M. Ballou & L. Brown (Eds.), *Theories of personality and psychopathology* (pp. 70–79). New York: Guilford.

Keeney, B. (1983). *Aesthetics of change*. New York: Guilford.

Kegan, R. (1982). *The evolving self: Problem and process in human development*. Cambridge, MA: Harvard University Press.

Kelly, E. W. (1989). Social commitment and individualism in counseling. *Journal of Counseling and Development, 67*(3), 341–344.

Kohlberg, L. (1969). Stage and sequence: The cognitive developmental approach to socialization. In D. Goslin (Ed.), *The handbook of socialization theory and research* (pp. 347–480). Chicago: Rand McNally.

Kohlberg, L. (1971). From is to ought: How to commit the naturalistic fallacy and get away with it in the study of moral development. In T. Mischel (Ed.), *Cognitive development and epistemology* (pp. 151–235). New York: Academic Press.

Kohlberg, L. (1984). *Essays on moral development: Vol. 2. The psychology of moral development*. New York: Harper & Row.

Kuhmerker, L. (Ed.). (1991). *The Kohlberg legacy for the helping professions*. Birmingham, AL: R. E. P. Books.

Lator, B. (1993). *We have never been modern*. Cambridge, MA: Harvard University Press.

Lerman, H. (1992). The limits of phenomenology: A feminist critique of humanistic personality theories. In M. Ballou & L. Brown (Eds.), *Theories of personality and psychopathology* (pp. 8–19). New York: Guilford.

Lerner, R. M., & Kauffman, M. M. (1985). The concept of development in contextualism. *Developmental Review, 5,* 309–333.

Lewis, J. A. (1993). Farewell to motherhood and apple pie: Families in the postmodern era. *The Family Journal: Counseling and Therapy for Couples and Families, 1*(4), 337–338.

Lewis J. A. (Ed.) (1994). *Addictions: Concepts and strategies for treatment.* Gaithersburg, MD: Aspen.

Lewis, J. A., Dana, R. Q., & Blevins, G. A. (1988). *Substance abuse counseling: An individualized approach.* Pacific Grove, CA: Brooks/Cole.

Lewis, J. A., Sperry, L., & Carlson, J. (1993). *Health counseling.* Pacific Grove, CA: Brooks/Cole.

Liberman, R. (1981). Behavioral approaches to family and couple therapy. In G. D. Erickson & T. P. Hogan (Eds.), *Family therapy: An introduction to theory and technique,* (2nd ed., pp. 152–164). Pacific Grove, CA: Brooks/Cole.

Lickona, T. (1992). *Educating for character: How our schools can teach respect and responsibility.* New York: Bantam.

Loevinger, J. (1976). *Ego development.* San Francisco: Jossey-Bass.

Lupton-Smith, H. S., Carruthers, W. I., Flythe, R., Modest, K. H., & Goette, E. (1995). *Conflict resolution as peer mediation: Programs for elementary, middle, and high school students.* Unpublished manuscript.

Madanes, C. (1981). *Strategic family therapy.* San Francisco: Jossey-Bass.

Magnusson, D., & Allen, V. L. (1983). An interactional perspective for human development. In D. Magnusson & V. L. Allen (Eds.), *Human development: An interactional perspective* (pp. 3–34). Pacific Grove, CA: Brooks/Cole.

Marecek, J. (1995). Gender, politics, and psychology's ways of knowing. *American Psychologist, 50*(3), 159–161.

McWhirter, E. H. (1994). *Counseling for empowerment.* Alexandria, VA: American Counseling Association.

Miller, J. B. (1986). *Toward a new psychology of women* (2nd ed.). Boston: Beacon Press.

Miller, J. B. (1991). The development of women's sense of self. In J. Jordan, A. Kaplan, J. B. Miller, I. Stiver, & J. Surrey (Eds.), *Women's growth in connection* (pp. 11–26). New York: Guilford.

Minuchin, S. (1979). Constructing a therapeutic reality. In E. Kaufman and P. Kaufman (Eds.), *Family therapy of drug and alcohol abuse* (pp. 5–18). New York: Garner Press.

Minuchin, S. (1984). *Family kaleidoscope.* Cambridge, MA: Harvard University Press.

Monahan, J., & Vaux, A. (1980). The macroenvironment and community mental health. *Community Mental Health Journal, 16,* 14–26.

National Mental Health Association Commission on the Prevention of Mental-Emotional Disabilities (1986). *The prevention of mental-emotional disabilities: Report of the National Mental Health Association Commission on the Prevention of Mental-Emotional Disabilities.* Alexandria, VA: National Mental Health Association.

Phinney, J. S. (1990). Ethnic identity in adolescents and adults: Review of research. *Psychological Bulletin, 108*, 499–514.

Piaget, J. (1970). *Structuralism*. New York: Basic Books.

Ponterotto, J. G., & Pedersen, P. B. (1993). *Preventing prejudice: A guide for counselors and educators*. Thousand Oaks, CA: Sage.

Rigazio-DiGilio, S. (1989). *Developmental theory and therapy: A preliminary investigation of reliability and predictive validity using an inpatient depressive population sample*. Unpublished doctoral dissertation, University of Massachusetts, Amherst.

Satir, V. M. (1967). *Cojoint family therapy* (2nd ed.). Palo Alto, CA: Science and Behavior Books.

Satir, V. M. (1972). *Peoplemaking*. Palo Alto, CA: Science and Behavior Books.

Scheier, M. F., & Carver, C. S. (1987). Dispositional optimism and physical well-being: The influence of generalized outcome expectancies on health. *Journal of Personality, 55*, 169–210.

Sherwin, E. D., Elliott, T. R., Frank, R. G., & Hoffman, J. (1992). Negotiating the reality of care giving: Hope, burnout, and nursing. *Journal of Social and Clinical Psychology, 45*, 128–145.

Snyder, C. R. (1995). Conceptualizing, measuring, and nurturing hope. *Journal of Counseling and Development, 73*(3), 355–360.

Steenbarger, B. N. (1993). A multicontextual model of counseling: Bridging brevity and diversity. *Journal of Counseling and Development, 72*, 8–15.

Steenbarger, B. N., & LeClair, S. (1995). Beyond remediation and development: Mental health counseling in context. *Journal of Mental Health Counseling, 17*(2), 173–187.

Steinglass, P. (1978). The conceptualization of marriage from a systems theory perspective. In T. J. Paolino & B. S. McCrady (Eds.), *Marriage and marital therapy: Psychoanalytic, behavioral, and systems theory perspectives* (pp. 298–365). New York: Brunner/Mazel.

Sue, D. W., Ivey, A. E., & Pedersen, P. D. (1996). *A theory of multicultural counseling and development*. Pacific Grove, CA: Brooks/Cole.

Sue, D. W., & Sue, D. (1990). *Counseling the culturally different: Theory and practice*. (2nd ed.). New York: Wiley.

Thomas, S. C. (1996). A sociological perspective on contextualism. *Journal of Counseling and Development, 74*(6), 529–538.

Umbarger, C. C. (1983). *Structural family therapy*. New York: Grune & Stratton.

von Bertalanffy, L. (1968). *General systems theory*. New York: Braziller.

Watson, D. L., & Tharp, R. G. (1993). *Self-directed behavior: Self-modification for personal adjustment* (6th ed.). Pacific Grove, CA: Brooks/Cole.

Young-Eisendrath, P. (1988). Making use of human development theories in counseling. In R. Hayes & R. Aubrey (Eds.), *New directions for counseling and human development* (pp. 66–84). Denver, CO: Love Publishing.

CHAPTER 5

CLIENT ADVOCACY

INTRODUCTION

Limitations of Direct Counseling

The community counseling model stresses clients' potential strengths rather than their weaknesses. Though many clients appear to have numerous needs, perpetual dependence on counselors must be discouraged. Although these considerations may seem obvious, Lewis and Lewis (1989) note that "counselors have traditionally had difficulty following them" (p. 173).

Through counseling, clients often experience a reduced level of stress and an increased sense of support. Even so, an overdependence on direct counseling services presents two major limitations.

First, the number of U.S. mental health professionals (e.g., counselors, psychologists, social workers) is grossly insufficient in terms of the country's general mental health needs. Numerous studies consistently show that the overall need for mental health services far exceeds available services (Albee, 1986; Albee & Gullotta, 1986; Conyne, 1987). For example, Conyne (1987) reports that though 43 million adults in the United States are diagnosed with some form of mental or emotional problem, both public and private mental health-care systems can only serve about 7 million clients each year. In short, there are just not enough professionals to provide direct counseling to everyone.

Second, direct counseling services can promote an increased dependence on the counselor/therapist. People seeking counseling services often feel a lack of power over their own lives, a sense that they are being forced to relinquish control over environmental contingencies to others. Therefore,

> how we [counselors] structure the services we offer to clients may
> have a significant impact on their perceived personal power. If
> services are structured in such a manner that experiences seem
> non-contingent to clients, we are encouraging learned helplessness
> and a perceived external control both of which promote an unhealthy
> sense of personal powerlessness. (Stensrud & Stensrud, 1981, p. 301)

While this sort of dependence may be manifested in a variety of subtle and not so subtle ways in counseling, it frequently inadvertently leads to an erosion in the client's own sense of empowerment (Ivey, 1995; McWhirter, 1994). The notion that traditional counseling approaches may sometimes unintentionally lead to an erosion in any client's sense of personal power (however temporary) is a serious ethical issue that practitioners need to vigilantly strive to avoid.

This chapter discusses the ways mental health practitioners can expand their practice by working indirectly to promote their clients' psychological health and personal well-being. It specifically addresses the counselor's role as an advocate, consultant, and coalition builder. Finally, it stresses the importance of indirect helping strategies in light of the rapid cultural diversification of the United States in the 21st century.

Distinguishing Client Advocacy from Counseling

Recognizing problems associated with overusing direct counseling services, counselors can expand their overall effectiveness by incorporating client advocacy strategies as a central component of their work. Brown (1988) explains some of the similarities and differences between counseling and advocacy services as follows:

> Counselors are regularly engaged in the process of directly assisting
> clients to mobilize their personal resources so that they can more
> effectively function in their environments. This direct process of
> personal empowerment is typically referred to as counseling. Less
> often, but frequently, counselors work indirectly to alter systems or to
> facilitate change in individuals which will result in enhanced personal
> functioning on the part of clients. . . . Advocacy, like counseling and
> consultation, is an empowerment process. That is, it is concerned
> with the transfer of personal power to the client. However, unlike
> counseling, it is usually an indirect method of assisting clients. (p. 5)

Advocacy services are designed to serve two basic purposes: (1) increasing clients' sense of personal power and (2) fostering environmental changes that reflect greater responsiveness to their personal needs.

Counselors can provide client advocacy services in a number of ways. For instance, they can encourage clients to participate in self-help groups or foster changes in families, schools and universities, business organizations, or communities that make these environments more responsive to their clients' needs. These actions, in turn, can help mitigate a variety of problems that occur when clients are stigmatized by others because of their unique problems and/or circumstance.

STIGMATIZATION

A person is stigmatized when labels become central to his or her interactions with others. In his now classic work, Goffman (1963) explains how stigmatization negatively impacts people who might otherwise have been received easily in ordinary social intercourse. Too often, Goffman notes, people from stigmatized groups tend to be rejected and distanced by others primarily because of the labels imposed on them by others.

He notes further that people tend, unconsciously or consciously, to view the differences in stigmatized individuals in undesirable terms. According to Goffman (1963), this sense of undesirability is often rooted in the belief that stigmatized individuals are not competent, are inferior to nonstigmatized people, and are "by definition . . . not quite human" (p. 5).

Labeling Resulting from Disability or Impairment

When an individual suffers some disability or impairment, whether mental or physical, he or she is labeled as such. Unfortunately, such labels often imply dependence and limited worth.

Almond (1974) describes the process by which individuals are labeled as deviant and therefore stigmatized and devalued. He notes that people receive various labels (diagnoses) from mental health professionals often because their behavior has aroused increasing anxiety in others until finally they become

> characterized by [their] problem behavior. . . . As such, [they] may be
> dealt with differently; [their] deviance becomes the overriding
> consideration and [they] may be arbitrarily deprived of certain rights
> and freedoms. Handling [them] becomes the special province of
> experts in [their] sort of deviance. (p. xxiii)

Whether the "expert" involved is a physician, a psychotherapist, or a corrections officer, individuals exiled to the province of professional care often become separated from their families and peers, as well as wholly or partially excluded from normal community life. Their unique differences from people in the mainstream of society become viewed as overriding conditions, emphasized to the point that those differences frequently become a focus of their lives. Similar forms of stigmatization and labeling occur as a result of racial and cultural stereotyping.

Racial/Cultural Stereotyping

Since the founding of the United States, people of color have been labeled negatively by the dominant culture. Numerous scholars have explained how the various forms of racial and cultural stigmatization, still perpetuated in this country, fuels a heightened level of interracial tension that is unhealthy for the economic, social, psychological, physical, and moral well-being of this country (Allen & Niss, 1990; Carter & Wilson, 1989: D'Andrea & Daniels, 1994; Magner, 1989). This tension has led to increasing numbers of racially motivated violence in the United States over the past decade (Harvey, 1991).

Such stigmatization has also been reinforced by and perpetuated within the mental health professions. In this regard, it has been noted that counseling practitioners, researchers, and theorists have referred to people of color in many negative and condescending terms. Labels such as "culturally deprived" and "culturally disadvantaged" have been frequently used to describe individuals from various cultural/ethnic/racial groups in the past (Atkinson, Morten, & Sue, 1993; D. W. Sue, Ivey, & Pedersen, 1996). Unfortunately, this sort of stereotypic labeling has frequently translated into various forms of discrimination and racism in schools, workplaces, communities, and even within the fields of counseling and psychology (D'Andrea, 1992; Gibbs & Huang, 1990; Ridley, 1995).

The Counselor's Role

REDUCING VICTIMIZATION BASED ON LABELS AND STEREOTYPES To address the problem of stigmatization, counselors must (1) work to reduce the victimization that results from labeling and (2) increase the value stigmatized individuals and groups place on themselves. Thus, when community counselors work with socially devalued populations, they assume that it is possible to

1. End the self-devaluing that results from external limitations, which often occur from being labeled
2. Bring labeled individuals currently excluded from various aspects of school or community life into the mainstream of social interaction
3. Facilitate efforts to increase the power of the stigmatized group to fight for needed social changes

TABLE 5.1
CLIENT ADVOCACY
AND THE COMMUNITY COUNSELING MODEL

	COMMUNITY SERVICES	CLIENT SERVICES
Direct		
Indirect		Self-help groups Class advocacy Fostering a responsive helping network

4. Increase community responsiveness to the needs and rights of all labeled individuals and groups who have been intentionally or unintentionally stigmatized

In the long run, one can overcome stigmatization and labeling only through changes in perception and efforts to adapt society itself to new ways of accommodating every person's humanness. In the short run, however, counselors can address stigmatization by developing empowerment strategies aimed at strengthening the psychological health and well-being of people hurt by labeling.

The community counseling framework rests on the premise that one cannot reach such goals solely through individual and small-group counseling. For this reason, counselors must embrace other, indirect methods of helping their clients such as bringing clients into contact with self-help groups, fostering the development of other helping networks, and using one's consultation skills to create positive changes in their social environment. The place of such advocacy efforts in the community counseling model is shown in Table 5.1.

AVOIDING EXCLUSIONARY COUNSELING PRACTICE When individuals accept or are assigned the role of a client, the gap between them and their community is, if anything, typically widened. This gap is part of a broader exclusionary process that many one-to-one counseling interventions often promote. In discussing this exclusionary process, Stensrud and Stensrud (1981) point out that counselors help foster this process when they (1) work with clients apart from other people who may either be sources of their psychological stress or important support people and (2) do not consistently nurture the client's own sense of empowerment in the counseling process.

Marriage and family therapists (Hanna & Brown, 1995; Satir, 1972) and advocates of peer counseling programs (Sprinthall, Hall, & Gerler, 1992) have long recognized the importance of being more inclusive by involving other people from the client's social environment in the helping process. Also, while developmental counseling models emphasize the need to focus on clients' personal strengths (Ivey, 1986; Mosher & Sprinthall, 1971), several theorists have recently outlined practical ways to foster clients' personal empowerment and psychological liberation within the context of individual counseling sessions as well (Ivey, 1995; Ivey, Ivey, & Simek-Morgan, 1993; McWhirter, 1994). In these ways, marriage and family counselors as well as those practitioners who incorporate developmental models in their work both help reduce the negative impact of client stigmatization and promote their personal empowerment.

Counselors can also greatly facilitate the empowerment process by strengthening their clients' ties to the mainstream of normal life. They can accomplish this, in part, by providing opportunities for clients to interact in meaningful ways with others in the greater school and/or community context. One of the best ways to help clients develop such ties is to encourage them to join self-help groups and organizations.

EMPOWERMENT THROUGH SELF-HELP GROUPS

In self-help organizations, people with common bonds can connect with and mutually support one another, request or offer active assistance, and deal with common problems in an understanding but realistic group setting. In most self-help organizations, group members are not categorized as service givers or service receivers, and all of the members make decisions collectively. By operating in this manner, the members of self-help groups are considered as both "helpers" and "helpees."

Steele (1974) lists several important ways self-help groups nurture clients' sense of empowerment. In such groups, people can do the following:

1. Gain a positive personal identification within a peer group
2. Have their attitudes altered as a result of being around other people who emphasize the importance of taking collective and constructive action to address the common challenges and problems the group faces

3. Feel more confident about the way in which they communicate with others because of the common experiences shared by the group members
4. Avoid many of the cultural, racial, and ethnic barriers traditional counseling settings often manifest
5. Find opportunities and experiences that generally improve their socialization (p. 106)

Self-help groups provide an environment in which clients can have free and open discussions about issues of common interest to others. As members of a "common community," they can also receive emotional support and understanding in ways that differ from the support and empathy experienced in traditional counseling. Because of their commonalties, individuals in self-help groups can be confronted by their peers in ways that remove their defensiveness and encourage them to take greater personal responsibility for their own lives.

Most important, individuals find opportunities to develop and exercise leadership skills in the context of such groups. Although some self-help organizations allow professional participation or sponsorship, the participants in such groups recognize that their potential for success always rests on the active involvement and commitment of their members.

When new members enter a self-help organization, they are encouraged to believe that the group and its members are special and that they can share in this specialness. Full membership is valued and is based on behaving according to the particular norms of the group. When a person first agrees to become a member of a self-help organization, she or he typically accepts the role of an "initiate." As an initiate, the individual must conform to the expectations of the group and behave in ways that affirm his or her commitment to the organization's ideology.

This sort of group conformity is expected from every member of the organization. Moving from the role of an initiate to a full-fledged group member requires the individual to demonstrate her or his willingness and ability to help other members in the organization rather than just accept help.

The fact that each member of a self-help group becomes a caregiver is the key to the empowering potential of this approach. As Gartner (1982) states,

> Self-help converts problems or needs into resources. For instance, instead of seeing 32 million people with arthritis as a problem it is possible to see these people as resources, service givers, for dealing with the everyday concerns of the arthritic. . . . At the same time, people will acquire a new sense of independence and empowerment as a consequence of dealing effectively with their own problems. (p. 64)

The "Helper-Therapy" Principle

The "helper-therapy" principle provides a good explanation for why self-help groups succeed. Skovholt (1974) discussed the benefits of "helper therapy" more than two decades ago by noting that, although receiving help is beneficial, giving help is even more so. Elaborating on this principle, Skovholt (1974) outlined the following benefits that people in self-help groups normally experience by providing help to others. That is, the effective helper often

1. Feels an increased level of interpersonal competence as a result of making an impact on another's life
2. Feels a sense of equality in giving and taking between himself or herself and others
3. Receives valuable personalized learning acquired while working with a helpee
4. Receives social approval from the people he or she helps
   (p. 62)

Gartner and Riessman (1984) point out three additional benefits that are related to the helper-therapy principle:

1. The helper becomes less dependent.
2. In struggling with the problem of another person who has a similar problem, the helper has a chance to observe his or her problem at a distance.
3. The helper obtains a feeling of social usefulness by playing the helping role. (p 20)

A good example of the helper-therapy principle in action is Recovery Incorporated, an organization for self-described "nervous and former mental patients." Though the organization's initial impetus in 1937 came from a professional, Dr. Abraham Low, the group's leaders are now all lay people who came to the group as patients. In this context *patients* are people recently discharged from inpatient settings or others who identify themselves as under psychiatric care or as having symptoms such as anxiety or depression.

At weekly Recovery Incorporated meetings, group discussions are combined with structured panel presentations during which members contrast old and new ways of dealing with their personal problems. By planning and participating in these activities, the members experience an increased sense of psychological health and personal well-being by recognizing that they are not alone in their problems, by being exposed to successful and relevant role models, and by realizing that they can assist others while helping themselves.

In addition to their regular meetings, experienced members of this group also present educational programs to other community groups. This service increases public knowledge and awareness about mental health issues and points to another strength of self-help groups: They can potentially give stigmatized people a collective voice that they would not have as individuals.

Although the idea of helper therapy has existed for more than 25 years, counselors have been slow to incorporate this principle into counseling practice. Recognizing its potential utility, D'Andrea (1994) reports on the success of using helper therapy among a group of chronically mentally ill clients who attended an adult day-treatment program in a community mental health center.

All the clients who participated in this community-based program were African Americans diagnosed with serious mental health problems. Besides receiving a variety of traditional psychotherapeutic services, such as individual and small-group psychotherapy, these clients also met twice a week as a self-help group to plan various activities that addressed other specific needs of theirs.

Recognizing that much of the stress they experienced related directly to racism, these clients agreed to develop a strategy to address it. As a result, the clients designed and implemented a psychoeducational class entitled, "Coping with Racism in Contemporary America," which was held at the community mental health center.

This class consisted of several meetings in which the clients examined the different ways they experienced racism in their own lives and brainstormed effective strategies for coping with these and other types of racism. These meetings provided the clients with opportunities to develop a greater sense of their own collective support and power as a group of adults who had traditionally been viewed as being limited in terms of their ability to develop and implement practical solutions that enhanced their own psychological health and well-being.

A second project this group of clients developed involved planning and implementing several strategies that enhanced their participation in the community's political process. To this end, they selected representatives from their group who were responsible for contacting local elected officials to set up times to discuss various issues related to mental health services in the community and the need to expand services for people with serious mental health problems. This project was primarily developed in response to proposed cutbacks in local and state spending for mental health services.

Not only did the clients meet with their elected officials, they also testified at a number of legislative hearings organized to help state lawmakers better understand the potential impact of cutting funding for mental health services in the area. Though one of the counselors at the mental health center served as a resource person for the clients to turn to for help if needed, the clients were ultimately responsible for planning and implementing these and other self-help projects.

Because they participated in these self-help projects, several positive changes occurred in the clients' overall psychological disposition. These changes included an increased sense of social purpose and self-esteem, the development of more effective interpersonal and problem-solving skills, and an enhanced pride in their identification with other members in the therapeutic community (D'Andrea, 1994).

The Ideology of Self-Help Groups

Self-help organizations usually expect their members to adhere to some mutual belief system regarding the problems or issues on which the group focuses. As Gartner and Riessman (1984) point out, the ideological character of self-help groups demands involvement beyond the self. This extension of oneself fuels the members' sense of commitment and gives the organization its "force and conviction" (p. 22).

Another aspect of the ideology of self-help organizations relates to the value individuals place on *experiential knowledge,* or one's firsthand knowledge about a specific problem. According to Borkman (1984), "experiential knowledge is developed within self-help groups through a process in which individuals reflect upon and trust as valid their experiences in a context of other people with similar experiences" (p. 207).

The specific content of an organization's ideology may be less important than the fact of its existence as a unifying force and as an explanation for members' successes. In general, however, the longest-lived of the self-help organizations tend to have coherent philosophies readily understood by new members and capable of inspiring lifelong adherence, whether or not science has proven them valid.

Among the numerous self-help organizations in the United States, none has been more successful than Alcoholics Anonymous (AA) in affecting the belief systems of its adherents (Riordan & Walsh, 1994). The ideology of Alcoholics Anonymous has its basis in the Twelve Steps that guide each person's recovery and Twelve Traditions that promote a sense of solidarity among its members. The Twelve Steps fit Borkman's experiential knowledge framework in that they were based on the experiences of AA's earliest members. Here are the Twelve Steps of AA:

1. We admitted we were powerless over alcohol—that our lives had become unmanageable [as a result of abusing alcohol].
2. Came to believe that a Power greater than ourselves could restore us to sanity.

3. Made a decision to turn our will and our lives over to the care of God *as we understood Him*.
4. Made a searching and fearless moral inventory of ourselves.
5. Admitted to God, to ourselves, and to another human being the exact nature of our wrongs.
6. Were entirely ready to have God remove all these defects of character.
7. Humbly asked Him to remove our shortcomings.
8. Made a list of all persons we had harmed, and became willing to make amends to them all.
9. Made direct amends to such people wherever possible, except when to do so would injure them or others.
10. Continued to take personal inventory and when we were wrong promptly admitted it.
11. Sought through prayer and meditation to improve our conscious contact with God *as we understood Him*, praying only for knowledge of His will for us and the power to carry that out.
12. Having had a spiritual awakening as a result of these steps, we tried to carry this message to other alcoholics, and to practice these principles in all our affairs. (*Alcoholics Anonymous*, 1976, pp. 59–60)

These Steps are meant to guide individuals toward long-term recovery. Created by Alcoholics Anonymous, these Steps have also been adapted to fit the needs of other populations. Other "twelve-step groups" that are currently in operation include Al-Anon, Alateen, Narcotics Anonymous, Families Anonymous, and Overeaters Anonymous (Bristow-Braitman, 1995).

The Twelve Traditions, designed to give unity and coherence to AA as an organization, consist of the following:

1. Our common welfare should come first; personal recovery depends upon A.A. unity.
2. For our group purpose there is but one ultimate authority— a loving God as He may express Himself in our group conscience. Our leaders are but trusted servants; they do not govern.
3. The only requirement for A.A. membership is a desire to stop drinking.
4. Each group should be autonomous except in matters affecting other groups or A.A. as a whole.
5. Each group has but one primary purpose—to carry its message to the alcoholic who still suffers.

6. An A.A. group ought never endorse, finance or lend the A.A. name to any related facility or outside enterprise, lest problems of money, property and prestige divert us from our primary purpose.
7. Every A.A. group ought to be fully self-supporting, declining outside contributions.
8. Alcoholics Anonymous should remain forever nonprofessional, but our service centers may employ special workers.
9. A.A., as such, ought never to be organized; but we may create service boards or committees directly responsible to those they serve.
10. Alcoholics Anonymous has no opinion on outside issues; hence the A.A. name ought never be drawn into public controversy.
11. Our public relations policy is based on attraction rather than promotion; we need to always maintain personal anonymity at the level of press, radio and films.
12. Anonymity is the spiritual foundation of all our Traditions, ever reminding us to place principles before personalities. (*Alcoholics Anonymous*, 1976, p. 564)

The Twelve Traditions have helped Alcoholics Anonymous maintain its integrity as a self-help organization. Over the decades, AA has avoided such pitfalls as dependence on outside funding, cooptation by other institutions, and deference to individual personalities. Instead, the fellowship has successfully combined autonomy for its separate groups and commonality of purpose for the organization as a whole (Le, Ingvarson, & Page, 1995).

Mutual Support in Self-Help Groups

People join self-help groups often because they need social support. Typically, these people experience gaps in their own social support networks but may not be particularly attracted to traditional counseling services that reflect a predominately individual, intrapsychic, and remedial approach to helping.

Even the person who does seek professional help may find that his or her family members, friends, and others do not offer enough support or even deny that there is a problem. This sort of unresponsiveness commonly reflects a general lack of understanding of various types of physical or mental health problems which, in turn, leads them to relate poorly to the person, or react only to the negative consequences of his or her problems. Thus, they can actually reinforce the negative stigma associated with being a mental health client.

Sometimes this unsupportiveness is subtle, sometimes overt. Borkman (1984) has coined the phrase *stigmatizing reactions* to describe how people commonly react to others labeled with a particular physical or psychological problem. Such behaviors include ignoring, denying, or minimizing the problem; manipulating situations to protect the troubled individual and thereby avoiding stigmatization; stereotyping the individual; or reacting to interactions with the individual with unease, embarrassment, or discomfort. When counselors recognize that their client's natural support systems are not responsive to her or his needs, they must recommend alternatives, such as self-help groups.

Indeed, anyone dealing with special problems may benefit from developing mutually supportive relationships with others who understand these problems firsthand. Self-help groups provide an opportunity for emotional and social support that might be difficult to find in everyday interactions. This need seems especially important for individuals with health-related problems. In this regard, participation in mutual self-help groups enables clients to realize that they are not alone in their fears and struggles and, at the same time, instills hope by introducing them to others striving positively to confront the challenges that characterize their lives. A partial list of national health-related self-help groups follows:

Alcoholics Anonymous
AMEND (Aid to Mothers Experiencing Neonatal Death)
American Schizophrenic Association
Association for Children with Learning Disabilities
Candlelighters (for parents of young children with cancer)
The Compassionate Friends (for bereaved parents)
Daughters United (for young women who have been
    victims of incest)
DES-Watch (for women who took DES during pregnancy and for
    their daughters)
Emotions Anonymous (a twelve-step program for people with
    emotional problems)
Epilepsy Foundation
Families Anonymous
Gamblers Anonymous
Gay Men's Health Crisis (for gay men concerned about AIDS)
Gray Panthers
Heart to Heart (a one-to-one visitation program for people with
    coronary problems)
Juvenile Diabetes Foundation
La Leche League
Make Today Count (for people with cancer and for their families)

Muscular Dystrophy Association
Narcotics Anonymous
National Alliance for the Mentally Ill
National Association for Retarded Citizens
National Federation of the Blind
National Foundation for Sudden Infant Death
National Gay Task Force
National Society for Autistic Children
Neurotics Anonymous
Overeaters Anonymous
Parents Anonymous
Parents of Stillborns
Parents Without Partners
Parents of Premature and High Risk Infants
Reach to Recover (for women who have had mastectomies)
Recovery, Inc.
Resolve, Inc. (for individuals who are infertile)
Sisterhood of Black Single Mothers
Share (for parents who have lost an infant)
Smokenders
Theos Foundation (for the widowed and their families)
United Cerebral Palsy
Widowed Persons

The length of this partial list indicates the pervasiveness of the self-help phenomenon. Ironically, because of the important services they provide, self-help groups have entered the social mainstream. In these and other organizations designed to foster mutual help and support, people can experience a sense of empowerment. McWhirter (1994) describes *empowerment* as a multifaceted process in which people (1) "become aware of the power dynamics in their life context," (2) "develop the skills and capacity for gaining some reasonable control in their lives," (3) "which they exercise," (4) "without infringing on the rights of others but actively supporting the empowerment of others in their community" (p. 12).

Each of the self-help organizations just mentioned addresses these dimensions of empowerment to a greater or lesser degree. In doing so, they facilitate the empowerment of people who are either vulnerable to or currently experience mental health problems. Central to the empowerment process is clients' motivation and ability to help themselves and others who share similar threats to their psychological well-being (McWhirter, 1994). As Riessman (1985) notes,

> When people help themselves . . . they feel empowered; they are able to control some aspect of their lives. . . . Empowerment expands

energy, motivation, and help-giving power that goes beyond helping one's self or receiving help. In addition, this self-help-induced empowerment may have significant political relevance because, as people are enabled to deal with some aspects of their lives in a competent fashion, the skills and positive feelings they acquire may contagiously spread and empower them to deal with other aspects of their lives. (pp. 2–3)

Self-Help and Political Action: Disability Rights

Riessman (1985) notes that self-help groups have traditionally been non-political, focusing on strengthening individuals rather than on ameliorating adverse social conditions. Some organizations, however, have become more politically oriented, recognizing that the power and competencies their members have developed can affect larger issues.

Researchers have reported many benefits clients derive from advocacy services that include political and social action strategies (Albee, Joffe, & Dusenbury, 1988; D'Andrea, 1994). These sorts of services reflect a natural progression in the empowerment process and typically come into play when clients and counselors come to understand the effect that environmental conditions have on one's psychological health and personal well-being. In this regard Riessman (1985) states,

> An advocacy focus may appear as the self-helpers discover the external causes of their problems. In some cases this takes the form of criticism regarding the provision of services, in other cases it is concerned with the media and the images presented of the particular self-help problem or condition. Underlying all of this is the basic self-help ethos that emphasizes the indigenous strengths of the people involved in contrast to a dependence on external, elite experts. (pp. 3–4)

The Center for Independent Living (CIL), an organization operated by and for disabled people since 1972, exemplifies this self-help ethos. Based on the idea that "disabled people know what is best for disabled people," CIL began in Berkeley, California, as a support service for blind and physically disabled people and as a movement advocating for the rights of the disabled. CIL's brochure describes the accomplishments of this groundbreaking organization:

> CIL is a non-profit organization operated by and for disabled people. It was founded in 1972 in Berkeley by a small group of disabled people who wished to live independent lives away from isolating and costly institutions or dependency upon family. Funding first came from the University of California at Berkeley and private foundations, soon to be followed by government grants for pilot and model

programs never before offered. CIL quickly grew to become the nation's leading advocate for people with all types of disabilities. A pioneer in the disability movement, CIL offered hope and opportunity for many disabled people whose lives had been locked behind institutional doors or similar dependent situations. Disabled people came from all over the country to form an umbrella organization which led to major changes for disabled people. By the late 70s, barriers were broken in all areas as curb cuts opened accessibility; ramps replaced stairs; doors widened as did opportunities in the classroom, workplace, transportation and housing.

For thousands of disabled people and their families these changes opened a world of choices, making a difference between unnecessary confinement, which meant a tax burden as well as isolation, and full participation in our society as tax paying and productive members. Thanks to the efforts of CIL and our many friends, disabled people take their rightful places alongside students, employees in all kinds of corporations and businesses, commuters on the bus and BART [Bay Area Rapid Transit], and in all kinds of social and recreational activities as self-sufficient people demonstrating their abilities. Because CIL's staff members are primarily disabled people, they provide a positive role model for other disabled people seeking to live independently. Because of CIL over 200 similar organizations have sprung up throughout the world. (Center for Independent Living, n.d., p. 1)

CIL offers several programs designed to help its clients live independently in the community. Although which specific services are offered at a given time depends on funding, CIL's basic programs include the following:

Attendant Referral: Interviewing and referral of prospective attendants for disabled and elderly clients who need special housekeeping and personal care in order to live independently

Benefits Counseling: Counseling, education, and representation to ensure that disabled individuals receive the financial and medical benefits to which they are entitled

Blind Services: Instruction in mobility and orientation, reader referrals, talking-book certification, counseling, information, referral services for the visually impaired, and special outreach to visually impaired elderly people

Deaf Services: Peer counseling, referral, and special services to give deaf and hearing-impaired individuals access to all CIL services

Housing Department: Providing disabled and elderly clients assistance in locating and securing accessible and affordable housing; consultation on issues such as building ramps and moving

Independent Living Skills Classes: Instruction by peer counselors on practical issues such as home modifications, cooking, budgeting,

homemaking, nutrition, personal care, vocational planning, and
socialization

Job Development: Assistance in job seeking; offering disability-
awareness workshops with employers and affirmative-action
officers

Mental Disabilities Independent Living Program: Peer counseling and
training in independent living skills for mentally disabled
individuals

Peer Counseling: Personal support for individuals, groups, couples,
and families attempting to cope with stressful interpersonal issues
and social situations

Youth Services: Programs to help young disabled people and their
families make the transition from dependence to independent
living at the earliest possible age, including on-site
psychoeducational training programs at schools

Wheelchair Repair: Servicing and modification of wheelchairs, sale of
wheelchair accessories as well as provision of advice about
purchasing orthopedic equipment

Though important, CIL direct services are offered within a context of
advocacy. Staff members recognize that independent living depends not just
on disabled people's skills and attitudes but also on the degree to which the
environment allows their integration into the greater community. Thus,
CIL members take pride in the changes that have taken place in their home
city of Berkeley and throughout the country since the organization's formation in 1972. As CIL's executive director wrote at the outset of the center's
15th year,

> Fifteen years ago in Berkeley/USA, severely disabled individuals were
> living in nursing homes and institutions.
>
> Fifteen years ago a group of disabled people had an idea, a dream, a
> vision, that they and other people in similar situations should and
> could live in the community.
>
> Fifteen years ago disabled people had to protest in the streets of
> Berkeley in order for the city to provide curb cuts.
>
> Fifteen years ago parents of disabled children had to fight for the
> right of disabled children to be educated alongside non-disabled
> children in public schools.
>
> Ten years ago over 100 disabled persons sat in front of the federal
> building for over 100 days until their civil rights bill, Section 504, was
> signed into law by Jimmy Carter. Just within 10 years disabled people
> had to wage a fight to have bus lifts and make BART accessible. As a
> result of CIL and the independent living movement . . . the ruling
> philosophy is that disabled people should live in the community and
> not in institutions. (Winter, 1986, p. 1)

Self-Help and Volunteerism

Volunteers can provide a valuable link between client populations and the community at large. At one time, the use of volunteers to provide services seemed necessary because of the limited number of professionals available to deal with problems. It is becoming more apparent, however, that volunteers also offer a resource base that benefits community members. Frequently, they offer a depth of personal involvement, a freshness of approach, and a link to the community that salaried personnel cannot duplicate.

Volunteerism has traditionally meant helping others who are less fortunate. By this definition, the distance between the volunteer and the person being helped might be as great as that between the person and a traditional professional mental health worker. However, the idea of who constitutes a potential volunteer and what volunteers do has expanded greatly over the past two decades.

Several pioneers have helped counselors recognize the positive links between volunteerism and self-help efforts. In this regard, Wilson (1976) points out that "instead of being the privilege of the already privileged, volunteering must become the right of everyone: minorities, youth, seniors, the handicapped, blue-collar workers, business people, the disadvantaged" (p. 118). Giving an early voice to empowerment, Cull and Hardy (1974) have noted that volunteer work should move "away from the notion of 'doing for' toward the concepts of 'doing with' and 'helping to help themselves'" (p. 112).

This orientation is particularly important when volunteers work with socially devalued people. Such people can, indeed, help themselves. However, volunteers can play an important role in linking individuals from devalued populations with the greater community by the following:

1. Facilitating two-way communication between the excluded population and the community at large
2. Helping shed light on the particular concerns of the group being served
3. Mobilizing community support for needed programs and changes that foster the empowerment of devalued people

The empowerment process is nurtured when volunteer programs emphasize the importance of having volunteers and the people they serve work together, grow together, and learn together. With this ethic in mind, the best volunteer programs do not replace self-help initiatives but complement them.

These principles of volunteerism were discussed as early as 1972 by Wolfensberger, who described a three-day course during which developmentally disabled adults and volunteers took a trip together.

The nonretarded often arrive with the thought that they are to be the teachers, and the retarded will be their pupils. However, soon after arriving, all participants discover that they are taking part in a course common for all. As tourists, they are going to learn and be enriched through new experiences and meeting new people. All are given the same amount of money for budgeting their weekend needs and activities, such as meals, shopping, sightseeing, and entertainment. When they are exploring the city in small mixed groups of three or four persons (which are changed at intervals), they gradually learn not only about the life and assets of this new city, but they also learn from being together. They find out about public transit, price levels of various restaurants, the amusement possibilities for their Saturday night, and the interesting places for their Sunday morning walk. (p. 182)

Through these experiences, occasional lectures, and comparative reports and discussions, the nondisabled gradually learned more and more about the proper ways of being together with the developmentally disabled, and vice versa. When they later listened to the report from the disabled adults, especially their reactions to the attitudes of the nonretarded people they have met, the volunteers commonly experienced that they were the pupils and the disabled adults the teachers (Wolfensberger, 1972).

Volunteers in programs such as this one certainly do help the people with whom they work. At the same time, however, the volunteers also gain new knowledge and new perceptions they take back to their communities. While strengthening the stigmatized group, volunteers' efforts also help counter stigmatization in the community.

A similar process takes place when volunteers work in corrections. Ways they can help offenders include developing personal relationships with juvenile offenders, probationed offenders, or prison inmates; locating job possibilities for ex-offenders; providing tutoring, vocational training, or other educational opportunities to prison inmates; helping to create recreational programs or other services within prisons; and working with the families of inmates.

Most important, the volunteers recognize correctional facilities as a community responsibility and offenders as a part of the entire community. That is, volunteers create links through their presence and through their recognition of the humanness of the offender and his or her family. As this attitude spreads, the corrections process leaves behind its customary isolation, and the community at large can begin to actively and effectively address problems traditionally consigned to so-called experts.

No expert can solve the problems of the stigmatized. Too many of these problems lie in the attitudes of the community itself; responsibility for solutions therefore falls on the community. Many citizens are beginning to recognize this responsibility and seek their own roles in fulfilling it.

Contemporary efforts to develop effective volunteer programs thus break from traditional forms of volunteerism. The 21st-century volunteer cannot be viewed as someone with excessive leisure time, someone who can fit in to perform whatever task has been left or overlooked. What the volunteer can give is, in many ways, as valuable as what the professional can offer. For all these reasons, 21st-century volunteers have the right to expect new attitudes about their value and be provided opportunities to promote the psychological health of others as well as nurture the general well-being of their communities in the process.

Professionals should encourage volunteers to examine their own needs and develop work styles and assignments that meet them. They should receive immediate training during an orientation period, followed by in-service education that responds to questions they themselves raise. They should have the opportunity to use their volunteer work to develop their own careers, whether in receiving academic credit or in being considered for paid human service positions. Most important, practitioners should encourage volunteers to use their own creativity to develop roles and programs that meet needs they have observed in the community.

Volunteerism, along with self-help groups, "may be the treatment of choice for many individuals whose need to become involved with other community members is greater than their need to become clients. When community members help themselves and one another, resources increase geometrically" (Lewis, Lewis, & Souflee, 1991, p. 101).

FOSTERING A RESPONSIVE HELPING NETWORK

Although self-help groups and volunteers play an important role in the empowerment process, clients sometimes need help from other human services agencies and institutions. In most communities, several organizations offer such help. Examples include the following:

- Mental health facilities that attempt to treat or prevent psychological problems
- Educational and religious institutions
- Specialized agencies that deal with specific problems such as substance abuse, legal or medical problems, family conflicts, disabilities, poverty, or homelessness
- Agencies that provide services to specific populations, such as women, gays and lesbians, children, adolescents, or the elderly

- Crisis or suicide prevention centers
- Employment or rehabilitation centers that help individuals gain the skills and opportunities they need to achieve independence and economic security
- Employee assistance programs that provide services at the work site

These entities may be government-supported, charitable, or self-help; large or small; formal or informal. They all, however, help people experiencing personal difficulties, especially those coming from devalued and stigmatized populations.

Individuals may also help in this way, particularly those whose occupation gives them a special opportunity to work with people. For example, teachers, police officers, welfare workers, and employers can all act as important helping resources if they are sensitive to the human needs of the people around them.

These individuals in combination with self-help groups constitute a *helping network* that makes up an important part of the social environment in every community. But the helping network is helpful only if it responds to the needs of the people it seeks to serve. Further, one can call it a network only if all its parts connect intentionally and purposefully. Several mechanisms, including class advocacy, community-based planning, and consultation, can foster a responsive helping network.

Class Advocacy

Though self-help efforts expand people's ability to control their own lives, true empowerment often depends on changes beyond the individual or the group, as you have already seen. Making the social, political, and economic environment conducive to the development of people with special needs requires active advocacy efforts. As mentioned earlier in this chapter, *advocacy* refers to the act of speaking up for people whose rights might be in jeopardy. In addition, *class advocacy* involves working to protect the rights of an entire category of people.

MOTIVATION TO ACT When community counselors see the rights of less powerful individuals or groups compromised, they take action. Ideally, counselors act to empower and strengthen oppressed individuals or groups to the point where they can protect themselves. In the interim, however, mental health professionals may need to act as advocates, defending those who cannot defend themselves and working to limit the power of those who abuse others.

Advocates fight not just against dehumanization but also for humanization. That is, people's rights extend beyond simply not being mistreated.

People have the right to develop their own creativity and their own values, to access all the benefits society offers, and to increase the numbers and kinds of choices they may make in their lives. When counselors see a client being confined and restricted, they seek to alter the situation, whether by trying to change a policy or by attempting to make those in authority accountable. They struggle not just to eliminate constraints but also to create opportunities.

Thus, when community counselors in school settings learn of an unfairly punished child, they confront the school authorities. They also confront those authorities when children are denied the opportunity to learn in nurturing, exciting classroom environments. Similarly, when community counselors see their clients being treated without dignity by agency personnel, they confront those personnel. They also fight for their clients' rights to access services that facilitate their empowerment and sense of personal well-being. Finally, when community counselors see individuals denied their right to privacy in mental health residential settings, they act to safeguard that right. At the same time, they seek the recognition of clients' rights to a comfortable and stimulating environment.

Ideally, advocacy is motivated not by an immediate crisis but by a sensitivity to potential problems. In *preventive advocacy*, the community counselor recognizes a situation that may deprive individuals of rights or opportunities and acts to change the environment before individual clients suffer. This sort of advocacy arises most frequently when counselors have identified a population as having special needs that the environment could help them to meet or as needing support in protecting their freedom and dignity. Acting on behalf of the group as a whole can prevent much harm to individuals identified as being at-risk for physical or mental health problems, part of a socially devalued group, or persons who have been stigmatized because of their differences with other persons in the mainstream of society.

CITIZEN ADVOCACY   Fortunately, community counselors do not need to bear the burden of advocacy alone. With the development of *citizen advocacy*, large numbers of people are available to work on behalf of others. Among the first to define this term, Wolfensberger and Zauha (1973) say a *citizen advocate* is

> a mature, competent citizen volunteer representing, as if they were his [or her] own, the interests of another citizen who is impaired in his [or her] instrumental competency (meaning the ability to solve practical problems of everyday living), or who has major expressive needs which are unmet and which are likely to remain unmet without special intervention. (p. 11)

Riessman (1985) points out that when self-help efforts move from pre-political to advocative actions, they often progress through three stages. First, a sense of empowerment begins to emerge in the group as a result of participating in self-help endeavors. Second, as individuals gain a greater understanding of the importance of addressing environmental factors to realize fully their individual and collective potential, they start to plan and implement advocacy strategies. Finally, groups and organizations begin to see the interconnections among issues and form coalitions with other groups and organizations in the community. As Riessman (1985) emphatically states, class advocacy works best when a variety of self-help and citizens' groups work together to address their mutual needs.

Advocacy in a Multicultural Society

People from nonwhite, non-European backgrounds often view counseling as an intimidating process that conflicts with many of their traditional values and customs. As such, counselors have turned to alternative strategies to help individuals from diverse cultural, ethnic, and racial backgrounds (Locke, 1992; D. W. Sue et al., 1996). With this in mind, several multicultural counseling theorists have noted that client advocacy may, in fact, be the service of choice for such people (Atkinson et al., 1993) for several reasons.

First, as Atkinson et al. (1993) point out, the dominant society by definition oppresses, to some degree, all people from ethnic-racial minority groups in the United States. Some individuals in these groups have developed skills that help them deal with this daily oppression. Others, particularly those who have recently immigrated to this country, may lack the English-speaking skills and economic resources that buffer oppressive environments. In these situations, the client may need advocacy services more than direct counseling services.

> As an advocate, the counselor speaks on behalf of the client, often confronting the institutional sources of oppression that are contributing to the client's problems. The counselor need not represent a particular client or group of clients; rather the entire minority culture experiencing an injustice may function as client. In this role the counselor represents a client or group of clients who have brought a particular form of discrimination to the counselor's attention. Being an empathic counselor who suggests alternative ways of coping with a particular problem is not enough; the counselor must be willing to pursue actively alternative courses with or for the client, including making a personal contact for the client, who is overwhelmed with the bureaucracy of social service, legal, and/or employment agencies. (Atkinson et al., 1993, p. 301)

In many instances, the problems nonwhite clients experience are externally based. For this reason, advocacy services intentionally designed to ameliorate the stressful conditions that exist in daily environments, such as fostering a helping network or soliciting help from citizen advocacy groups, represent more relevant and appropriate ways to help these people than direct counseling services do.

Second, advocacy may be the intervention of choice because some cultural groups consider seeking help for their personal problems shameful. For instance, several investigators have noted that Asian Americans tend not to seek help from mental health professionals because they see it as shameful. This is of particular concern given that many Aisan Americans finally turn to counseling only when their psychological health has seriously deteriorated (Atkinson et al., 1993; S. Sue & McKinney, 1975; S. Sue & Sue, 1974). Thus, counselors may find working indirectly as an advocate for these clients a useful intervention strategy.

Third, discomfort at having to explore highly personal issues with a stranger (e.g., a counselor) is common among most people. Given that most mental health practitioners in the United States come from European backgrounds, however, people of color will likely experience greater discomfort than white clients, especially if the former have been discriminated against by the dominant social group. Given the level of racial tension that continues to exist in this country, the indirect advocacy approach will most likely be a relatively appealing and effective form of intervention for many culturally diverse clients (Atkinson et al., 1993).

Fourth, counselors can greatly facilitate the empowerment of clients in culturally diverse populations by advocating for the development of coalitions among groups and organizations that share common goals even though their constituencies come from different backgrounds. Although infrequently used by many traditional counselors, coalition-building strategies represent a vital part of the community counseling model.

Coalition Building

A *coalition* is a group of organizations working together for a common purpose. The combined resources of these groups can have a greater impact than can the same constituency groups working by themselves.

Organizations may come together to address multiple issues affecting their constituencies. Coalitions can also arise to address a single unifying issue (Kahn, 1991). The length of time that groups and organizations stay together in a coalition largely depends on the issue(s) to be addressed. In commenting on the different types of coalitions that have emerged in communities across the nation, Kahn (1991) notes,

Short-term coalitions are often easier to put together because they ordinarily require only that each participating organization be in favor of the particular issue in question. A single-issue coalition can bring together organizations that would otherwise have difficulty working together. In the long run, though, there is also a need to build coalitions that can fight on a number of issues and that involve many different kinds of constituencies and organizations. (p. 238)

THREE STAGES OF COALITION BUILDING   When planning to build a coalition with other mental health, educational, and advocacy groups in their community, counselors should keep in mind the following three stages:

1. *The Planning Stage:* In the planning stage, counselors must identify those constituency groups that might link with their organization to address an issue of common concern. This task includes making sure that those invited to attend the first coalition-building meeting really do have a common interest and stake in the given issue(s).

2. *The Consultation Stage:* Coalition building involves more than simply presenting an issue to each organization in a way that makes the members appreciate its importance and value. During the consultation stage, representatives from various organizations must discuss the ways in which joining into a coalition with other groups will benefit each constituency.

3. *The Planning and Implementation Stage:* The planning and implementation stage of the coalition-building process determines the level of interest and commitment individuals genuinely have regarding the issues of common concern to them. This is critical because individuals will likely demonstrate an increased commitment to a coalition when they feel they have been directly involved in the planning and implementation of beneficial strategies. Given their training and expertise in human relations, community counselors are well equipped to deal with the challenging task of facilitating group discussions that involve all participants during the planning and implementation stage.

Indeed the overall success of a coalition requires that all members own the work they have agreed to do. This sense of ownership increases when individuals (1) feel as though they have received the opportunity to express their views and (2) feel their views have been heard and respected by the other members in the coalition during this stage.

Coalition building represents another way counselors can foster a helping network that promotes the well-being of people from stigmatized and socially devalued groups. Counselors must keep in mind, however, that the primary purpose of building these networks is to help their clients become more responsible and empowered participants in society.

AN EXAMPLE OF COALITION BUILDING   One successful coalition-building effort took place in the state of Washington, where organizations concerned with developmental disabilities have broadened their focus to speak on behalf of all citizens who experience any sort of mental, emotional, or physical challenge. In early 1983, representatives from several groups concerned with disability issues met to explore the possibility of increasing their strength through unified action. As a result of this meeting, three separate organizations were formed.

The Washington Assembly for Citizens with Disabilities would function as a lobbying and political body. The Disabilities Political Action Committee would handle financial contributions to political campaigns and work on behalf of selected candidates for election. The Developmental Disabilities Research and Information Coalition would conduct research and disseminate information on issues affecting people with disabilities. These three organizations have continued to grow steadily ever since, complementing one another's efforts on behalf of stigmatized and devalued citizens.

The Washington Assembly for Citizens with Disabilities (WACD) affects the political process by rating candidates and endorsing issues. The assembly also organizes political activity for and against legislative issues regarding habilitation rights, services, and related issues.

The goals of WACD include the following:

1. Increase community support for developmental services.
2. Increase citizen participation in the political process to obtain and maintain developmental and support services.
3. Build a broad-based coalition to support adequate human service systems.
4. Improve the quality and quantity of services to citizens with various types of mental, emotional, or physical challenges by working for the continued development of a comprehensive service system that promotes (1) the protection of individual interests in the areas of health, human, and legal rights, (2) the presence of citizens with disabilities in the community, (3) community participation, and (4) competency building and status enhancement. (Washington Assembly for Citizens with Disabilities, 1987)

WACD accomplishes these goals by coordinating activities such as voter registration and education, coalition building, rating legislators, administering questionnaires on candidates, community organizing, endorsing issues, operating a hot line, lobbying, providing advocacy services, and statewide networking. The assembly includes representatives from groups throughout the state concerned with a broad range of issues stemming from the situations their clients encounter in their daily lives.

A key to the assembly's structure is the *core group*, or those citizens who accept the responsibility of organizing and maintaining the communications network for a specific region of the community, city, or state. The communications network is vital to any coalition because it allows members to share information and unite citizens for their cause.

The core group thus brings together parents, consumers, service providers, professionals, and local advocacy groups to help develop and implement the coalition's action plan. The core group provides a structure through which the power of individuals from diverse groups and populations can be fostered and tapped. It also provides a means for these people to contribute to the assembly's discussions of important local issues. Further, the core group enables the assembly and other statewide organizations to mobilize local citizens for lobbying efforts.

The second component of this statewide coalition, the Disabilities Political Action Committee (D-PAC), focuses specifically on the electoral process. The D-PAC raises money for candidates who support adequate funding for special education and human services. The organization also uses contributions to support legislation in favor of programs and services that expand helping networks throughout the state of Washington.

Third, the Developmental Disabilities Research and Information Coalition provides information to the community, legislature, administrative agencies, and others concerned with issues related to developmental disabilities. Except for providing information, the coalition engages in no political activity. Rather, it provides a nonpartisan forum for generating and exchanging information on budgetary and other issues affecting special education and human services for people with various types of mental, emotional, and/or physical challenges. The coalition does this by disseminating the results of their research in a newsletter distributed to the state legislature and the general public.

By working together in these sorts of coalitions, the statewide organizations representing people with disabilities in Washington can powerfully and uniquely support self-help groups, promote a greater awareness of volunteerism, and safeguard the rights of people with special needs. A small sampling of the legislation in Washington State over the past decade illustrates the combined impact of these coalitions. This included the passing of numerous legislative bills that resulted in

- A mandate for preschool programs to be available for children with disabilities
- An expansion in learning assistance programs for students from kindergarten through ninth grade
- Maintenance of a special education office within the Office of the Superintendent of Public Instruction

- Increased spending for programs that provide family support and home-aid services
- The reinstatement of dental services for people with disabilities
- The passage of a safe-medication bill that allows people with minimal cognitive or physical skills who take medication to live in the community
- Funding for community residential placements
- Fiscal support for employment programs for previously unserved adults with developmental disabilities
- The passage of habilitation rights legislation declaring that all people have a right to habilitative services
- An amendment of a state law, making verbal or physical harassment of persons with physical, mental, or sensory disabilities a criminal offense
- Measures to ensure that people who are deaf or hard of hearing will have certified interpreters when involved in the criminal justice system
- The provision of adaptive telecommunication devices at the public's expense
- Protection of clients' privacy when their records are used for research purposes
- The establishment of the right of clients and their families to design and have funded less restrictive, alternative programs for themselves (Washington Assembly for Citizens with Disabilities, 1987)

The legislation supported by the Washington-based coalitions is noteworthy for its sensitivity to human needs. At all governmental levels, policies that affect the helping network need to be responsive, well-coordinated, and carefully planned.

Community-Based Planning

The effectiveness of the helping network in any community depends on the care people have taken in planning it. Responsive and well-organized helping networks share several distinctive characteristics, as follows.

1. Both those who deliver and those who use services actively plan and evaluate programs.

When using traditional approaches to helping, an agency or institution plans what services they will offer, then hires workers to perform specified roles in the service delivery system. Responsive helping networks tend to use community-based planning, whereby agency workers at all levels continuously attempt to evaluate community needs and create or adapt programs to meet them. A fluid process, community-based planning has no clear beginning and no end. Often, when workers or community members recognize the need for a particular kind of program, they use existing skills and resources in newly created programs or new locations.

Ongoing assessment of services by those who actually use an agency's services works most effectively in small agencies. Because such agencies lack the power and resources to influence community-wide planning, they need other means to this end.

2. Agencies work together in cooperative helping networks.

In small agencies, workers and community members can feel a sense of ownership, a sense that the agency belongs to them. Small agencies can also provide ample opportunities for workers and community members alike to participate in planning the agency's programs.

Yet, every community needs some kind of centralized planning. Because almost all communities have limited resources, each community must allocate them according to chosen priorities. Without cooperative networks, agencies find themselves simply competing against one another for limited funds. United, however, they can identify gaps in the community's services, plan joint programs when appropriate, and share valuable resources. Most important, agencies working together can influence the decisions of government officials and of established social-planning agencies. Only then can the people who actually deliver services participate in community-wide planning.

3. The network has a coordinating organization that facilitates ongoing planning and includes workers and community members in the process.

If members of the helping network are to be adequately represented in the planning process, they must be able to rely on some ongoing, stable structure—an organization or group of people assigned to keep track of community needs and changes in available resources. The advantages of such a body include the following: (1) Network members can maintain ongoing relationships with other groups in the community; (2) planning can be continuous and developmental instead of reactive and limited; and (3) support can be mobilized immediately whenever needed. An ongoing group can recognize problems when they arise and see the positive potential in legislative changes. As long as it maintains effective communication, a coordinating group can call on the participating agencies when necessary and keep them informed of changes in the community.

4. The network has a mechanism through which it can react to specific issues.

In addition to making long-range plans, the network should be prepared to take advantage of opportunities when they arise and to deal intensively with specific issues when they emerge in the community. By forming alliances or coalitions with other community groups, network members develop a mechanism by which groups can act en masse to a relevant issue or opportunity. Such actions are most efficient when these groups communicate regularly. If a situation requires joint planning, separate organizations can quickly unite and forge effective work units.

Another mechanism that can facilitate the network's response to specific issues is a task force or research group that focuses on a particular topic. Research task forces can intensively study a community's needs and resources in relation to particular areas. They can gain in-depth knowledge, create concrete plans, and share the results of their studies with other network members. This planning strategy is particularly efficient because it combines the strength of large numbers with the specialization of small groups.

5. Conventional planning agencies within the network are open to broad participation.

So that volunteers and agency workers do not merely parallel the efforts of conventional planning agencies, they all must constantly exchange information and ideas. Such an exchange proves most effective when the planning agencies are open to participation by individuals representing a variety of community groups. Therefore, successful planning requires broad-based community involvement in not only direct service agencies but also agencies that allocate funds. After all, a community implements its real priorities in its financial decisions.

6. Governmental agencies, social-planning agencies, direct service agencies, and community groups maintain an ongoing dialogue.

Planning is most effective when the participants of a community's helping network are interdependent and maintain a continuous exchange of ideas. Because people may feel compelled to promote the mission and philosophy of their own group, however, this exchange may, at times, prove confrontational rather than collaborative. As such, planners should try to resolve their philosophical differences in the interest of delivering efficient and relevant services.

When diverse agencies and institutions can work together this way, the resulting plan will likely be efficient. Through open dialogue, participants can realistically analyze community needs and allocate resources. Networks make the most of each available dollar, property, and worker; consequently, competition for scarce resources decreases.

Further, instead of duplicating services, agencies and community members can plan programs and services that complement one another well. Most important, the efficiency engendered by a broad-based planning process allows networks to give priority to the rights and interests of those who will ultimately be served by such programs and services.

7. The rights of consumers, as well as the uniqueness of each agency, are protected at all stages of the planning process.

Community-based planning allows planners to remain sensitive to the needs of individuals and to the will of the community. Planners working in isolation can inadvertently overlook the rights of individuals. When a broad coalition of persons does the planning, however, the decision making will more likely represent all interests of the community. Further, agencies will also more likely retain the flexibility and informality they need to maintain their roots in the community. Thus, as the community changes, its helping network can change with it.

The recent development and implementation of school-community-parent management systems in the public schools across the United States provides a good example of how coalition-building strategies can give parents and others a greater say in how schools are organized and managed. Regardless of the setting and participants, though, counselors need to use their human relations skills to facilitate the coalition-building process. The degree to which counselors can help facilitate this process depends on their ability to consult effectively with people from varied backgrounds and positions within school, business, and community settings.

Consultation

During the 1960s and 1970s, counseling theorists began emphasizing the importance of using consultation services (Caplan, 1970; Schein, 1969). A classic definition of consultation frequently used since came from Caplan (1970), who described consultation as the following:

> A process of interaction between two professional persons—the consultant, who is a specialist, and the consultee, who invokes the consultant's help in regard to a current work problem with which he [or she] is having difficulty and which he [or she] has decided is within the other's area of specialized competence. (p. 19)

In this definition, the traditional role of the consultant is seen primarily as remedial and problem oriented. However, since then, the idea of the consultant's role has shifted from this focus to a more proactive, preventive, and systemic interpretation. Thus, rather than helping consultees target specific factors and individuals for change, the contemporary view of consultation emphasizes the importance of helping others develop more expansive conceptual abilities that enhance what Kurpius and Fuqua (1993a) call *paradigm shift thinking*. In describing this thinking, they note the following:

> A paradigm is how we see things and what we choose to believe
> about those observations. It is our internal frame of reference that
> frames our view of reality. Marilyn Ferguson (1980) proposed that the
> old paradigm for change and helping followed a theme of separation,
> which posed dichotomies such as past and future, cause and effect,
> and mind and body. The newly emerging paradigm according to
> Ferguson proposes seamlessness, which is embedded in collaboration,
> participation, and other forms of interpersonal and intrapersonal
> connectedness. In this regard consultation is neither just an expert
> who inserts an intervention for all to accept nor just a processor of
> what exists, but is a connected combination of human and structural
> helping with a heavy emphasis placed on helping the persons
> involved to better understand the paradigm issues, human and
> structural, that support and hinder the growth, development, and
> desired change. (Kurpius & Fuqua, 1993b p. 596)

Counselors can use consultation services to help others (1) better understand current paradigm shifts in society, (2) learn how these paradigm shifts affect the way people think about and behave in different environments, and (3) consider new strategies to promote human development in light of the paradigm changes that will continue into the 21st century. In this way, counselors can help administrators, policy-makers, and program planners think in more creative and expansive ways about the organization and management of our schools, businesses, and communities.

Consultation can thus help others think about how they might make school, work, and community environments more conducive to nurturing human potential. Successful consultation efforts in this regard lead to what others have referred to as collaborative schools (West & Idol, 1993), learning organizations (Senge, 1990), and empowering communities (Werner & Tyler, 1993).

Contrary to the idea that only professionals engage in consultation, most members of a helping network find themselves acting sometimes as consultants and at other times as consultees—that is, sometimes they help their colleagues, sometimes they ask for help. The role they play does not always depend on their formal roles or specializations. Their practical knowledge of and competence in dealing with specific aspects of human behavior and development are far more relevant.

Generally, consultation efforts consistent with the community counseling model include the following characteristics:

1. *The consultee asks for help.* Participation in a consultation is voluntary. When the consultee recognizes that (1) a real problem, (2) a potential problem, or (3) a chance to promote an organization's wellness and empowerment exists, he or she may request assistance from someone he or she considers competent to offer it.

2. *The consultant has no power over the consultee's actions.* The relationship between the consultant and the consultee is cooperative. Just as the consultee chooses whether or not to participate in the process, he or she can choose whether to follow the consultant's recommendations or not. Though the two work together to solve immediate problems and to increase the consultee's skills, the consultee decides which actions or solutions to implement.

3. *The consultation process is educational.* The consultee may request help with an immediate situation or with long-term planning to enhance the organization's ability to empower its members. Thus, consultation strives to improve an organization in two ways: (1) how it solves its problems and (2) how it realizes its potential as an environment that promotes collective learning and development (Senge, 1990).

Consultants can help counselors learn to work more effectively with a particular type of client or deal with a special problem. They can encourage organizations to examine the benefits of changing current policies and operating principles. In both cases, the consultant educates and motivates the consultees.

4. *The consultant uses holistic strategies.* To be effective, the consulting process must deal with the consultee's feelings, attitudes, and values. In this way, the consulting relationship resembles a counseling relationship; however, the desired end is different. The consultee's personality is dealt with primarily in terms of its effect on his or her work in a given professional, community, school, or other organizational setting. The goal, therefore, is to increase the consultee's effectiveness in this aspect of living.

5. *Consultation focuses on an external individual, group, or organizational issue.* The long-term beneficiaries of the consultation process include the individuals or groups affected by the consultee's development. Although the consultee may learn a great deal through participation in the process, what he or she learns is intended to impact the development and well-being of others in the consultee's environments.

In general, then, consultation involves equal communication between the consultant and consultee. Both focus on how the consultation might positively affect the people and systems counselors will likely serve as consultants (such as clients, community agencies, schools, and businesses).

MULTICULTURAL CONSULTATION CONSIDERATIONS   The knowledge counselors have about the process and potential benefits of consultation has
greatly increased over the past three decades. The consultation models presented in the professional literature, however, often lack sensitivity to multicultural issues. Jackson and Hayes (1993) have been among the first to
strongly assert that "consultation models are deficient in the areas related
to ethnic, racial, and cultural diversity" (p. 144).

With the increasing cultural diversity of the United States, counselors
must be aware of the potential impact cultural factors may have in consulting, such as the following issues that were adapted from Jackson and Hayes
(1993, pp. 144–145):

1. The integration of multicultural concerns into consultation is
   necessary to ensure that ethnically diverse organizations will have
   their members' needs, goals, and missions achieved.
2. Consultants need to be aware that individuals, organizations, and
   communities usually struggle with problems and issues that reflect
   cultural differences.
3. When working in culturally diverse settings, consultants' overall
   effectiveness will largely depend on how comfortably they can
   discuss cultural and ethnic issues as they relate to the concerns
   and challenges confronting individuals in schools, organizations
   and work places.
4. Lack of familiarity with a particular culture does not preclude
   a consultant from working with culturally diverse consultees.
   The consultant must, however, demonstrate a genuine
   willingness to learn about the ways cultural dynamics influence
   the consultation process. Certainly, some of this learning should
   precede the consultant's efforts to assess the consultee's needs
   and challenges.
5. Although consultants recognize that resistance commonly
   emerges at some point in the consultation process, the
   culturally competent consultant should be particularly sensitive
   to the ways racial-ethnic differences may inadvertently
   contribute to increased levels of resistance and tension during
   consultation.
6. Consultants must know the differences in the formal and
   informal communication patterns, structures, and power
   dynamics that typically exist in organizations comprising people
   from diverse backgrounds.

In short, culturally competent consultants recognize that they must
address culture when consulting with people who come from different back-

grounds and traditions, whether consultants work with individuals, organizations, or entire communities.

CONSULTATION WITH INDIVIDUALS   A network of helpers may possess more resources among themselves than one might guess. Instead of considering only a small group of experts as potential consultants, helping professionals should recognize that everyone in the larger helping network has expertise to share. What can result is cross-consultation among cooperating equals who take turns as consultants and consultees, depending on the specific issue being discussed and the particular need and expertise of the helping professionals involved.

Counselors routinely assist such diverse service providers as school personnel, police officers, correctional workers, and family service workers. Yet, special situations frequently occur in which they must in turn seek consultation from these same professionals. For instance, substance-abuse counselors often act as consultants to educational institutions and as consultees of health-care providers. These roles reverse, however, if the counselor needs help setting up an educational program or the health-care provider requires information about a particular client. Thus, one should not consider consultation as hierarchical.

Helping professionals are responsible for recognizing when they need assistance from others and when they can provide help to their colleagues. Further, by demonstrating their willingness to consult with others, commuity counselors strengthen the link so important within any helping network.

Consultation often involves a dyadic collaboration with the consultant assisting another helper with some aspect of service delivery (Brown, 1993). In most cases, this type of consultation aims at helping the consultee gain greater skill or objectivity in working with problems he or she will likely face again. For instance, the consultant might share specific information concerning the needs of certain client groups or the likely effects of specific behaviors.

Rarely, however, does the consultant present solutions in a vacuum; rather, he or she considers how to improve the long-term effectiveness of individual helpers and their agencies. Whether the consultant is working with a co-worker or with a colleague in another agency, he or she should (1) facilitate the consultee's exploration of the problem; (2) emphasize the importance of considering cultural, contextual, and systemic factors; (3) encourage the consultee to search actively for alternatives; and (4) collaborate with the consultee in developing a concrete plan for resolving the problem.

A large group of potential consultees exists outside of professional human service agencies. Many people have jobs that place them in close contact with others or give them a degree of power over other people's lives. Consultation can enable these members of the informal helping network to serve others more constructively and sensitively. It also enables them to handle many problems without turning to an agency for help.

For instance, an employer who has just hired an ex-offender or a physically challenged person may either overemphasize the new employee's difference from others in the organization or be unaware of the importance of other issues, such as confidentiality. Consultation can help such an employer find a responsive middle road that reflects an increased awareness of the person's similarities with other employees and a better understanding of the importance of respecting his or her differences.

Similarly, a teacher may encounter a student with a unique learning problem or unusual behaviors. Talking with a consultant may enable the teacher to devise, try, and evaluate new approaches to the situation while becoming more aware of his or her own attitudes toward the child. A consultant's support may mean the difference between effectively teaching the child in a regular classroom or sending him or her to special education facilities.

Often the first to make contact with people in crisis, police officers can respond most appropriately if they have access to information about the psychological aspects of a situation and the most effective methods of communicating personal concern.

In these and other situations, a consultant can help community members deal with difficult problems in the settings in which they occur. If the practice of consultation spreads, many of these problems can actually be prevented.

CONSULTATION WITH ORGANIZATIONS   Because of their human relations skills, counselors are often called on to act as consultants within their own and other work settings, not only to help develop individual competencies but also to improve the climate of the organization as a whole. Through *organizational development* efforts, they can help bring about planned change in whole systems.

To create these sorts of changes, consultants typically develop a process that helps the organization assess its own challenges, plan ways to address these challenges effectively, and set their plans in motion. In doing so, consultants should try to help organizations (1) take full advantage of available human resources, (2) support input from persons at all levels of the organization, and (3) reinforce individuals' willingness to plan and implement needed changes (Beer & Spector, 1993).

To help organizations find ways to identify and meet their unique challenges, consultants can apply any combination of interventions, including the following:

1. Group process interventions, such as team building, laboratory training, or observation and feedback concerning group dynamics
2. Intercultural-intergroup process interventions, including conflict-resolution strategies, intergroup confrontations, and joint problem-solving sessions
3. Training programs designed to enhance interpersonal, intercultural, and organizational communications skills
4. Survey feedback, which involves collecting, analyzing, and disseminating assessment data about the organization
5. Action research interventions in which behavioral science technologies are used to develop strategies for change
6. Advocating for changes in organizational structure that are based on members' consensus about such changes (Lewis et al., 1991)

CONSULTATION WITH COMMUNITIES By working collaboratively with other groups, counselors can also serve as consultants to improve the problem-solving capacities of entire communities. Consultation at the level of formal intergroup interactions is often called *community organizing*. Kahn (1991) discusses three components of community organization: locality development, social planning, and social action. Distinguishing these components can help community counselors adapt consultation procedures to community settings.

In *locality development*, as in organizational development, good communication can help people with common interests identify them. Here, the consultant serves to facilitate this communication by using such tactics as leading small problem-solving groups, planning and implementing intergroup meetings, and fostering clear and respectful communication among people from different cultural, ethnic, and racial backgrounds.

Seeing self-help and empowerment as the community's primary goals, the community consultant concentrates on helping it become the kind of environment that nurtures effective collaboration regarding the challenges and problems that confront the community. Counselors can use this approach with either the entire community or a specific segment of it. This process-oriented approach to locality development is commonly used for the following:

1. To encourage the development of self-help groups for various people in the community
2. To build more effective support systems and helping networks for individual community members
3. To generate creative solutions both to current problems and to long-range issues

4. To enhance the problem-solving capacities of the community
5. As a first step in readying community groups for social action (Lewis et al., 1991, p. 191)

Next, consultants taking a *social planning approach* to community organization recognize they can help solve specific problems in a rational manner that respects the unique cultural, racial, and ethnic differences within the community. Following this approach, the consultant gathers data through research and makes substantive recommendations based on her or his analysis of the data. Community counselors use this approach when asked to assess a community's needs, to conduct empirical studies, or to make suggestions based on their knowledge of social and psychological systems. Such content-oriented consultation might prove appropriate in the following circumstances:

1. When community groups have set clear goals for themselves and require only technical assistance to achieve their goals
2. When identifiable ecosystem changes are important to clients' well-being
3. When future agency plans will be affected by the results of the research
4. When those sponsoring the planning process have the power, resources, and commitment needed to implement specific changes in the community (Lewis et al., 1991, p. 191)

Finally, in *social action approaches,* counselors assume that a certain group within the community is entitled to a more equitable share of available resources and power than it actually receives. Social action consultants see themselves as accountable to this segment of the community, with the ultimate goal of consultation being a shift of power. Consultants thus serve to facilitate the development of leaders within the group and to help plan and implement community-based, sociopolitical action strategies.

Counselors might use this approach for the following reasons:

1. To increase the community's responsiveness to the needs of community members
2. To enhance the feelings of potency and self-esteem among community members who might be unable to affect their environment as individuals
3. To improve environmental influences impinging on healthy human development
4. To develop local leaders (Lewis et al., 1991, p. 191)

SUMMARY

Indirect client services serve to make the environment more responsive to the rights and needs of people in specific populations. Often, clients who need specialized services possess some disability that might cause them to be stigmatized or devalued by the larger community. The act of becoming a client may actually exacerbate the problem by increasing the individual's feelings of dependence and powerlessness.

When counselors follow the community counseling model in their work with such clients, they endeavor to put the label or problem in perspective as only one part of the individual's total being, to end clients' self-devaluation, to bring excluded individuals into the mainstream of social interaction, to increase the power of stigmatized groups to fight for needed social changes, and to increase the community's responsiveness to the needs and rights of devalued people. To accomplish these ends, counselors encourage self-help and voluntary efforts while working to make the community's helping network more responsive.

In self-help organizations, people dealing with common issues or problems meet one another, provide mutual support, and have the opportunity to both seek and offer assistance. That each member can act as a helper to others is key to the effectiveness of such groups. According to the helper therapy principle, giving help can be even more beneficial to the individual than receiving it.

Another key to the effectiveness of self-help organizations is their adherence to a common ideology. A good example of such an ideology can be found in the Twelve Steps and Twelve Traditions of Alcoholics Anonymous (AA). The Twelve Traditions have helped AA maintain its integrity as a self-help organization, while the Twelve Steps have provided guidelines for the recovery of individual members. Self-help groups also provide social support that can make up for gaps in an individual's natural support network. Because these organizations are so empowering, the self-help phenomenon has evolved into an important movement that has grown substantially in the United States and other parts of the world.

Although many self-help efforts focus on the ability of individual members to control their lives, some have developed strong advocacy components because members have become aware of the external causes of their problems. A good example of the marriage between self-help and advocacy is the disability rights movement as implemented by such agencies as the Center for Independent Living (CIL).

Though CIL provides several direct services by and for disabled individuals, the agency's staff members recognize that independent living depends as much on the environment as on the individual's skills and attitudes. For this reason, the agency has remained at the forefront of the disability rights effort, addressing such issues as community integration and accessibility in transportation and housing.

Self-help and voluntary groups form one part of the total network of caregivers in a given community. For clients who sometimes need additional help, almost all communities possess a number of individuals, agencies, and institutions that together constitute a helping network. Counselors who use the community counseling model try to improve the responsiveness of this helping network through such strategies as class advocacy, community-based planning, and consultation.

Clients' well-being also depends on a cohesive network of service agencies. Well-planned service networks involve both service deliverers and consumers in planning and evaluation; coordinate the work of separate agencies; maintain an ongoing dialogue among governmental agencies, social-planning agencies, direct service agencies, and community groups; and protect the rights of consumers.

In the final analysis, consultation among members of the helping network may be the best means counselors can use to improve the network's effectiveness. Consultation serves three purposes: helping individuals and organizations deal with immediate problems, improving their ability to solve future problems, and engendering new ways of operating that enhance the quality of life within the organization. The community counseling framework encourages counselors to act as consultants to individuals, organizations, and communities, using a variety of methods to make the helping network more responsive to their clients' needs.

SUPPLEMENTAL ACTIVITIES

1. Understanding stigmatization is difficult without actually experiencing it. Although you can never duplicate the experience of another individual or group, you can attempt, at least temporarily, to learn something about how social devaluation affects people. Choose one population, preferably one you hope to work with professionally. Find a way to experience what a member of that population might face as a part of everyday living. Spend at least part of one day seeking services or relating to others as though you had a disability that you have not experienced before. Examine the differences between your usual interactions with others and those you have when others perceive you as disabled.

2. Considering again the hypothetical agency or program you have been creating, try to fill in the fourth facet: client advocacy. How would you

go about making the community and the helping network more responsive to your clients' needs? What self-help options can you identify for this specific group?

REFERENCES

Albee, G. (1986). Toward a just society: Lessons from observations on primary prevention and psychopathology. *American Psychologist, 41*, 891–898.

Albee, G., & Gullotta, T. (1986). Facts and fallacies about primary prevention. *Journal of Primary Prevention, 6*, 207–218.

Albee, G. W., Joffe, J. M., & Dusenbury, L. A. (1988). *Prevention, powerlessness, and politics: Reading on social change*. Newbury Park, CA: Sage.

Alcoholics Anonymous (3rd ed.). (1976). New York: Alcoholics Anonymous World Services.

Allen, B., & Niss, J. (1990). A chill in the college classroom. *Phi Delta Kappan, 71*, 607–609.

Almond, R. (1974). *The healing community: Dynamics of the therapeutic milieu*. New York: Aronson.

Atkinson, D. R., Morten, G., & Sue, D. W. (Eds.). (1993). *Counseling American minorities: A cross-cultural perspective* (4th. Ed.). Madison, WI: Brown & Benchmark.

Beer, M., & Spector, B. (1993). Organizational diagnosis: its role in organizational learning. *Journal of Counseling and Development, 43*(6), 642–650.

Borkman, T. (1984). Mutual self-help groups: Strengthening the selectively unsupportive personal and community networks of their members. In A. Gartner & F. Riessman (Eds.), *The self-help revolution* (pp. 205–216) New York: Human Sciences Press.

Bristow-Braitman, A. (1995). Addiction recovery: Twelve-step programs and cognitive-behavioral psychology. *Journal of Counseling and Development, 73*(4), 414–418.

Brown, D. (1988). Empowerment through advocacy. In D. J. Kurpius & D. Brown (Eds.), *Handbook of consultation: An intervention for advocacy and outreach* (pp. 5–17). Alexandria, VA: Association for Counselor Education and Supervision.

Brown, D. (1993). Training consultants: A call to action. *Journal of Counseling and Development, 72*(2), 139–143.

Caplan, G. (1970). *The theory and practice of mental health consultation*. New York: Basic Books.

Carter, D., & Wilson, R. (1989). *Minorities in higher education*. Washington, DC: American Council on Education.

Center for Independent Living. (n. d.). Brochure. [Available from the Center for Independent Living, 2539 Telegraph Avenue, Berkeley, CA 94704]

Conyne, R. K. (1987). *Primary preventive counseling: Empowering people and systems*. Muncie, IN: Accelerated Development.

Cull, J. G., & Hardy, R. E. (1974). *Volunteerism: An emerging profession*. Springfield, IL: Thomas.

D'Andrea, M. (1992). The violence of our silence: Some thoughts about racism, counseling, and development. *Guidepost, 35*(4), 31.

D'Andrea, M. (1994, April). *Creating a vision for our future: The challenges and promise of the counseling profession*. Paper presented at the annual meeting of the American Counseling Association, Minneapolis, MN.

D'Andrea, M., & Daniels, J. (1994). The different faces of racism in higher education. *Thought and Action, 10*(1), 73–90.

Daniels, J., & D'Andrea, M. (1996). MCT theory and ethnocentrism in counseling. In D. W. Sue, A. E. Ivey, & P. B. Pedersen (Eds.), *A theory of multicultural counseling and therapy* (pp. 155–174). Pacific Grove, CA: Brooks/Cole.

Ferguson, M. (1980). *The aquarian conspiracy*. Los Angeles, CA: Tarcher.

Gartner, A. (1982). Self-help/self-care: A cost effective health strategy. *Social Policy, 12*(4), 64.

Gartner, A., & Riessman, F. (Eds.). (1984). Introduction. In A. Gartner & F. Riessman (Eds.), *The self-help revolution* (pp. 17–23). New York: Human Sciences Press.

Gibbs, J. H., & Huang, L. N. (Eds.). (1990). *Children of color: Psychological interventions with minority youth*. San Francisco: Jossey-Bass.

Goffman, E. (1963). *Stigma: Notes on the management of spoiled identity*. Englewood Cliffs, NJ: Prentice-Hall.

Hanna, S. M., & Brown, J. H. (1995). *The practice of family therapy: Key elements across models*. Pacific Grove, CA: Brooks/Cole.

Harvey, W. B. (1991). Faculty responsibility and racial tolerance. *Thought and Action, 7*(2), 115–136.

Ivey, A. E. (1986). *Developmental therapy*. San Francisco: Jossey-Bass.

Ivey, A. E. (1995). Psychotherapy as liberation: Toward specific skills and strategies in multicultural counseling and therapy. In J. G. Ponterotto, J. M. Casas, L. A. Suzuki, & C. M. Alexander (Eds.), *Handbook of multicultural counseling* (pp. 53–72). Newbury Park, CA: Sage.

Ivey, A. E., Ivey, M. B., & Simek-Morgan, L. (1993). *Counseling and psychotherapy: A multicultural perspective*. Boston: Allyn and Bacon.

Jackson, D. N., & Hayes, D. H. (1993). Multicultural issues in consultation. *Journal of Counseling and Development, 72*(2), 144–147.

Kahn, S. (1991). *Organizing: A guide for grassroots leaders*. Washington, DC: NASW Press.

Katz, P. A., & Taylor, D. A. (1988). *Eliminating racism: Profiles in controversy*. New York: Plenum Press.

Kurpius, D. J., & Fuqua, D. R. (1993a). Fundamental issues in defining consultation. *Journal of Counseling and Development, 71*(6), 589–600.

Kurpius, D. J., & Fuqua, D. R. (1993b). Introduction to the special issues. *Journal of Counseling and Development, 71*(6), 595–597.

Le, C., Ingvarson, E. P., & Page, R. C. (1995). Alcoholics Anonymous and the counseling profession: Philosophies in conflict. *Journal of Counseling and Development, 73*(6), 603–608.

Lewis, J. A., & Lewis, M. D. (1989). *Community counseling.* Pacific Grove, CA: Brooks/Cole.

Lewis, J. A., Lewis, M. D., & Souflee, F. (1991). *Management of human service programs* (2nd ed.). Pacific Grove, CA: Brooks/Cole.

Locke, D. C. (1992). *Increasing multicultural understanding: A comprehensive model.* Newbury Park, CA: Sage.

Magner, D. K. (1989, April). Blacks and whites on campuses: Behind ugly racist incidents. *Chronicle of Higher education*, p. 1.

McWhirter, E. H. (1994). *Counseling for empowerment.* Alexandria, VA: American Counseling Association.

Mosher, R., & Sprinthall, N. (1971). Psychological education in secondary schools: A program to promote individual and human development. *American Psychologist, 25*, 911–924.

Ridley, C. R. (1995). *Overcoming unintentional racism in counseling and therapy: A practitioner's guide to intentional intervention.* Thousand Oaks, CA: Sage.

Riessman, F. (1985). New dimensions in self-help. *Social Policy, 15*(3), 2–5.

Riordan, R. J., & Walsh, L. (1994). Guidelines for professional referral to Alcoholics Anonymous and other twelve step groups. *Journal of Counseling and Development, 72*(4), 351–355.

Satir, V. (1972). *Peoplemaking.* Palo Alto, CA: Science & Behavior Books.

Schein, E. H. (1969). *Process consultation: Its role in organizational development.* Reading, MA: Addison-Wesley.

Senge, P. M. (1990). *The fifth discipline: The art and practice of the learning organization.* New York: Doubleday.

Skovholt, T. M. (1974). The client as helper: A means to promote psychological growth. *Counseling Psychologist, 4*, 58–64.

Sprinthall, N. A., Hall, J. S., & Gerler, E. R. (1992). Peer counseling for middle school students experiencing divorce: A deliberate psychological education model. *Elementary School Guidance and Counseling Journal, 26*(4), 279–294.

Steele, R. L. (1974). A manpower resource for community mental health centers. *Journal of Community Psychology, 2*(2), 104–107.

Stensrud, R., & Stensrud, K. (1981). Counseling may be hazardous to your health: How we teach people to feel powerless. *Personnel and Guidance Journal, 59*, 300–304.

Sue, D. W., Ivey, A. E., & Pedersen, P. B. (Eds.). (1996). *A theory of multicultural counseling and therapy.* Pacific Grove, CA: Brooks/Cole.

Sue, D. W., & Sue, D. (1993). *Counseling the culturally-different: Theory and practice.* New York: Wiley.

Sue, S., & McKinney, H. (1975). Asian Americans in the community mental health care system. *American Journal of Orthopsychiatry, 45*, 111–118.

Sue, S., & Sue, D. W. (1974). MMPI comparisons between Asian American and non-Asian students utilizing a student health psychiatric clinic. *Journal of Counseling Psychology, 21*, 423–427.

Washington Assembly for Citizens with Disabilities. (1987). *Assembly consensus agenda results.* [Available from the Washington Assembly for Citizens with Disabilities, P. O. Box 2577, Olympia, WA 98507]

Werner, J. L., & Tyler, M. (1993). Community-based interventions: A return to community mental health centers' origins. *Journal of Counseling and Development, 43*(6), 678–683.

West, J. F., & Idol, L. (1993). The counselor as consultant in the collaborative school. *Journal of Counseling and Development, 43*(6), 678–683.

Wilson, M. (1976). *The effective management of volunteer programs.* Boulder, CO: Volunteer Management Associates.

Winter, M. (1986, Winter). Disabled community: Fifteen years on the move with CIL and independence. *Friends of CIL,* p. 1. [Available from the Center for Independent Living, 2539 Telegraph Avenue, Berkeley, CA 94704]

Wolfensberger, W. (1972). *Normalization.* Toronto, Canada: National Institute on Mental Retardation.

Wolfensberger, W., & Zauha, H. (1973). *Citizen advocacy and protective services for the impaired and handicapped.* Toronto, Canada: National Institute on Mental Retardation.

CHAPTER 6

THE COMMUNITY
COUNSELOR AS SOCIAL
CHANGE AGENT

Chapter 5 discussed the gap between the need for mental health services and the actual number of counseling services provided to the U.S. public. Because of this gap, counselors are encouraged to expand their impact by adopting indirect counseling strategies. While admitting that direct counseling services are vital, the community counseling model emphasizes the importance of engineering positive changes in clients' surroundings to affect a greater number of people. In addition to providing advocacy and consultation services, then, community counselors can act as social change agents to promote constructive environmental changes that enhance positive outcomes for clients.

Community counselors know that human beings constantly interact with their surroundings and that these interactions influence their development. Knowing this, they recognize that they must consider the impact of social, political, and economic factors on their clients' lives. Therefore, confronting social issues is a natural extension of the counseling process. For community counselors, providing direct counseling services to clients in need and dealing with sociopolitical systems are two aspects of the same task.

THE ROLE OF SOCIAL CHANGE AGENT

Barriers and Challenges

Although mental health professionals are increasingly becoming aware of the limited overall impact of direct counseling services, many continue to overuse these services. Further, many such counselors often avoid working indirectly as a client advocate or social change agent. The following sections present five reasons many practitioners continue to embrace the individual-remedial-intrapsychic helping paradigm, which has dominated the counseling profession for the past 50 years, and hesitate to use advocacy and social change strategies.

PRESSURE FROM FUNDING SOURCES Funding sources continue to favor mental health professionals who provide traditional counseling services (e.g., individual and small group counseling services) to clients. These fiscal restrictions discourage many counselors from planning and implementing other types of counseling services. As many have emphatically pointed out, though, the relevance and viability of the mental health professions in the 21st century will largely depend on practitioners' ability to affect the psychological development of greater numbers of people than the U.S. mental health-care system currently serves (D'Andrea, 1994; Germaine, 1991). Thus, from a community counseling perspective, counselors and their professional associations must look for ways to secure fiscal support for advocacy, consultation, and social change initiatives, or those services that enhance the psychological health of large numbers of people. Otherwise, counselors run the risk of becoming an increasingly nonviable professional group in the future.

GRADUATE TRAINING PROGRAMS   Many graduate schools place an inordinate emphasis on direct, remedial counseling services in their training programs. This sort of training limits many counselors' understanding of alternative ways to promote the psychological health and personal well-being of larger numbers of clients in their schools and communities.

Made almost two decades ago, Bronfenbrenner's (1979) assessment still applies to many counseling training programs in the United States today. In this regard, he asserts the following:

> Though human development is a product of the interaction between the growing human organism and its environment, there is a marked asymmetry, a hypertrophy of theory and research focusing on the properties of the person and only the most rudimentary conception and characterization of the environment in which the person is found. (p. 16)

Several people have supported Bronfenbrenner's analysis by criticizing the tendency of counseling training programs to focus primarily on intrapsychic considerations rather than spending an equal amount of time helping students learn ways to assess the negative impact of environmental conditions (Aubrey & Lewis, 1988; Conyne, 1985; D'Andrea, 1994). These critics point out that many counseling educators generally ignore Lewin's (1951) formulation that B = f(P × E)—that is, behavior is a function of the interaction between the person and the environment. Instead, many tend to operate from a far more limited formula: B = f(P); that is, behavior is a function of the person (Conyne, 1985). As a result, counseling programs still perpetuate the individualistic-remedial-intrapsychic approach even though the general population's need for mental health services far exceeds this limited modality.

LACKING THE COURAGE TO PROMOTE SOCIAL CHANGE   D'Andrea (1994) points out that many mental health practitioners seem to lack the courage to incorporate social change strategies into their work. Doing so requires not only the ability to analyze human behavior systemically and contextually (Ivey, 1995; Merrick, 1995; Slaughter-Defoe, 1995), but also the courage to confront aspects of the status quo that negatively affect clients' general health and well-being. Counselors manifest this sort of courage when they (1) consistently take time to assess their clients' psychological well-being from a systemic and contextual perspective (Sue, Ivey, & Pedersen, 1996) and (2) initiate actions designed to alter the impact of negative environmental conditions in their clients' lives; these interventions often include social and political action strategies (D'Andrea, 1994; Netting, Kettner, & McMurtry, 1993).

The helping professions as a whole have awakened in recent years to the need to participate in social and political action in schools and communities (Albee, Joffe, & Dusenbury, 1988). However, many practitioners—new or experienced—continue to hesitate in this regard. Aubrey and Lewis (1988) state that counselors are most likely to recognize and address sociopolitical issues if they first make a "transition in their own thinking from assuming intrapsychic causality of their clients' problems to recognizing that political explanations are sometimes more appropriate" (p. 300).

LACKING THE ANALYTICAL SKILLS TO THINK SYSTEMICALLY   The transitional thinking Aubrey and Lewis (1988) refer to involves a fairly high level of analysis on the part of mental health professionals. This analytical competence includes

(a) the ability to accurately identify individual and intrapsychic factors that contribute to a client's problems, (b) differentiating those systemic conditions that promote psychological health from those that negatively affect clients' well-being, and (c) understanding the ways in which mental health practitioners can foster social and political changes in order that larger numbers of persons from diverse backgrounds might more fully realize their health potential. (p. 287)

Iscoe (1981) discusses many instances in which mental health professionals have inaccurately assumed intrapsychic causes for problems clearly caused by sociopolitical phenomena. He also describes the backlash mental health professionals have experienced from trying to create societal changes for their clients' sake; that is, the intrapsychic causes others ascribed to them:

> In the late '60s and early '70s . . . there was concern about ethnic minorities, the distribution of power, the rights of subordinate counselors, and persons who generally did not fit into the clinical mold. It is instructive to note, however, that many explanations given about those persons in the mental health professions who articulated these issues were often similar to the explanations given to individuals who used drugs, were involved in urban riots, and demonstrated on university campuses. These explanations were often cast into clinical molds. Thus, concepts like acting-out behavior and unresolved hostility towards authority were invoked to explain the motivation of those mental health professionals who became involved in social change efforts. (Iscoe, 1981, pp. 125–126)

Of course, the motives to become involved in social change initiatives are more complex. Counselors who take such action may do so because they have consistently analyzed their client's situation from both an intrapsychic and a systems perspective. As such, they do not emphasize one perspective at the expense of the other. Further, by taking this comprehensive approach, community counselors can see how their clients' intrapsychic problems relate to various sociopolitical dynamics, and thus they find motivation to change negative environmental factors.

The community counseling model thus provides a comprehensive, balanced approach by emphasizing the following:

1. Analyzing issues related to clients' mental health and personal well-being from both an individual and a systemic perspective
2. Developing multifaceted intervention strategies that facilitate clients' personal development through the use of direct and preventive counseling services
3. Using indirect counseling and community interventions to impact clients' social environments

LACKING KNOWLEDGE OF SOCIAL CHANGE STRATEGIES   Although many counselors possess the courage and motivation to promote social change for their clients, they often do not understand how to initiate practical strategies. The rest of this chapter should help counselors overcome this problem, as well as the other four described, by doing the following:

1. Increasing counselors' understanding of the importance of implementing social action strategies to promote clients' empowerment
2. Describing the ecological systems that comprise clients' social environments
3. Enhancing counselors' knowledge of how ecological systems contribute to clients' well-being
4. Providing a framework for conducting an ecological assessment
5. Presenting examples of programs and services counselors have used to promote change in their clients' social environments

Promoting Clients' Empowerment Through Social Activism

Counselors need to address the general environmental factors that make their clients susceptible to problems, such as the unequal distribution of power in contemporary society. Specific environmental factors that directly or indirectly affect many community members must also be addressed by the ecologically minded mental health practitioners. These factors include the chemical toxification of land, air and water; increased noise levels in cities; and the challenge of disposing of society's trash and garbage safely (Tester, 1993). Going beyond being concerned about how these systemic issues impact their clients, community counselors do what they can to help change negative aspects of the social environment.

Counselors can use their advocacy and consultation skills in many ways to promote changes in clients' families, schools, neighborhoods, and/or communities (see Chapter 5). In doing so, community counselors remain constantly focused on the importance of intervention strategies that foster their clients' sense of personal and collective empowerment.

They see the importance of clients' empowerment also because they realize that feeling powerless to control one's own life is, in itself, a major mental health problem, especially if it occurs throughout a community.

Further, mental health and feelings of self-competence depend on a level of self-esteem rooted in the belief that one's behavior can affect the world. Such confidence predominately comes from overcoming environmental obstacles rather than from an in-depth exploration of intrapsychic experiences.

Community counselors also recognize that the well-being of schools, neighborhoods, and businesses rests on the same sense of power, effectiveness, and self-determination that emerges from this empowerment process.

Thus, because these ecological systems significantly impact the way individuals develop, community counselors realize that they cannot simply wait on the sidelines until people show up at their offices.

SPECIFIC ROLE OF THE SOCIAL CHANGE AGENT   According to Egan (1985), *change agent* refers to "anyone who plays an important part in designing, redesigning, running, renewing, or improving any system, subsystem, or program" (p. 12). When counselors incorporate environmental and social change strategies into their work, they necessarily move beyond providing direct counseling services by becoming a more visible and integral part of the school, neighborhood, business, and/or community in which they work.

Here are the two main reasons community counselors accept the role of social change agent:

1. They have come to a new understanding of the strengths and limitations of the traditional counseling model.
2. They readily recognize that one of the greatest challenges to the mental health professions in the 21st century is finding new ways to increase their professional impact on an ever more culturally diverse client population.

Many researchers and theorists have supported these considerations in writing about the powerful and positive results of fostering constructive systemic changes. They cite a variety of social change strategies implemented by mental health professionals to help families (Gordon & Scales, 1988; Hilliard, 1988), schools (D'Andrea & Daniels, 1995; Levin, 1988), and larger communities (Albee, 1988; Clark, 1988; Konopka, 1988; Trotter, 1988).

Lewis and Lewis (1989) present additional factors that help explain why community counselors are committed to promoting changes in the social environment. These include

1. The awareness that specific aspects of the family, school, neighborhood, business, and/or community environment may be detrimental to the healthy development of individuals
2. An understanding that other aspects of the social environment can nurture the development of individuals and groups in society.
3. The realization that mental health practitioners cannot facilitate and sustain long-term improvement in the psychological health and well-being of large numbers of clients unless they take a more active role as a sociopolitical change agent
4. The belief that the social environment will become more responsive to its members' needs when mental health practitioners, clients, parents, students, members of the business community, elected officials, and others work together toward common goals

Despite the many advantages derived from playing a more socially active role in their clients' environments, many counselors fear implementing social action strategies because they might generate controversy. Regarding the importance of overcoming this reluctance, Martin (1991) states the following:

> Does the mental health professional best serve the welfare of patients or clients by limiting services to direct professional care, or can that be combined with advocacy and social action to press for policy changes and needed public services? This issue must be addressed as the rapid erosion and decline of the standard of living faced by children and families during the past decade continue into this one. . . . As professionals, we attempt the therapeutic amelioration or correction of existing illnesses through the use of a variety of traditional services. But vital as these contributions are, they are not enough. If we are to fulfill our roles appropriately, we must address ourselves to prevention as well as to morbidity. To do so in the present cultural and political climate, it becomes necessary to be advocates and activists. (p. 488)

ECOLOGICAL CONSIDERATIONS IN COUNSELING PRACTICE

Bronfenbrenner (1976, 1988), a pioneer in community counseling, has dedicated most of his career to describing how ecological factors impact human development. According to Bronfenbrenner (1976),

> The ecology of human development is the scientific study of the progressive, mutual accommodation, throughout the life span, between a growing human organism and the changing immediate environments in which it lives, as this process is affected by conditions within and between these immediate settings and the larger social contexts, both formal and informal, in which the settings are embedded. (p. 2)

Ecological theories emphasize that one's growth and development is affected both by the immediate systems in which one directly participates and by broader ecological forces that indirectly affect one's life. Thus, from an ecological perspective, problems derived from social systems must be addressed through interventions in these systems. From a counseling perspective, this means that mental health interventions can take place at any of several systemic levels that constitute the client's broader social environment.

However, to use an ecological approach effectively, counselors must be able to do the following:

1. Distinguish among the different systems that compose the broad ecological environment
2. Understand how transactions between clients and their social environments impact their development
3. Recognize how their clients are currently impacting their social environment
4. Consider how their clients *could* impact various ecological systems (their families, schools, neighborhoods, work settings, and communities) in the future

In his theory of the ecology of human development, Bronfenbrenner (1988) describes the following systems: the microsystem, the mesosystem, the exosystem, and the macrosystem. Collectively, these systems form a nest composing the total social environment.

A *microsystem* includes those immediate settings of which the developing person is directly a part, such as home, school, and work place). The microsystem significantly impacts and, to a large degree, determines individuals' pattern of activities, roles, and interpersonal relationships.

The *mesosystem* refers to dynamic interactions or linkages that occur among microsystems at a particular point in a person's development (Bolger, Caspi, Downey, & Moorehouse, 1988; Bronfenbrenner, 1988). As Merrick (1995) notes, the mesosystem includes "the linkages and processes taking place between two or more settings containing the developing person; these may conflict with or complement each other" (p. 290). For example, one mesosystem is the linkage between the home and the school. Thus, counselors who use an ecological perspective within school settings might want to assess how this linkage affects students' motivation and sense of academic competence (Bolger, Caspi, Downey, & Moorehouse, 1988).

An extension of the mesosystem, the *exosystem* includes those social structures, both formal and informal, that impact the microsystems. These formal and informal structures do not themselves necessarily include the developing person. Rather, they encompass those major societal institutions that indirectly influence people in their microsystems. Examples of exosystems include the world of work, the mass media, the distribution of goods and services, and various informal social networks (Bronfenbrenner, 1988).

Macrosystems refer to those overarching societal and cultural institutions that directly and indirectly impact the way individuals develop and behave. Examples include the economic, social, educational, legal, and political institutions any society comprises. According to Merrick (1995), the macrosystem differs from the preceding systems in that it "refers not to

TABLE 6.1
SOCIAL POLICY STRATEGIES
AND THE COMMUNITY COUNSELING MODEL

	COMMUNITY SERVICES	CLIENT SERVICES
Direct		
Indirect	Interventions at the microsystem, mesosystem, exosystem, and macrosystem levels.	

specific contexts affecting the life of a particular person but to general pro-totypes that set the pattern for the way society is structured" (p. 291).

Community counselors intervene at all of these levels. Table 6.1 shows the place of these systemic interventions in the community counseling model. Here, you can see that interventions aimed at systemic change require community counselors to use indirect methods.

Often, these efforts are directed toward people not necessarily identi-fied as having mental health problems. As such, many have viewed ecolog-ical interventions as a powerful preventive strategy that can strengthen the well-being of large numbers who are already psychologically healthy (Netting et al., 1993). For instance, as Cowen (1985) has pointed out, macrosystem interventions are broad enough to address the profound and widespread social injustices that lie at the root of a significant number of psychological problems that individuals from diverse cultural, ethnic, racial, and socioeconomic backgrounds commonly experience.

Using an Ecological Approach with Culturally Diverse Clients

Multicultural counseling experts have repeatedly criticized mental health practitioners for failing to take contextual and ecological factors into con-sideration when assessing a client's situation and planning helping inter-ventions. These critics have pointed out further that when counselors primarily focus on a client's intrapsychic reactions to particular problems within her or his social environment, they tend to ignore the powerful impact of other systemic factors that characterize the client's life and nega-tively affect his or her well-being (Atkinson, Morten, & Sue, 1993; Ivey, 1995; Sue et al., 1996).

This narrow approach to counseling reportedly leads some clients to feel blamed for their problems even though they see that much of the impetus for these problems comes from factors in their social environment. Because many counselors use theories that generally fail to incorporate a systems perspective, their helping is prone to communicate inadvertently a sense of blame toward the very victims of unhealthy and dehumanizing social environments (Lee & Richardson, 1991; Locke, 1992; Sue et al., 1996).

> Blaming the victim means application of a psychological intervention that is aimed at fitting an individual into existing social conditions, which are presumed to have victimized him or her in the first place. Implied is the notion that the individual has some sort of deficit or emotional difficulty that is the basis of his or her problem in living. . . . It matters little whether one applies the medical model or any other if the interventions are victim blaming while the problems are social systemic in nature. (Rappaport, Davidson, Wilson, & Mitchell, 1975, p. 525)

By using an ecological approach to assess the culturally diverse client's situation, counselors can more accurately understand the many ways discrimination, racism, and oppression negatively affect the client (Atkinson et al., 1993; Banks & Banks, 1993; Ivey, 1995). Counselors who use an ecological approach when working with such client populations will inevitably need to address the social and political issues that negatively impact these people (Martin, 1991).

The most basic rationale for community counselors' involvement in social and political issues is that many clients—especially people of color, poor people, women, gays and lesbians, the elderly, and the physically challenged—are often victimized by negative economic, employment, political, and social policies and conditions perpetuated in the greater social environment. Therefore, to help reduce this sort of victimization, counselors must work actively to modify the environment (Sue & Sue, 1990).

Several multicultural theorists have underscored the importance of fostering environmental modifications that enhance the well-being of individual clients and at-risk groups (Atkinson et al., 1993). These theorists strongly urge counselors to incorporate social change strategies into their overall approach in order to provide more effective services to large numbers of clients from culturally diverse populations.

> As a change agent, the counselor attempts to change the social environment that oppresses racial/ethnic minorities. A major criticism of the traditional counseling model is the focus on intrapsychic sources of the client's problem and on psychotherapy as the primary intervention for resolving the problem. As a change agent, the counselor helps the client identify the external sources of

his or her problem as well as the methods of resolving the problem. Rather than encouraging the client to "own the problem," the counselor helps the client become aware of the oppressive forces creating the problem. Then together the counselor and client develop a strategy for eliminating or reducing the effect of oppression on the client's life. This is often done by facilitating the formation of racial/ethnic minority political groups. Through political power, racial/ethnic minorities and other disenfranchised groups are able to bring about change in their social and physical environment. The counselor serving as a change agent frequently assumes a low-visibility profile, often finding it useful to mobilize other influential persons in the offending institution [or system] so as to bring about change. (Atkinson et al., 1993, p. 302)

Prior to developing and implementing social change strategies, community counselors must first accurately assess their clients' situation from an ecological perspective. The following discussion examines how counselors and other mental health professionals might go about conducting an ecological assessment.

ASSESSING TEENAGE PREGNANCY FROM AN ECOLOGICAL PERSPECTIVE The United States has one of the highest rates of teenage pregnancy and childbearing among all of the industrialized nations in the world (United Nations, 1992). Further, the rate of adolescent childbearing in lower socioeconomic, urban, African-American communities is twice that in white communities (Children's Defense Fund, 1996).

These pregnancy and childbearing rates clearly suggest that direct counseling services to youths at-risk for adolescent pregnancy have not reduced the number of teenagers who actually become parents each year in this country. With this in mind, many experts have recommended replacing traditional counseling approaches with a broader ecological assessment and intervention plan (D'Andrea & Daniels, 1992; Geronimus & Korenman, 1990; Merrick, 1995).

An ecological approach will inevitably require a dramatic shift in the way many counselors think about and try to address adolescent pregnancy. For example, Merrick (1995) points out that from an ecological view, one would not necessarily think of adolescent childrearing in lower socioeconomic, African-American communities as a "problem." Rather, by becoming aware of the limited life options the social environment allows these teenagers, one might more accurately interpret teenage childbearing as a realistic "career choice" (p. 288) for many in this sort of devalued population.

Microsystems.   Regarding ecological assessment, Merrick (1995) notes that counselors should first evaluate the degree to which factors in the client's microsystems (such as parents, peers, and teachers) influence adolescents' development in general and their thoughts about human sexuality in particular. For example, when working to reduce teenage childbearing in a school or community setting, counselors should focus on how students' microsystems influence their sexual behavior, use of birth control, and attitudes about teenage childbearing. Important factors counselors would need to assess in this regard include the following:

1. The quality of the adolescents' relationships with their parents
2. The degree to which parents influence their sons' or daughters' attitudes toward teenage childbearing
3. The degree to which the teenagers' peers accept and/or encourage unprotected sexual behavior during adolescence
4. Gathering information about the teenage pregnancy prevention programs and services that exist (or do not exist) at the adolescent's school

The information generated from this sort of assessment helps mental health practitioners determine useful microsystem interventions. Possible strategies include the following:

1. Providing family consultation and outreach services designed to enhance relationships and communication between parents and adolescents
2. Initiating adolescent peer "rap groups" in which youths have opportunities to discuss various topics related to human sexuality (e.g., issues related to teen pregnancy, sexually transmitted diseases, HIV/AIDS, gay and lesbian lifestyles)
3. Organizing a meeting with representatives from local adolescent programs to discuss the problems associated with teenage childrearing

Mesosystems. The next step in conducting an ecological evaluation involves assessing the degree to which factors in the mesosystem encourage teenagers to abstain from getting pregnant or giving birth during adolescence. To do this, community counselors should consider how formal and/or informal linkages, such as those between family and school or neighborhood and family, impact adolescent development in general and encourage a reduction in the number of teenage childbirths in particular.

Questions counselors might find useful in assessing the adolescent's mesosystem include the following:

1. What programs or services currently provide opportunities for positive parent-adult-adolescent interactions?
2. Which key people in the neighborhood (role models, religious leaders, athletic coaches) may already be playing an important

role by informally helping adolescents strive toward positive life choices and experiences?

3. Are there any specific neighborhood- or community-based pregnancy-prevention projects currently in operation in which parents and teenagers could become involved?

Exosystems.   When assessing the exosystem, counselors examine how such social structures as the mass media influence teenagers' views about getting pregnant and becoming a parent during their adolescence. The following questions might prove helpful in evaluating factors that exist (or do not exist) in the exosystem.

1. It has been recognized that socioeconomic factors are more powerful determinants of adolescent childbearing than a teenager's racial or ethnic background (Merrick, 1995). Thus, counselors would do well to investigate what sort of efforts have been directed toward developing comprehensive career development projects for youth identified as at risk for giving birth during adolescence?

2. Have there been any efforts to promote a teenage pregnancy prevention campaign through the mass media in the past? If not, is there any interest to do so in the future? What resources currently available in the exosystem might help develop this sort of intervention in the future?

3. How easily can adolescents access birth control products at their schools and in their communities? Where are these products most accessible? How could one increase the distribution of these products to at-risk youth?

Macrosystems.   A macrosystem assessment involves evaluating the ways cultural patterns impact one's attitudes about human sexuality and teenage parenting. Thus, when assessing adolescent childbearing from a macrosystem perspective, Merrick (1995) suggests that counselors should do the following:

1. Consider how the liberalization of society's views of teenage childbearing impacts this phenomenon.

2. Assess how the adolescent's background (e.g., cultural, racial, ethnic factors) contribute to the development of his or her sexual attitudes and behavior.

THE IMPORTANCE OF ECOLOGICAL ASSESSMENT   When community counselors take time to conduct an ecological assessment, they gain a much more comprehensive and accurate picture of their clients' situations than traditional assessment methods typically offer (D'Andrea, 1994). Another important reason for conducting an ecological assessment is that it provides practitioners and program planners with a great deal of information, which they can use to design interventions aimed at fostering positive changes in their clients' social environments.

The past two decades have seen an increase in the number of interventions designed to impact different systems within clients' social environments. These systemic interventions represent models that other mental health practitioners may find useful when planning and implementing new programs and services in their own schools, neighborhoods, and communities.

Microsystems: School-Based Programs

Bronfenbrenner (1977, 1988) has cited the school as an example of a microsystems setting; clearly, interventions in schools can strongly affect young people's development. Such interventions, though, are difficult to implement, largely because the educational status quo is often highly resistant to change. As Aubrey (1972) has pointed out, "non-negotiable factors" within the educational system thwart the aspirations of many counselors who are genuinely interested in planning organizational development strategies that promote positive systemic changes within the school system.

> These non-negotiable factors are institutional constraints that have been ingrained and long-established by custom and tradition, e.g., the ultimate authority of the principal in instructional and noninstructional matters, the inviolate sovereignty of the teacher in his [or her] classroom, the rigid time schedule in schools, the inflexible methods in the grouping of children, the premium placed on docility and conformity, and so on. In the course of time, they become sanctioned and therefore present themselves to counselors as routine procedures, structural patterns, organizational practices, hierarchical processes, and conventional observances. Collectively, these school heirlooms represent tremendous impediments to counselors wishing to innovate programs and practices for children. (Aubrey, 1972, p. 90)

These "heirlooms" remain as much a part of U.S. school systems today as they were in 1972. Consequently, most efforts at primary prevention, even those aimed at young children, tend to focus on individuals instead of environment (Wolff, 1987).

However useful direct competency building and other similar school-based prevention interventions are, more programs must focus concurrently on the total school environment, if not to change it, then at least to understand its effects.

Thus, when programs are developed in schools we want to know something about the impact on the teachers, the administrators, the social climate, and the educational policies. We want to know about more than changes in test scores. We want to understand how it is that some children grow up with a sense of their own ability to influence the outcomes of their life and the life of their various communities, while other children do not. (Rappaport, 1987, p. 133)

THE QUALITY OF SCHOOL LIFE PROGRAM   Adults and children can work together to bring about positive changes within the entire school environment as the Quality of School Life program (QSL) implemented in Washtenaw County, Michigan, demonstrates.

The Quality of School Life for Elementary Schools Program (QSL-E) of the Washtenaw County Community Mental Health Center is a social systems intervention whose goal is to promote a beneficial school climate through improved pupil and staff participation and more positive mutual expectancies. (Schelkun, Cooper, Tableman, & Groves, 1987, p. 8)

Based on the Quality of Work Life/Quality Circle programs developed for business and industry, the systemwide QSL-E program uses a variety of organizational development methods to enhance participation and problem solving within the school setting. Funded by the Michigan Department of Mental Health, the program has been described by its developer as follows:

QSL procedures join with other efforts associated with the movement toward excellence and effectiveness in the schools, focusing on the following issues and objectives:

- *Appropriate school climate:* the attainment of a safe, friendly, and orderly learning environment.
- *Effective student/staff motivation and morale:* a realistic belief in one's ability to affect the outcomes of relevant decisions, with resulting staff/student support and acceptance of school and classroom activities, rules, and norms.
- *Congruent staff/student/parent expectations:* the explicit sharing of expectations in a context which encourages consensus.
- *Mutual understanding:* the development of a shared vocabulary, conceptual base, and systematic operating guidelines for problem-solving at all levels of the system.
- An *effective participative organizational culture:* a realistic and predictable system of communication, structures, and procedures for involving others in problem identification, problem-solving, and decision-making—where appropriate—in the entire school as well as in the classroom.

The total QSL program consists of four levels: (1) Pupil Involvement (PI) clubs, (2) Teacher/Staff Involvement (TI/SI) groups, (3) School Climate Coordination (SCC), and (4) Family/Community Involvement (FI & CI) groups.

Pupil Involvement Clubs

The Pupil Involvement (PI) process encourages students and their teachers to cooperate in identifying, researching, goal-setting, planning, implementing, and evaluating activities which contribute to solving problems and maximizing opportunities in their own classrooms. Teachers utilize a standard curriculum to teach children concepts and skills that are helpful for group problem-solving activities. During PI club meetings, students and their teacher meet regularly—first, to learn the skills and concepts, and then to apply these to their ongoing classroom challenges and opportunities. . . .

Training goals include improved problem-solving by individuals and groups, cooperativeness in the classroom, improved individual and group responsibility, and mutually understood expectations regarding ability to learn and do. Students learn the "chain of command" functions and responsibilities within the school district, effects of changing the physical environment of the classroom, the need for developing explicitly stated classroom norms, the various stages and techniques related to problem-solving and action planning, and various skills needed for responsible self-control. They are encouraged to apply these skills throughout the school day.

Teacher Involvement/Staff Involvement

At the building level, the Teacher Involvement (TI) or Staff Involvement (SI) steering committee is the primary problem-solving mechanism in the participating elementary school. This group always includes the building administrator and, where bargaining units exist, a representative of the relevant bargaining units(s). In addition, volunteers are recruited from the rest of the school's personnel. Professional staff development training in QSL processes is offered to all participants, operating guidelines are presented and refined, and the TI/SI steering committee then meets regularly for the remainder of the school year. The group identifies building-based problems and opportunities; engages in fact-finding; suggests goals; reviews recommendations of volunteers, task forces, and work groups; develops and utilizes feedback procedures for the entire staff; makes recommendations to the building administrator; and assists the administrator in other activities which affect his or her decisions. In this way, the TI/SI group serves as a facilitating bridge between administrator and staff. . . .

School Climate Coordination Structure

Once a school district legitimizes the creation of TI/SI steering committees, it is important to monitor and standardize the operating procedures and guidelines of the various buildings so that changes in administrative personnel will not unduly disrupt the participatory process. There is no standard set of coordination and communication structures; however, the program suggests a number of ways a district may choose to ensure the durability and usefulness of participatory methods in a manner which suits the style and structure of the system.

Family Involvement/Community Involvement

Increasingly, school districts are seeking ways to involve parents and community leaders in identifying and solving related problems. One major difficulty lies in the various expectations and styles which "outsiders" bring to such endeavors, and school personnel are frequently frustrated to find that family or community participation takes problem-solving in so many directions that it ends nowhere or, even worse, into seemingly insurmountable conflicts.

The QSL model suggests that community/family participation can be coordinated in the same way that TI/SI participation is managed: a central figure coordinates, communicates, and monitors these activities, and participatory groups are trained in similar skills and concepts before getting down to work. Operating guidelines and procedures are clarified in advance, boundaries are established, and staff responsibilities to the group and to the school district are clearly established (Michigan Department of Mental Health, 1987).

The strength of the QSL program lies in its systematic attempt to bring so many people into the problem-solving process. Significant effort has been put into designing and implementing a curriculum that directly enhances children's competencies. What makes the program unusual is its complementary effort to make each school an environment in which children can use their problem-solving skills meaningfully. Adults and children in the targeted school systems also have a chance to learn new skills and, because of the program's participatory structure, they also have a chance to practice them.

Mesosystem: Projects for School Development

As mentioned earlier, a mesosystem comprises the linkages among various microsystems. In his description of the mesosystem, Bronfenbrenner (1988) acknowledges that the interactions between settings probably have as much impact on human development as the settings themselves. Thus, mesosystem interventions tend to focus on the interaction between two settings, such as between a child's home and his or her school. Mesosystem interventions may also address ecological transitions, such as a child's entry into preschool or when a student transfers from one school to another.

In 1979, Bronfenbrenner hypothesized that the quality of home-to-school and school-to-school connections might be found to affect children's development over the long run. Years later, when the American Psychological Association's (APA) Task Force on Promotion, Prevention, and Intervention Alternatives sought to identify programs proven to be effective, several of the 14 "showcase" programs it selected dealt in some way with the sort of childhood transition issues that Bronfenbrenner had discussed a decade earlier (Bales, 1987).

THE PERRY PRESCHOOL PROJECT   The High/Scope Perry Preschool Project was one of these programs. Implemented in Ypsilanti, Michigan, the project provided a preschool program for children from "poor, undereducated families" and followed the participants up through age 19. As described by one of the project's codirectors, the preschool experience proceeded from the following set of assumptions about the components of high-quality programs:

1. A developmentally appropriate curriculum
2. Supervisory support and in-service training for program staff
3. Low enrollment limits and an adequate number of adults with teaching/caregiving teams assigned to small groups of children
4. Staff trained in early childhood development
5. Parents involved as partners with program staff
6. Sensitivity to the noneducational circumstances of the child and family
7. Developmentally appropriate evaluation procedure (Schweinhart, 1987, p. 9)

The Perry Preschool Project, which included home visits by teachers, has been heavily researched. Participating children were compared with a matched group of children who did not attend preschool. The results of these investigations revealed that members of the Perry preschool group did better in their later school years: They scored significantly higher on standardized tests, fewer of them were classified as mentally retarded, and as a group they spent fewer years in special education. The differences between the two groups remained significant as the participants approached adulthood.

> Interviews at age 19 showed the preschool group dropped out of school less, relied on welfare less, had lower arrest and self-reported delinquency rates, and higher employment rates than the control group. Those who went to the preschool also had lower illiteracy rates, were more likely to go on to college, and the women had fewer pregnancies. (Bales, 1987, p. 18)

THE TRANSITION PROJECT   Another exemplary program identified by the APA task force dealt with a specific ecological transition: entering high school. Several researchers have noted that young people at risk for school failures are especially vulnerable during this transition (Felner, Ginter, & Primavera, 1982; Ing, 1995). A key factor influencing this sort of transition is the nature of the setting itself.

> One feature of the school setting which may exacerbate students' difficulties in coping with the transition into high school is that the entire local social system is in a state of flux with all incoming students . . . attempting to adapt to the new setting at the same time. All students in the entering class are simultaneously confronted by a new physical environment and a larger and generally unfamiliar set of peers and school personnel. . . . Teachers and counselors are confronted with getting to know and providing information and support for large numbers of new students. Thus in addition to those tasks typically confronted by a student transferring into a new school, the students entering high school are also confronted by a less stable, less predictable environment in which the resources available to aid them in their coping efforts may be seriously taxed. (Felner et al., 1982, p. 279)

Under Felner's direction, the Transition Project was designed to increase the level of support available to vulnerable students from both peers and teachers during this important period of change. Interventions included both restructuring the role of homeroom teachers and reorganizing the school environment to reduce the degree of flux students encountered and to facilitate the establishment of new peer support systems.

Randomly selected students participated in the project, which assigned them to homerooms and primary academic classes with other project students. Their teachers—all volunteers—were selected on the basis of the physical proximity of their classrooms. Thus, for these students, the school became a stable, cohesive, and familiar environment.

Like the Perry Preschool Project, the Transition Project had clear positive results. Compared with controls, project students coped more successfully with the transition to high school, showing significantly better grade point averages, attendance records, and self-concepts, as well as expressing more positive views of the school environment.

> This study demonstrates that low-cost changes in the roles of school personnel and the social ecology of the high school environment can effectively prevent academic and personal difficulties associated with school change by increasing the levels of social support available to students and decreasing the confusion and complexity of the setting being entered. . . . Overall, these findings support the arguments that attempts to understand and modify social environments . . . can be

adapted fruitfully to preventive programs designed to increase people's ability to cope with the adaptive tasks of life transitions. (Felner et al., 1982, p. 288)

Exosystems: Neighborhood Organizations

The exosystem affects the developing person indirectly, through its impact on the microsystems it encompasses. Of the many exosystems, such as the world of work, mass media, and informal social networks, Bronfenbrenner (1979) emphasizes the neighborhood.

In discussing the influence of the exosystem, he notes,

> The developmental potential of a setting is enhanced to the extent that there exist direct and indirect links to power settings through which participants in the original setting can influence allocation of resources and the making of decisions that are responsive to the needs of the developing person and the efforts of those who act in his [or her] behalf. (Bronfenbrenner, 1979, p. 256)

Accordingly, the potential of the neighborhood to promote human development can be realized through neighborhood organizations. That is, these organizations allow people to change their environments. These organizations both deal with specific local issues and affect how community decisions are made.

The process of organizing neighborhoods and communities may be as important as the outcomes attained. As Alinsky (1969), the dean of American community organizers, writes,

> If people are organized with a dream of the future ahead of them, the actual planning that takes place in organizing and the hopes and the fears for the future give them just as much inner satisfaction as does their actual achievement. The kind of participation that comes out of a people's organization in planning, getting together and fighting together, completely changes what had previously been to John Smith, assembly-line American, a dull, gray, monotonous road of existence that stretched out interminably, into a brilliantly lit, highly exciting avenue of hope, drama, conflict, with, at the end of the street, the most brilliant ending known to the mind of man—the future of mankind.
>
> This, then, is our real job—the opportunity to work directly with our people. It is the breaking down of the feeling on the part of our people that they are social automatons with no stake in the future, rather than human beings in possession of all the responsibility, strength, and human dignity which constitute the heritage of free citizens of a democracy. (pp. 49–50)

The most effective neighborhood and community organizations win reforms that bring concrete improvements to people's lives, give participants a sense of their own potential, and alter existing power relations (Midwest Academy, 1973). Although outsiders may help with the organizing and share concrete skills, real leadership must emerge from within the group. Only then can the group trust that the issues most meaningful to neighborhood residents will be addressed. Only then can a genuine, enduring power base develop.

Neighborhood organizations should be structured to allow maximum participation and to take advantage of all opportunities for positive change. This means selecting appropriate issues and targets for action and developing the strongest possible organization within the neighborhood or larger community.

Experience indicates that community organizations work most effectively when they begin by focusing on concrete issues amenable to change. People will rally around a practical issue they find important. Working together on an issue both relevant and manageable thus lends cohesiveness to the group. Further, once the group experiences success—once it actually accomplishes a necessary change—the organization attracts more people to take on new projects. Success can break through people's apathy, countering the feeling of helplessness common among many, by giving participants a sense of their own power. Many successful organizations begun in response to one problem have gone on to build successful coalitions dealing with many related issues thereafter.

Coalitions enable organizations to combine active citizen involvement and the strength of numbers. Individuals tend to become most actively involved in small organizations with which they identify closely and in which they feel important. The smaller the organization, the more central to its success or failure each member can feel. Strength, however, lies in numbers. By banding together, small, close-knit organizations enjoy the advantages of both an active, involved membership and large numbers.

For a community organization to work successfully, then, it must do the following:

1. Allow leadership to emerge from within the group
2. Attack specific, concrete issues, then deal with broader goals from a base of success
3. Use coalitions to combine both active involvement and large numbers of people

The Woodlawn Organization, based in Chicago, demonstrates the kinds of gains a group organized along these lines can make. Its history exemplifies community organization concepts in action.

THE WOODLAWN ORGANIZATION   Woodlawn is a mile-square neighborhood in the heart of Chicago, Illinois. Close to Lake Michigan, to Chicago's thriving downtown areas, to some of the world's finest museums, and to the University of Chicago, it has the potential to be an exceptional place to live.

Yet, in 1960—the year its citizens decided to organize—Woodlawn's potential seemed grim. Though the University of Chicago bordered it to the north, a barbed wire fence clearly separated it from the university.

In Woodlawn, the rates of unemployment, school dropouts, infant mortality, venereal disease, and premature births were among the highest in the city. The people of Woodlawn paid high rent for substandard housing, high prices for low-quality food and clothing. Health care, social services, and educational facilities were all inadequate. No one in the public or private sector took responsibility for making either goods or services more accessible, and every day more local businesses disappeared. To wipe out hopelessness and bring community self-determination in its place, the Temporary Woodlawn Organization (TWO) was created.

TWO's Beginnings.   As the 1950s drew to a close, four of Woodlawn's religious leaders realized that unless something was done to break the cycle, the community's descent into despair would never stop. Doctors Leber and Blakely of the First Presbyterian Church, Father Farrell of the Catholic Church, and Reverend Profrock of the Woodlawn Emanuel Lutheran Church examined the problems they saw around them and turned to their churches for help. By 1960, Leber, Blakely, and Farrell had secured funds from the Catholic Archdiocese of Chicago, the Schwarzhaupt Foundation, and the First Presbyterian Church of Chicago. Forming the Greater Woodlawn Pastors' Alliance from what had been the entirely Protestant Woodlawn Ministers' Alliance, they took the first major step toward community organization. They called in Saul Alinsky and his Industrial Areas Foundation (IAF), formed to provide technical assistance to communities attempting to build their own people's organizations.

The IAF's strategy for change involved the development of indigenous people's organizations, which provide the only possible means for obtaining broadly based power. In a community such as Woodlawn, the only resource available to the residents is their number. Initially, the IAF tried to (1) attract people by dealing with the concrete issues most important to them, (2) give them an avenue through which they could raise and resolve conflict, and (3) provide an opportunity for local leadership to arise.

In January 1961, a meeting of representatives of the Woodlawn Block Club Council, the Woodlawn Businessmen's Association, the Greater Woodlawn Pastors' Alliance, and the United Woodlawn Conference (which subsequently dropped out) resulted in the creation of the Temporary

Woodlawn Organization, with the IAF serving as technical advisor. It was important that the organization be deemed "temporary," because the goal of those present was to build a community-based organization that would respond to the needs and desires of a broad range of civic groups in Woodlawn. Toward this end, the Temporary Woodlawn Organization embarked on a series of activities aimed at resolving the most important issues immediately facing the community, while building a base that could support a permanent organization.

South Campus. The most difficult and immediate concern of the Woodlawn community in 1960 was an expansion plan that the University of Chicago had announced the previous summer. The university intended to clear a strip of land one mile long and one block wide along the southern boundary of the campus, on which it would then build its South Campus. Having the area declared a blighted slum would mean that the university could expand cheaply, while the city would benefit by becoming eligible for federal urban renewal funds.

The residents of Woodlawn were concerned not just about that parcel of land but also about the expansion's long-range implications for the community. TWO wanted an overall plan for urban renewal, a plan that would involve community members as full participants, that would set out objectives with the people's interests in mind, and that would prevent the university from swallowing up the whole Woodlawn community over time.

The fledgling organization rallied support within the community, opposed the plan in Washington on the basis of lack of citizen participation in its planning, and embarked on a long and bitter conflict with a seemingly unbeatable adversary. TWO even hired independent city planners to draw up alternatives to the plans developed by the university and by the city.

Finally, an agreement was reached. A citizens' committee, a majority of whom came from TWO, would take part in all plans for urban renewal in Woodlawn. The South Campus plan would not take effect until the broken-down nonresidential buildings on another large plot of land were cleared and low-cost, low-rise housing replaced them.

By organizing an action plan and working with members of the community to implement it successfully, TWO won recognition as the organization that could speak for Woodlawn. It also won recognition of the right of Woodlawn residents to participate in all planning affecting their lives. At the same time, this struggle brought the organization into a new and long-lived stage in its own development.

With the support of the Kate Maremont Foundation, TWO developed the newly acquired land under the auspices of the TWO-Kate Maremont Development Association. As a result of investing their time and energy to develop the social environment in this way, the TWO-Kate Maremont

Development Association built, owns, and manages the 502 apartment units of Woodlawn Gardens.

Business Exploitation.   Just as important to many Woodlawn residents as the university's expansion plan was the exploitation of residents by businesses within their own neighborhood. The primary problems in this regard involved false advertising, unfair credit practices, overcharging, and, in the case of food stores, inaccurate weighing. Because Woodlawn residents had few shopping alternatives to these businesses, they felt powerless as individuals to deal with these problems. At the same time, honest business owners within the community were concerned about these grievances, too.

In attempting to address community concerns regarding these unscrupulous business practices, TWO created the Square Deal campaign. It began with a large parade along one of Woodlawn's main shopping streets. The follow-up to this highly visible form of community action included setting up a checkout counter in the yard of a church. People who had just completed their grocery shopping could bring their purchases there, have them weighed accurately, have their cash register totals checked, and find out immediately whether or not they had been cheated. Stores identified as exploitive received widespread negative publicity and threats of a boycott. Cheated individuals were encouraged to tell their neighbors.

This concerted campaign resulted in Woodlawn merchants' agreeing to sign a code of business ethics drawn up by a group of community leaders and representatives of the Woodlawn Businessmen's Association. They also agreed to develop a board of arbitration, composed of representatives from the Businessmen's Association and consumer groups, that would deal with future problems. Through these tactics, the people of Woodlawn not only improved local business practices but also became increasingly aware of the power of their community.

Poor Living Conditions.   Another primary motivation for organizing was the actual physical deterioration of the buildings in which Woodlawn residents lived. Many of these buildings had been subdivided several times and allowed to fall into disrepair by absentee landlords. Such neglect often included refusal to make emergency repairs such as broken windows, faulty plumbing, and lack of heating. With no alternatives, tenants had to pay high rents for substandard housing.

Recognizing the negative impact of these conditions on the well-being of the residents, TWO agreed to support those residents committed to taking action. Thus, when a majority of tenants within one of these buildings formed a tenants' committee, TWO helped them negotiate with the landlord, sometimes turning to such tactics as going to the owner's suburban neighborhood to picket in front of his or her home.

When all else failed, rent strikes were organized, with the tenants putting their rent checks into an escrow account until needed repairs were made. They hoped the landlords would complete the needed repairs upon notification of the committee's demands. However, this only happened consistently after the tenants won a few hard-fought battles in the court system. All these efforts helped to strengthen the young TWO, which was beginning to have an increasingly visible impact on concrete problems in the Woodlawn community.

Public Schools.   Another emotionally charged issue of great concern to members of TWO involved the public school system. In Woodlawn, parents saw their children packed into overcrowded schools and forced to attend in double shifts, while a few miles away, white, middle-class children studied in half-empty classrooms. Recognizing that these conditions and the policies that allowed them to continue reflected institutional racism and oppression, TWO again turned to dramatic demonstrations of community concern.

"Truth squads" visited white schools and took pictures of vacant classrooms to point up the fact that Chicago's schools were, in fact, segregated. Hundreds of community members appeared at a citywide public hearing to discuss the findings of these squads. At their own hearing in Woodlawn, parents heard reports from masked schoolteachers, afraid of reprisals if their identities were known. In addition, each Board of Education meeting was attended by the "Death Watch," groups of parents wearing black capes to symbolize the fate of their children in the Chicago public schools.

Awareness of TWO.   Along with major voter registration campaigns, these activities made the Temporary Woodlawn Organization a powerful force in the community. As a result, people with political and economic power in Chicago were becoming increasingly aware of the organization. More important, the community members themselves were becoming aware of TWO and the power of citizens coming together in collective planning and action. In the minds of many in the Woodlawn area, it was clearly time to create a permanent organization.

As a result, The Woodlawn Organization (still TWO) was set up not as an association of individual members but as an umbrella organization for Woodlawn groups, including block clubs, religious institutions, business associations, and other civic-action groups. Each group would send delegates to meetings and to the annual convention, with ongoing functions carried on by a steering committee and several standing committees. Through this mechanism, TWO had in the beginning—and continues to have—the ability to speak for the entire Woodlawn community. The organization could now turn its attention to building programs that could provide long-range solutions.

TWO and Community Development. In the 1970s, TWO created the Woodlawn Community Development Corporation (WCDC) to implement programs in real estate development and management, commercial development, workforce training and education, neighborhood improvement, and health. TWO/WCDC, as always a people's organization, now creates and maintains a variety of its own human service programs, such as programs for children and youth, including day care and Head Start; youth advocacy programs; adoption and foster-care programs; child-abuse prevention projects; employment and training programs; and counseling and residential programs for special groups, such as Woodlawn citizens with developmental disabilities. Real estate development has continued over the years, with the organization involved in the building, renovation, and management of many housing and business projects. Commercial ventures have also brought financial investments to the area.

In the decades since its creation, The Woodlawn Organization has continued to represent the people of its neighborhoods. Although the issues have changed over the years, the organization's priorities have kept pace with new challenges. The basic meaning and purpose of the organization, however, has remained constant; what was true in 1970 remains true today. Compared with other poor, urban neighborhoods, "there is an important difference which distinguishes Woodlawn. . . . The Woodlawn Community has a voice" (The Woodlawn Organization, 1970, p. 28).

Macrosystems: Shaping and Changing Society

Policies at the macrosystem level reveal the way a society as a whole solves its problems and treats its members. If social injustice and a lack of personal power interfere with healthy human development, "it follows that informed social action, policy change and reform, based on concepts such as justice, empowerment, and provision of life opportunities, rather than changing people, are keys to achieving primary prevention's ultimate goal" (Cowen, 1985, p. 32).

To prevent problems and promote health, reforms must aim at eliminating *oppression,* or "that state or condition within an ordered society where one segment of the society is differentially and involuntarily limited access to all the available opportunities, resources, and benefits of that particular society" (Wilson, 1987, p. 19). When working to create changes in the macrosystem, therefore, community counselors seek to counter oppressive policies and conditions by "enhancing the possibilities of people to control their own lives" (Wilson, 1987, p. 20). That is, they promote empowerment strategies in the macrosystem.

Many theorists doubt that one can translate these ideals into concrete, practical programs; however, such efforts can and do occur in a political context. To create the type of macrosystem changes that both reduce oppression and promote human empowerment, one must ask the following, adapted from Vasconcellos, 1986: How do we provide environments (including human relationships) that enable people to develop into healthy human beings? How do we nurture people to be

- Self-aware and with self-esteem
- Self-realizing and self-determining
- Free and responsible
- Competent and caring
- Faithful rather than cynical
- Open rather than closed
- Gentle rather than violent
- Ecologically responsible
- Motivated rather than apathetic
- Moral rather than immoral or amoral
- Political rather than apolitical (pp. 1–2)

In 1986, Vasconcellos introduced a legislative program entitled "Toward a Healthier State—California '86." This comprehensive agenda for change included several separate pieces of proposed legislation, all linked by a common concern for fostering personal power and promoting healthy development. This legislative agenda demonstrates how idealism can lead to real changes, how empowerment ideals can become accepted policies.

Many of the proposals contained in this package have, in fact, already become law in California. The proposed bills that together form this legislative agenda address public, social, economic, family, environmental, governmental, political, and educational health; public safety; and human survival.

The diverse issues addressed by specific bills submitted to the state legislature included the following:

- Incentives for development of an AIDS vaccine
- Establishment of a statewide commission on self-esteem
- Reforms in the state's unitary tax
- Establishment of free-standing, humane birthing clinics by addressing malpractice liability insurance problems and implementing standards for training lay and nurse midwives
- A comprehensive survey of parent-education programs, as well as a directive to counties to inform parents of such services
- Reforms in the state licensing of marriage, family, and child counselors
- Measures to protect against toxic wastes
- Campaign-funding reforms

- Establishment of a pilot project for an individualized educational program for troubled youths
- Establishment of an academic exchange and sister-state program with Russia
- Designation of a "Peace Day" and provision of an honorarium for peace prizes to California residents
- Training teachers to encourage critical thinking about conflict-resolution strategies and alternative solutions to current world problems
- A study of the needs of adults who were molested as children
- Demanding that the Department of Health Services be required to develop a feasibility plan for implementing AIDS hospice treatment services
- Allowing the Department of Corrections to place inmates with AIDS in appropriate care facilities, such as hospices

Some of these bills have yet to pass, but many have become law. Among the latter, AB 3659 established the California Commission to Promote Self-Esteem, Social and Personal Responsibility. In his discussion of the rationale for that bill, Vasconcellos (1986) states,

> We need not resign ourselves to a malfunctioning society. To do so is fatalism at best, self-fulfilling prophesy at worst. If we continue merely to treat symptoms rather than search for causes, we abandon hope of solutions. Continually treating symptoms is neither cost-effective nor responsible. It's like looking for better ways to drag bodies out of the river instead of attempting to fix the bridge.

The 1986 California initiative demonstrates the possibility of implementing broad, systemic policies that can help prevent many kinds of problems. In each state and locality, comparable issues can be identified, and changes that address their citizens' specific needs can be fostered in similar ways within the macrosystem.

INDIRECT COMMUNITY PROGRAMS AS EMPOWERMENT STRATEGIES

Whether they operate at the level of the individual, institution, community, or society at large, indirect community programs are, in fact, empowerment strategies designed to increase the degree of control people have over their lives. Rappaport (1986) clarifies the importance of empowerment strategies for the community counseling framework as follows:

> By empowerment I mean that our aim should be to enhance the possibilities for people to control their own lives. If this is our aim,

then we will necessarily find ourselves questioning both our public policy and our role relationship to dependent people. We will not be able to settle for a public policy that limits us to programs we design, operate, or package for social agencies to use on people, because it will require that the form and the metacommunications as well as the content be consistent with empowerment. We will, should we take empowerment seriously, no longer be able to see people as simply children in need or as only citizens with rights, but rather as full human beings who have both rights and needs. We will confront the paradox that even the people most incompetent, in need, and apparently unable to function, require, just as you and I do, more rather than less control over their own lives. (p. 154)

The directions that empowering programs take must depend precisely on the priorities set by the people most affected, for "locally developed solutions are more empowering than single solutions applied in a general way" (Rappaport, 1987, p. 141). Individuals, groups, and communities can all move toward empowerment with the help of interventions that create helpful environmental conditions.

Like other citizens, community counselors need to participate in organized action affecting public policy. Most community counselors who participate in such action, however, are entering a new arena. Many have been trained primarily in one-to-one or small-group counseling techniques; their concern for social change arises from their experiences rather than their training. Thus, they must forge a new identity as professionals concerned both with individuals and with the environment. They should define that identity according to the unique attributes they as counselors can bring to organized action.

1. Community counselors have a unique awareness of the common problems faced by community members.

Counselors become aware of the recurring difficulties and obstacles faced by people in the schools, neighborhoods, and communities where they work. This awareness enables counselors to identify specific aspects of the environment that may be detrimental. Trying to help each affected individual, however, can become an exercise in frustration, because new victims of unhealthy environmental systems continually appear.

This frustration typically occurs when community counselors work in neighborhoods overwhelmed by poverty. It also occurs when career counselors become aware of inequitable hiring practices, when rehabilitation counselors note the obstacles to equal treatment, when school counselors encounter inhumane educational practices, when agency counselors dealing with special populations try to stop the community from stigmatizing particular groups. It happens whenever counselors find their helping power eroded and ultimately overwhelmed by environmental forces.

Community counselors' special perspective allows them to recognize the seriousness of community problems and help others in the search for new solutions. When they become aware of specific difficulties within the environment, such counselors help bring these problems to the surface and encourage action for change by doing the following:

- Making the community as a whole aware of problems and their consequences
- Alerting organizations that might have an interest in the issue at hand
- Joining others to support citizens fighting for change on their own behalf

2. Community counselors can encourage the development of new leadership and provide support to new organizations.

Because of the nature of their work, community counselors have intimate contact with the least powerful segments of the population. In the past, many mental health practitioners have used this contact to teach these groups ways to adjust to the demands of the larger community. More and more, however, community counselors are trying to encourage and support the growth of self-help organizations that try to influence the social environment constructively.

Human services workers often bring together groups of community members who wish to share mutual concerns and develop new coping skills. When leadership emerges from within, the group has taken its first step toward becoming a self-help organization and toward building a coalition for action. Thus, a natural transition from direct to indirect community services can occur. Groups of people participating in a workshop or a class may evolve into groups ready to confront community problems more actively than before. Counselors can provide support to such groups while allowing local leadership to emerge.

3. Community counselors can share their human relations skills with groups trying to help themselves.

If effective community counselors share one skill, it is interpersonal relations and communication. They can contribute significantly to a community by sharing these skills with people attempting to organize for change. Community counselors can act as consultants to such groups and can provide training in the skills that the community members value. Specifically, counselors might provide leadership training, analyze communication patterns within the group, and train members in skills that can help them function as an effective unit.

Counselors might also help community organizations develop expertise in research and evaluation—that is, in gathering the hard data that they need to support their concerns. Ideally, community counselors can also share their understanding of social systems and the nature of change itself.

4. Community counselors can help coordinate groups working to bring about change.

Effective community counselors have their fingers on the pulse of the community. Familiar with the local agencies that provide direct services, they can also get to know the groups and organizations working more directly to bring about changes in the social environment. Counselors can also link individuals and groups addressing specific mutual needs and interests.

Many agencies—particularly those serving special populations—act as clearinghouses for information and as home bases for a number of self-help groups. Along with others, community counselors can participate in actions that will help their clients. Often, several organizations join forces to act on a specific issue. Community counselors and their agencies can, whenever appropriate, be a part of such a force for change.

SUMMARY

Because environmental factors make a powerful impact on the well-being of community members, indirect, community-wide interventions play an important part in the work of the community counselor. Because problems develop within social systems, counselors must address them through systemic interventions.

Bronfenbrenner's ecological model of human development defines four systemic levels: microsystems, mesosystems, exosystems, and macrosystems. An example of a microsystem is a school, which directly affects the development of its students. The Quality of School Life program in Michigan exemplifies intervention at this level. The mesosystem involves the relationships between microsystems. The Perry Preschool Project and Felner's Transition Project are programs designed to facilitate ecological transitions in mesosystems. The neighborhood is an exosystem; neighborhood organizations such as The Woodlawn Organization demonstrate the process of local empowerment. Finally, policies at the level of the macrosystem concern the way society as a whole treats it members. Macrosystem interventions involve social action, policy change, and reform.

All these interventions represent empowerment strategies designed to increase the degree of control people have over their own lives. Community counselors play a unique role in the empowerment process because of their particular awareness of the common problems faced by community members. The contributions they can make include increasing community awareness of problems, encouraging the development of new leaders and organizations, sharing human relations skills with people organizing for change, and helping to coordinate groups and organizations.

SUPPLEMENTAL ACTIVITIES

1. Read through a current local newspaper. As you read, try to spot those issues that might affect the clients of a local community counseling program. Do aspects of your community environment strike you as potentially detrimental? Are there things going on that you feel should be changed? After assigning priorities to the issues you identify, choose one thing in your community to change. Consider this change in relation to the following questions:
   a. What other individuals or groups might share a concern about this issue?
   b. What individuals or groups might actively oppose this change?
   c. Can the desired change be broken down into smaller objectives that might be more easily met?
   d. What specific activities might help bring about this change?

2. Consider again the hypothetical agency you have been designing. What policy changes might make the school, neighborhood, business sector, and community as a whole more responsive to the needs of the population you plan to serve? Does your program deal with problems that could be prevented through changes in social policy? Try to detail this facet.

REFERENCES

Albee, G. W. (1988). Toward a just society: Lessons from observations on the primary prevention of psychopathology. In G. W. Albee, J. M. Joffe, & L. A. Dusenbury (Eds.), *Prevention, powerlessness, and politics: Readings on social change* (pp. 549–556). Newbury Park, CA: Sage.

Albee, G. W., Joffe, J. M., & Dusenbury, L. A. (Eds.). (1988). *Prevention, powerlessness, and politics: Readings on social change*. Newbury Park, CA: Sage.

Alinsky, S. D. (1969). *Rules for radicals*. New York: Vantage.

Atkinson, D. R., Morten, G., & Sue, D. W. (1993). *Counseling American minorities: A cross-cultural perspective* (4th ed.). Madison, WI: Brown & Benchmark.

Aubrey, R. F. (1972). Power bases: The consultant's vehicle for change. *Elementary School Guidance and Counseling, 7*(2), 90–97.

Aubrey, R. F., & Lewis, J. A. (1988). Social issues and the counseling profession in the 1980s and 1990s. In R. Hayes & R. Aubrey (Eds.), *New directions for counseling and human development* (pp. 286–303). Denver, CO: Love Publishing.

Bales, J. (1987, April). Prevention at its best. *APA Monitor*, pp. 18–19.

Banks, J. A., & Banks, C. A. (Eds.). (1993). *Multicultural education: Issues and perspectives*. Boston: Allyn and Bacon.

Bolger, N., Caspi, A., Downey, G., & Moorehouse, M. (1988). *Persons in context: Developmental processes*. New York: Cambridge University Press.

Bronfenbrenner, U. (1976). *Reality and research in the ecology of human development*. Master lectures on developmental psychology. Washington, DC: American Psychological Association.

Bronfenbrenner, U. (1977). Toward an experimental ecology of human development. *American Psychologist, 32*(4), 513–531.

Bronfenbrenner, U. (1979). *The ecology of human development*. Cambridge, MA: Harvard University Press.

Bronfenbrenner, U. (1988). Interacting systems in human development. In N. Bolger, A. Caspi, G. Downey, & M. Moorehouse (Eds.), *Persons in context: Developmental processes* (pp. 25–49). New York: Cambridge University Press.

Children's Defense Fund. (1996). *Teenage pregnancy: An advocate's guide to the numbers*. Washington, DC: Adolescent Pregnancy Clearinghouse.

Clark, K. B. (1988). A community action program. In G. W. Albee, J. M. Joffee, & L. A. Dusenbury (Eds.), *Prevention, powerlessness, and politics: Readings on social change* (pp. 461–470). Newbury Park, CA: Sage.

Conyne, R. K. (1985). The counseling ecologist: Helping people and environments. *Counseling and Human Development, 18*(2), 1–12.

Cowen, E. L. (1985). Person-centered approaches to primary prevention in mental health: Situation-focused and competence-enhancement. *American Journal of Community Psychology, 13*(1), 31–48.

D'Andrea, M. (1994, April). *Creating a vision for our future: The challenges and promise of the counseling profession*. Paper presented at the annual meeting of the American Counseling Association, Minneapolis, MN.

D'Andrea, M., & Daniels, J. (1992). A career development program for inner-city black youth. *Career Development Quarterly, 40*(3), 272–280.

D'Andrea, M., & Daniels, J. (1995). Helping students learn to get along: Assessing the effectiveness of a multicultural developmental guidance program. *Elementary School Guidance and Counseling Journal, 30*(2), 143–154.

Egan, G. (1985). *Change agent skills in helping and human service settings*. Pacific Grove, CA: Brooks/Cole.

Felner, R. D., Ginter, M., & Primavera, J. (1982). Primary prevention during school transitions: Social support and environmental structure. *American Journal of Community Psychology, 10*(3), 277–289.

Germaine, C. (1991). *Human behavior in the social environment: An ecological view*. New York: Columbia University Press.

Geronimus, A. T., & Korenman, S. (1990). *The socioeconomic consequences of teen childbearing reconsidered* (Report No. 90–190). Ann Arbor, MI: Population Studies Center.

Gordon, S., & Scales, P. (1988). Preparing young people for responsible sexual parenting. In G. W. Albee, J. M. Joffe, & L. A. Dusenbury (Eds.), *Prevention, powerlessness, and politics: Readings on social change* (pp. 328–341). Newbury Park, CA: Sage.

Hilliard, T. O. (1988). Prevention of psychopathology of blacks. In G. W. Albee, J. M. Joffe, & L. A. Dusenbury (Eds.), *Prevention, powerlessness, and politics: Readings on social change* (pp. 342–358). Newbury Park, CA: Sage.

Ing, J. (1995). *ASSET: A school-based classroom guidance program to aid students in making the transition to intermediate school.* Unpublished master's thesis, University of Hawai'i, Honolulu.

Iscoe, I. (1981). Conceptual barriers to training for the primary prevention of psychopathology. In J. M. Joffe & G. W. Albee (Eds.), *Prevention through political action and social change* (pp. 110–134). Hanover, NH: University Press of New England.

Ivey, A. E. (1995). Psychotherapy as liberation: Toward specific skills and strategies in multicultural counseling and therapy. In J. G. Ponterotto, J. M. Casas, L. A. Suzuki, & C. M. Alexander (Eds.), *Handbook of multicultural counseling* (pp. 53–72). Newbury Park, CA: Sage.

Konopka, G. (1988). Social change, social action as prevention. In G. W. Albee, J. M. Joffe, & L. A. Dusenbury (Eds.), *Prevention, powerlessness, and politics: Readings on social change* (pp. 337–348). Newbury Park, CA: Sage.

Lee, C. C., & Richardson, B. L. (Eds.). (1991). *Multicultural issues in counseling: New approaches to diversity.* Alexandria, VA: American Association for Counseling and Development.

Levin, H. M. (1988). Changing the schools. In G. W. Albee, J. M. Joffe, & L. A. Dusenbury (Eds.), *Prevention, powerlessness, and politics: Readings on social change* (pp. 441–460). Newbury Park, CA: Sage.

Lewin, K. (1951). *Field theory in social science.* New York: Harper.

Lewis, J. A., & Lewis, M. D. (1989). *Community counseling* (2nd ed.). Pacific Grove, CA: Brooks/Cole.

Locke, D. C. (1992). *Increasing multicultural understanding: A comprehensive model.* Newbury Park, CA: Sage.

Martin, J. M. (1991). The mental health professional and social action. *American Journal of Orthopsychiatry, 61*(4), 484–488.

Merrick, E. N. (1995). Adolescent childbearing as a career "choice": Perspective from an ecological context. *Journal of Counseling and Development, 73*(3), 288–292.

Michigan Department of Mental Health. (1987). *The Quality of School Life program: Improving school and classroom climate by problem-solving with people.* Washtenaw, MI: Washtenaw County Community Mental Health Center.

Midwest Academy. (1973). *Building the community: Modes of personal growth.* Chicago: Author.

Netting, F. E., Kettner, P. M., & McMurtry, S. L. (Eds.). (1993). *Social work: Macro practice.* New York: Longman.

Rappaport, J. (1986). In praise of paradox: A social policy of empowerment over prevention. In E. Seidman & J. Rappaport (Eds.), *Redefining social problems* (pp. 141–164). New York: Plenum.

Rappaport, J. (1987). Terms of empowerment/exemplars of prevention: Toward a theory for community psychology. *American Journal of Community Psychology, 15,* 121–148.

Rappaport, J., Davidson, W. S., Wilson, M. N., & Mitchell, A. (1975). Alternatives to blaming the victim or the environment. *American Psychologist, 30*(5), 525–528.

Schelkun, R. F., Cooper, S., Tableman, B., & Groves, D. (1987). Quality of School Life for Elementary Schools (QSL-E): A system-wide preventive intervention for effective schools. *Community Psychologist, 20*(2), 8–9.

Schweinhart, L. J. (1987, Fall). When the buck stops here: What it takes to run good early childhood programs. *High Scope Resource,* pp. 8–13.

Slaughter-Defoe, D. T. (1995). Revisiting the concept of socialization: Caregiving and teaching in the 90s—a personal perspective. *American Psychologist, 30*(4), 276–286.

Sue, D. W., & Sue, D. (1990). *Counseling the culturally different: Theory and practice.* New York: Wiley.

Sue, D. W., Ivey, A. E., & Pedersen, P. B . (Eds.). (1996). *A theory of multicultural counseling and therapy.* Pacific Grove, CA: Brooks/Cole.

Tester, F. J. (1993). In an age of ecology: Limits to volunteerism. In F. E. Netting, P. M. Kettner, & S. L. McMurtry (Eds.), *Social work: Macro practice* (pp. 75–99). New York: Longman.

Trotter, S. (1988). Neighborhood change. In G. W. Albee, J. M. Joffe, & L. A. Dusenbury (Eds.), *Prevention, powerlessness, and politics: Readings on social change* (pp. 471–482). Newbury Park, CA: Sage.

United Nations. (1992). *Demographic yearbook 1990* (pp. 313–331). New York: United Nations, Department of International Economic and Social Affairs, Statistical Office.

Vasconcellos, J. (1986). *A new human agenda* (Capitol Report, 23rd Assembly District). Sacramento: State of California.

Wilson, M. (1987). Classnotes on the psychology of oppression and social change. *Community Psychologist, 20*(2), 19–21.

Wolff, T. (1987). Community psychology and empowerment: An activist's insights. *American Journal of Community Psychology, 15,* 151–166.

The Woodlawn Organization. (1970). *Woodlawn's model cities plan: A demonstration of citizen responsibility.* Northbrook, IL: Whitehall.

CHAPTER 7

APPLICATIONS OF THE COMMUNITY COUNSELING MODEL

REVIEW OF THE COMMUNITY COUNSELING MODEL

In the preceding chapters, we have described the four components the community counseling framework comprises: direct client, direct community, indirect client, and indirect community services. Mental health practitioners can use these intervention modalities to foster the psychological health and personal well-being of more people more effectively into the 21st century.

These four modalities can work in any counseling setting. Regardless of the nature of a given agency or institution, effective programs should include both services to individuals and efforts to improve the environment. Regardless of the specific problems addressed, community counseling's main goal is to foster clients' healthy development and well-being. To accomplish this, the community counselor focuses on ways to enhance individuals' personal competency and to prevent dysfunction.

Community counselors intervene not only directly, with their clients, but indirectly, to facilitate positive changes in clients' social environments. In this latter intervention, counselors act as advocates, consultants, and change agents. The nature of a given intervention depends on the setting in which the counselor works and the needs of his or her particular group of clients. Because community counseling represents an approach rather than a job title, one can find community counselors in a multitude of mental health agencies, in other professional helping organizations, in schools and universities, and in business settings across the country.

To make the community counseling model more concrete and understandable, we have outlined several applications of this framework in diverse settings. We have selected programs that tend to employ many kinds of helpers with different specializations and training backgrounds. Even so, the programs presented in this chapter represent only a few of the many ways one might incorporate the community counseling framework into educational, business, and helping organizations. Each mental health practitioner must find the most appropriate adaptation of the model to fit his or her own setting.

MENTAL HEALTH AGENCIES

Community mental health agencies address the psychological concerns of a general population residing within specific geographical boundaries, often referred to as *catchment areas*. Agencies serving catchment areas can develop particularly well-coordinated services and can play a powerful role in helping the local population remedy detrimental environmental conditions.

Whether small agencies dedicated to outpatient care or major centers offering comprehensive services, community mental health centers and agencies can provide multifaceted services. Table 7.1 presents an example of a multifaceted program that community counselors might implement in such agencies.

Direct Community Services

As noted in Table 7.1, direct community services offered by local human service agencies comprise preventive education programs designed to promote a variety of life skills and competencies. For these programs to work well, the entire community must be able to access them. Fundamentally, developers should design these direct community services to (1) educate community members about issues related to mental health and personal wellness; (2) provide experiences that foster the development of community members' personal, social, and/or career competencies, and thereby (3) help to prevent serious problems, particularly among at-risk groups.

Programs that teach people about mental health should aim at clarifying those factors that promote health and effectiveness in everyday living. They should help the participants understand the relationship that exists

TABLE 7.1
COMMUNITY COUNSELING
IN COMMUNITY MENTAL HEALTH AGENCIES

	COMMUNITY SERVICES	CLIENT SERVICES
Direct	Educational programs on the nature of mental health	Counseling and rehabilitation programs
	Preventive educational programs teaching mental health–related life skills	Crisis intervention
		Outreach programs for populations dealing with life transitions or other high-risk situations
Indirect	Helping the local community organize to work for environmental changes	Advocacy for groups such as people with chronic mental health problems
	Action on policies affecting community mental health	Consultation within the helping network
		Promotion of self-help programs
		Linkage with other helping systems

among individuals, their psychological wellness, and their environments. Mental health education programs sponsored by community agencies can do much to help erase the stigma all too often placed on people who have received counseling services for psychological problems.

A mental health agency's educational programs should also define how the agency is trying to contribute to the community. As previous chapters have stressed, community members must participate in the planning of agencies' educational programs and services. As such, agencies must actively solicit input from community members about their needs, goals, and interests as well as involve them in the planning and ongoing evaluation of the educational services offered.

Community mental health centers usually deal with relatively large, heterogeneous populations and strive to meet a broad range of their psychological needs. Particularly appropriate to such agencies are programs that help members of the community become more self-sufficient in dealing with personal and interpersonal needs as they arise. That is, a mental health agency's educational programs should help community members develop the skills and awareness that will enhance their effectiveness, or help them learn to create and maintain healthful environments. In the following sections, we present some programs useful in promoting these skills.

TRAINING PROGRAMS Mental health practitioners can use training programs to help foster a host of personal competencies among a broad range of people, of different ages and from diverse backgrounds. Such programs can make help readily available to community members when they need it and may prevent serious impairment. These programs can also boost people's sense of community because they make the development of competencies and mutual help everyone's responsibility instead of the special province of professionals.

The Nashville Youth Network (Daniels & D'Andrea, 1991) is a good example of an effective community-based educational and training program for teenagers. Designed to promote the empowerment of adolescents, this youth network used a variety of formal and informal educational and training services within the community that emphasized the importance of tapping into the members' strength and knowledge (thereby promoting self-help principles). As the teenagers planned and implemented a host of community service projects intended to impact positively various systems (e.g., schools, neighborhood youth agencies, state legislative committees) within their social environments, they found validation and support for their self-determination (Daniels & D'Andrea, 1991).

GROUP EXPERIENCES Counselors working within community mental health centers can use various group interventions to help their clients develop better interpersonal relationships with one another. Such groups focus on development and education rather than remediation of existing problems.

Sayger (1996) aptly describes the use of group experiences to foster the development of effective interpersonal skills among children and families experiencing multiple stressors in their environment. This preventive intervention focuses on educating parents and children about the impact of high-risk environments on healthy family functioning.

As Sayger (1996) notes by fostering the empowerment of the whole family unit, these psychoeducational groups provide a valuable alternative to traditional family and crisis counseling services. Using Sayger's model to facilitate family empowerment, counselors are encouraged to do the following:

1. Use an educational approach to foster the development of new interpersonal competencies among family members
2. Discuss issues of trust and social support with family members during the educational group meetings

3. Focus on the families' positive strengths
4. Provide opportunities for family members to exercise their newly developed interpersonal skills in a safe and supportive environment.

SKILL-BUILDING PROGRAMS   Skill-building programs provide another way counselors can offer direct community services that help individuals learn to live more effectively and deal with issues more competently. Many community members can be reached through skill-building programs presented in a large-group format or through a mass medium.

In the past, skill-building programs have typically required participants to attend classes that offered information about various life skills and provided opportunities to practice these new skills through role playing. However, with the advancement of technology, counselors can now use computer-based skill-building programs and provide online educational services to people in their homes. Continued advancements in computer technology will revolutionize the ways mental health practitioners think about and offer skill-building services to large numbers of people in the 21st century (Gerler, 1995).

EDUCATION FOR EVERYDAY LIVING   The overall effectiveness of direct community service programs largely depends on the degree to which they help individuals develop competence in meeting the issues they face every day. Competence-building programs usually direct attention to such areas as family relationships, career planning, stress management, decision-making strategies, time management, and other issues community members see as important. See Nelson-Jones (1993) for a helping framework mental health professionals may find useful for planning preventive education programs aimed at enhancing individuals' living competencies.

Direct Client Services

One of the important roles mental health agencies play in their communities is providing counseling for people who need or want more active intervention in their lives. These services must be easily accessible and affordable. When working directly with clients, community counselors should operate from a broad conceptualization of mental health. In this way, they can provide assistance with almost any everyday problem or developmental challenge their clients face.

When helping people who are having trouble coping with their lives, community counselors strive to recognize and build on their clients' strengths and do all they can to prevent the need for inpatient treatment. However, if clients' problems interfere with their self-sufficiency or require more intensive treatment, the counselor must try to provide rehabilitation services in accordance with clients' own goals.

Community counselors have a particular responsibility to help former inpatients live and work effectively in mainstream society. Thus, direct client services offered to these clients should include the following:

1. Helping clients address environmental conditions that interfere with their growth and well-being
2. Individual, group, and family counseling services as needed
3. Promoting clients' involvement in self-help organizations
4. Intervention strategies that help clients acquire life skills that facilitate their successful integration into the larger community

Counselors in community mental health settings can also recognize and address situations that put individuals at risk for psychological problems. During the past three decades, mental health centers across the United States have developed and implemented various types of outreach programs for people affected by such crisis-provoking situations as the loss of a family member, marital disruption, financial problems, and health concerns (Lewis & Lewis, 1989). These programs have often succeeded in providing temporary assistance and support, enabling individuals to deal more effectively with their problems.

Indirect Community Services

Because of their close association with the community in which they work, counselors in mental health agencies are particularly well positioned to recognize factors in the environment that interfere with healthy human development. They are also positioned to see the strengths and resources available within the greater community.

When a mental health center or agency is an integral part of their community, staff members help residents organize in order to support the community's goals. In doing so, the agency can serve as a coordinating base where mental health professionals work together with other community members to do the following:

1. Plan services that can best meet the needs the members themselves have defined
2. Outline strategies for confronting negative political, social, and economic forces within the community to ensure that local organizations and institutions respond to community needs and that decision making within the business, educational, and health-care sectors is open to citizen participation
3. Act to meet community members' immediate needs, especially education, housing, sanitation, transportation, employment, and medical care

Although mental health workers can implement indirect community services that support and encourage these activities, the long-term success of these initiatives ultimately depends on leadership by local citizens. Further, the interest and leadership that mental health practitioners themselves exhibit in such services can bring about changes in the community as well as the mental health system. Thus, when mental health agencies incorporate indirect community services, counselors often find themselves acting as advocates for the general consumers of mental health services and fighting for the provision of educational and career opportunities in place of incarceration, for alternatives to institutionalization, and for the development of public and organizational policies that recognize and respect human dignity.

Indirect Client Services

Counselors working in comprehensive mental health agencies are also in a good position to forge links with the whole human services network within the community. Dealing with the mental health needs of a local population and treating clients holistically necessitates having regular ongoing contact with a broad range of other community agencies, health-care providers, and educational specialists.

To attain mental health, clients must have their practical needs met. Counselors in mental health agencies provide important links between clients and services that meet these and other needs. Such counselors are well positioned to serve as a first contact and coordinator, ensuring that the maze of services and facilities available in the community is reasonably clear and accessible to clients.

Because the mental health of an individual largely depends on her or his interactions with other people, the counselor also works with that individual's family members as well as with any others who might be contributing to the client's problem or be part of a solution. In doing so, the community counselor goes beyond linking, to advocating. Finally, mental health professionals may act as consultants, helping members of the helping network learn more effective ways of working with the people whose lives they touch.

CAREER DEVELOPMENT AGENCIES

Many agencies primarily help clients through job placement, vocational rehabilitation, or career development. These programs succeed when their clients find work appropriate to their abilities, interests, and goals.

Yet, such agencies often go far beyond their traditional image as places where individuals are merely "fitted" with—or perhaps trained for—new jobs. Effective career development agencies emphasize the following:

1. Helping individuals formulate and act on career goals and strategies
2. Helping clients develop the skills they need to enter and succeed in the work world
3. Working with employers to increase job opportunities and support for their clients
4. Directing time and energy toward influencing policies that affect career development opportunities for their clients and for the community at large

The work of the community counselor in such an agency must, in fact, be multifaceted. Possible adaptation of the community counseling model for career development and vocational rehabilitation agencies is shown in Table 7.2.

Direct Community Services

Agencies focused on helping clients make career decisions should offer developmental programs that allow individuals to explore their values, goals, and occupational options. Group workshops can provide much training that might otherwise have to occur in one-to-one counseling. If participation

TABLE 7.2
COMMUNITY COUNSELING
IN CAREER DEVELOPMENT AGENCIES

	COMMUNITY SERVICES	CLIENT SERVICES
Direct	Workshops and educational programs on career planning and work-related skills	Counseling, evaluation, and placement services
		Programs for workers with special needs
Indirect	Support of efforts to promote job safety and the humanization of workplaces	Consultation with employers
		Linkage of clients with other services
	Action against discriminatory hiring practices	Advocacy for workers with special needs

were open to all interested community members, regardless of their current job status, such workshops might help prevent job crises, thus increasing the community's well-being. Through structured workshops, individuals can examine their current work situations and lifestyles, explore their values and goals, and develop problem-solving and decision-making skills.

Given the rapid cultural diversification of the United States and the increasing number of people from nonwhite, non-European backgrounds who need career development services each year, counselors must develop group workshops sensitive to the unique needs and perspectives of such individuals. A good example of a culturally sensitive career development workshop has been reported by Kim, Gaughen, and Salvador (1995). Testing the effectiveness of a one-day career development workshop offered to more than three thousand people from Japanese, Chinese, Filipino, Hawaiian, and Samoan backgrounds over five years, they noted significant improvements in the participants' level of career self-efficacy.

Direct Client Services

Of course, counselors must place a high priority on meeting the immediate goals of people needing training, employment, or rehabilitation. Counselors working in career development agencies will use individual counseling to help clients evaluate their own interests and abilities, consider their alternatives, and plan strategies.

Direct services to individuals and groups should also take into account the strong impact of unemployment. In this regard, Herr and Cramer (1996) have discussed the many ways unemployment as well as employment in unhealthy and stressful environments negatively impact one's psychological health and personal well-being. Brenner (1973) has also found long-standing correlations between economic changes and hospital admissions for emotional disturbances.

Individuals seem to find sudden unemployment most stressful when they cannot point to broad economic trends as the reason for their problem. As Brenner (1973) notes, "The more an individual feels that he or [or she] is among a minority of the economically disadvantaged, or the closest he [or she] comes to be singled out by economic loss, the more likely he [or she] is to see the economic failure as a personal failure, one due to his [or her] own incompetence" (p. 236).

When economic downturns affect a community, counselors working in career development agencies can help prevent adverse effects. Monahan and Vaux (1980) describe the role mental health practitioners can play when negative economic conditions hit a community:

> When a social stressor cannot be prevented, the role of mental health professionals lies in mitigating the adverse effects of social stress.

> Monitoring the economic changes in a region should . . . allow the development of primary prevention programs. . . . These programs would aim at preparing the population to deal with the psychological ramifications of an economic downturn. Techniques such as anticipatory guidance . . . could be used to persuade those about to be unemployed that their situation is not of their own doing. . . . They should not view themselves, nor be seen by family and friends, as failures. (pp. 22–23)

Counselors can be most effective in their direct work with clients if they combine this service with others, preventing work-related problems by addressing relevant issues before employment crises occur.

Indirect Community Services

The workplace affects every actual or potential client of vocational and career development agencies. Accordingly, counselors working in these agencies would do well to make the work world more responsive to the needs of all community members.

In this regard, agencies should focus on the hiring, training, and promotion practices of businesses in the community. Combating sexism and racism in employment practices is an obvious and necessary part of improving the work environment. Counselors should also look for unjust practices such as culturally biased screening tests or those that measure aptitudes irrelevant to the job, or bias against ex-offenders, former psychiatric patients, or individuals with disabilities.

Counselors must extend their awareness not only to the hiring process but also to what happens to clients once they have begun working. Though counselors by themselves may not have the power to change the work environments of large corporations and bureaucracies, they can lend their active support to groups seeking to improve industrial safety, to expand the role of workers in making decisions that affect them, and to make workplaces better in general.

Indirect Client Services

Community counselors may act as advocates for either workers in general or individual clients. In agencies that focus on career development issues, client advocacy is most likely to be needed in instances of employment discrimination or other unfair practices.

As in any other setting, the counselor must focus on the client as a whole person as well as on the interaction between individual and environment. One cannot separate career development from human development, nor one's work from the rest of one's life. In the employment setting, the counselor should pay particular attention to those aspects of clients' immediate surroundings that affect their vocational decisions and likelihood of job success.

Community counselors therefore often help clients with matters not directly related to employment but that may nonetheless affect their career development. In many instances, the career counselor may act as a consultant, helping others serve clients more effectively. Just as often, he or she may consult with others to better understand the social, psychological, or physical factors affecting clients' vocational development.

SPECIALIZED AGENCIES

A *specialized agency* deals with a specific population or concern. Such agencies may focus on the members of a specific group—such as women, adolescents, gays and lesbians, or the elderly—or on a specific problem—such as substance abuse or family violence. Such agencies recognize that their individual clients may need a variety of direct services. Primarily, however, these agencies deal with those aspects of the environment that most directly affect the people they serve. Table 7.3 show the kinds of services a specialized agency might implement.

Direct Community Services

In specialized agencies, direct community services often take the form of courses or workshops that provide knowledge or skills that a given population considers important. For instance, women's centers often provide courses on women's health concerns, assertiveness training, self-defense, and career development. Agencies for the elderly may include educational services related to health care, retirement planning, social security and other benefits, and second careers. Finally, youth agencies typically provide courses related to drug and alcohol use, sexuality, decision making, and life planning. All these agencies should maintain close ties to the people they serve, involving them actively in setting priorities for educational programs and other services.

In some specialized agencies, counselors deal with a specific area of concern on an everyday basis. This gives them a special sensitivity to the issues related to that concern. If they work with individuals affected by a particular disability, for instance, they become quite aware of both the effect of the disability and the strengths of their clients. By learning how similar their clients are to the rest of the community, counselors can place problems or disabilities in perspective. Further, by providing educational programs for the community at large, they can help prevent the problem their agency treats and increase public awareness about its effects.

TABLE 7.3
COMMUNITY COUNSELING IN SPECIALIZED AGENCIES

	COMMUNITY SERVICES	CLIENT SERVICES
Direct	Preventive educational programs for the community at large	Accessible counseling services using volunteers and peer counselors when possible
	Training and skill-building programs for members of the population being served	Outreach programs for clients with special needs
		Rehabilitation services focused on independent living
Indirect	Efforts to change legal, economic, and political policies affecting the targeted problems or population	Advocacy for the population being served
	Identification of aspects of the social environment that affect the prevalence or severity of the targeted problem	Consultation with other helpers concerning the special needs and interests of the population being served
		Linkage with other agencies and individuals in the helping network
		Linkage with self-help groups

For instance, workers who help people with drug and alcohol abuse often provide educational programs to the community at large, offering lectures and discussions to students at all levels, parents' groups, and civic or church-related organizations. Such programs can play an important role in the community if they avoid scare tactics and present accurate, up-to-date information on dealing with drug or alcohol use as a decision based on personal values, correct misinformation, involve community members in planning preventive strategies, and eliminate stereotyped images of substance-dependent individuals.

Breaking through stereotypes is also important when counselors provide information about physical or mental disabilities. Educational programs should help participants understand that people with disabilities are individuals with the same needs, desires, and rights as other citizens. Such programs often deal with the causes and effects of particular disabilities and with the special needs of disabled individuals, but they should always emphasize the community's responsibility for integrating all its members into the mainstream. Further, as they inform the public, these programs can enlarge the pool of volunteers ready to devote time and energy to building necessary bridges.

Direct Client Services

Agencies serving specific populations often develop a mechanism for helping people in crisis, partly because such people often turn first to agencies with close ties to the community. Also, such agencies are uniquely aware of—and usually better prepared for—the kinds of crises most likely to occur among the populations they serve. Thus, many youth agencies offer short-term housing and assistance to runaways. Women's centers develop crisis-intervention services for women who have been raped or battered. Many counseling centers serving gays and lesbians have developed AIDS information hot lines.

Because they recognize the types of situations that tend to make their clients vulnerable to problems, counselors in specialized agencies can provide timely and appropriate outreach services. Ongoing counseling must be highly accessible, with peer counseling services provided whenever possible.

Specialized agencies dealing with a specific problem or disability also provide rehabilitation programs to help each individual become self-sufficient. Effective rehabilitation involves the whole person—in many cases, a whole family—and the immediate environment or microsystem (see Chapter 6). Multifaceted, this approach includes the following:

1. Individual counseling on personal or career issues
2. Group counseling that includes interpersonal, support, and skill-building components
3. Family counseling
4. Locating appropriate financial resources and benefits
5. Helping clients find ways to meet their physical needs
6. Providing equipment (such as hearing aids) to enable clients to remain financially and personally self-reliant
7. Having clients help plan and implement new training or educational programs
8. Placement in training programs or jobs
9. Assistance in developing necessary support systems
10. Assistance in finding avenues for recreation and positive social interaction

Of course, in choosing services, rehabilitation counselors should follow the client's own needs, interests, and goals.

The focus of a particular agency will of course, affect the kinds of programs its counselors design. An agency dealing with substance abuse, for instance, will pay particular attention to training individuals on how to prevent relapses. An agency that serves people with physical disabilities will concentrate on helping them maintain the greatest possible mobility and independence, while an agency assisting people with developmental disabilities might emphasize normalization and personal care. These services vary as greatly as the problems they answer. What all specialized programs that use the community counseling model have in common, however, is that they attempt to deal with the whole individual, helping them make the most of their strengths and live as fully and as independently as possible.

Indirect Community Services

Working to create a better environment by fostering changes in social policies is the core of community counselors' work in specialized agencies. Through such efforts, counselors address whatever environmental factors affect the agency's clientele. For instance, youth agencies might focus on school policies or on job and recreational opportunities available to young people in the local community. Women's centers fight discriminatory practices and support women's rights to make personal choices without governmental interference. Counselors working with the elderly may take a stand to help solve urgent economic and health-care problems.

Through these actions, counselors in specialized agencies can play an important part in promoting broad-based efforts for social change while they are addressing immediate, local issues and community needs. Furthermore, specialized agencies can serve as places in which local groups come together, learn to organize, and begin actively to seek solutions to common problems they face in the social environment.

Indirect Client Services

Counselors should see themselves as advocates not only for the populations with which they work but also for individual clients. Public policy can make a difference only when individuals know their rights and can safeguard them. Community counselors can act on their clients' behalf if they are aware of clients' rights and have the courage to confront inequities. Further, community counselors must maintain close ties with other agencies in order to help clients contact the most appropriate agencies and facilities for their needs.

Because community counselors in specialized agencies develop expertise in dealing with a specific area of human concern, they often act as consultants to other helpers. By sharing their knowledge of the specific problems and the special needs of the unique populations they serve, they help to make the human services network more responsive to those populations.

A major factor in the client's struggle for autonomy involves independence from professional helpers themselves. Accordingly, counselors should encourage the formation of self-help groups that allow individuals to receive support by helping others and by developing relationships with successful and productive people.

Thus, from a community counseling perspective, specialized agencies should strive to enhance the strength and resources of the clients they serve. They should also make the environment more conducive to clients' psychological health and personal well-being.

BUSINESS AND INDUSTRY

Counseling programs for employees in their work settings have become more and more widespread, with the number of consultants involved in such programs increasing rapidly. Counseling programs in business settings, usually called *employee assistance programs (EAPs)*, have traditionally focused on helping troubled workers return to their former levels of productivity. In fact, corporations fund and support employee assistance programs mainly because of their positive effects on employee performance.

In the past, employee assistance programs have tended to emphasize treatment rather than prevention. As Hollmann (1981) notes,

> EAPs tend to be treatment-oriented. By stressing referral to
> professional assistance, an EAP is focusing on activities designed to
> get the employee's performance back to an acceptable level. While
> there certainly is nothing wrong with improving the employee's
> performance, this approach neglects to initiate any activity to reduce
> or eliminate factors causing or contributing to the problem. The
> employee's "problem" (e.g., stress, marital, family, drug abuse) may
> actually be a symptom of the real problem or combination of
> problems, such as a boring job, improper placement . . . insufficient or
> too much job responsibility, undue pressure to achieve results, or lack
> of recognition for superior performance. (pp. 213–214)

Service providers could improve the effectiveness of EAPs if they would concentrate on both enhancing employees' coping skills and reducing stressors in the work environment. Table 7.4 illustrates a multifaceted approach to employee assistance programs.

Direct Community Services

Programs based on community education models are well suited for business and industrial settings. Such programs may focus specifically on stress management. Murphy (1982), for example, reports the successful delivery of

TABLE 7.4
COMMUNITY COUNSELING
IN BUSINESS AND INDUSTRY

	COMMUNITY SERVICES	CLIENT SERVICES
Direct	Stress-management programs	Assessment, short-term counseling, and referral of individual employees
	Health-promotion programs	
		Outreach programs for employees in transition
	Life-skills training	
Indirect	Efforts to reduce stressors in the workplace	Consultation and training for supervisors
	Efforts to improve the organizational climate	Linkage with the local helping network
		Promotion of employee participation in self-help programs

programs teaching stress-reducing techniques such as biofeedback, muscle relaxation, and meditation. However, one can also introduce workshops, seminars, and self-instructional programs at the work site, making such programs accessible to people who might otherwise not attend them. For example, workshops on communication skills, parenting, alcohol and drug information, time management, assertiveness training, and preparing for retirement can take place at lunchtime or after hours.

An employee assistance program can also form part of a company's total approach to employee health and wellness. Corporations have increasingly taken responsibility for providing health-care services to their employees (Offerman & Gowing, 1990). When corporations stress prevention as well as treatment and rehabilitation, EAPs tend to include fitness programs and other health promotions, which help everyone in a company (Gebhardt & Crump, 1990; Ivancevich, Matteson, Freedman, & Phillips, 1990).

Direct Client Services

Counseling services constitute a major part of employee assistance in any company. Normally, counseling provided at the work site is limited to short-term assistance in problem solving, decision making, or coping with situational stress. If employees need more assistance, they are referred to community agencies. The EAP thus serves as "a method for disentangling employee problems from routine personnel concerns" (Sonnenstuhl & O'Donnell, 1980, p. 35).

In counseling, an employee may focus on alcohol or drug abuse, family conflicts, legal or financial crises, stress, or interpersonal difficulties. Help offered at the workplace can be particularly timely. When use of the service is confidential, employees tend to choose the free and accessible service provided by their employers rather than an agency they assume serves people with serious psychological problems.

Counselors sensitive to organizational factors can also reach out to employees facing job-related transitional crises. Joining a new company, promotion, relocation, retirement, change in the organization's structure, or downsizing can each cause such a crisis. In any transition, employees may need help exerting control and taking responsibility for themselves. They may also need strengthened support systems.

In their workshops for employees in transition, Leibowitz and Schlossberg (1982) try to ensure that employees receive three types of support:

1. Support from other participants experiencing the same type of transition
2. Support from workshop facilitators
3. Support from employees who have dealt successfully with similar transitions

Of course, the nature of the transition and the characteristics of the employees must dictate the type of direct client service used. For example, an employee's level of psychological maturity and racial/ethnic identity development (see Chapter 4) are particularly important factors to consider. In general, however, effective outreach counseling strategies all do the following:

1. Demonstrate the organization's commitment to assist in the transition
2. Use whatever sources of support are available, including peers, counselors, and models of successful coping
3. Give affected employees maximum opportunities to help themselves and one another
4. Provide information concerning the characteristics of the new role or situation they will face in their transition
5. Assist employees in self-assessment, goal setting, and strategy formulation (Lewis & Lewis, 1986, p. 176)

Indirect Community Services

The organization of a company may itself contribute to stressors, including role conflict, role ambiguity, work overload, responsibility for the activities of other people, career development problems, and physical factors that limit or impede work performance. Of particular importance is the degree of social support in the work setting, which can buffer even the most severe stress.

> If social support is to be effective in reducing stress, preventing health problems, and increasing workers' ability to adapt to the irreducible stresses at work, all people must be able to obtain support from the persons with whom they routinely work—superiors, subordinates, and co-workers or colleagues. (House, 1981, p. 120)

Like other community counselors, employee assistance counselors can attempt to make the environment as a whole less stressful and more conducive to the health of employees:

> Employee assistance counselors can have a major impact on organizational efforts to enhance social support systems and decrease environmental stressors. Because they see the victims of stress every day, they tend to be among the first to recognize problem areas. Moreover, they have the kinds of human relations skills that are needed to bring about positive changes in the work environment. . . . Efforts to change the way an organization addresses its problems can take a number of forms, including intervening in group processes, developing conflict resolution strategies, conducting training programs, gathering and sharing diagnostic data about the work environment, and suggesting changes in the organizational structure. All of these activities should be seen as part of the effective EAP consultant's role. (Lewis & Lewis, 1986, pp. 148–149)

Indirect Client Services

A counseling program in the work setting can offer an alternative to disciplinary measures, but only if supervisors know how to use it. For this reason, counselors in virtually all EAPs provide training for managers and line supervisors, teaching them how to recognize incipient employee problems, to confront issues directly while facilitating communication, and to make appropriate referrals. An effective supervisory training program makes the organization more responsive to the needs of employees facing either personal or work-related problems.

The community counselor also provides a link between troubled employees and the local helping network. When an individual needs social, psychological, medical, or other services, the counselor identifies and contacts the appropriate service system, and even acts as a personal advocate when needed.

Counselors can obviously be more effective links when they know all the available options for help. They should place a high priority on finding options that cause the least disruption in clients' lives and offer the greatest opportunity for them to help themselves. Lewis and Lewis (1986) have suggested the following guidelines in this regard:

1. Locate and use self-help options available in the community
2. Develop a personal knowledge of local resources
3. Develop methods for evaluating local services
4. Offer objective choices to each client regarding the unique challenges she or he is currently facing
5. Provide ongoing linkage between the client and the helping network (pp. 82–85)

That counselor who is familiar with both the issues affecting individual employees and the company and local community can provide the kind of consultation needed to ensure that systems work not against troubled employees, but for them.

EDUCATIONAL SETTINGS

One can consider counselors in educational settings as community counselors because they serve two separate but interrelated communities: the school itself and the school's neighborhood or district.

We have defined *community* as a system of interdependent people, groups, and organizations that meets the individual's primary needs, affects the individual's daily life, and acts as an intermediary between the individual and the larger society. With this definition in mind, one can see that schools and universities function as communities. Accordingly, counselors have a responsibility to deal with the school environment as it affects the people who work and study there. Because the school belongs to a larger community, though, counselors must also deal with people in the broader social environment, such as students' parents, law enforcement officials, health-care professionals, members of the business sector, and elected officials.

In an educational setting, perhaps more than in any other, community counselors can create programs that promote human growth and development instead of concentrating on remediation. The school community itself offers counselors the possibility of creating the best possible setting for learning and growth. To do this, counselors try to provide dynamic, nurturing programs for learning and to foster personal development. Community counselors in schools create and implement the following services:

1. Direct community services that provide developmental learning experiences for students and community members
2. Direct client services that provide special experiences, such as individual and group counseling, for students and/or other members of the community
3. Indirect community services aimed at improving the learning environment within the school as a whole
4. Indirect client services intentionally aimed at making both the school and the community more responsive to the needs of individual students, especially those at risk for dysfunction

One can adapt all four facets of the community counseling framework to meet the special needs of elementary and secondary schools as well as institutions of higher education.

Elementary and Secondary Schools

Elementary and secondary schools touch the lives of all citizens. Free, compulsory public education means that most individuals in the United States have experienced schooling at some time in their lives. It also means that the school plays a central role in virtually every community.

TABLE 7.5
COMMUNITY COUNSELING
IN ELEMENTARY AND SECONDARY SCHOOLS

	COMMUNITY SERVICES	CLIENT SERVICES
Direct	Educational programs for students on issues such as career development, interpersonal skills, value clarification, problem solving, and health and family issues	Individual and group counseling
		Peer counseling
		Outreach to children in high-risk situations
	Community and parent education	
Indirect	Action on social policies affecting children and youth	Consultation with school personnel and members of the community's helping network
	Efforts to improve the school's learning environment	Linkage with community agencies
		Child advocacy

This role gives community counselors a unique opportunity to affect their work settings. It also presents the challenge of meeting diverse human needs in a variety of ways. Counselors can begin to meet that challenge by taking a multifaceted approach to the task of school counseling. Table 7.5 shows the kind of program such an approach might yield.

DIRECT COMMUNITY SERVICES   Direct community services are intended to provide opportunities to grow and learn among a broad range of individuals, not just to those who need special counseling services. Counselors can use schools' unique combination of human and physical resources to meet the educational needs of both students and community members.

To realize their potential to promote psychological development in the school setting, counselors need to reassess and in many cases redefine their professional roles. For many, this will necessitate moving beyond individual and quasiadministrative services such as monitoring students during lunch and recess, completing attendance forms, tracking tardy and absent students, and supervising students during study hall, which affect a limited number of students (Baker, 1996). New roles within educational settings include (1) providing leadership in planning innovative educational programs, (2) responding to the requests for various types of psychoeducational and life-skills training, and (3) directing particular attention toward creating learning opportunities for adults likely to affect the lives of students, such as parents and community workers.

Counselors who use the community counseling framework in elementary and secondary schools strive to find ways to promote the psychological development and well-being of all students. Clearly, students have the chance to develop personally as well as academically during the school day. Thus, schools that treat youngsters as whole people offer a curriculum that allows them to learn about themselves and their relationships with others.

In some cases, community counselors may create and implement special programs available to any student who wishes to participate. More often, however, efforts to promote personal awareness and the development of life skills are integrated into the general curriculum. To affect a large number of students, counselors can use several strategies, such as the following:

1. Going into classrooms to both teach students and demonstrate interpersonal skills to teachers. This might include teaching students decision-making, problem-solving, and conflict-resolution skills as well as modeling effective classroom-management techniques and group-process skills for teachers (Barell, 1991; Gerler, Ciechalski, & Parker, 1990)

2. Helping teachers select appropriate materials for planning and implementing new classroom-based programs and activities that promote students' psychological development (Barell, 1991)
3. Helping teachers integrate new subject areas into the curriculum (Paisley & Hubbard, 1994)
4. Using resources from the community to enhance the school's educational and health-promotion programs (Barth, 1990)
5. Helping groups of students develop educational programs in accordance with their own needs, interests, and goals (Gerler et al., 1990)
6. Encouraging the implementation of multicultural educational and guidance programs (D'Andrea & Daniels, 1995)

These strategies introduce students to many aspects of the human condition—aspects previously unmentioned in many school settings. Currently, many counselors provide programs related to AIDS education (Brutvan & Mejta, 1987), prevention of alcohol abuse (Spoth & Rosenthal, 1980), social problem solving (Albert & Rosenfield, 1981), assertiveness training (Jean-Grant, 1980), premarital education (Martin, Gawinski, Medler, & Eddy, 1981), democratic values (Hayes, 1982), moral development (Kohlberg, 1981; Mosher, 1980), and affective education (Dinkmeyer & Dinkmeyer, 1980). Topics such as career development, personal and interpersonal understanding, value clarification, decision making, and intergroup relationships are now as much a part of many curricula as any subject matter or academic discipline (Baker, 1996).

Educating parents is also central to community counselors' work in elementary and secondary schools. Although many schools serve as centers for adult education, offering community members a variety of learning experiences, effective parenting should receive the greatest attention. Community counselors in many schools participate in planning and implementing courses or study groups designed to help parents function effectively, thereby having long-range effects on students themselves.

Working in groups gives parents a chance to share their feelings, frustrations, and successes and to support one another in the difficult task of parenting. Even unstructured or loosely structured groups can be helpful. Most important, this service and others should be made available to *any* parent who wishes to participate, not just those with children who have particular academic, psychological, or physical problems.

Several structured parenting programs effectively promote parenting skills. These include evening programs for parents based on such approaches as Systematic Training for Effective Parenting, or STEP (Dinkmeyer & McKay, 1976) and STEP/Teen (Dinkmeyer & McKay, 1983). Parent-education programs effective with people from diverse cultural backgrounds include a framework for young African-American parents (D'Andrea, 1981), a preventive-training model for Latino families (Szapocznik, Santisteban, Kurtines, Perez-Vidal, & Hervis, 1984), and an effectiveness-training program for parenting bicultural children (Szapocznik, Santisteban, Rio, Perez-Vidal, & Kurtines, 1986). These programs offer useful guidelines for counselors planning parenting groups. By providing direct community programs and services, school counselors can foster the healthy growth and development of the parents and students with whom they work.

DIRECT CLIENT SERVICES   For many children and adolescents, group experiences in the classroom will provide all the personal assistance they want or need in the school setting. As they grow up, however, young people often encounter situations in which they need extra support. For this reason, the option of participating in one-to-one or small-group counseling should remain open to all young people, not just those labeled problem students.

Counseling should be a process through which the clients can learn about themselves through self-examination, learn about the environment and its effects, set realistic goals, try and evaluate new ways of behaving, and solve immediate problems while learning long-range problem-solving skills. This kind of process is particularly important to children and adolescents as they strive to develop personal identities and learn to relate effectively with others. As they struggle with these personal challenges, they must develop their own value systems and goals. In the process, they must also contend with the immediate, practical pressures of family, school, and peers.

Students have the right to have someone in the school setting spend time helping them through these important aspects of their personal growth. They have the right to quick, informal access to a counselor, at least for short-term assistance with situational problems.

School counselors should, of course, set a high priority on being ready to provide individual counseling and support as needed. Effective counseling, however, tends to create an even greater demand for the service. As this occurs, counselors need to look beyond themselves for resources to meet this increasing demand. For instance, they can train others as helpers. Training students as peer counselors brings double benefits: not only more helpers but also counseling that is more psychologically accessible to students. For some young people, going to another student for help is preferable to seeking assistance from an adult; shared experiences and mutual concerns make turning to peer counselors easier for many students.

Whether these helpers are students or other community members, the training process is essentially the same. Usually working together in small groups, potential helpers do the following in training:

1. Discuss the kinds of issues they are likely to encounter in peer counseling
2. Discuss their role as helpers
3. Observe demonstrations of the helping process
4. Evaluate the interaction they observe, according to clearly defined criteria
5. Practice the helping process repeatedly, under supervision
6. Receive feedback on their helping skills
7. Give feedback to other group members on their helping skills
8. Evaluate their own strengths and weaknesses as helpers

After the initial training period, active helpers should have the opportunity for ongoing training and supervision, particularly as their actual participation brings up new questions and concerns. Thus, for community counseling programs to be effective and far-reaching in public educational institutions, school counselors must be accessible as helpers, trainers, and supervisors.

The school setting provides a prime opportunity for outreach to young people. Counselors recognizing situations that put children at risk can intervene to offer help before serious problems start. Family pressures, for instance, may make children vulnerable at certain times of their lives, making short-term group interventions appropriate. Groups for children whose parents have recently divorced (Omizo & Omizo, 1987; Pedro-Carroll & Cowen, 1985; Stolberg & Garrison, 1985) and for children of alcoholics (Lewis, 1987; Morehouse, 1986) address this concern.

INDIRECT COMMUNITY SERVICES   Their intense involvement in needs of children and adolescents makes school counselors conscious of how the community provides—or fails to provide—a nourishing, responsive environment for young people. For this reason, it is often appropriate for school counselors to confront detrimental public policies and to participate in creating healthful alternatives. For example, counselors have often helped bring about changes in police or court policies regarding youth, in sensitizing community agencies to the needs of children and families, in creating social or recreational programs for the young people of a community, and in encouraging local businesses to create meaningful job opportunities for students (Lewis & Lewis, 1989).

More immediately, however, the environment of the school itself must stay or be made responsive to the needs of the students it was created to serve. Ideally, if local educational leaders are open to change, the counselor can act as an internal advocate and consultant, encouraging the development of democratic decision-making mechanisms and improving communication among students, teachers, parents, administrators, and community members. In this situation, the counselor can play an important role in helping to formulate policies and procedures that make the school a more responsive institution.

Unfortunately, schools are not usually easy to change. Sometimes, only political action can bring about such change. Because of their unique role in the school setting, counselors have several attributes they can use as a power base for promoting changes in school policies. These unique attributes include the following:

1. A global perspective relative to a targeted individual or a group of individuals with an understanding of the individual's many environments and the impact that they have on his or her development
2. Flexible roles and functions that allow counselors to adapt readily to new circumstances
3. The opportunity to interact readily with targeted individuals and members of all significant referent groups
4. Access to confidential information regarding targeted populations
5. A role of gatekeeper as evidenced in information dispensation, placement, and referral functions (Erpenbach & Perrone, 1985, pp. 4–5)

According to Erpenbach and Perrone (1985), counselors can use their strengths on behalf of students if they (a) recognize their power base, (b) accept the responsibilities that go along with exercising this power, and (c) use their power as a beginning point for gaining wider support to create additional changes that foster the creation of healthier school and community environments (p. 5).

Positive changes that the concerted efforts of counselors alone could not bring about can take place through the united efforts of counselors, teachers, parents, and other school and community members (Daniels & D'Andrea, 1991). A collective power base can begin to develop if counselors assume the leadership in bringing members of various groups together to work on projects related to their common concerns.

The school environment can become more responsive and more stimulating when power is distributed widely and when many individuals and groups play an active part in decision making. The school counselor can play an instrumental role in initiating these kinds of processes.

INDIRECT CLIENT SERVICES   The school counselor is a key link between the school and local community agencies. Often, individual students need services more specialized than those a school can offer. Such services may be medical, legal, social, psychological, or vocational. In any case, the counselor can help locate the appropriate agency and then follow through by maintaining close communication with that agency. Such an ongoing liaison is important because it allows the student's school program and professional helpers in the greater community to work along the same lines but in a complementary way. The counselor is well positioned to coordinate this effort, working closely with school administrators, teachers, parents, and professionals in the community.

School counselors also act as consultants in the local community. As such, these counselors often help develop community programs or services for youths or help train workers likely to have close contact with young people. Many school counselors, for instance, maintain close ties with local police officers who primarily work with youth in various neighborhoods in a given community (Lewis & Lewis, 1989).

Just as important is the counselor's role as a consultant to people within the school itself. Counselors must work closely with administrators, teachers, and other school personnel to make school practices and policies responsive to the needs of all students and to ensure that the special needs of individual youngsters are met.

Teachers tend to ask for help in dealing with individual children, immediate problems, or special challenges and situations they face in their classrooms. Often, however, this can lead to discussions about ways in which the teacher might create a more effective learning environment for all of her or his students. Through consultation, counselors can help teachers examine current practices, generate new ideas, consider alternatives, and select and evaluate new plans for action. Though consultants cannot solve their consultees' problems, they can help teachers examine how their personal and professional values and goals might be manifested in their interactions with students.

Consultees are assumed to be willing to learn and to change, because they voluntarily seek help. The counselor cannot always wait for such willingness, however. Often, an individual child or group of children will need an advocate to initiate change, who can either pave the way for the creation of beneficial services or halt detrimental policies or practices. Thus, counselors in school settings have a dual responsibility: to help young people develop into healthy, mature adults and to work as youth advocates to foster learning environments that nurture growth, creativity, psychological health, and personal wellness.

Colleges and Universities

In higher education, two longstanding traditions are gradually dying. First, many have in the past considered the university as an island in the midst of a community, isolated from the life of the town or city surrounding the campus. This tradition is crumbling, however, as college personnel and students reach out to the world around them and as community members' interest in higher education and its role in community life grows. The integration of such institutions into local communities is evidenced by the growth of community colleges, the very name of which suggests a new role and a new mandate for higher education.

Second, tradition has treated the college counseling center as another isolated island, this time in the midst of the college or university campus. However, more and more college counselors are searching for new ways to reach out to the populations they seek to serve in order to make a real difference in the whole campus community.

Counselors at colleges or universities must now act as community counselors, treating the college campus as an environment that affects every student and staff member. They must also bridge the gap between the institution and the surrounding community. These tasks can be very complex, particularly in large institutions. Table 7.6 illustrates the form that community counseling might take at a college or university.

DIRECT COMMUNITY SERVICES   Providing direct community services includes offering outreach services to persons in those communities in which colleges and universities are located. Often, these services include helping community members examine their vocational, educational, and career goals. Many who would not seek assistance from a community agency might be comfortable participating in a program connected with a local college or university, especially if considering the possibility of further education for themselves. Instead of simply recruiting new students, therefore, college counselors can help community members examine the place of education in their lives and make decisions based on their values, strengths, and knowledge of concrete options.

Outreach programs directed to the greater community have particularly helped women, people seeking career changes, retirees searching for new vocations or avocations, and people who need job retraining. Brief courses or workshops also provide educational experiences to community members (Lewis & Lewis, 1989).

College counselors should direct some of their time to assessing the educational needs of the local community. Then, the counselor can examine the resources of the college or university to determine how they could best meet these needs. In this way, counselors can effectively plan and implement educational and training programs for people who would otherwise go without.

Most college and university programs are, of course, designed for students formally enrolled. To offer meaningful educational and training programs accessible to all such students, counselors have had to move beyond

TABLE 7.6
COMMUNITY COUNSELING IN COLLEGES AND UNIVERSITIES

	COMMUNITY SERVICES	CLIENT SERVICES
Direct	Educational programs for the community at large	Outreach counseling
	Preventive, skill-building programs on issues such as stress management, career development, loneliness, and young-adult transitions	Supportive services for specific groups of students Peer counseling
Indirect	Efforts to improve campus life	Consultation with faculty and staff
	Facilitation of conflicts between the campus and neighborhood	Efforts to make the institution more responsive to the changing student population

the one-to-one services that have traditionally characterized most campus-based counseling centers.

During the late 1970s and early 1980s, several pioneers in college counseling centers began implementing new programs and services intentionally designed to promote the personal development of larger numbers of university students. These efforts included the development of workshops and seminars that focused on problems common to many students across the country. Among these pioneers, Frew (1980) and Meeks (1980) discussed how minicourses could be used to teach students ways of dealing with issues related to loneliness. These minicourses approached the problem of loneliness both as a pressing concern for many students on college campuses and as a universal in life. Barrow (1981) reported many benefits derived from using intensive, structured workshops to help university students develop competencies in (1) stress management and relaxation techniques, (2) strategies for managing test anxiety, and (3) ways to feel more comfortable with others.

Self-instructional methods have also been developed for college campuses. Some of the earliest efforts include interventions to help university students deal with career and personal issues. In this regard, Katz (1980) was among the first to provide college students with opportunities to develop more effective decision-making skills related to their careers and personal development through the use of interactive computer programs.

In another pioneering effort, Thurman, Baron, and Klein (1979) introduced taped self-help messages accessible by telephone on college campuses. Recognizing the powerful potential of electronic media, Warrington and Method-Walker (1981) provided students with self-instructional videos on personal development.

More recently, great strides have been made at the university level in employing a group format to teach life skills and interpersonal effectiveness. Groups have become especially common for helping college and university students develop skills in decision making and career planning, with many university counseling centers offering workshops in self-assessment, time management, goal setting, gathering information, and interviewing (Astin, 1993).

An excellent example of a broad-based group intervention strategy used to help students develop effective study skills and healthy lifestyles, the Community Contracting Project was initiated at Mankato State University (MSU) (Reason, Lee & Bixler, 1995). This project was designed to foster the development of a host of academic and other life skills that helped students realize their educational and personal potential while they lived in several of the university's high-rise residential halls.

The project planners recognized that the impersonal isolation in many high-rise residential halls could be transformed into positive communities that reinforced healthy personal development. With this in mind, Reason et al. (1995) designed a creative direct community service program for the residents of several of the high-rises at MSU. Here, they describe the program:

> Through the community contracting process implemented at MSU's
> Gage Complex, students set GPA goals, explicitly state behavioral
> expectations, and plan celebrative programs when goals are met. The
> community contract itself allows students a vehicle through which
> they may discuss what it means to be an educationally purposeful
> community where expectations are well-defined and the well-being of
> each member of the community is supported.
>
> In implementing this project, two one-hour floor meetings were
> scheduled within the first week of the school year among groups of
> students in targeted residential halls. During the first floor meeting, a
> contract outline was introduced to all residents. Each issue on the
> contract was discussed using returning residents as group facilitators.
> Positive peer pressure was exerted to arrive at tentative decisions
> concerning noise, visitation, cleanliness, and alcohol use. At the
> conclusion of the group meeting, each resident submitted his/her
> GPA goal for the quarter. All GPA goals were later averaged to
> obtain a community GPA.
>
> During the second floor meeting, residents discussed the academic
> focus of the floor, the GPA goal of the contract, a list of alphabeti-

cally-focused floor programs, and its study-lounge usage/noise policy. They then proceeded to vote on each of the tentative decisions suggested for inclusion in the community contract during the previous gathering. The community contract was completed and ratified by students at the completion of this meeting. (Reason et al., 1995, pp. 289–290)

This direct community service caused several positive outcomes, including the following:

1. All three of the campus-based residence halls that participated in the community contracting had higher GPAs during the academic year than did those residence halls that were not included in the project.
2. The preventive benefit of the project was demonstrated as vast improvements were noted in the number of conduct cases reported among the contracted residents versus violations reported in the other residential halls.
3. Other specific behavioral changes, especially related to alcohol misuse and noise problems, were evident. That is, students involved in the community contracting project were noted to have drunk less alcohol during the academic year and were more cognizant of their noise level and its impact on other students in their residential hall community in comparison with students who lived in residential halls that were not a part of the contracting program. (Reason et al., 1995, p. 290)

In the 1990s, the role of college counselors has greatly expanded, as the change in the title of many suggests. Now referred to as student affairs professionals, college counselors have a title that more accurately describes the global mission they attempt to fulfill as they plan and implement services that effectively address the psychological, educational, and career-development needs of large numbers of students on college and university campuses across the United States.

DIRECT CLIENT SERVICES   No matter how many preventive programs are offered, many students will need or want individual counseling; some will experience crises that call for immediate, intensive intervention. In the past, when counseling centers were isolated from the mainstream of college and community life, only a small percentage of students benefited from the services counselors offered. Outreach programs and crisis intervention make counseling services more accessible and more likely to be used by a greater number of people before they develop chronic problems.

Counselors in many colleges and universities now set up satellite counseling offices to provide services closer to campus life. Counseling seems more a normal part of college living when counselors themselves are part of the scene in dormitories, classroom buildings, student recreational centers, and other high-traffic locations rather than a single administrative office. Their presence conveys that counseling is natural and accessible.

This message is underscored when counselors train others to act as helpers. Though professional counselors cannot realistically meet the total demand for services, they can train students to provide effective help. College campuses have provided much of the impetus for the peer counseling movement, with students in many institutions taking advantage of the chance to help others.

In addition, counselors at colleges and universities often train other members of the campus community, such as residence-hall supervisors, health service workers, administrative staff, and faculty members, teaching them to recognize potential problems and make appropriate referrals to the counseling center.

INDIRECT COMMUNITY SERVICES   In college settings, indirect community services address both the community in which the institution is located and the environment of the campus itself. One important aim of environmental programs is to ensure that the college or university is a resource rather than a deficit for the community. The growth of an institution and the well-being of the community may occasionally conflict, particularly when large, sprawling universities lie in crowded urban areas. Disagreements may arise because of such issues as land use, traffic, construction, or the destruction of parks or homes to make room for campus development. Sometimes, severe conflict can be avoided by involving citizens in making decisions that affect their environment and, therefore, their lives. Community members will always be dissatisfied at some level unless they feel that the institution belongs, at least in part, to them and that policy makers are willing to face the problems of the locality in genuine and ongoing ways.

Community counselors trying to help college students develop competency and effectiveness cannot overlook the powerful effects of the institutional environment. That environment can promote human development or interfere with it, support the institution's stated goals or counter them. The climate of an institution may have more influence on students' development, particularly when students are in full-time residence, than any other factor in their college experience. The college is their community—the place where their needs are met, where they interact with others, and where they express their competence and individuality.

Institutions of higher education—particularly large ones—can be impersonal and depersonalizing. They can allow students to go through their college years feeling both isolated and powerless. Professionals in student affairs must recognize and act on their responsibility for building a sense of community and finding ways to make use of the human resources the campus has to offer.

One way of reducing the sense of depersonalization many college students experience is to link on-campus resources with the needs of the greater community. For example, one can do this by integrating community service projects into college courses (Cotter, Ender, Gindoff, & Kowalewski, 1995).

Although many universities have developed various community service projects over the past 35 years, Levine and Hirsch (1991) have noted a resurgence of community projects used as part of students' learning experiences in schools across the United States. These projects usually target vulnerable groups in the community where the university or college is located. They include tutoring at-risk youth in poor urban areas, providing health-care services in local hospitals and nursing homes, preparing prison inmates for their General Education Degree (GED) examinations, serving meals in soup kitchens, providing support services in homeless shelters, working in battered women's homes, doing carpentry and painting in apartment areas for low-income and disabled families, providing educational services to teenage mothers and fathers in rural Appalachia, helping to create after-school programs to help gang members stay out of trouble, and working in local hospices (Levine & Hirsch, 1991).

Community counselors working in university and college campuses can play a important role in helping to organize such service projects. By working with various groups and organizations in the community, acting as an advocate for people in vulnerable populations, and consulting with faculty members and administrators, counselors can facilitate the planning necessary to integrate community service projects into the college curriculum.

These projects provide benefits for all involved. For instance, they offer direct assistance to groups in the greater community who have been identified as vulnerable to various personal problems. Without assistance from university-supported projects, many of these individuals' personal, educational, and mental health needs would go unmet. Also, given the continuing reduction in governmental spending for programs that serve at-risk populations, university-sponsored service projects help lessen the burden many communities are currently experiencing as a result of inadequate funding.

University students also benefit in many ways from participating in community service projects. These benefits include

> (1) helping freshmen and sophomore students gain a positive
> acquaintance with local community members, (2) fostering the
> establishment of a personal network of local contacts which junior
> and senior students can use in establishing an internship, an
> independent study, or the opportunity to seek upper-level courses

focusing exclusively on community service and learning, and
(3) providing opportunities to secure part-time, temporary, or
full-time paid employment positions in the community. (Cotter et al.,
1995, p. 87)

Beyond these pragmatic advantages, students benefit by attaining an increased awareness of others' needs, gaining greater sensitivity regarding their social consciousness, manifesting positive gains in terms of their own level of moral development and responsibility, and experiencing lower levels of depersonalization than students who do not participate in community service projects (Cairb & Kielsmeier, 1991).

INDIRECT CLIENT SERVICES   In many colleges and universities, faculty members as well as students may feel isolated. Counselors can take the initiative in breaking through the barriers that separate people, if for no other reason than to bring to the surface the helping skills that many members of the university community possess.

In colleges and universities, even more than in elementary or secondary schools, academic and nonacademic aspects of the educational process have traditionally been separate and distinct. Consultation between university counselors and instructors has been rare. Individual development, however, does not occur separately from educational experiences; rather, students' academic and personal growth are inseparable. Faculty members, as well as other workers in the college setting, constantly interact with students. This interaction can help students if faculty and staff view themselves as potential helpers. Consultation with faculty members can make them part of the college's helping network, able to recognize situations that require specialized assistance and to relate more effectively with all students. Promotion of this kind of attitude can make the campus setting more responsive to the special needs of individual students as these needs surface.

Counselors can also prevent many problems by helping to make the campus environment more responsive to the needs of particular groups of students. Many colleges and universities have been organized to meet the needs of a student population that is homogeneous in terms of age, culture, and academic background. The demography of student bodies, however, is diversifying. Though many schools have failed to keep pace with cultural diversification, they must either adapt their curricula, student services, housing, and activities to make college life more welcoming to students from diverse backgrounds or run the risk of becoming increasingly irrelevant and alienating in the future.

It is often difficult for those in power to respond to the needs of all students and the community. Counselors can be the links that facilitate communication among diverse groups and individuals on campus and in the greater community.

SUMMARY

The four components of the community counseling model can be suitably applied in a variety of agencies and institutions. Any application should include both services to individuals and efforts to improve the environment; it should also make the prevention of dysfunction a priority. Though the types of interventions community counselors implement depend on the nature of the setting and the clientele being served, the four components of the model—direct client, direct community, indirect client, and indirect community services—remain the same. In this chapter, we have examined examples of how one might use these components in various settings.

In community mental health agencies, direct services include providing educational programs to community members that enhance skills and competencies related to mental health and reaching out to client groups at risk for psychological problems. Indirect services include advocating for policies that positively affect community members' and clients' mental health, consulting within the helping network, and promoting self-help options for clients.

In career development agencies, community counselors use a multifaceted approach to focus on vocational issues. Workshops and counseling programs address career planning and job placement; indirect efforts address job safety, the humanization of the workplace, and discriminatory hiring practices.

Specialized agencies also take a multifaceted approach to specific issues. Such agencies typically focus either on the members of a specific population or on a particular problem. Indirect services address those aspects of the environment that most directly affect the people they serve, while direct services aim at building clients' personal resources. Special efforts are made to strengthen the client group through peer counseling and self-help intervention strategies whenever possible.

Counseling in business and industry, a rapidly growing specialization, represents another setting to which the community counseling model can easily be applied. Counselors in employee assistance programs are well positioned to help prevent employee problems by providing stress-management, health-promotion, and life-skills training as well as attempting to reduce stressors in the workplace.

Because we define a community as a system of interdependent people, groups, and organizations that meets the individual's primary needs, affects the individual's daily life, and acts as an intermediary between the individual and the society as a whole, we consider schools and colleges as unique communities. School counselors and workers in student affairs are, in fact, responsible to two communities: the school itself and the neighborhood in which it is located. In schools, as in agencies, community counselors focus on prevention and provide services that enhance the learning environment while strengthening the personal resources of students, parents, and community members.

SUPPLEMENTAL ACTIVITIES

1. Now that you know how community counseling concepts can be applied in various settings, you will find visiting a community agency helpful. Using the community counseling model as a guide, try to evaluate the methods used by this agency. Are the activities comprised by the agency's programs likely to meet the agency's goals? Keeping the four components of the community counseling framework in mind, determine what sort of programs and services the agency could include in the future to serve clients and the community more effectively.

2. Reexamine your own hypothetical program. Are the methods you have designed for reaching your goals appropriate to these goals? Next, review the applications presented in this chapter. Do you see additional services you could include in your own program to meet the needs of your clients more effectively?

REFERENCES

Albert, J. L., & Rosenfield, S. (1981). Consultation and the introduction of problem-solving groups in schools. *Personnel and Guidance Journal, 60*, 37–40.

Astin, A. (1993). *What matters in college? Four critical years revisited.* San Francisco: Jossey-Bass.

Baker, S. B. (1996). *School counseling for the twenty-first century.* Englewood Cliffs, NJ: Merrill.

Barell, J. (1991). *Teaching thoughtfulness: Classroom strategies to enhance intellectual development.* New York: Longman.

Barrow, J. C. (1981). Educational programming in stress management. *Journal of College Student Personnel, 22*, 17–22.

Barth, R. S. (1990). *Improving schools from within: Teachers, parents, and principals can make a difference.* San Francisco: Jossey-Bass.

Brenner, M. H. (1973). *Mental illness and the economy.* Cambridge, MA: Harvard University Press.

Brutvan, E., & Mejta, C. (1987, August 27). *AIDS education*. Paper presented at the Illinois Institute on Drugs and Alcohol, Peoria, IL.

Cairb, R. W., & Kielsmeier, J. C. (1991). *Growing hope: A sourcebook on integrating youth service into the school curriculum*. St. Paul, MN: National Youth Leadership Council.

Cotter, D., Ender, M. G., Gindoff, P., & Kowalewski, B. (1995). Integrating community service into introductory college courses. *Journal of College Student Development, 36*(1), 87–88.

D'Andrea, M. (1981). *Becoming parents during adolescence: A transactional developmental analysis of the effects of parenthood among unmarried, black females*. Unpublished doctoral dissertation, Vanderbilt University, Nashville, TN.

D'Andrea, M., & Daniels, J. (1995). Helping students learn to get along: Assessing the effectiveness of a multicultural developmental guidance project. *Elementary School Guidance and Counseling Journal, 30*(2), 143–154.

Daniels, J., & D'Andrea, M. (1991). *The Nashville Youth Network*. Unpublished manuscript, Honolulu: University of Hawai'i.

Daniels, J., & D'Andrea, M. (1995). *Promoting the wellness of at-risk youth*. Paper presented at the meeting of the American Counseling Association, Reno, NV.

Dinkmeyer, D., & Dinkmeyer, D., Jr. (1980). An alternative: Affective education. *Humanist Educator, 19*, 51–58.

Dinkmeyer, D., & McKay, G. (1976). *STEP: Systematic training for effective parenting*. Circle Pines, MN: American Guidance Service.

Dinkmeyer, D., & McKay, G. (1983). *STEP/Teen*. Circle Pines, MN: American Guidance Service.

Erpenbach, W. J., & Perrone, P. A. (1985). School counselors: Using power and influence to better meet students' needs. *Counseling and Human Development, 17*(8), 1–10.

Frew, J. E. (1980). A group model with a loneliness theme for the first year college student. *Journal of College Student Personnel, 21*, 459–460.

Gebhardt, D. L., & Crump, C. E. (1990). Employee fitness and wellness programs in the workplace. *American Psychologist, 45*(2), 262–272.

Gerler, E. R. (1995). Applications of computer technology [Special issue]. *Elementary School Guidance and Counseling Journal, 30*(1).

Gerler, E. R., Ciechalski, J. C., & Parker, L. (Eds.). (1990). *Elementary school counseling in a changing world*. Alexandria, VA: American Association for Counseling and Development.

Hayes, R. (1982). Democratic schools for a democratic society. *Humanist Educator, 20*, 101–108.

Herr, E. L., & Cramer, S. T. (1996). *Career guidance and counseling through the lifespan* (5th ed.). New York: Harper Collins.

Hollmann, R. W. (1981). Beyond contemporary employee assistance programs. *Personnel Administrator, 11*(3), 213–218.

House, J. S. (1981). *Work stress and social support*. Reading, MA: Addison-Wesley.

Ivancevich, J. M., Matteson, M. T., Freedman, S. M., & Phillips, J. S. (1990). Worksite stress management interventions. *American Psychologist, 45*(2), 252–261.

Jean-Grant, D. S. (1980). Assertiveness training: A program for high school students. *School Counselor, 27*(3), 230–237.

Katz, M. R. (1980). SIGI: An interactive aid to career decision-making. *Journal of College Student Personnel, 21,* 34–40.

Kim, B., Gaughen, D., & Salvador, D. (1995). Enhancing students' development through community-based research and service projects: The UH-JOBS orientation program. *Educational Perspectives, 29*(2), 3–10.

Kohlberg, L. (1981). *Essays on moral development.* New York: Harper & Row.

Leibowitz, A. B., & Schlossberg, N. K. (1982). Critical career transitions: A model for designing career services. *Training and Development Journal, 36*(2), 12–19.

Levine, A., & Hirsch, D. (1991). Undergraduates in transition: A new wave of activism on American college campuses. *Higher Education, 22,* 119–128.

Lewis, J. A. (1987). Children of alcoholics. *Counseling and Human Development, 19*(9), 1–9.

Lewis, J. A., & Lewis, M. D. (1986). *Counseling programs for employees in the workplace.* Pacific Grove, CA: Brooks/Cole.

Lewis, J. A., & Lewis, M. D. (1989). *Community counseling.* Pacific Grove, CA: Brooks/Cole.

Martin, D., Gawinski, B., Medler, B., & Eddy, J. (1981). A group premarital counseling workshop for high school couples. *School Counselor, 28,* 223–226.

Meeks, C. (1980). On loneliness seminar. *Journal of College Student Personnel, 21,* 470–471.

Monahan, J., & Vaux, A. (1980). The macroenvironment and community mental health. *Community Mental Health Journal, 16,* 14–26.

Morehouse, E. R. (1986). Counseling adolescent children of alcoholics in groups. In R. J. Ackerman (Ed.), *Growing in the shadow* (pp. 97–121). Holmes Beach, FL: Learning Publications.

Mosher, R. L. (1980). *Moral education: A first generation of research.* New York: Praeger.

Murphy, L. R. (1982). Worksite stress management programs. *EAP Digest, 2*(3), 22–25.

Nelson-Jones, R. (1993). *Lifeskills helping: Helping others through a systematic people-centered approach.* Pacific Grove, CA: Brooks/Cole.

Offermann, L. R., & Gowing, M. K. (1990). Organizations of the future: Changes and challenges. *American Psychologist, 45*(2), 95–108.

Omizo, M., & Omizo, S. (1987). Group counseling with children of divorce: New findings. *Elementary School Guidance and Counseling, 22*(1), 46–52.

Paisley, P. O., & Hubbard, G. T. (1994). *Developmental school counseling programs: From theory to practice.* Alexandria, VA: American Counseling Association.

Pedro-Carroll, J. L., & Cowen, E. L. (1985). The children of divorce intervention program: An investigation of the efficacy of a school-based prevention program. *Journal of Consultation and Clinical Psychology, 53,* 603–611.

Sayger, T. V. (1996). Creating resilient children and empowering families using a multifamily group process. *Journal for Specialists in Group Work, 21*(2), 81–89.

Sonnenstuhl, W. J., & O'Donnell, J. E. (1980). EAPs: The why's and how's of planning them. *Personnel Administrator, 25,* 35–38.

Spoth, R., & Rosenthal, D. (1980). Wanted: A developmentally oriented alcohol prevention program. *Personnel and Guidance Journal, 59,* 212–216.

Stolberg, A. L., & Garrison, K. M. (1985). Evaluating a primary prevention program for children of divorce. *American Journal of Community Psychology, 13,* 111–124.

Szapocznik, J., Santisteban, D., Kurtines, W. M., Perez-Vidal, A., & Hervis, O. (1984). Bicultural effectiveness training: A treatment intervention for enhancing intercultural adjustment in Cuban-American families. *Hispanic Journal of Behavioral Sciences, 6,* 317–344.

Szapocznik, J., Santisteban, D., Rio, A., Perez-Vidal, A., & Kurtines, W. M. (1986). Bicultural effectiveness training (BET): An experimental test of an intervention modality for families experiencing intergenerational/intercultural conflict. *Hispanic Journal of Behavioral Sciences, 8*(4), 303–330.

Thurman, C. W., Baron, A., & Klein, R. L. (1979). Self-help tapes in a telephone counseling service: A three-year analysis. *Journal of College Student Personnel, 20,* 546–550.

Warrington, D. L., & Method-Walker, Y. (1981). Career scope. *Journal of College Student Personnel, 22,* 169.

CHAPTER 8

MANAGING THE COMMUNITY COUNSELING PROGRAM

Effective community counseling programs depend on thoughtful planning, deliberate organization, rigorous evaluation, and responsive and visionary leadership. Such programs can take place in a variety of settings, including public agencies, private nonprofit organizations, educational settings, and for-profit institutions.

Regardless of the setting, managing any community counseling program involves developing a plan to achieve a desired outcome, organizing the people and resources needed to carry out the plan, motivating workers who will perform the tasks, and evaluating the results. Clearly, community counselors must be competent in these managerial functions in order to control the direction their programs take. However, like many other human service workers, community counselors are often forced to choose between actively participating "in the administration of their own programs or leave leadership in the hands of others who may have little understanding of the helping process. Many are being forced to manage their programs or to lose them altogether" (Lewis, Lewis, & Souflee, 1991, p. 2).

Because such programs are innovative, multifaceted, and philosophically clear, only people who understand their goals and overall mission can lead them. Therefore, community counselors have little choice but to acquire the managerial skills that can guarantee the effective operation of programs and services that reflect a preventive, group-oriented, culturally responsive approach to mental health and human development. These skills include planning, budgeting, organizing, supervising, and evaluating.

PLANNING

By moving beyond traditional counseling roles and functions, which focus primarily on individual change and development, community counselors embody a multifaceted approach to professional helping. They serve as change agents, advocates, consultants, advisors, administrators, supervisors, evaluators, organizational development specialists, and multicultural experts.

No matter which roles they assume, their overall goal remains the same: to assist the largest number of people in the most efficient and cost-effective way. As such, community counselors need to develop programs and services designed to address the needs of the community. They must therefore base each program on a careful assessment of the community's needs.

The overall task of planning a community counseling program involves several steps. First, counselors should assess which needs in the community are not currently being met. By taking time to do this, counselors position themselves to develop realistic and relevant program goals, objectives, and services that may better fulfill the identified needs than programs not based on careful assessment. On implementing their plans, counselors should also periodically evaluate their efforts to assess whether they are meeting the community's needs adequately.

Needs Assessment

In any human service setting, the planning process must begin with a careful evaluation of the needs, interests, and desires of community members. By taking these considerations into account, community counselors attempt to determine the community's problems and resources so they can develop services that would help fill the gaps in the current delivery system.

Community need refers to a condition that negatively affects the well-being of people in the community. For example, the recent influx of a large number of immigrants from southeast Asia into a small midwestern community that lacks adequate housing for them has created a community need.

More positively, one can see community needs as unique challenges that could be solved when human and material resources are pooled. Using the example just provided, the lack of housing represents a specific community problem that might be remedied by assessing available resources, such as vacant houses or apartment buildings.

Keep in mind that the identification of community needs fundamentally involves a value judgment. In other words, what may appear to be a serious need by some members of the community may not be perceived as such by others (Barton, 1978; McKillip, 1987).

NEEDS ASSESSMENT AND PROGRAM DEVELOPMENT   McKillip (1987) describes several ways one might use needs assessments to develop and manage community counseling programs, including the following:

1. *Fostering community advocacy:* By accurately identifying specific community needs, counselors can advocate for people in vulnerable populations whose physical and/or psychological needs remain unmet as a result of a lack of resources in the community. Armed with this information, counselors are positioned to solicit funding (e. g., by writing grants) to help at-risk populations.

2. *Facilitating responsible fiscal planning:* In a period of continuing cutbacks in spending for mental health and educational programs and services, community needs assessments can help identify funding priorities.

3. *Enhancing public support for counseling initiatives:* The results of a community needs assessment can foster public awareness and support for various issues by highlighting a community's specific problems.

4. *Documenting the effectiveness of counseling interventions:* The data from a community needs assessment can help counselors evaluate the impact of new programs and services developed to address specific community problems.

5. *Program planning:* Gathering data related to the community's resources and needs allows counselors to make more responsible and informed decisions when planning and preparing to implement new program initiatives.

6. *Lobbying support from policy makers and others with access to funding sources:* Using information generated from needs assessments to describe specific types of community needs is a powerful way to lobby support in both the public and the private sector.

Although the main objective in such assessments is to identify specific problems or unmet goals, the perception of the community members concerning the seriousness of any situation must always be taken into account. Therefore, counselors must actively include community members in the needs assessment process rather than try to identify problems themselves.

CONSIDERATIONS FOR CULTURALLY SENSITIVE SETTINGS   To promote community involvement in the assessment of culturally diverse settings, Butler (1992) indicates that counselors should do the following:

1. Be knowledgeable, sensitive, and respectful regarding the various cultural groups in the community

2. Be aware of the political, social, and cultural needs of those involved in the assessment and implementation of programs
3. Advocate for the establishment of a review committee that includes representatives from the different cultural, ethnic, and racial groups in the community
4. Assess what types of questions and methods of data collection would be most appropriate for people from different backgrounds
5. Be sure to use multiple sources when collecting data, including key members of the community, formal and informal leaders of various cultural groups, such as religious/spiritual leaders, school personnel, and indigenous health-care providers
6. Use culturally appropriate methods to disseminate the results of the needs assessment in an attempt to increase the awareness of the greatest number of people in the community

TOOLS OF ASSESSMENT   One can effectively conduct a comprehensive needs assessment by using any one or a combination of evaluation tools. "The choice of instruments or approaches depends on how the information will be used and the time and resources available. . . . Most needs assessments utilize a combination of approaches because comprehensiveness requires different tools for the measurement of different factors" (Lewis et al., 1991, p. 39). Approaches commonly used to conduct community needs assessments include the following:

1. *Surveys:* Community members may be asked through mailed questionnaires, telephone contacts, or personal interviews for information related to their characteristics or needs. One can administer such surveys to all members of a target population or to a sample. The information generated can be used to lobby support for new programs, to evaluate existing programs, and to update data from previous needs assessments.

2. *Community meetings and/or focus groups:* Community forums or focus groups serve two purposes. First, they reveal local priorities. Second, they provide a means for community members to have direct input and thus feel more involved in the development of programs and services designed to serve the needs of the greater community.

These meetings may include formal public hearings or informal discussion groups. Often, these meetings help to identify needs and strategies that might not have emerged through other assessment methods. Community counselors should go to great lengths to make sure that groups overlooked because of their relative lack of power and status gain a voice in the needs assessment process.

3. *Social indicators:* The community counselor can use existing quantitative information on aspects of the community that might directly or

indirectly relate to service needs. They can find this secondary data in sources such as census and other governmental reports, private compilations of local and national statistics, and reports from other local health and planning agencies.

Social indicators include demographic characteristics, health and education statistics, socioeconomic variables, employment patterns, and family patterns. For instance, if community counselors wanted to assess the needs of teens in a given area, they might begin by reviewing local statistics such as the juvenile delinquency rate, suicide rate, school dropout rate, or divorce figures.

4. *Surveys of local agencies:* One can survey local agencies to determine what services are currently being offered in the community. Questionnaires dealing with services and client profiles can help identify service gaps and avoid needless duplication.

5. *Interviews with key informants:* Local leaders or informal caregivers might also be able to provide important information concerning unmet community needs. This information can provide the basis for developing other assessment tools, such as questionnaires. "Their sensitive analysis of current situations can never replace more broadly based needs assessments, but they can help narrow the focus of the assessment so that appropriate meetings, surveys, or social indicator approaches can be designed" (Lewis et al., 1991, p. 42).

Needs assessment tools provide a means of identifying priorities on which one should base a program's objectives. This sort of assessment provides counselors with valuable data that can be used to (1) select and prioritize problems and target populations, (2) identify and implement specific programs, and (3) evaluate the impact of these programs on the community (Hadley & Mitchell, 1995; Walsh & Betz, 1995).

Goal Setting

Once an initial needs assessment has been completed, community counselors can turn their attention to setting specific program goals. Setting clear goals may be the single most important task in managing a community counseling program. As an assessment tool, program goals determine precisely what services will be provided. Those services that aim at clearly articulated goals will be included in the program, while services with vague goals or that do not specifically relate to given objectives will be eliminated. Providing a coherent set of services thus depends on clearly stated goals agreed on by policy makers, service deliverers, and consumers.

The goals of a community counseling program should be in accord with the outcomes desired by the community members. They should be systematically related to objectives that are measurable, realistic, and acceptable to all groups affected by the success or failure of the program. The desired outcomes provide the basis for all subsequent decisions concerning the nature of the services.

Decision Making

Another way community counselors break from traditional roles is by avoiding what Odiorne (1974) calls the "activity trap." When human service professionals get caught in this trap, their activity (such as individual counseling) becomes an end in itself. They get so used to performing the same tasks that they lose sight of their overall purpose (i.e., promoting psychological wellness) and do not consider alternative helping methods and strategies to help them be more effective.

In contrast, the community counseling framework requires the use of multifaceted approaches to achieve a program's goals. In making decisions concerning program development, for example, community counselors should consider a broad range of services, weigh the negative and positive implications of each, and make choices based on a reasonable search of available data. The key to this decision-making process is openness, with counselors considering innovative activities as freely as they consider familiar services, such as one-to-one counseling.

When choosing services to be included in the design of their programs, counselors should carefully consider the following questions:

1. Does this kind of service fit our program goals?
2. What resources are available for delivering this service?
3. Are community members and consumers interested in this service?
4. Does this service complement the values and worldviews of community members from different cultural/ethnic backgrounds?
5. Do the potential benefits of this service outweigh the projected costs?
6. How can we measure the effectiveness of this service?

Planning for Implementation

Once the set of services to be delivered has been selected, community counselors can plan the delivery process. For each service, counselors must perform a series of specific activities to get the program into motion. Young (1978) has outlined the following questions, which counselors may find helpful when planning the delivery process:

1. What are the major activities necessary to implement the methods selected?
2. Who will be responsible for performing each activity?

3. What are the starting and completion dates for the major
activities?
4. What are the basic resources needed to perform each activity?
(p. 16)

A timeline can help counselors carry out plans on schedule. While
this initial plan is being developed, methods for evaluation should also be
devised. This careful planning process enables community counselors to
carry out other management tasks more efficiently.

BUDGETING

Developing a budget means translating plans into financial terms. Community counselors must be involved in or at least understand the budgeting
process, because it brings plans into reality. Here, Mayers (1989) describes
the important relationship between budgeting and planning:

> Budgeting is one of the singular most important activities that takes
> place in the human service agency. As an activity, budgeting involves
> planning for the acquisition and allocation of resources for future
> agency programs. The outcome of the process is one or more budget
> documents that not only delineate resources assigned to personnel,
> materials, and programs, but also to a large extent reflect agency goals
> and priorities. (p. 25)

A *budget* is a projected plan of action that usually spans a fiscal year.
Based on the goals of the given community counseling program, it "should
be the servant, rather than the master of planning. As a decision making
tool, it helps transform goals into service realities" (Lewis et al., 1991,
pp. 155–156).

The traditional budgeting process has always assumed the growth of
resources. Thus, human service agencies have most commonly used a *line-
item budget*, with expenditures categorized by function, such as personnel,
consultation costs, supplies, travel, telecommunications, and capital outlay.
Normally, a budget request is made each year, with estimations of the necessary resources based on a slight increment over the current year's budget.
This process usually emphasizes expenditures rather than specific programs.

A negative consequence of this budgeting approach is that the program's accountability often becomes more closely linked to limiting expenditures than to accomplishing program goals. Fortunately, however, several
alternatives to line-item budgeting more effectively complement the community counseling framework.

Program budgeting involves categorizing expenditures by program area
rather than by line item, and it holds programs accountable for accom-

plishing their goals. *Zero-based budgeting*, a related strategy, requires each program to justify its existence in order to obtain funding. Decision makers judge each program according to its success in meeting agency goals, so that existing programs compete equally with new ones. These budget reforms use cost-benefit or cost-effectiveness analysis to relate costs to program accomplishments.

Using complex rational analyses may lie beyond the funds and technical expertise available to many small community counseling programs. Even without highly sophisticated statistical analyses, though, counselors can adopt the idea of relating budgets to program priorities. As part of the planning process, a yearly budget may be developed using the line-item approach in conjunction with the plans for implementation. Budget makers can determine the costs of each of the activities to be carried out, then use these figures to make an accurate estimate of a program's costs. These costs can then be integrated into the line-item budget of the agency or institution. If the plans have been reasonably detailed, the creation of a budget involves simply translating activities into dollar amounts.

Sources of Revenue

The creation of an annual budget depends on estimates of both expenditures and expected revenues. Community counseling programs receive revenues most frequently through appropriations, grants and contracts, fees, contributions, or a combination of these and other sources.

APPROPRIATIONS   Money allocated by the legislative branch of government, or *appropriations*, directly supports mandated public services. Often, programs are also affected indirectly, through contracts received from public agencies that depend on appropriations each year. Dependence on legislative appropriations makes an agency subject to variations in funding due to economic stress or political changes. Planners at such agencies need to develop a high degree of sensitivity to economic and political forces so they can make accurate programmatic and budgetary forecasts.

Funding based on appropriations has advantages and disadvantages in terms of the budgetary process and issues of accountability.

> On-going use of public funds does tend to allow for continuity and consistency in agency mission and goals. There is still a strong tendency, however, for accountability to be measured in terms of community impact. Because agencies are held accountable for the means they use rather than for the ends they seek, they tend to have difficulty reforming budgetary processes or attempting innovations in service delivery unless these innovations have gained political acceptance. (Lewis et al., 1991 p. 167)

GRANTS AND CONTRACTS   Another way to receive funding is through *grants and contracts*, which one can acquire from private foundations or public funders. A *grant* is a sum of money awarded to an agency to enable it to meet certain goals and objectives. A *contract* is similar, but it specifies in greater detail the amount and types of activities that must be carried out to meet a program's goals and objectives, even before the recipient has been chosen. Both grants and contracts typically allocate funds only to specific projects that meet the priorities of the funder.

Proposals that meet funding guidelines are usually considered on the basis of the completeness of the needs assessment, the clarity and attainability of the project's objectives, the suitability of the plan of action, the appropriateness of the budget, the stringency of the evaluation plan, and the track record of the agency seeking funds. An agency that uses effective planning processes can therefore put those same procedures to good use in applying for earmarked funding.

FEES   Community counseling programs may also charge *fees*, either directly to the client or through third parties such as insurance companies and medicaid, medicare, or other public agencies. Unfortunately, the fee structure tends to encourage direct, rehabilitative services and to discourage the kinds of indirect, preventive programs that form the heart of community counseling. Because fees tend to be paid for direct services to individuals, community counselors must seek other forms of funding to support the innovative preventive programs and services that form a major part of the community counseling framework.

CONTRIBUTIONS   *Contributions* also add significantly to the operating budgets of most agencies. For those contributions restricted to specific purposes, agencies need to educate contributors concerning the kinds of programs that can best meet clients' needs. That is, people making contributions to programs may be unfamiliar with innovative approaches to human services, so public relations efforts need to be designed and implemented to make people aware of them.

FUNDING FROM SEVERAL SOURCES   Getting funding from a variety of sources can help sustain an agency's autonomy. Eliminating one source of funding should not throw a program into crisis.

Regardless of the kind of funding involved, community counselors need to keep their primary mission clearly in mind. When funds become available, it is tempting to take on new projects, even if they do not fit the organization's overall goals and objectives. Yet continual implementation of tangential projects can move an organization away from its focus on programs and clients' assessed needs.

ORGANIZING

The way a program, school, or agency is organized should be based on its mission and approach to helping. When they have finished planning, program developers need an organizational structure to carry out the planned activities. Given the tremendous variations in organizational design, community counselors should keep in mind that the organizational structures chosen can have major implications for their work. Such design largely determines how activities will be divided among individuals or groups, who makes decisions, how specialized roles and jobs are defined, how activities are to be coordinated, and how communication is to take place.

Contrasting Two Organizational Models

Management experts have discussed the impact of using various organizational structures to facilitate decision making and management within different types of organizations, which range from "closed bureaucratic organizations" to more dynamic "open and future-oriented organizations" (Mink, Mink, Downes, & Owen, 1994). By examining differences between these poles, counselors can assess where their own agency or program might fit on a continuum between the two.

1. **Organizational structure:** Bureaucratic organizations are rigid, static, ritualistic, and procedurally oriented. Open organizations are flexible, holistic, and responsive; they use task forces and networks to make decisions and accomplish tasks.
2. **Organizational atmosphere:** Bureaucratic organizations are formal, based on a hierarchical chain of command; they operate on a low level of trust and are competitively oriented. Open organizations, in contrast, are people centered, informal, and goal oriented.
3. **Organizational leadership:** Bureaucratic organizations value seniority, emphasize tasks over relationships, encourage taking minimal risks, and use a controlling leadership style. Open organizations are innovative and team centered, emphasize both tasks and relationships, and value risk taking and experimentation.
4. **Organizational planning:** Bureaucratic organizations use top management officials to conduct planning efforts and focus on rational and legalistic methods for decision making. Open organizations conduct planning with those affected by the planning process; they emphasize collaboration—group decision making and problem solving.

5. **Motivation:** Bureaucratic organizations use external rewards and punishment to motivate employees. Open organizations focus on individuals' intrinsic motivation and positive expectations; they use learning contracts to stimulate employees' personal and professional development.

6. **Communication:** Bureaucratic organizations use one-way hierarchical communication and value the suppression of employee feelings. Open organizations value multichannel communication that supports the respectful expression of feelings.

7. **Evaluation:** Bureaucratic organizations use performance-based evaluations that are conducted by a supervisor and tend to be subjective. Open organizations use a goal-focused evaluation process that is both objective and subjective (Mink et al., 1994).

Many human service agencies are characterized by traditional, bureaucratic structures because their organizational designers were unaware of alternatives. As such, each individual is expected to report to one direct supervisor; each manager is responsible for the activities of his or her subordinates. In such an organization, routine is important. Each employee depends on written regulations and procedures to provide guidelines for action. Specifically, when tasks in a human service agency are specialized, one employee or department typically does individual counseling, another does community outreach, another performs managerial tasks, another does consultation and advocacy, and still another conducts groups. Members of the organization tend to become highly involved in their own specialty, with only executive-level managers seeing the workings of the whole agency.

In comparison, an agency that embraces a more open system has a flexible structure responsive to the changing environment. That is, such an agency is structured around work teams and networks that shift according to its goals and needs. As Mink et al. (1994) explain,

> Open organizations focus on achievement of goals through collaboration and working together rather than through application of authority. . . . Open organizations are proactive rather than reactive in relation to their environments. They can therefore anticipate and prepare for changes rather than make decisions after crises have developed. (p. 8)

Open systems rely on a human relations approach to address personnel needs and to promote organizational development. They are also characterized by freedom of action and broad-based employee participation in organizational decision making.

Instead of departmentalizing work responsibilities by function as traditional human service agencies have done, open organizations divide activities according to their purpose or to the population being served. Thus, individuals working in open systems function as members of a team responsible for determining the types of activities that might best serve the organization's goals.

The power and control in an open organization are shared, whereas in bureaucratic systems they are centralized. Theoretically, this sharing of power and control among the workers leads to an increased sense of responsibility and fosters a heightened motivation to achieve the goals on which all have agreed.

The community counseling model goes a step further by emphasizing the importance of receiving direct input from consumers as well as workers. This necessitates the use of task forces and consultation teams in which program administrators, mental health practitioners, and residents of targeted service areas work together to design intervention strategies aimed at promoting the mental health and psychological wellness of the community. Agency employees and community members are thus involved in policy making as well as program planning and evaluation.

By using this sort of community-team approach, work is divided along project lines rather than lines of specialization. Further, by working closely with community residents, program planners and service providers maintain an awareness of their clients' needs rather than identify solely with their own management philosophy and expertise.

Managing an agency that truly reflects the characteristics of an open organization is difficult. To do so, administrators, mental health practitioners, and community residents typically have to be encouraged and trained to adapt to a structure that is less familiar to them than a traditional bureaucracy.

Of course, no one type of organizational design suits all human service agencies. By becoming familiar with a range of organizational structures, however, community counselors can enable themselves to recommend a management approach that best fits the unique needs and characteristics of their agency and the community in which they work.

Contingency theorists (T. Burns & Stalker, 1961; Lawrence & Lorsch, 1967; Woodward, 1965) suggest that the most effective type of structure for a specific organization depends on the contingencies that agency faces. Traditional mechanistic, bureaucratic organizational structures may work best when environmental conditions are stable and efficiency is a high priority. Organic, less formalized structures, on the other hand, may be more appropriate when organizations face internal challenges or must deal with rapid external change and problems in the community. If the organization or community is in a state of flux, mechanisms need to be in place that

(1) encourage communication among workers at all levels of the agency, (2) foster consultation among community residents, and (3) facilitate the flow of information between the agency and the community. These mechanisms can help administrators, counselors, and other human service practitioners consider ways to exercise greater flexibility when facing challenges within the organization and in the greater community.

Future Organizational Challenges

The critical challenges organizations face in the 21st century involve adapting to a host of new and unprecedented changes in society. In this regard, experts have noted that to be effective in the 21st century, organizations will have to deal with the following:

1. The continuing shift from an industrial to a postindustrial, highly technological society (Mink et al., 1994).
2. The shift from a national economy to a global economy, which will greatly affect how schools and universities prepare students to be future workers (Senge, 1990).
3. The rapid cultural/racial/ethnic diversification of the United States (Atkinson, Morten, & Sue, 1993; Sue, Ivey, & Pedersen, 1996). This factor will force those who work in organizations and community agencies to grapple headfirst with their co-workers, administrators, clients, and community members regarding the challenge and promise of multiculturalism (Sue, 1995).

Acknowledging the impact and magnitude of these challenges, Mink et al. (1994) discuss the importance of creating new types of organizations designed to enhance workers' ability to adapt to life in the 21st century:

> If organizations are to respond successfully to diversity and change, they need people who can think, learn, and adapt, who are flexible and creative, innovative, and collaborative. . . . To function and excel in today's global economy while coping with the challenges of an increasingly diverse work force and constantly changing information and technologies, modern organizations must create new paradigms that focus on adaptability, learning and openness. Forward-thinking organizations must thus acknowledge that human life is organic and fluid rather than mechanistic. (p.14)

The organizational structures just discussed are presented to help counselors more effectively understand and manage the particular agency or school in which they work. By reviewing these organizational models, counselors can consider ways to foster the development of their own organization by initiating new program initiatives and management strategies.

LEADERSHIP AND SUPERVISION

Community counseling programs depend on the cooperative efforts of many people, including service providers, support personnel, and community members. Counselors who wish to improve the quality of counseling services must exercise effective leadership when working with other practitioners, administrators, and community members. The following discussion examines issues related to the counselor's leadership style and her or his ability to supervise other mental health practitioners.

Leadership Style

Effective leadership involves the ability to help others realize their potential to contribute to the organization's overall goals and purposes. Thus, the effectiveness of a true leader is largely measured by the degree to which he or she facilitates the personal and professional development of other people within an agency or organization.

Leadership style refers to the manner in which leaders interact with other people within an organization. Over the past three decades, several theorists have discussed various leadership styles (J. M. Burns, 1978; D'Andrea, 1989; Deal & Kennedy, 1982; Senge, 1990). These theorists have typically focused on ways leaders might facilitate the other people's development in a given organization. Here follows a brief discussion of four models of leadership particularly relevant to community counseling.

THEORY X AND THEORY Y LEADERSHIP STYLES   A pioneer in the study of leadership, J. M. Burns (1978) presents two classic theories that have guided much of the thinking done in this area over the past two decades: Theory X and Theory Y.

According to J. M. Burns (1978), a Theory X leader assumes that people lack interest in their work, lack intrinsic motivation, and try to avoid responsibility. In sharp contrast, Theory Y leaders assume that people are genuinely interested in the work they do, are motivated by extrinsic and intrinsic factors, and desire greater responsibility within their organizations.

Managers who aspire to these two leadership models manifest quite different styles when supervising workers. For instance, supervisors demonstrating Theory X leadership characteristics tend to use a structured supervisory approach in which they carefully monitor employees' actions. To motivate workers, Theory X leaders rely on rewards and punishments designed to maintain a smooth and predictable organizational structure and to keep employees in line.

Theory Y managers, on the other hand, usually delegate decision making and responsibility. Their willingness to do so stems from the belief that most people are self-motivated and can meet challenges effectively and creatively.

While Theory X and Theory Y provide a general way of thinking about leadership styles, most organizational leaders and supervisors fall somewhere between the two. At one end of this continuum, supervisors are authoritarian and highly structured in their interactions with others in the organization. At the other end, supervisors emphasize the importance of democratic decision making and exhibit flexibility as they encourage employees to contribute to the organization in their own ways. To avoid implying the superiority of one of these theoretical frameworks over the other, remember that aspects of both Theory X and Theory Y leadership may be appropriate and necessary, depending upon the specific challenges facing the organization, changes occurring within the community, the particular supervisee with whom one is working, and the goals of the organization.

THE MANAGERIAL GRID AND TEAM MANAGEMENT LEADERS   Blake and Mouton's (1978) "managerial grid" provides another way of conceptualizing different types of leadership styles. Their two-axis model distinguishes two orientations: a "concern for people" and a "concern for production." According to Blake and Mouton, supervisors and managers may demonstrate a preference for one, both, or neither when supervising employees.

Blake and Mouton (1978) describe effective organizational managers and supervisors as "team management leaders." Such leaders combine a high degree of concern for production with a heightened and genuine concern for people. Although they see these two concerns as complementary, team management leaders often view their concern for people as being potentially more important in enhancing workers' overall level of productivity.

THE SITUATIONAL LEADERSHIP MODEL   Hersey and Blanchard (1993) emphasize the importance of adapting one's leadership style to different situations and challenges that emerge within the organization. Their "situational model" assumes that effective organizational leadership requires managers to use different supervisory styles to meet the professional and personal needs of workers.

This leadership model suggests that the appropriateness of leadership behavior depends on the worker's maturity level. Thus, a supervisor would use a highly structured, task-oriented approach with people who have not yet developed enough expertise and internal motivation to complete given tasks effectively.

In contrast, managers should use a task-and-relationship-oriented approach with workers who have a greater degree of internal motivation but need help in developing specific job-related competencies. Hersey and Blanchard (1993) also stress the importance of using a relationship-oriented

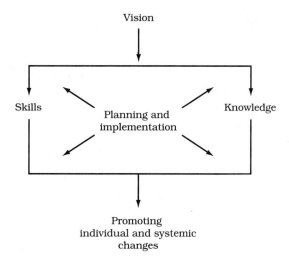

FIGURE 8.1   D'Andrea's leadership model

approach when working with individuals who lack motivation and confidence in themselves. Finally, these theorists encourage organizational leaders to delegate responsibility to those supervisees who demonstrate the confidence, maturity, willingness and ability to accomplish work-related tasks without much assistance.

The Five Components of Effective Leadership

Based on the work of Senge (1990), D'Andrea's (1996) model of organizational leadership is particularly relevant for the community counseling model, because it emphasizes the ways counselors can foster individual and systemic changes in and among clients, colleagues, and organizations. D'Andrea's leadership model comprises five distinct components, as portrayed in Figure 8.1. Rather than viewing this model from a linear or hierarchical perspective, D'Andrea (1996) emphasizes the fluid and dynamic relationship among the model's components. Thus, these factors constantly interact.

According to D'Andrea (1996) and Senge (1990), leadership stems from the individual's vision of what their clients, colleagues, and organization can accomplish. Formulating such a vision requires counselors to picture how their clients, colleagues, and members of the greater community contribute to the organization's development. One's capacity to develop a vision for the organization requires knowledge of it; that is, knowledge about an organization helps one develop a clearer mental picture of where one could imagine the agency/business/school going. Further, as one's vision becomes clearer, the desire to gain more information about the organizational change process tends to increase. When striving to develop their own professional vision, then, community counselors and educators should increase their knowledge related to organizational development, human development, and multicultural counseling theories as a way of fueling their emerging mental pictures of their agency, business, or school (D'Andrea, 1996).

Beyond developing a vision and acquiring knowledge about one's organization, leaders have to use leadership skills effectively in planning and implementing strategies that help realize their vision. Thus, while the planning and implementation component represents the heart of the model, the leader's level of organizational skills represents the energy that fuels it, determining the degree to which the leader's vision will be realized.

As noted in Figure 8.1, all five of these components foster individual and systemic changes in organizations. Community counselors try to stimulate in their organizations those changes that ultimately foster the consumer's (i.e., clients'/students') psychological well-being as well as the personal and professional development of the other workers in their organization. One of the most direct ways leaders can influence other workers' personal and professional development is through supervision.

The Supervisory Relationship

Like counseling clients, supervising human service workers requires an understanding of the complex needs that affect human behavior and relationships. The effectiveness of the supervisory process depends on the fit among the supervisor's leadership style, the work to be accomplished, and the supervisory relationship.

Most community counselors act as supervisors at least occasionally, in directing the work of volunteers, paraprofessionals, inexperienced professionals, or a staff of experienced mental health workers. Providing effective supervision requires supervisors to do the following:

1. Offer appropriate levels of challenge, support, and structured guidance to supervisees (Bernard & Goodyear, 1992)
2. Stimulate workers' level of motivation (Lewis et al., 1991)
3. Foster the supervisee's overall level of counseling skills (Lewis et al., 1991)
4. Address diversity and cultural dimensions within the process of supervision (D'Andrea & Daniels, 1996; Leong & Wagner, 1994)
5. Help supervisees integrate their personal and professional identities (Bradley, 1989)

All these tasks and responsibilities help supervisees provide services that promote their clients' psychological health and personal wellness effectively.

Community counselors who supervise view their relationship with supervisees as comprehensive and fluid. In other words, community counselors pay attention to the ramifications of how supervision is structured and of the dynamic exchange of thoughts and feelings commonly communicated during supervision. Further, they can and do impact the supervisee, the supervisor, and the supervisory relationship itself. Thus, it is important for supervisors to know about everyone involved and to structure the supervisory experience in ways that foster everyone's personal and professional development, including their own.

THE PERSON-PROCESS MODEL OF SUPERVISION   D'Andrea (1989) has outlined a comprehensive theory of supervision that one can use in a variety of settings. The Person-Process Model of supervision outlines several important points for supervisors to consider when they work from a comprehensive and fluid perspective:

1. The supervisee's level of development
2. The supervisee's level of motivation
3. The degree to which the supervisor's style matches the supervisee's level of development and motivation
4. In what stage of supervision both are currently engaged (D'Andrea, 1989)

Using Loevinger's (1976) theory of ego development as a guide, D'Andrea (1989) discusses ways supervisors can (1) determine the developmental stage of each supervisee and (2) design specific strategies that effectively match this stage. In doing so, supervisors can more effectively stimulate their supervisees' personal and professional growth (D'Andrea, 1989).

Assessing the maturity level and skills of a supervisee can be difficult because supervisees, however mature and competent in delivering familiar services, may lack the skills and confidence to adopt new methods of work. Effective supervision requires sensitivity to the difficulties human service providers face in adapting their work to changing client needs. As such, both supervisor and supervisee need to work together (1) to determine what professional knowledge and skills the supervisee needs to optimize his or her performance in the organization and (2) to address personal issues or concerns either thinks may be influencing the supervisee's job performance.

Once supervisors have accurately assessed their supervisees' competencies, they can begin to implement supervisory strategies that build on these skills (D'Andrea, 1989; Lewis et al., 1991). As individuals grow in competence and self-esteem, they usually become more confident in their ability to contribute to their organization.

ASSESSING THE SUPERVISEE'S LEVEL OF MOTIVATION   Another important role supervisors play, already mentioned briefly, lies in motivating workers. Motivating human service workers takes on different forms, depending on their needs, maturity, and competence. The needs that determine how actively an individual will work toward job-related goals have been examined from several perspectives.

One perspective managers may find useful is Maslow's hierarchy of needs (Maslow, 1954). This hierarchy includes, from the lowest to the highest, the need for (1) physiological well-being; (2) safety and security; (3) belonging, love, and social interaction; (4) esteem and status; and (5) self-actualization.

According to this theory, individuals become motivated to satisfy higher-order needs only when their lower-order needs have been met. The relevance of this theoretical framework to work-related motivation becomes clear when one considers that lower-order needs are limited to the degree to which they can serve as motivators. Lower-order needs are limiting because they focus primarily on the individual's need for survival. Higher-order needs, in contrast, are associated with a drive to work in a more democratic and egalitarian matter with others (Maslow, 1954). Therefore, when the worker's need for economic and emotional security has been satisfied, he or she can best be motivated when supervisors direct attention to his or her higher-order needs, such as the need for belonging, positive social interactions, sense of professional esteem, and achievement. Thus, supervisors would do well to consider where their supervisees are in terms of Maslow's hierarchy and adjust their supervisory approach accordingly.

The emphasis placed on the supervisor's role in fostering workers' personal development distinguishes this model of supervision from others that address only the supervisor's responsibility in promoting supervisees' professional competence. Bradley (1989) was one of the first to write about the importance of helping supervisees integrate their personal and professional identities.

Because the community counseling model (a) reflects a holistic perspective, (b) emphasizes the importance of fostering empowerment, and (c) embraces the value of building community with others, the leadership styles and supervisory relationships that complement this framework are those that are intentionally designed to promote workers' total development. Thus, the value community counselors place in fostering their supervisees' personal and professional development are central considerations throughout all the stages of supervision.

STAGES OF SUPERVISION   Supervision normally proceeds through a set of predictable stages (Bernard & Goodyear, 1992; D'Andrea, 1989; Glatthorn, 1990). Reflecting changes in the supervisory relationship, these stages are marked by tasks and issues that emerge predictably at certain points in the process. The way supervisors attend to their supervisees' personal and professional development—how they address issues of motivation, present challenges, and provide support—will vary by stage.

Several researchers have noted that supervision generally involves a three-stage process (Lewis et al., 1991; Littrell, Lee-Borden, & Lorenz, 1979). First, a working relationship is established between the supervisor and the supervisee. During this initial stage, the supervisor serves as a counselor, teacher, and mentor. This stage requires active involvement by the supervisor, who takes the lead in negotiating with the supervisee about the goals and objectives to be accomplished in supervision.

In the second stage, supervisees are encouraged to take more initiative and responsibility in setting work-related goals. To help accommodate the changes associated with this stage, supervisors serve as consultants; though they provide less structure, they continue to offer information and support to their supervisees. This approach fosters a greater sense of personal confidence as the supervisee strives to heighten his or her professional competence.

The goal of the final stage is to help supervisees develop skills that will allow them to meet future challenges on their own, particularly to monitor and supervise themselves effectively (Lewis et al., 1991). Thus, in this final stage, supervisees develop a more mature sense of their own professional identity, growing confident about working effectively and autonomously. However, as Lewis et al. (1991) point out,

> Autonomy does not mean isolation. Through the supervisory process, the relationship between the supervisor and supervisee remains important. Although the need for active intervention may lessen, the supervisory dyad thrives in an atmosphere of trust and supportiveness. The supervisee in a human service setting is not just learning to perform tasks but is learning to use the self as an instrument for helping others. That process implies a need for continual growth and nondefensiveness. (p. 219)

While the knowledge base related to supervision has greatly increased over the past 20 years, counseling researchers and theorists have only recently directed attention to the multicultural issues related to supervision (D'Andrea & Daniels, 1996; Leong & Wagner, 1994). In light of the rapid diversification of society, supervisors in all sectors of society, such as business and industry, schools, universities, and mental health agencies, must learn to address the goals and challenges of supervising people from diverse backgrounds (Jackson & Hayes, 1993).

Multicultural Supervision

Recently presented in the professional literature, the phrase *multicultural supervision* describes those supervisory situations affected by cultural factors (Pope-Davis & Coleman, 1996). Examples of multicultural supervision include the following:

1. White counselors supervising white supervisees who work with clients from diverse cultural/racial/ethnic backgrounds
2. White supervisors working with nonwhite supervisees
3. Nonwhite supervisors supervising people from diverse cultural/racial/ethnic backgrounds (D'Andrea & Daniels, 1996)

Multicultural theorists emphasize the importance of dealing openly with cultural/ethnic/racial issues within the context of supervision (Leong & Wagner, 1994). To do so effectively, supervisors need to be aware of the overall goals of multicultural supervision as well as the issues and dynamics that commonly emerge in the process.

THE GOALS OF MULTICULTURAL SUPERVISION   Multicultural supervision serves several goals similar to those of counseling supervision in general. These goals include (1) providing an environment and set of experiences that facilitate the supervisee's personal and professional development, (2) fostering the development of more effective counseling and consultation skills, and (3) increasing overall accountability for the quality of counseling services clients receive (Bradley, 1989). In addition, multicultural supervision aims at addressing the specific ways supervisors', supervisees', and clients' cultural backgrounds and levels of ethnic/racial identity development affect both counseling and supervision (D'Andrea & Daniels, 1996).

Because no one escapes the influence of culture, researchers have emphasized the importance of understanding people's ethnic and racial identity development when counseling (D'Andrea & Daniels, 1992) or supervising them (Cook, 1994; Leong & Wagner, 1994). Several counseling theorists have developed models to explain the stages of ethnic/racial identity development. These include the Black Racial Identity Development model (Cross, 1971, 1995), the Asian-American Development model (Kim, 1981), the Minority Identity Development (MID) model (Atkinson et al., 1993), and various white identity development models (Hardiman, 1982; Helms, 1995; Helms & Carter, 1990; Ponterotto & Pedersen, 1993).

As noted in Chapter 4, counseling practitioners use these models to better understand their clients' psychological development. In doing so, they become positioned to design interventions that effectively complement each client's current level of personal development. The ethnic-racial identity development models just listed play a similar role in supervision settings. Specifically, D'Andrea and Daniels (1996) outline how one might use these models to (1) assess the supervisor's and supervisee's own level of ethnic/racial identity development and (2) gain insight regarding challenges likely to occur during multicultural supervision sessions.

Being able to assess which stage(s) of ethnic-racial identity development supervisors and supervisees are likely to be operating in is a critical consideration in multicultural supervision. It is important, therefore, that supervisors and supervisees/counselors take time to consider how their own ethnic/racial identity development and level of multicultural competence impacts their views of counseling and supervision.

By knowing the stages of various ethnic and racial identity development models, supervisors and supervisees can begin to assess their own level of development in these areas. In doing so, they will likely (1) gain a better understanding of how cultural/racial/ethnic factors have influenced their own development and (2) use these theoretical models to guide the work they do in both counseling and supervision.

USING THE MID THEORY IN SUPERVISION   People in the *Conformist Stage* of the Minority Identity Development (MID) model reflect two noticeable psychological characteristics: (1) an unequivocal preference for the values of the dominant white, European culture and (2) self-deprecating attitudes about people from their own ethnic-racial background as well as other nonwhite minority groups (Atkinson et al., 1993). Those who operate at this developmental stage usually prefer to work with white professionals because they consider nonwhite counselors and supervisors as generally less qualified and competent than their white counterparts (D'Andrea & Daniels, 1996).

At the *Resistance/Immersion Stage*, individuals are characterized by their strong positive feelings and pride in their cultural/racial background. These positive characteristics are accompanied by a heightened sense of distrust and dislike for white people. At this stage, people strongly prefer to work with members of their own cultural/ethnic/racial group or members of other minority groups in the United States. This generalized distrust of white people represents a major challenge to white supervisors, which they should prepare to address when supervising people at the Resistance/ Immersion Stage.

Individuals who have developed the characteristics associated with the *Synergistic Stage* of the MID model experience a sense of self-fulfillment regarding their own cultural/ethnic/racial identity. They reflect a high level of regard for themselves as individuals and as members of a particular cultural group. However, unlike people at the Resistance/Immersion Stage, they are "not characterized by a blanket acceptance of all the values and norms of their minority group" (Ponterotto & Pedersen, 1993, p. 49).

Many people functioning at the Synergistic Stage are politically active in their communities (Atkinson et al., 1993). This activism springs from a desire to eliminate various forms of oppression and discrimination that negatively impact their cultural group as well as other oppressed groups in the United States.

When working with individuals at this stage, supervisors should take time to initiate discussions about the cultural dimension of counseling. In doing so, they provide opportunities in which they can share their own views of multicultural counseling and supervision and learn from their supervisees' views of multiculturalism as well.

Supervisors should also bring up political and social action strategies when discussing how to help clients from diverse groups (D'Andrea & Daniels, 1996). By taking the time to make this important point, supervisors can explicitly communicate their respect for the synergistic supervisee's commitment to this sort of activism.

USING THE WHITE IDENTITY DEVELOPMENT THEORY IN SUPERVISION
Though the vast majority of counseling supervisors in the United States come from white, European backgrounds, little attention has been directed to the impact of their racial identity development on work with nonwhite supervisees or white counselors who provide services to nonwhite clients. Researchers, though, have presented several models that describe white identity development. The stages (Cook, 1994; Ponterotto & Pedersen, 1993) and developmental statuses (Helms, 1995; Helms & Carter, 1990) these models comprise offer supervisors and supervisees helpful insights into the different ways white professionals think about and respond to multicultural issues. The following discussion is based on Cook's (1994) White Identity Development theory as it applies to supervision.

According to Cook (1994), white supervisors operating at the Contact Stage do not consider race or culture as important factors in a person's psychological development. Instead, individuals at this stage focus on the "common humanity" of all. When discussing cultural, ethnic, and racial concerns, they typically express the view that there is only one race—the human race.

Workers operating at this stage usually have not acquired the knowledge base necessary to implement multicultural counseling or supervision interventions effectively. Some supervisors operating at this stage may even demonstrate resistance to the suggestion that one needs to address cultural, ethnic, and racial issues in all counseling sessions.

In contrast, people functioning at the Pseudo-Independence Stage have developed a broader understanding of how race, ethnicity, and culture impact psychological development. However, they tend to discuss racial differences primarily with people of color rather than whites. Cook (1994) notes that these discussions usually manifest generalized (and sometimes inaccurate) assumptions and beliefs about people of color. Further, though many supervisors and supervisees functioning at this stage recognize the cultural biases inherent in most counseling theories, they usually lack the knowledge or skills necessary to adapt traditional counseling approaches to the unique needs and different worldviews of culturally diverse clients (Cook, 1994).

In contrast, people at the Autonomy Stage know a lot about the ways racial and cultural factors influence psychological development. Supervisors and supervisees at this stage go beyond simply discussing the cultural biases that underlie many traditional counseling theories and techniques by demonstrating the willingness to implement culturally sensitive strategies in supervision or counseling.

DIFFERENT COMBINATIONS: INTERESTING SUPERVISORY CHALLENGES
Many interesting challenges and potentially conflictual interactions will likely ensue when supervisors and supervisees operating at different stages of these models must work together. For instance, a nonwhite supervisee at the Conformist Stage of the MID model should find comfort working with a Contact Stage supervisor, who generally ignores the racial and cultural dimensions of counseling and supervision. However, this same supervisee will predictably be uninterested and perhaps even frustrated when supervisors in the Autonomy Stage insist on discussing racial and cultural issues during their supervision sessions (D'Andrea & Daniels, 1996).

In contrast, supervisees functioning at the Resistance/Immersion Stage will likely be dissatisfied with supervision when matched with white supervisors operating from the Contact Stage. This supervisor's general cultural naiveté and lack of sensitivity to racial/cultural differences sharply conflict with this supervisee's heightened interest and pride in such differences.

When people at the Synergistic and Autonomy Stages work together, though, their expansive understanding and high level of respect for cultural diversity represent unique conditions in supervision. In this relationship, a great deal of mutual learning about multicultural counseling is likely to occur for both parties, especially when the supervisor encourages a collaborative approach in discussing multicultural counseling issues with the supervisee (D'Andrea, 1996).

The MID (Atkinson et al., 1993) and White Identity Development model (Cook, 1994) thus provide practical frameworks one can use to evaluate prospective supervisors' and supervisees' level of development in these areas. (See Table 8.1 for a summary of these identity models.) The insights gained from this sort of assessment can help mental health program planners and administrators successfully match people in supervisory situations. Using assessment strategies such as these to determine the impact of cultural factors in the supervision process provides another example of the importance of using evaluation techniques within the community counseling framework.

Regardless of their setting or the people with whom they work, community counselors are distinguished from other traditional mental health practitioners by the emphasis they place on conducting evaluations at all phases of their work. This includes making assessments before one actually begins supervision (or initiates a counseling intervention), during supervision (or while the counseling intervention is in process), and at the conclusion of supervision (or when the intervention has ended). Because evaluation strategies are such an important part of the community counseling model, the following section examines several practical evaluation issues and strategies that counselors may employ in a variety of settings.

EVALUATION

Evaluating community counseling programs facilitates the decision-making process, providing useful data that counselors can use to plan new projects or adjust current services. Attkisson and Broskowski (1978) have defined program evaluation as

1. A process of making reasonable judgments about program efforts, effectiveness, efficiency, and adequacy
2. Based on systematic data collection and analysis
3. Designed for use in program management, external accountability, and future planning
4. Focused especially on accessibility, acceptability, awareness, availability, comprehensiveness, continuity, integration, and cost of services (p. 24)

Program evaluation is an important part of the management cycle. This cycle begins with planning and moves to implementation, then to evaluation, and finally to replanning. Although evaluation uses many of the same methods and techniques as research, its central purpose is to inform program planning. Thus, evaluation helps in managerial decision making, brings about improvement in current programs, makes services accountable,

TABLE 8.1
STAGES OF THE MINORITY AND WHITE IDENTITY
DEVELOPMENT MODELS

MINORITY IDENTITY DEVELOPMENT	WHITE IDENTITY DEVELOPMENT
CONFORMIST STAGE • Unequivocal preference for the values of dominant white culture • Self-deprecating attitudes about minority groups, including own	*CONTACT STAGE* • Race or culture not considered important to development; there is only one race—the human race • Some resistance to implementing cultural, racial, and ethnic issues in counseling
RESISTANCE/IMMERSION STAGE • Pride in own cultural/racial background • General distrust and dislike of white people	*PSEUDO-INDEPENDENCE STAGE* • Recognition of cultural bias but lack of skills to adapt to culturally diverse clients • Tendency to discuss racial differences with peole of color rather than whites
SYNERGISTIC STAGE • Self-fulfullment regarding own cultural/ethnic/racial identity • Political activism on behalf of own community/group	*AUTONOMY STAGE* • Willingness and ability to implement culturally sensitive strategies

Minority Identity Development Model based on *Counseling American Minorities: A Cross-Cultural Perspective* (4th ed.), by D. R. Atkinson, G. Morten, and D. W. Sue (Eds.), 1993, Brown & Benchmark. White Identity Development Model based on *Preventing Prejudice: A Guide for Counselors and Educators,* by J. G. Ponterotto and P. B. Pedersen, 1993, Sage Publications.

and can even increase public support. It can accomplish these purposes, of course, only if the results are widely disseminated to policy makers, managers, service deliverers, consumers, and the public at large.

Comprehensive evaluation looks at both processes and outcomes. In *process evaluation*, one determines whether or not services have actually been carried out in accordance with plans. In *outcome evaluation*, one assesses whether or not services have had the expected impact on the target population.

Process Evaluation

Process evaluation assesses whether or not the expected number of people in target populations were served and whether or not the services provided had the quality and quantity expected. Because process evaluation depends on clear, measurable program objectives, process evaluators begin by specifying such objectives and developing management information systems that provide the data required for evaluation.

When programs are being planned, the decision makers should specify the kind of information that will be needed for process evaluation. Then, appropriate data can be gathered routinely, from direct observation and service records as well as service providers and program participants. The information system should include client demographics, information about the community, details about services and staff, and data related to available resources. Services can then be monitored, so that progress toward objectives can be easily assessed at any time.

Professional evaluators cannot carry out these procedures alone. They obviously require the active involvement of all human service workers within the organization, because appropriate objectives must be set and data must be gathered continually. If service providers are involved from the beginning of the evaluation process, they can help ensure that the objectives are appropriate and that the monitoring procedures are workable. Because they are often well aware of any problems that exist in the service delivery system, consumers can also play a useful role in planning and evaluation.

Outcome Evaluation

Outcome evaluation measures the degree to which services have impacted clients and the community. One might measure community outcomes by changes in the incidence of a target problem, while changes in clients are normally evaluated in terms of their level of functioning before and after receiving services.

The real goals of community counseling programs, which tend to emphasize prevention, are difficult to assess, because only a combination of many programs can lead to measurable differences in the community.

> Prevention research is faced with two separate problems. The first is to determine the effects on behavior of specific intervention programs. The second is to link proximal objectives such as effective behavior change (if the program was successful) with the ultimate reduction in rates for the end-state goals in question. . . . When the data are in on how separate risk factors can be modified, we would be in a better position to mount intervention programs that combine a number of interventions which would be likely to impact on the distal goal. (Heller, Price, & Sher, 1980, p. 292)

Thus, one might best evaluate prevention programs by assessing the effectiveness of the interventions in bringing about client changes that can reasonably be expected to affect risk factors and, ultimately, the incidence of a disorder. For instance, programs that demonstrate effectiveness in enhancing developmental levels and life skills can be assumed to affect real-world functioning (Sprinthall, 1981). A combination of many evaluation studies, measuring several client competencies, can reveal those interventions with greatest prevention potential.

Like process evaluation, outcome evaluation depends on clear objectives. Routine measurement of outcomes can provide ongoing assessment of the impact of services. Criteria and standards can be developed to make real objectives measurable. For many objectives, standardized instruments for assessing client functioning are available. In addition, measures of client satisfaction are helpful when used in conjunction with other measures. In this regard, community counselors can also use experimental or quasiexperimental designs to gain useful information about the efficacy of specific programs (Isaac & Michael, 1995).

The most important aspect of any evaluation—whether process or outcome—is measuring objectives congruent with the real goals of service providers and consumers. Program developers must always search for ways to measure the real goals of those who have a direct stake in a program's effectiveness, rather than settle for objectives easily measurable but less central to the agency's mission and the community's needs.

UNIQUE MANAGERIAL CHALLENGES

Because of their comprehensiveness and sensitivity to multiculturalism, mental health programs based on the community counseling framework present a host of unique managerial challenges. The complexity of the community counseling model reflects the importance of using a multifaceted approach to promote the psychological health and personal well-being of persons from a broad range of backgrounds within the context of constantly changing environments.

As families, businesses, schools, and communities change, so do the needs of the people they comprise. For this reason, mental health practitioners must be prepared to modify the focus of the services they offer so they can meet clients' needs effectively.

The multifaceted nature of community counseling programs makes good planning and evaluation particularly necessary. Goals and objectives must be clear so that services match community needs.

At the same time, service providers must participate in ongoing training and educational workshops designed to enhance their professional development. By committing themselves to professional development, counselors can learn creative ways to promote clients' psychological health and, as a result, become better positioned to act in an effective and innovative way when new challenges emerge in the community.

However, counselors cannot effectively deal with these challenges unless they are closely involved in the organization's decision-making process. For this reason, community counseling programs virtually require a participatory approach to management.

Because community counselors deliver highly innovative services, they need to maintain vigilance concerning the central mission of their programs. Funding methods and reward structures usually support traditional methods. Managing community counseling programs often requires developing bases that support innovation and working doubly hard at evaluation and accountability.

SUMMARY

Successful community counseling programs require effective management, and counselors should expect to perform a number of managerial tasks. The task of management in human service settings includes planning, budgeting, organizing, supervising, and evaluating.

Effective planning begins with a careful assessment of the needs and desires of community members. Using surveys, meetings, social indicators, and interviews, community counselors can begin to lay the groundwork for setting appropriate goals. Once goals and objectives have been set, one can decide which services will best meet identified needs.

A program's budget translates plans into reality by allocating financial resources for specific activities. Although people have traditionally used the line-item budget, reforms have tied the budget more consciously to program accomplishments. Even without using highly sophisticated analyses, program planners can create a budget centered on the activities selected in the planning process.

Community counselors should be careful to keep the agency's central mission in mind, both in seeking funds and in establishing an organizational structure. Many agencies are structured along traditional, hierarchical lines, with each member of the organization specializing in a particular function. An alternative approach is to organize agencies or programs more organically, encouraging widespread participation in decision making. Departmentalization can be designed either by function or by the population being served. The design that is chosen has major implications for the kinds of services that are ultimately provided.

Because community counseling programs depend on the cooperative efforts of many people, supervision is particularly important. Whether of professionals, paraprofessionals, or volunteers, supervision involves providing encouragement, building motivation, and enhancing competence in service delivery. The supervisory process is largely determined by the supervisor's leadership style, the supervisee's motivation, and the nature of the supervisory relationship.

Finally, the cycle of management also includes evaluation. Comprehensive program evaluations assess the success of services delivered. Process evaluation attempts to measure whether or not services were provided in the quantity and the quality expected. Outcome evaluation assesses the impact of the services on clients and the community.

Although the effectiveness of all human service programs depends on good planning, budgeting, organizing, supervising, and evaluating, community counseling programs present unique challenges. Because these programs are multifaceted, community based, and innovative, they require widespread involvement in decision making and vigilance concerning their central mission.

SUPPLEMENTAL ACTIVITIES

1. Try to describe the behavior of the best manager you have known (preferably in a place you yourself have worked). What was it about this manager that made him or her effective? Would the approaches he or she used in that setting be effective in a community counseling program, or would they have to be adapted?

2. Suppose that you had an immediate opportunity to implement the community counseling program you have been designing. What skills do you have now that would help you manage your school, agency, or mental health program? What skills would you need to develop? Lay out a plan of action that would help you develop your managerial effectiveness.

REFERENCES

Atkinson, D. R., Morten, G., & Sue, D. W. (Eds.). (1993). *Counseling American minorities: A cross-cultural perspective* (4th ed.). Dubuque, IA: Brown & Benchmark.

Attkisson, C. C., & Broskowski, A. (1978). Evaluation and the emerging human service concept. In C. C. Attkisson, W. A. Hargreaves, M. J. Horowitz, & J. E. Sorensen (Eds.), *Evaluation of human service programs* (pp. 3–26). New York: Academic Press.

Barton, A. K. (1978). A problem, policy, program model for planning community mental health services. *Journal of Community Psychology*, 6(1) 37–41.

Bernard, J. M., & Goodyear, R. K. (1992). *Fundamentals in clinical supervision.* Needham Heights, MA: Allyn and Bacon.

Blake, R. R., & Mouton, J. S. (1978). *The new managerial grid.* Houston, TX: Gulf.

Bradley, L. J. (Ed.). (1989). *Counselor supervision: Principles, process, practice* (2nd ed.). Muncie, IN: Accelerated Development.

Burns, J. M. (1978). *Leadership.* New York: Harper & Row.

Burns, T., & Stalker, G. M. (1961). *The management of innovation.* London: Tavistock.

Butler, J. P. (1992). Of kindred minds: The ties that bind. In M. A. Orlandi, R. Weston, & L. G. Epstein (Eds.), *Cultural competence for evaluators* (DHHS Publication No. 92-1884, pp. 23–74). Rockville, MD: Department of Health and Human Services.

Cook, D. A. (1994). Racial identity in supervision. *Counselor Education and Supervision, 34*(2), 132–141.

Cross, W. E. (1971). The negro-to-black conversion experience: Toward a psychology of black liberation. *Black World, 20,* 13–19.

Cross, W. E. (1995). The psychology of nigrescence: Revising the Cross model. In J. G. Ponterotto, J. M. Casas, L. A. Suzuki, & C. M. Alexander (Eds.), *Handbook of multicultural counseling* (pp. 93–122). Newbury Park, CA: Sage.

D'Andrea, M. (1989). Person-process model of supervision: A developmental approach. In L. J. Bradley (Ed.), *Counselor supervision: Principles, process, practice* (2nd. ed., pp. 257–298). Muncie, IN: Accelerated Development.

D'Andrea, M. (1996). *A syllabus for a course dealing with problems with school adjustment.* Unpublished manuscript, Department of Counselor Education, University of Hawai'i, Honolulu.

D'Andrea, M., & Daniels, J. (1992). A career development program for inner-city black youth. *Career Development Quarterly, 40*(3), 272–280.

D'Andrea, M., & Daniels, J. (1996). Multicultural counseling supervision: Central issues, theoretical considerations, and practical strategies. In D. B. Pope-Davis & H. L. K. Colemen (Eds.), *Multicultural counseling competencies: Assessment, education, and supervision* (pp. 290–309). Newbury Park, CA: Sage.

Deal, T. E., & Kennedy, A. A. (1982). *Corporate culture: The rites and rituals of corporate life.* Reading, MA: Addison-Wesley.

Glatthorn, A. A. (1990). *Supervisory leadership: Introduction to instructional leadership.* Glenview: IL: Scott, Foresman.

Hadley, R. G., & Mitchell, L. K. (1995). *Counseling research and program evaluation.* Pacific Grove, CA: Brooks/Cole.

Hardiman, R. (1982). *White identity development: A process oriented model for describing the racial consciousness of white Americans.* Unpublished doctoral dissertation, University of Massachusetts, Amherst.

Heller, K., Price, R. H., & Sher, K. J. (1980). Research and evaluation in primary prevention: Issues and guidelines. In R. H. Price, R. F. Ketterer, B. C. Bader, & J. Monahan (Eds.), *Prevention in mental health: Research, policy, and practice* (pp. 285–313). Newbury Park, CA: Sage.

Helms, J. E. (1995). An update of Helms' white and people of color racial identity models. In J. G. Ponterotto, J. M. Casas, L. A. Suzuki, & C. M. Alexander (Eds.), *Handbook of multicultural counseling* (pp. 181–198). Newbury Park, CA: Sage.

Helms, J. E., & Carter, R. T. (1990). Development of the white racial identity development inventory. In J. E. Helms (Ed.), *Black and white racial identity: Theory, research, and practice* (pp. 67–80). New York: Greenwood Press.

Hersey, P., & Blanchard, K. H. (1982). *Management of organizational behavior: Utilizing human resources* (4th ed.). Englewood Cliffs, NJ: Prentice-Hall.

Isaac, S., & Michael, W. B. (1995). *Handbook in research and evaluation: For education and the behavioral sciences* (3rd ed.). San Diego, CA: Edits/Educational and Industrial Testing Services.

Jackson, D. N., & Hayes, D. H. (1993). Multicultural issues in consultation. *Journal of Counseling and Development, 72*(2), 144–147.

Kim, J. (1981). *Process of Asian-American identity development: A study of Japanese American women's perceptions of their struggle to achieve positive identities.* Unpublished doctoral dissertation, University of Massachusetts, Amherst.

Lawrence, R. R., & Lorsch, J. J. (1967). *Organization and environment.* Cambridge, MA: Harvard University Press.

Leong, F. T. L., & Wagner, D. A. (1994). Cross-cultural counseling supervision: What do we know? What do we need to know? *Counselor Education and Supervision, 34*(2), 117–131.

Lewis, J. A., Lewis, M. D., & Souflee, F. (1991). *Management of human service programs* (2nd ed.). Pacific Grove, CA: Brooks/Cole.

Littrell, J. M., Lee-Borden, N., & Lorenz, J. (1979). A developmental framework for counseling supervision. *Counselor Education and Supervision, 19*(2), 129–136.

Loevinger, J. (1976). *Ego development: Conceptions and theories.* San Francisco: Jossey-Bass.

Maslow, A. H. (1954). *Motivation of personality.* New York: Harper & Row.

Mayers, R. S. (1989). *Financial management for nonprofit human service agencies.* Springfield, IL: Thomas.

McKillip, J. (1987). *Need analysis: Tools for the human services and education.* Newbury Park, CA: Sage.

Mink, O. G., Mink, B. P., Downes, E. A., & Owen, K. Q. (1994). *Open organizations: A model for effectiveness, renewal, and intelligent change.* San Francisco: Jossey-Bass.

Odiorne, G. S., (1974). *Management and the activity trap.* New York: Harper & Row.

Ponterotto, J. G., & Pedersen, P. B. (1993). *Preventing prejudice: A guide for counselors and educators.* Newbury Park, CA: Sage.

Pope-Davis, D. B., & Coleman, H. L. K. (1996). *Multicultural counseling competencies, assessment, education, and supervision.* Newbury Park, CA: Sage.

Senge, P. M. (1990). *The fifth discipline: The art and practice of the learning organization.* New York: Doubleday.

Sprinthall, N. A. (1981). A neo-model for research in the service of guidance and counseling. *Personnel and Guidance Journal, 59,* 487–494.

Sue, D. W. (1995). Multicultural organizational development: Implications for the counseling profession. In J. G. Ponterotto, J. M. Casas, L. A. Suzuki, & C. M. Alexander (Eds.), *Handbook of multicultural counseling* (pp. 474–492). Newbury Park, CA: Sage.

Sue, D. W., Ivey, A. E., & Pedersen, P. B. (1996). *A theory of multicultural counseling and therapy*. Pacific Grove, CA: Brooks/Cole.

Walsh, W. B., & Betz, N. E. (1995). *Tests and assessment*. Englewood Cliffs, NJ: Prentice-Hall.

Woodward, J. (1965). *Industrial organization: Theory and practice*. London: Oxford University Press.

Young, K. M. (1978). *The basic steps in planning*. Charlottesville, WV: Community Collaborators.

NAME INDEX

Subject Index